ROUTLEDGE HANDBOOK OF SPORT, RACE AND ETHNICITY

Few issues have engaged sports scholars more than those of race and ethnicity. Today, globalization and migration mean all major sports leagues include players from around the globe, bringing into play a complex mix of racial, ethnic, cultural, political and geographical factors. These complexities have been examined from many angles by historians, sociologists, anthropologists and scientists. This is the first book to offer a comprehensive survey of the full sweep of approaches to the study of sport, race and ethnicity.

The *Routledge Handbook of Sport, Race and Ethnicity* makes a substantial contribution to scholarship, presenting a collection of international case studies that map the most important developments in the field. Multidisciplinary in its approach, it engages with a wide range of disciplines, including history, politics, sociology, philosophy, science and gender studies. It draws upon the latest cutting-edge research to address key issues such as racism, integration, globalization, development and management.

Written by a world-class team of sports scholars, this book is essential reading for all students, researchers and policy makers with an interest in sports studies.

John Nauright is Professor and Chair of the Department of Kinesiology, Health Promotion and Recreation at the University of North Texas, USA. Until May 2016 he was Professor of Sport and Leisure Management at the University of Brighton, UK. He is the author and editor of many books including the award-winning *Making Men: Rugby and Masculine Identity*, the *Routledge Companion to Sports History* and *Sport Around the World: History, Culture and Practice*. He is currently co-editing the *Routledge Handbook of Sport in Africa* with Mahfoud Amara and editing the *Routledge Handbook of Global Sport*.

David K. Wiggins is Professor and Co-director of the Center for the Study of Sport and Leisure in Society at George Mason University, USA. He has published many articles, book chapters, edited books and monographs. His publications include *Glory Bound: Black Athletes in a White America*, *The Unlevel Playing Field: A Documentary History of the African American Experience in Sport* and *Out of the Shadows: A Biographical History of African American Athletes*. He is the former editor of the *Journal of Sport History* and an Active Fellow in the National Academy of Kinesiology. With Nauright and Alan Cobley, he also co-edited *Beyond C.L.R. James: Race and Ethnicity in Sport*.

ROUTLEDGE HANDBOOK OF SPORT, RACE AND ETHNICITY

Edited by John Nauright and David K. Wiggins

Routledge
Taylor & Francis Group

LONDON AND NEW YORK

First published 2017
by Routledge
2 Park Square, Milton Park, Abingdon, Oxon OX14 4RN

and by Routledge
711 Third Avenue, New York, NY 10017

Routledge is an imprint of the Taylor & Francis Group, an informa business

British Library Cataloguing-in-Publication Data
A catalogue record for this book is available from the British Library

Library of Congress Cataloging in Publication Data
Names: Nauright, John, 1962- editor. | Wiggins, David Kenneth, 1951- editor.
Title: Routledge handbook of sport, race and ethnicity / edited by John
Nauright and David K. Wiggins.
Other titles: Handbook of sport, race and ethnicity
Description: Abingdon, Oxon ; New York, NY : Routledge, 2016. | Includes
bibliographical references and index.
Identifiers: LCCN 2016014379| ISBN 9781138816954 (hardback) | ISBN
9781315745886 (ebook)
Subjects: LCSH: Racism in sports. | Racism in sports--Case studies. | Sports
and globalization--Social aspects. | Sports and globalization--Social
aspects--Case studies. | Sports--Sociological aspects. |
Sports--Sociological aspects--Case studies.
Classification: LCC GV706.32 .R68 2016 | DDC 306.4/83--dc23
LC record available at https://lccn.loc.gov/2016014379

ISBN: 978-1-138-81695-4 (hbk)
ISBN: 978-1-315-74588-6 (ebk)

Typeset in Bembo
by Saxon Graphics Ltd, Derby

CONTENTS

Contents

CONTRIBUTORS

Daryl Adair is Associate Professor of Sport Management at the University of Technology Sydney, Australia. His research interests include diversity, inclusion and anti-racism in sport. In that context he has edited special issues of the journals *International Review of the Sociology of Sport, Sport Management Review, Sport in Society, Sporting Traditions, Australian Aboriginal Studies* and *Cosmopolitan Civil Societies*. Adair is also the editor of the book *Sport, Race and Ethnicity: Narratives of Difference and Diversity* (2011). In addition to this work he is author of *Wearing of the Green: A Cultural History of St. Patrick's Day* (with Mike Cronin) and *Sport in Australian History* (with Wray Vamplew).

Sine Agergaard is Associate Professor at Aarhus University, Denmark, where she is undertaking research on sport and migration. She is Principal Investigator of a Nordic collaborative research project on sports labour migration as a challenge and opportunity for Nordic civil society, and manager of the International Network for Research in Sport and Migration Issues.

Sergey Altukhov is Deputy Director of the Sport Management Centre, Lomonosov Moscow State University in Russia. He is a Member of the Expert Council for Physical Culture and Sport of the Council of the Russian Federation; Chief Editor of the web portal Sportdiplom.ru and author of the book *Event Management in Sport* (2013). He is the coordinator of the 2016 World Hockey Forum and Summit in St. Petersburg in association with the International Ice Hockey Federation.

Mahfoud Amara joined Qatar University in autumn 2015. He is Assistant Professor in Sport Management and Policy at the College of Arts and Sciences (Sport Science Programme). Before joining Qatar University he was Assistant Professor in Sport Policy and Management and Deputy Director of the Centre for Olympic Studies and Research in the School of Sport, Exercise and Health Sciences, Loughborough University. Mahfoud has a specific interest in sport business, culture and politics in Arab and Muslim contexts. In 2012 he published a new book, *Sport Politics and Society in the Arab World*, with Palgrave Macmillan. He recently co-edited *Sport in Islam and in Muslim Communities* with Alberto Testa (Routledge, 2016) and is currently co-editing the *Routledge Handbook of Africa and Sport* with John Nauright.

Chris Bolsmann is a South African sociologist with a research and teaching interest in the social history of sport. He is Associate Professor in the Department of Kinesiology at California State University Northridge. He received his PhD in Sociology from the University of Warwick in the United Kingdom in 2006 and completed his MA and BA at the University of Pretoria in South Africa. He has taught, among others, at the universities of Pretoria and Johannesburg in South Africa, the University of Seoul in South Korea and the universities of Warwick and Aston in the United Kingdom. He has published a range of articles primarily in sports history and the sociology of sport, and co-edited two books: *South Africa and the Global Game* and *Africa's World Cup*.

Sebastian Braun is University Professor at the Humboldt-Universität zu Berlin. He is head of the Department of Sport Sociology at the Institute for Sport Sciences and head of the Department of Sport, Integration and Football at the Berlin Institute for Integration and Migration Research (BIM). Prior to this position he worked as a University Professor at the University of Paderborn, as a Research Fellow in the Emmy Noether Program of the German Research Foundation (DFG) and as a Research Associate in the Commission of Inquiry on the 'Future of Civic Engagement' in the German Bundestag. His current research priorities focus on civic engagement, civil society and non-profit organizations, integration and social capital, as well as CSR.

Paul Darby is Reader in the Sociology of Sport at Ulster University in Northern Ireland. He is author of *Gaelic Games, Nationalism and the Irish Diaspora in the United States* and *Africa, Football and FIFA: Politics, Colonialism and Resistance*. He also co-edited *Emigrant Players: Sport and the Irish Diaspora* and *Soccer and Disaster: International Perspectives*. He sits on the editorial board of *Soccer and Society* and *SportsWorld: The Journal of Global Sport*, as well as the advisory board of *Impumelelo: The Interdisciplinary e-Journal of African Sport*.

Meghan Ferriter (PhD, Sociology, University of Glasgow, 2011) is an Anthropologist and Interdisciplinary Researcher. Her doctoral thesis explored the extent of change in discourses of mediated sport concerning race, gender and age. Meghan's research examines the communication of cultural beliefs through media technologies and discourse and ways these resources are used to refine social relationships. She manages collaboration with volunteers and staff as the Project Coordinator with the Smithsonian Transcription Center, increasing access to Smithsonian Institution collections and creating new institutional workflows. She has presented extensively on crowdsourcing best practices and project design. In recent research, Meghan has investigated the intersections of identity and participatory knowledge within temporal communities and social networking platforms, including Tumblr and Twitter.

Thomas Fletcher is Senior Lecturer at Leeds Beckett University, UK. His personal research interests focus on race and ethnicity, families and equality and diversity issues in sport and leisure. He is editor of *Cricket, Migration and Diasporic Communities* (Routledge, 2015) and co-editor of *Sport, Leisure and Social Justice* (Routledge, in press), *Diversity, Equity and Inclusion in Sport and Leisure* (Routledge, 2014) and *Sports Events, Society and Culture* (Routledge, 2014). He is a member of the editorial boards of *Sport in Society* and *Sociological Research Online* and Secretary to the Leisure Studies Association. He has undertaken research on behalf of Sport Wales, the England and Wales Cricket Board (ECB), Yorkshire Cricket Foundation, Economic and Social Research Council (ESRC) and Meetings Professional International (MPI) in the United Kingdom.

Luke J. Harris is Researcher in Sport Studies and History at Canterbury Christ Church University, UK. He is an expert in the Olympic Games, national identity and racism within sport. He is the author of *Britain and the Olympic Games, 1908–1920: Perspectives on Participation and Identity*.

Mari Haugaa Engh is a Postdoctoral Research Fellow at the School of Applied Human Sciences at the University of KwaZulu-Natal, where she is undertaking research on gender and migration. Mari completed her PhD at Aarhus University, where she was part of a Nordic project on transnationalism, migration and women's football. Her research interests are gender and sexuality studies, migration studies and the sociology of sport.

Kevin Hylton is Professor of Equality and Diversity in Sport, Leisure and Education, Carnegie Faculty, Leeds Beckett University, UK. Kevin is the first black professor to hold this title. His early research focused on race equality in local government and has continued research into the nature and extent of racism in sport, leisure and education. Kevin has published extensively in peer-reviewed journals and book projects. Kevin authored *'Race' and Sport: Critical Race Theory* and is currently writing *Contesting 'Race' and Sport: Shaming the Colour Line* for Routledge. Kevin is Patron of the Equality Challenge Unit's Race Equality Charter, and on the boards of the *International Review for the Sociology of Sport* and the new *Journal of Global Sport Management*.

Rasmus Bysted Møller is Assistant Professor at the research group Sport and Body Culture, Section for Sport Science at the Department of Public Health, Aarhus University, Denmark. His research focuses particularly on moral philosophy and sport ethics.

Verner Møller is Professor of Sport and Body Culture at the Department of Public Health, Aarhus University, Denmark. His research focuses particularly on elite sports and body cultural extremes. His edited and authored books include: *The Doping Devil*; *The Essence of Sport*; *Elite Sport Doping and Public Health* (2009); *The Ethics of Doping and Anti-doping: Redeeming the Soul of Sport?* (2010); *The Scapegoat: About Michael Rasmussen's Tour de France Exit* (2011); *Doping and Anti-doping Policy in Sport: Ethical, Legal and Social Perspectives* (2011); and most recently, *The Routledge Handbook of Sport and Drugs* (2015).

John Nauright is Professor and Chair of the Department of Kinesiology, Health Promotion and Recreation at the University of North Texas in the USA. Through May 2016 he was Professor of Sport and Leisure Management at the University of Brighton in the UK. He is the author and editor of many books, including the award-winning *Making Men: Rugby and Masculine Identity*; *Rugby and the South African Nation*; and *Sport Around the World: History, Culture and Practice*, as well as *Beyond C.L.R. James: Race and Ethnicity in Sport*; *Long Run to Freedom: Sport, Cultures and Identities in South Africa*; *Making the Rugby World: Race, Gender, Commerce*; *The Essence of Sport: The Routledge Companion to Sports History* and *The Rugby World in the Professional Era*. He holds a PhD in African History from Queen's University in Canada. He is currently co-editing the *Routledge Handbook of Africa and Sport* with Mahfoud Amara, and editing the *Routledge Handbook of Global Sport*. He is also Honorary Professor of Sport Management at Lomonosov Moscow State University in Russia; Visiting Professor of Cultural Studies at the University of the West Indies, Cave Hill in Barbados and Adjunct Professor of Sport Management at the University of Ghana.

Tina Nobis is Assistant Professor at the Berlin Institute for Integration and Migration Research (BIM) and the Department of Sport Sociology at the Institute for Sport Sciences at the Humboldt University of Berlin. She teaches, researches and publishes in the fields of migration and integration, social capital, civic engagement, non-profit organizations and political socialization. She was and still is involved in different research and evaluation projects that deal with integration, socialization and participation achievements of sports associations and other volunteer associations – from a theoretical and empirical perspective.

Farah Palmer is Director of the Māori Business and Leadership Centre and a Senior Lecturer in the School of Management, College of Business, Massey University. Her teaching and research interests are in sport sociology, sport management, leadership and governance as they relate to Māori and women in particular. Farah was a member of the New Zealand women's rugby team (Black Ferns) from 1995 to 2006, and captained the team to victory in three World Cups (1998, 2002 and 2006). Her work in sport and women's rugby was acknowledged in 2007 when she became an Officer of the New Zealand Order of Merit (ONZM) and in 2014 when she was inducted into the IRB Rugby Hall of Fame.

Rob Ruck is Professor of History at the University of Pittsburgh, where he teaches and writes about sport. His work focuses on how people use sport to tell a collective story about who they are to themselves and the world. His books include: *Sandlot Seasons: Sport in Black Pittsburgh* (1987); *The Tropic of Baseball: Baseball in the Dominican Republic* (1991); *Rooney: A Sporting Life* (2010); and *Raceball: How the Major Leagues Colonized the Black and Latin Game* (2011), as well as two documentaries, *Kings on the Hill: Baseball's Forgotten Men* (1993) and *The Republic of Baseball: Dominican Giants of the American Game* (2006). He is currently finishing a book about American football and *fa 'a samoa* (in the way of Samoa) in American Samoa and among the Samoan diaspora.

Greg Ryan is Professor and Dean of the Faculty of Environment, Society and Design at Lincoln University in Christchurch, New Zealand. He has published various academic and popular press articles and chapters on sport in New Zealand; edited *Tackling Rugby Myths: Rugby and New Zealand Society 1854–2004* (2005) and *The Changing Face of Rugby: The Union Game and Professionalism Since 1995* (2008); and has written three books – *The Contest for Rugby Supremacy: Accounting for the 1905 All Blacks* (2005); *The Making of New Zealand Cricket 1832–1914* (2004); and *Forerunners of the All Blacks: The 1888–89 New Zealand Native Football Team in Britain, Australia and New Zealand* (1993). He is currently co-authoring a general history of New Zealand sport and writing a social history of beer and brewing in New Zealand.

Rob Steen is an internationally renowned sportswriter and co-leader of the BA (Hons) Sport Journalism course at the University of Brighton. He has written extensively for, among other major newspapers, the *Guardian*, the *Independent*, *Financial Times*, the *Melbourne Age*, the *Hindustan Times*, the *Sunday Telegraph* and *Sunday Times*, where he was Deputy Sports Editor. Winner of the 1995 Cricket Society Literary award for *David Gower: A Man Out of Time* and the UK section of the 2005 EU Journalism Award 'For Diversity, Against Discrimination' for an investigation into the decline of Anglo-Caribbean cricketers, he has also twice been shortlisted for the William Hill Sports Book of the Year for *Spring, Summer, Autumn: Three Cricketers, One Season* (1991) and *Floodlights and Touchlines: A History of Spectator Sport* (2014), and also shortlisted for the 2014 Lord Aberdare Literary Prize for Sports History. He has published over a dozen books and contributed to a multitude of magazines and journals, and is also a long-standing columnist for *Cricinfo*. He co-edited *The Cambridge Companion to Football* (2013) and is currently co-editing the *Routledge Handbook of Sports Journalism*.

Sasha Sutherland is a Lecturer in the Academy of Sport Cave Hill, Department of Management Studies, at the University of the West Indies, Cave Hill Campus in Barbados. Her research interests are centred on women, sport, leadership and anti-doping in the Anglophone Caribbean, and the intersections of sport, culture and ideology in the organization and development of Caribbean sport and society, particularly among girls and women.

Geoff Watson is a Senior Lecturer in History at Massey University, Palmerston North, New Zealand. His research focuses on sports history. He is the principal author of *Seasons of Honour: A Centennial History of New Zealand Hockey 1902–2002* (2002) and *Sporting Foundations of New Zealand Indians: A Fifty Year History of the New Zealand Indian Sports Association* (2012). He was also one of the editors of and a contributor to *Legends in Black: New Zealand Rugby Greats on Why We Win*, which was published by Penguin in 2013. He is presently working on a general history of sport in New Zealand.

David K. Wiggins is Professor and Co-director of the Center for the Study of Sport and Leisure in Society at George Mason University. Educated at San Diego State University and the University of Maryland, he has a particular interest in the history of American sport, especially as it relates to the interconnection among race, sport and culture. He has published many scholarly articles, book chapters and edited books and monographs. Among his publications are *Glory Bound: Black Athletes in a White America*; *The Unlevel Playing Field: A Documentary History of the African American Experience in Sport*; *Out of the Shadows: A Biographical History of African American Athletes*; *Rivals: Legendary Matchups that made Sports History*; *Beyond C.L.R. James: Race and Ethnicity in Sport*; and *DC Sports: The Nation's Capital at Play*. He is the former Editor of *Quest* and the *Journal of Sport History* and an Active Fellow in the National Academy of Kinesiology.

INTRODUCTION

David K. Wiggins and John Nauright

The interconnection among race, ethnicity, and sport has drawn an enormous amount of scholarly attention from historians, sociologists, and other academicians representing a variety of disciplinary areas.[1] Fascinated by the impact that race and ethnicity have had on one of the most popular and influential cultural institutions, academicians have delved into the topic with much enthusiasm and earnestness that has resulted in a greater understanding of how minority groups and those considered 'Other' have sought to become full participants in sport at various levels of competition. Importantly, scholarship on the topic has generally been disseminated by means of more narrowly conceived academic journals and specialized anthologies and monographs, without a concerted effort to make available the research on the interconnection among race, ethnicity, and sport in one volume that takes an inclusionary and more global perspective. It is understandable why this is the case in an academic environment that continues to move rapidly towards more focused preparation and specialization that values silos over context and more expansive world-views.

The *Routledge Handbook of Sport, Race and Ethnicity* takes a decidedly different approach. Working under the premise that sports do matter and have impacted billions of people around the world, the book explores the complexities of race, ethnicity, and sport amid the historical transformations that have taken place both nationally and internationally. Leading the exploration is a number of outstanding scholars who have a passion for the subject and have been published widely on it. Included among the contributors are individuals who have written a plethora of articles, published multiple anthologies and monographs, served as editors of prestigious scholarly journals, directed or co-directed various centres and institutes of sport, garnered large amounts of external grant money for their research, and given a number of invited keynote addresses at local, regional, national, and international conferences.

The topics covered in the book are reflective of the expertise of the individual contributors while at the same time providing a broad overview of how race, ethnicity, and sport have impacted each other in an assortment of different ways in different geographical locations and over different periods of time. Although it is impossible to cover every topic in one volume, this book analyses, among other things, the contours of race and gender in sport; race, whiteness and sport; race and sports journalism; migration and racialization in sport; racism in European football; sport among Muslims; and the complexities of race, ethnicity, and sport in the countries of Aotearoa/New Zealand, Australia, Germany, Great Britain, Ireland, South Africa, Russia/Soviet Union, and the United States, among others.

A significant contribution the authors make is the furnishing of a large compilation of primary and secondary sources dealing with race, ethnicity, and sport. Those scholars interested in the topic will benefit enormously from the canvassing of the notes put together by each author in the volume. The contributors also provide a great service by making clear the trends in the research on race, ethnicity, and sport as well as the gaps in the literature that still need to be addressed. In addition, the contributors point out, with varying degrees of emphasis, both the progress in sport in regards to equality of participation and the persistent racialist thinking and discrimination that exists in relation to athletic ability and performance. Although sport has proven to be an important site of resistance, deep-seated stereotypical notions about character traits and mental and physical abilities based on race and ethnicity have been slow to dissipate, as has the belief on the part of some minority athletes that it is their biological cultural destiny to succeed in sport.

The contributors to this book, again with varying degrees of emphasis, point out the continued racialist thinking and discrimination in sport, but also make clear it can serve an integrative function among different groups irrespective of racial, ethnic, and cultural backgrounds. Although it is difficult to gauge genuine friendships established across racial and ethnic lines, sports have provided minority and immigrant groups with opportunities to realize lasting fame as well as material gain often not possible through other means. There is also little question that minority and immigrant athletes, particularly those of great talent who have produced outstanding performances, have garnered genuine respect and elicited a more complete understanding of those from different cultural backgrounds. Much of this depends on local identities, differences in political systems, class structure, citizenship, heritage, global communications, and social and cultural capital. Ultimately, and this is perhaps as true now as it was prior to the current period of globalization, the achievements of minority and immigrant athletes have served as important symbols of possibility in a world that still grapples with the differences among Others of various races and ethnicities.

A key feature of this volume is the move beyond traditional analyses of race, ethnicity, and sport in the English-speaking world to include work on Germany and Russia/Soviet Union for example. Russia and later the Soviet Union expanded across more than a continent and incorporated new territories and peoples throughout its history. Germany, a relatively young modern nation, has been at the epicentre of the global refugee crisis of the 2010s as well as a leading destination for sporting migrants. Indeed, a relatively new feature of the literature on migration, race and sport is discussed here with examination of women football (soccer) migrants who play in European leagues. With the expansion of strong professional football leagues for women beyond Scandinavia and Germany to England and the USA, the intersections of race, ethnicity, and gender will be important to understand and integrate into the literature on male sporting migrants.

There are some gaps in the collection that a purist might wish to see. We do not have a specific chapter on race and ethnicity in the sociology of sport and the cultural studies of sport as those overlapping fields and the significant contributions made by scholars such as Ben Carrington, Kevin Hylton (an author in this volume), Grant Farred, Karl Spracklen, Jennifer Hargreaves, Paul Darby, Daniel Burdsey, and others are utilized well beyond any disciplinary confines. Scholars normally identified as historians of sport or geographers have also contributed well beyond their original disciplinary fields, including John Bale, Douglas Booth, Brian Stoddart, Colin Tatz, and, we hope, at least to some degree, ourselves. Lastly, interdisciplinary scholars such as John Hoberman, Jennifer Hargreaves, and Malcolm MacLean, who have written excellent examinations of race and ethnicity in sport, point to a trans-disciplinary focus as the way to best understand race and ethnicity issues in sport. In this volume, therefore, we chose rather to concentrate on concepts including the historical development of race and ethnicity as an issue in sports; the role of anthropology, philosophy, and the sciences in, sometimes spurious, efforts to theorize and categorize humans as well as the implications for societal views of race and ethnicity as issues which have become reflected in the development of sports policies around the world. We follow with geographic case studies of race and ethnicity in sport around the world, particularly in the era of globalization of the twentieth and twenty-first centuries.

In sum, this book makes clear the complexity and powerful dynamics of the interconnection among race, ethnicity, and sport. It is about skin colour and ethnic background and how those factors impact who participates in sport and what social meanings are derived from that participation. It is about how racial and ethnic groups have found their way into sport, how they express their cultural identities through sport, and how they have integrated sport in their lives. Equally important, it is about sport as a cultural site where people construct their own ideas about race and ethnic background and the process of integration as well as exclusion. For this reason alone, the book should prove valuable to those interested in grasping more fully the institution of sport that historically has often stressed, yet not always realized, equality of opportunity regardless of race, creed, or colour.

We would like to thank the editorial team at Routledge for having the foresight to include this area of work into its *Handbook* series, as well as to patiently working with us and our team of authors to deliver this timely volume. We would also like to thank our authors, particularly those who rose to a late challenge created by a couple of people originally committed to the project who decided at a late stage to not deliver.

We would like to dedicate this volume to all athletes and spectators around the world, who, despite challenges and roadblocks thrown up by small-minded people, have persevered in their passion for sport, and particularly to those who have used sport as a vehicle to challenge racist assumptions and racial discrimination. There is much still to be done and we hope many more scholars will seek the challenge to lay bare one of the ugliest aspects of the twenty-first-century world. *A luta continua.*

Note

1 Most of the important works on race and ethnicity in sport are discussed within the chapters following; however, recent international conferences on Sport, Race and Ethnicity, the establishment of the Sport, Race and Ethnicity academic network (led by Australian scholar Daryl Adair) and volumes produced after the conferences have begun to pull together significant case studies which we expound upon here, namely, J. Nauright, A.G. Cobley, and D.K. Wiggins (eds), *Beyond C.L.R. James: Race and Ethnicity in Sport* (Fayetteville, AR: University of Arkansas Press, 2014); and D. Adair, *Sport, Race and Ethnicity: Narratives of Diversity and Difference* (Morgantown, WV: Fitness Information Technology, 2011).

PART I

Key themes of race and ethnicity in sport

1

HISTORY OF RACE AND ETHNICITY IN SPORTS*

David K. Wiggins and John Nauright

Introduction

In the white-dominated countries of Europe and North America, race and ethnicity are central to discussions of who is included in the nation and in local, regional, and national identities, what sports are played and how the media covers participation by athletes from differing backgrounds. Issues of racism among sport spectating groups, particularly in football (soccer) in Europe, remain, though there have been some positive improvements during the first two decades of the twenty-first century.

Victorian-era 'scientists' categorized humans on a continuum known as the 'Great Chain of Being', which placed Africans at one end of the spectrum and Northern Europeans at the other, with other 'races' in between, thus creating a dichotomy between blacks and whites that has been difficult to eliminate. In addition, many scholars have argued that blacks have been viewed primarily in physical terms at the expense of mental acuity, going back to the era of slavery: 'Classical racism involved a logic of dehumanization, in which Africans were defined as having bodies but not minds: in this way the superexploitation of the black body as muscle-machine could be justified. Vestiges of this are active today.'[1]

In 2010 we published a chapter on 'Race' in the *Routledge Companion to Sports History* and we base our discussion here on that overview, applying it specifically to the role of race and ethnicity in sport over time, examining major issues and events and how they have been interpreted by scholars. Several years after we published that work, there are still few issues that receive more attention from historians of sport internationally. Indeed, the massive international refugee crisis which sent millions of refugees from Syria and other parts of the Middle East, several African nations and beyond to other regions and continents, notably Europe and North America, has reignited debates about perceived cultural, religious, ethnic, and racial differences. Many stakeholders view sport as an ideal vehicle to help address integration of migrant communities as well as a tool to fight 'radicalization' in disaffected and impoverished communities in Europe with diverse ethnic and religious backgrounds.

For the entire history of modern sport, race and ethnicity have been key dividing concepts, particularly in relation to people with black and white skin colour. Race was a legitimating concept used during the age of Empire and in the dissemination of sport across European and

US empires. This soon led to debates about sporting merits of differing races, particularly in Africa and the Caribbean. More recently, the literature on race in Asia and Latin America has expanded as well, as has the focus in the USA on Hispanic-Americans and Asian-Americans in sport. As late as 1904, indigenous peoples were put on display during 'Anthropology Days' at the St. Louis World's Fair, which coincided with the 1904 Olympic Games. Among sport history research in the USA, race plays a prominent role, exceeding almost any other area of study. In Europe, examinations of race and ethnicity have largely taken place in the postcolonial context, though historians realize that race has a complex relationship to the expansion of European empires and the colonial and postcolonial contexts that emerged as a result.

In 'settler' and plantation societies such as the USA, Australia, South Africa, and the British West Indies, race and class were closely intertwined, which led to the development of a black underclass that took many decades to achieve equality of opportunity on the playing field. Barriers to participation in white-dominated competitions hardened in the imperial era of the late nineteenth and early twentieth centuries such that whether in the USA, Barbados, or South Africa, blacks were forced to participate in their own competitions segregated from white ones.

After the Second World War, though, these barriers to participation began to fall, with Jackie Robinson beginning the process of integrating white professional baseball in the USA in 1945 and the first black captain of the West Indies cricket team appearing in 1960 in the person of Frank Worrell. The Olympic Games opened increasingly to athletes from all countries, particularly as colonialism gave way to independence in Asia and then Africa in the 1950s and 1960s. Black African runners began to achieve success, beginning with Kenyan middle-distance runners at the 1954 Empire Games.[2] While South Africa was slower to integrate, by the 1990s competitions were open to all regardless of racial background.[3]

The role of race in sport is complex and one that has been examined from many angles by historians, sociologists, and biological scientists. In this chapter we outline the achievements in sport by racially and ethnically marginalized peoples and the reactions by analysts and historians to these achievements, most of whom have been white, conceding that the literature on race and sport has focused heavily on the black/white divide.[4] We also discuss in the conclusion the need to continue expanding on this line of research.[5]

The literature and experience of black athletes in the USA is most well developed and provides the majority of examples, though Rob Ruck specifically discusses the USA in this volume. Here we begin to break down the tradition of purely national-level analyses and view race and sport from a more global perspective. Indeed, an American myopia on race and sport has begun to be challenged by scholars working on issues of race and sport outside the USA.[6] A few key examples of why this is important will be given here. The famous late nineteenth-century black boxer Peter Jackson was born in the Danish Virgin Islands, and participated in famous bouts in the USA and Australia, the latter being where he died and is buried. American cyclist Marshall 'Major' Taylor achieved acclaim in Europe, the USA, and Australia. One of American boxer Jack Johnson's best known fights was held in Sydney, Australia and top West Indian cricketers by the 1920s and 1930s were playing league cricket in the north of England, most famous of whom was the great Learie Constantine.[7]

With the closer integration of ideas and better communication and transport in the world by the early 1900s, it was impossible for events in the USA, for example, not to appear in Caribbean and South African newspapers. Great black thinkers such as Marcus Garvey had a significant impact in the West Indies, Africa, USA, and beyond, and the sporting exploits of African-American boxer Joe Louis could be lauded in Johannesburg or Bridgetown as much as in Detroit. White-controlled newspapers targeting white audiences rarely mentioned black sport; newspapers focused on black readers, such as the *Pittsburgh Courier* or the *Baltimore Afro-American* in the USA or the *Bantu World* and *Umteteli wa Bantu* in South Africa, reported widely on black sporting activities. These sources have provided historians with a wealth of information that has aided in the recovery and wider presentation of histories of blacks in sport.[8] Without these sources, much of what we have learned has had to be unearthed via oral histories and the piecing together of a wide array of official and unofficial documents.

The history of black involvement in sport has been a tumultuous one. First, black athletes faced segregation until the latter decades of the twentieth century. When competitions operated in an integrated fashion, discrimination frequently occurred. In recent years there has been a more level playing field, with many athletes of colour in the West obtaining more equal opportunities in sport, at least once they reach the playing field. Finally, we have seen the emergence of what some scholars have suggested are post-racial athletes such as Michael Jordan and Tiger Woods, though this has certainly not applied universally to black athletes and began to dismantle with scandals surrounding Jordan, Woods, and other widely popular African-American sporting stars.[9] Opportunities for black men and women beyond the playing field have increased in recent years as well, though not as equally as on the playing fields and courts. As African-American activist and scholar Harry Edwards noted in 1999, 'Michael Jordan doesn't just want to be on the team – he wants to own the team.'[10] While positions for black leaders and owners in sport have been limited, aspirations in all areas of sport are not completely unrealistic for black athletes and former athletes internationally.

Contemporary analyses during the past century have tended to place black athletes in the category of Nature as either the 'primitive', unable to compete with intellectually superior whites, or as 'beast', linked to superior physicality.[11] Even in recent studies, these concepts about race and physicality and mental abilities have been central in debates about blacks and sport.[12]

These tensions when examining race in sport will be explored with reference to specific periods in the history of sport, along with approaches to the examination of race as problematic in sport history. In particular, recent work in sport history has begun to move beyond the 'recovery' phase of telling the his- and her-stories of forgotten sportsmen and women, or to paraphrase the title of one of our books, to move beyond merely bringing black sports Out of the Shadows, to a more sophisticated interrogation of the ways in which 'race' has been used in sport and wider society in the practice of sport, the telling of sports stories, and the memorializing of the sporting past and sporting heroes and heroines. Or to use Douglas Booth's taxonomy, much of the writing on race and sport history prior to 2000 involved 'reconstruction' of previously hidden pasts.[13] Recent scholarship has sought to more fully understand the historical operation of systems of power, interpretations of race, and how athletes have been constructed as racial beings.

Racial segregation in sport

In colonial societies blacks were initially exposed to different sports on plantations or in larger cities. In limited cases, some blacks appeared in competitions in the metropole as well. Before the 1860s, though, there were only a handful of recognized successes by black sportsmen (all women were largely excluded from sports), though a more complex picture of racial mixing in sporting activities before the mid-nineteenth century is beginning to emerge.[14] Tom Molineaux was perhaps the most famous international black athlete in the period before 1860 and the era of 'modern' sports. In 1810 and 1811 he famously fought Tom Cribb in England for the 'world' boxing championship. Cribb was a rare exception, though it appears that racial barriers in sport in many places were less rigid in 1860 than they became by the end of the 1890s.

A number of outstanding African-American athletes distinguished themselves in highly organized sport at both the amateur and professional levels of competition in the years immediately following the Civil War of 1861–65. Similarly, black athletes achieved success in South Africa in the sport of cricket.[15] Aboriginal Australians began to realize success in the same sport, and, though marketed as a novelty that was full of racial overtones, they toured England in the late 1860s.[16] In New Zealand, Māori players joined Pakeha (whites) in playing rugby and a New Zealand 'natives' tour of Britain took place in 1888–89.[17] Both of these tours preceded the first official national tours by Australia and New Zealand by many years. In England, the West African athlete Arthur Wharton excelled in association football and athletics in the 1880s and 1890s, including establishing the initial record for the 100 yard dash.[18] Yet, in many cases black athletes were presented to the public as novelties, much in the same way that African bodies were put on display in zoos and anthropological displays or as artefacts of Empire to be consumed by a curious public at 'home'.

By the latter years of the nineteenth century and certainly by the early 1900s, the large majority of black athletes were excluded from participating in most highly organized sports internationally, and forced to establish their own teams and leagues that operated without white support or interference. This was due to several factors. First, elites in Western society set themselves apart from the masses by forming exclusive clubs and competitions and defining what a 'sportsman' was by creating 'amateur' as opposed to 'professional' sport. As social divisions included race, blacks were excluded from these competitions such as the early modern Olympic Games. Some well-to-do blacks, though, who were deemed on the path to full 'civilization' were incorporated into sport via their participation at elite universities in the USA and England during the first few decades of the 1900s. Second, racial attitudes hardened as Western societies embarked fully on the Age of Imperialism from 1885 onward, which included the dividing up of much of the rest of the world into formal colonies controlled by Western metropoles.

This division of the world was justified on the basis of Western 'scientific' beliefs in European/white superiority over Others, as well as the 'white man's burden' of bringing civilization to the 'darker' races. Third, legal decisions reinforced racial exclusion, such as the US Supreme Court's 1896 decision in *Plessy* v. *Ferguson*, which stated that the provision of 'separate but equal' amenities for blacks and whites did not violate the US Constitution, thus ushering in an era of racist laws – particularly in the American South, referred to as the Jim Crow era. In South Africa, the 1913 *Group Areas Act* defined land ownership and use that led to further segregation and separate areas for all activities of life among different racial communities. Fourth, distinct physical characteristics were written onto the body as racial characteristics were linked to perceived differences in physicality between races in the Nature–Culture debates that continued well into the twentieth century. Yet, despite this, the historical literature on race and sport has not until recently focused primarily on racial embodiment and sport, which is fundamental to the understanding of the operation of racial codes and racial discrimination in sport.[19]

With the notable exceptions of boxing and international athletic contests, African-Americans, blacks in the Caribbean and in southern Africa, for example, established their own organizations behind segregated walls in such sports as football, basketball, baseball, cricket, and rugby union. These separate institutions were a source of great pride to black communities and served as visible examples of black organizational skill and entrepreneurship during the oppressive years of the first half of the twentieth century. Cricket clubs in Trinidad and Barbados were segregated according to race and within racial categories by class as well, as social convention prohibited playing beyond one's 'station'.[20]

In South Africa, racial distinctions mixed with class and religion such that in Cape Town mixed race or 'coloured' rugby competitions were divided between a league that allowed Muslim players and one that was exclusively non-Muslim, while African rugby players had yet another competition.[21] As Booth and Nauright make clear, however, the lure of 'civilization' for an emerging group of middle-class and Western-educated elites in South Africa led them to utilize the sport of cricket as 'a form of finishing school for the body, a place to learn correct posture, dress, deportment, and speech, and how to position one's body in space (respect the private space of social betters) and time (adopt a measured, self-assured tempo)'.[22] Odendaal refers to this group as South Africa's 'black Victorians' for adopting the vestiges of British Victorian elite culture.[23]

Sandiford confirms that the lure of British social norms conveyed via cricket were powerful in colonial Barbados: 'The blacks themselves bought enthusiastically into the Anglo-Saxon ideology and placed great store not only on cricketing prowess but on cricketing forms and formalities.'[24] The academic literature examining this period of segregation in sport has tended to laud black achievement despite great obstacles, and quite rightly celebrates the achievements of black athletes and entrepreneurs in an era of often virulent racism among white elites globally.[25]

In South Africa and the West Indies, though, historians discussing the role of sport have painted a complex picture of the tensions in black society between those who aspired to 'civilization' on European terms, those who clung to African traditions, and those caught in the middle, though Runstedtler's work on boxer Joe Louis, discussed below, demonstrates that blacks in the USA faced similar tensions. It is clear that the interwar period of the 1920s and 1930s was an era of great black achievement in education, theatre, literature, music, and indeed sport, but awareness of this was limited in white communities. An increasing number of liberal whites, though, began to promote the inclusion of black elites into mainstream society; however, the majority of whites, particularly poorer whites internationally, were resistant and viewed black achievement as a threat to their own social standing. These prejudicial thoughts were supported in part by a racial sports science that sought to isolate physical explanations for black achievement in sport. Initially, though, 'scientific' research that sought to determine the existence of race, carried out most famously at Harvard University, used this research to prove the 'natural superiority' of whites.[26] This physical racial science has been debunked within the wider scientific world; however, in sports science it has taken much longer to dissipate.[27] Fleming has highlighted how much public sway these discredited theories have had and the social impact and beliefs that have been created as a result.[28] At the end of the day, these studies have proven to be flawed in that there is no accepted method for controlling for 'race' and many times the only control has been skin colour.

While the social scientific critiques of racial sports science have been persuasive, there is still a public perception of black athletic superiority. Thus, internationally, there emerged clear tensions between those who wanted to protect whiteness and those who sought a more inclusive and somewhat colour-blind system based on culture and class. This battle has yet to be concluded. Black sportspeople were often caught in the middle as the old British notion of *mens sana in corpore sano* gave way to the brain versus brawn debate, which became an obsession in the USA and the United Kingdom in particular, especially after the Second World War. As a result, racial sports science set out to examine whether blacks had innate physical characteristics that predisposed them to sporting success. Wiggins shows that this work was being done as early as the 1930s. W. Montague Cobb, who did numerous experiments on Jesse Owens, determined that there was no scientific basis to explain Owens' success on the basis of race, and indeed that Owens possessed some physical characteristics more common to whites than blacks.[29] Cobb's findings did not end the debate, but merely presaged research to come after the Second World War. In the meantime, black athletes began to emerge from the shadows and into the mainstream within Western societies, though the process has been ongoing for several decades.

Black athletes in white-dominated countries

While black athletes in the USA, England, South Africa, Australia, and New Zealand made an impact on sport in the late nineteenth century, it was the emergence of a globalizing sporting culture centred on increasing international competitions that led many in the white-dominated Western world to 'discover' black sporting talent. Beginning with international football and followed by the first Modern Olympics in 1896, the trend towards international sport as the pinnacle of competition began to emerge. In the few sports where blacks were not completely segregated at this time, such as cycling and boxing, internationally recognized black sports figures began to appear.

Involvement of African-Americans in boxing has a long tradition, extending back to the early years of the nineteenth century when Molineaux fought Cribb. Though widely covered in England, this feat was ignored by the American press since boxing had yet to take hold in the USA.[30] Peter Jackson was an outstanding boxer during the 1890s, having won the Australian championship in 1886 and fighting several major bouts in Australia, the USA, and England. Irish-American world champion John L. Sullivan refused to fight Jackson. Scholars have argued that Sullivan's refusal was due to racial prejudice. Gorn, the leading historian of the bare-knuckle era, claims that Sullivan's refusal to fight Jackson in 1892 was due to the hardening of racial lines and his fear of losing white supporters. Yet, only a few years earlier, Sullivan had participated in a barnstorming tour in 1883–84 with the New Zealand Māori boxer Herbert A. 'Māori' Slade. Sullivan seems to have become more careful in his selection of opponents as he aged, and Wiggins points out that Sullivan's manager wanted to spare him the 'humiliation of being defeated by a Negro'.[31] Sullivan's distinction between the 'Māori' Slade and the 'black or negro' Jackson also illustrates a difference that was emerging between blacks and Latinos and native peoples within sporting worlds. A black Cuban could participate in professional baseball if defined primarily as a Cuban, but a 'negro' or black American player would be excluded.

George 'Little Chocolate' Dixon became the first black world boxing champion, winning the bantamweight title in 1890 and the featherweight title in 1891; so, by 1892 the race line was not yet complete, at least in the lighter weight divisions which did not carry the same symbolic importance as the heavyweight championship. Avoidance of competition with blacks was often used as an excuse by white athletes prior to full integration of sport. While the 'recovery' phase of sport history research on race has yielded much, there are still many gaps in the literature and many worthwhile research projects yet to be done, particularly on these variations and multiethnic distinctions that emerged between 1890 and the 1930s.

It was the success of two African-American boxers in the first decades of the twentieth century, along with the performance of Jesse Owens at the 1936 Olympics in Berlin, however, that finally generated significant international attention for black athletes across all forms of media in both black and white communities.

Jack Johnson became the first African-American to capture the world's heavyweight championship, holding on to the title for some seven years before losing to white American Jess Willard in 1915. As great as Johnson's exploits were in boxing, it was outside the ring that Johnson gained the most attention and caused the greatest controversy. He has often been referred to as 'Bad Nigger', a man who played on the worst fears of the dominant culture by marrying three white women and having illicit affairs with a number of others, often prostitutes whom he treated with an odd mixture of affection and disdain. He was absolutely fearless and attracted to dangerous escapades that challenged white conventions and mores. Although a hero for many members of his race, Johnson drew the wrath of segments of both the African-American and white communities because of his unwillingness to assume a subservient position and play the role of the grateful black. He was eventually convicted in the USA of violating the *Mann Act* for transporting a white woman across state lines for illicit purposes and was forced to leave the country for a short time before returning home to serve a jail sentence at the US federal prison in Leavenworth, Kansas.[32]

The reaction to Johnson's public persona was emblematic of a country built upon the exploitation of the Other. Racism was widespread in the USA and became more violent in the early twentieth century, particularly in the South, where lynchings were common and the Ku Klux Klan fuelled the flames of race hatred. The Klan's view was celebrated in the most famous American movie of the era, *Birth of a Nation*, where fear of the black male body and its threat to the white female body were vividly displayed. It was against this context that black athletes like Johnson were judged.[33]

The bitter aftertaste from Johnson's career, combined with continuing racial discrimination in American society, made it virtually impossible for African-American boxers to secure championship fights over the next two decades. That all changed in 1937, though, when Joe Louis, the superbly talented boxer from Detroit, became the second African-American heavyweight champion by defeating James Braddock. Louis was a decidedly different champion to Johnson and became a model for 'acceptable blacks' in sport in white-dominated societies. Possessing enormous strength and boxing skills, Louis was a quiet, dignified man who assumed the more subservient role whites expected from members of his race, but he became a hero of almost mythical proportions in the African-American (and global black) community by demolishing white fighters with remarkable regularity and serving as a symbol of possibility for those subjugated by continuing racial discrimination, becoming what was known at the time as a 'Race Man'.[34]

The coverage of Louis and his rise to stardom was not uniform, however. Praised in the black press as emblematic of racial advancement and discipline, Louis was disparaged by some in the white press for being 'lazy'. Louis' differential treatment was particularly striking in the lead-up to his 1935 fight against Italian Primo Carnera, which was held against the backdrop of Italy's looming invasion of Ethiopia. Fears of racial unrest nearly led to the cancellation of the fight, though the black press saw this as a diversionary tactic on the part of the white establishment that might be used to limit Louis' chances at top fights, echoing problems that went back to at least the time of John L. Sullivan and Peter Jackson. Indeed, NBC and CBS radio networks refused to broadcast the fight for fear of widespread racial unrest. There had never before been more security around a fight.[35] Runstedtler, in her account of Louis, examines the black and white press coverage alongside each other and focuses on competing discourses in each that placed Louis in differing contexts of racial advancement and pride, on the one hand, and white prejudice and racial embodiment of the black athlete, on the other. She thus advances the analysis of Louis as much more than an improvement on Jack Johnson or a major step forward in race relations, but uncovers the complexity of competing racial discourses surrounding the black male sporting body represented by Joe Louis. Indeed, after the Carnera fight there was debate in the black press as to how to cover Louis' success. Some argued it represented racial advancement while others argued that it took away from intellectual gains being made. Several decades later, the urban blacks' seeming 'obsession' with sporting success, which Hoberman argued in his 1997 book *Darwin's Athletes* and which was depicted in the 1994 documentary film *Hoop Dreams*, and the white-dominated media's equal 'obsession' with black physicality, demonstrated that those concerns were certainly legitimate and have remained so.[36]

Meanwhile, limited advances were nevertheless being made in the first decades of the twentieth century as white-dominated high schools and universities in the north-east and upper midwest regions of the USA began to have small numbers of black athletes on their sports teams, particularly in football and track and field. John Baxter Taylor, the great track star, was an example. He attended racially mixed Central High School and Brown Preparatory before enrolling in the University of Pennsylvania. Winner of the 440-yard dash in the 1904, 1907 and 1908 championships of the Intercollegiate Amateur Athletic Association, Taylor was a member of the gold medal-winning 400-metre relay team in the 1908 Olympic Games in London. Paul Robeson, the great singer, actor, athlete and civil rights activist, was one of three African-Americans among the 250 students at New Jersey's Somerville High School, where he starred in football, basketball, baseball, and track and field. After Somerville, Robeson enrolled at Rutgers University, where he was a member of Walter Camp's All-American football team in 1917 and 1918. Fritz Pollard starred in several sports at integrated Lane Technical High School in Chicago before becoming a student at Brown University, where he was selected to Walter Camp's All-American football team in 1916. He would eventually become a player with the Akron Pros in a league that evolved into the NFL and later achieved distinction as the first African-American head coach in a major team sport when he was hired to lead the Pros in 1921. Yet, as recent work makes clear, there are other stories of numerous African-American athletes that need to be told before we have a full picture of sport and race in the USA during the first half of the twentieth century, and this picture is true in other Western and colonial societies as well.[37]

Women, race, and sport

Ironically, African-American female athletes who participated in the Olympic Games often came from black colleges rather than predominantly white universities. The first wave of African-American women Olympians, including high-jumper Alice Coachman, the first African-American woman to capture an Olympic gold medal, had been members at various times of Cleveland Abbott's great track teams at Tuskegee Institute. The next outstanding group of African-American women Olympians, including such great athletes as Wilma Rudolph, Barbara Jones, Martha Hudson, and Lucinda Williams, were products of Ed Temple's famous Tigerbelles track teams from Tennessee State University.[38] The large number of women Olympians from historically black colleges perhaps resulted, as Cahn has suggested, from the fact that African-American women athletes were seemingly more accepted in their community than white women athletes were in their own. Although 'middle-class white women' avoided track and field because of its reputation as a 'masculine endeavor', African-American women athletes were training and honing their talents under the watchful eyes of African-American male coaches like Abbott and Temple. Unfortunately, the acceptance of African-American women in a sport such as track and field 'also reinforced disparaging stereotypes of black women as less womanly or feminine than White women'.[39] In other countries the literature on women, race and sport is less well developed, though a recent path-breaking study by Jennifer Hargreaves demonstrates the many hurdles that Afro-Caribbean and Asian women have had to navigate in Britain as well as the challenges black women in South Africa have faced in realizing opportunities in sport.[40]

Segregated 'opportunities'

Holding out as much interest to the African-American community as college sports were the all-black professional teams and leagues that were organized in the USA in the early twentieth century. A legacy from the late nineteenth century, a number of all-black teams and leagues were established in the three major sports of football, basketball, and baseball. Of these three, baseball was the most highly organized and popular among members of the African-American community; the sport enthralled thousands of fans, who found the game a meaningful experience and pleasurable counterpoint to the drudgery of everyday life.[41]

Black baseball's first successful league was formed in 1920 by Rube Foster, the once great pitcher and manager of the Chicago American Giants. Foster organized that year the National Negro Baseball League (NNL), an organization patterned along the lines of Major League Baseball and composed of teams from Chicago, Detroit, St. Louis, Kansas City, and Indianapolis. The NNL collapsed under the weight of financial instability and a host of other problems in 1931, just three years after the rival Eastern Negro League (ENL) ceased operation. In 1933, a second NNL was organized and four years later was in competition with the newly created Negro American League (NAL).[42] These two leagues were the cornerstone of black baseball over the next two decades, representing at once some of the worst features of American racism and the best creative energy of the African-American community. The NNL and NAL, although quite stable through much of the 1930s and 1940s, were never able to realize their financial potential because clubs lacked ownership of baseball parks and were forced to engage in bidding wars for outstanding players.

Clark Griffith and other moguls in Major League Baseball never allowed black teams to establish significant profit margins because of the high rent they charged for the use of their ballparks. This situation caused myriad other problems, including inadequate working and living conditions for the league's African-American players, who already suffered the indignities associated with being members of one of, if not the least esteemed minority groups in the USA. The players were forced to make long, confined road trips in buses and beat-up old cars, stay in segregated and sometimes dilapidated hotels, and survive on limited meal money. They also had to cope with the frustrations that resulted from being denied service at restaurants, hotels, and other public accommodations.[43] The more talented African-American players participated in the greatest spectacle in black baseball, the annual East–West All-Star Game. Played in Chicago's Comiskey Park, the East–West All-Star Game was a grand social event in the African-American community that drew literally thousands of fans each year from across the country. The large attendance for the East–West All-Star Game, with estimates as high as 50,000 spectators for some of the contests, resulted in much needed profits for Gus Greenlee and other entrepreneurs in black baseball. By 1935 half of the profits were placed into an emergency fund that would assist players who were not paid by financially strapped owners, while at the same time protecting owners against extended rainouts.

In South Africa segregated competitions in sport were the norm until the 1990s. Even in disadvantaged communities, differences between groups manifested themselves on the playing field. In Cape Town there was a rugby competition for whites, one for Africans and two for 'coloureds' (or mixed-race South Africans). Among coloureds one competition banned Muslims, while the other was not exclusionary but primarily Muslim in composition.[44] Local businessmen and gangs (protection rackets) in Cape Town and in other South African urban centres sponsored sports teams as a way to promote themselves and other businesses in the community.[45]

International moves to integrate white-dominated sport

Coinciding with the creation of all-black sporting organizations were bitter campaigns waged by various individuals and groups against the colour line in white organized sport. Of all the groups that hammered away at organized sport for its exclusionary policies, perhaps none were more significant than sportswriters from such well-known African-American weeklies as the *Baltimore*

Afro-American, Chicago Defender, New York Amsterdam News, and *Pittsburgh Courier*. Clamouring loudly for an end to discrimination in baseball that symbolically, and in actual practice, was most important to the African-American community, they led the battle against racism in white organized sport.[46] The historic signing of Jackie Robinson by the Brooklyn Dodgers in 1945 was the beginning of the end for separate sporting organizations in the USA and had a great symbolic effect internationally. It also helped usher in the reintegration of sport in the USA. The NFL followed baseball by beginning to integrate again in 1946. The NFL had a much shorter history of outright segregation, with no black players appearing in the league between the early 1930s and mid-1940s, though never more than two or three on a team at any one time.[47] By 1959, with the integration of the Boston Red Sox, all Major League Baseball teams finally had black players on their rosters. This was not an easy process and in some sports, such as basketball, coaches and officials attempted to ensure that the majority of players on the court or field at any one time were white. By the early 1970s this situation largely disappeared as the last major sports league in the USA, the Southeastern Conference in NCAA football integrated.[48]

In other countries desegregation of sports or the opening up of opportunities for new migrants gathered pace after the Second World War. The exceptions to this rule were the racially based regimes in southern Africa, most notably in South Africa and Rhodesia (now Zimbabwe). Indeed, international focus on these two countries led to isolation in the Olympics by the end of the 1960s and in other sports soon after. As early as 1967, though, the South African government realized that racial exclusion in sport was a problem, particularly when New Zealand postponed a planned visit to South Africa due to exclusion of its Māori players. The South African government relented and allowed Māoris to tour in 1970, generating the first crack in a solid racist sporting policy. After piecemeal changes were rejected internationally, sport moved to integrate by the early 1990s.[49]

In the USA, toward the latter part of the 1960s, African-American athletes became involved in the Civil Rights movement by actively protesting against racial discrimination in sport and the larger society both at home and internationally. The two major forums for protest were the Olympic Games and predominantly white university campuses, where African-American athletes staged boycotts and spoke out against the racial discrimination experienced by them and other members of the African-American community. Protests of athletes contributed to South Africa's exclusion from the 1968 Olympics, its expulsion from the Olympic Movement and a boycott of the 1976 Olympics in Montreal due to the participation of New Zealand, which maintained sporting ties with South Africa in rugby union. This activism sparked a rise in academic research on race and sport in the 1970s and 1980s, with much of the international work focused on the anti-apartheid issue and isolating white South Africa,[50] while in the USA a project of recovering black contributions to sport gathered force.

Rebellious African-American athletes fought for racial equality through very visible public protests. Certainly the most celebrated protest was the proposed boycott of the 1968 Olympic Games in Mexico City, led by Harry Edwards, then an instructor at San Jose State College, who assembled a group of outstanding African-American athletes who threatened to withdraw from the Games in Mexico City unless certain demands were met. The demands included the removal of Avery Brundage as president of the International Olympic Committee, restoration of Muhammad Ali's heavyweight boxing title, exclusion of Rhodesia and South Africa from Olympic competition, appointment of at least two African-Americans to the US Olympic Committee, complete desegregation of the New York Athletic Club (NYAC), and addition of at least two African-American coaches to the men's Olympic track and field team.

By the latter part of the 1960s, African-American athletes, sometimes in concert with white athletes, were creating chaos on college campuses by becoming active participants in the Civil

Rights movement and protesting racial discrimination in sport and society at large. Inspired by the examples set by such outspoken individuals as Jim Brown, Bill Russell, and Muhammad Ali, African-American college athletes shed their traditional conservative approach to racial matters and vehemently protested everything from the lack of African-American studies in the curriculum to the dearth of African-American coaches and athletic administrators. This path was sometimes paved with dire consequences; many African-American athletes endured the wrath of university administrations and jeopardized their careers by speaking out on behalf of themselves and other members of their race.[51]

One of the targets of black protests was the apartheid system in South Africa that kept black South Africans from competing internationally. During the 1970s and 1980s blacks and whites internationally worked tirelessly to bring about an end to racial discrimination in sport there.[52] By the 1990s official segregation in sport was abolished nearly everywhere in the world, though the issue of race in sport was nowhere near the 'end of its history'.

Beyond black and white: race and ethnicity in sport in the twenty-first century

In North American professional sport, players now come from many parts of the world. NBA teams boast of players from Argentina, Brazil, Canada, China, Croatia, Serbia, Spain, Greece, Lithuania, and a host of others. Professional baseball in the USA has had players from all over Central America, Venezuela, the Caribbean, Japan, the Netherlands, Australia, South Africa, and many more. The National Hockey League staffs its teams with players from all over Europe as well as from Canada and the USA, though it remains largely a white, non-Hispanic league. In Europe, most leagues and major teams are populated with players from other countries as well as other continents. It is common to find South Americans playing in Spain and Italy, Africans in England and the Netherlands. In *How Soccer Explains the World*, Frank Foer covers many cases of the globalization of soccer, including one about a Nigerian playing in the Ukraine.[53] As sport has globalized, athletes have moved with opportunities. While on the one hand this has had a deleterious impact on local competitions in places like Brazil, Argentina, and Nigeria, it has brought Empires home to play so to speak. As a result, there has been more direct exposure to players from different cultures. Fans, media, administrators, and analysts all have had to alter their perceptions and understandings as a result, not always to positive effect. This process has accelerated since the 1990s with the post-*Bosman* ruling era in European football, the fall of the Berlin Wall and migration of Eastern Europeans to North American and Western European leagues, and the global search for talent among universities in the USA. Historians of sport internationally have made a number of advances in this period as well, developing more sophisticated analyses utilizing a wider array of sources including oral histories, previously untapped media and club records, literary texts, and through the development of broader techniques of analysis drawing on postcolonialism and postmodernism.

The history of race and sport has effectively moved from the discovery and recovery phases to one in which the meanings of race as a category for discussion in sport are explored through an examination of embodiment, discourse, and political economy to understand the stubborn persistence of race. While great strides have been made in the recovery of the sporting histories of people of colour throughout the world, there remains much to be uncovered. Race and ethnicity remain powerful social constructions impacting contemporary sport and all too often perceptions of the past invade the present.

Notes

* This chapter is based on an earlier version entitled 'Race' by Wiggins and Nauright, which appeared in *The Routledge Companion to Sports History* (London: Routledge, 2010). It has been expanded and updated for this volume.

1 K. Mercer, *Welcome to the Jungle: New Positions in Black Cultural Studies* (London: Routledge, 1994), 138.

2 J. Bale and J. Sang, *Kenyan Running* (London: Frank Cass, 1996).

3 J. Nauright, *Long Run to Freedom: Sport, Cultures and Identities in South Africa* (Morgantown, WV: Fitness Information Technology, 2010); D. Booth, *The Race Game* (London: Frank Cass, 1998); for the 1904 Anthropology Days, see S. Brownell, ed., *The 1904 Anthropology Days and Olympic Games: Sport, Race, and American Imperialism* (Lincoln, NE: University of Nebraska Press, 2008).

4 In many former imperialist societies social divisions have diversified. In the USA, for example, there are now more people classified as Latino than African-American, and a sizable Asian minority also exists. In the United Kingdom racial divisions occur primarily between whites, African-descended people (Afro-Caribbean), and South Asians (most of whose families originated in India and Pakistan).

5 For the most recent collection of historical work on sport, race and ethnicity, see J. Nauright, A. Cobley, and D. Wiggins, eds, *Beyond C.L.R. James: Race and Ethnicity in Sport* (Fayetteville, AR: University of Arkansas Press, 2014).

6 See, for example, A. Saeed, 'What's in a Name: Muhammad Ali and the Politics of Cultural Identity', *Sport in Society* 5, 3 (2002), 52–72; K. Sandiford, 'Shooting Hoops Against Darwin's Athletes: A Barbadian Response to John Hoberman', *The Sports Historian* 19, 2 (1999), 112–27. *Note: In this chapter we use the contested term 'American' when referring to citizens of the USA, not as an exclusionary term as all peoples of the Americas are indeed Americans on a larger level.*

7 A. Calder, 'A Man For All Cultures: The Careers of Learie Constantine', *Culture, Sport, Society* 6, 1 (2003), 19–42.

8 As a result, though, we know much more detail about black sport in these areas; see, for example R. Ruck, *Sandlot Seasons: Sport in Black Pittsburgh* (Urbana and Chicago, IL: University of Illinois Press, 1993).

9 D. Andrews, ed., *Michael Jordan Inc.: Corporate Sport, Media Culture, and Late Modern America* (Albany, NY: SUNY Press, 2001); C.L. Cole, 'The Place of Golf in U.S. Imperialism', *Journal of Sport and Social Issues* 26, 4 (2002), 331–6.

10 Cited by C.K. Harrison in his Foreword to D. Andrews, ed., *Michael Jordan Inc.: Corporate Sport, Media Culture, and Late Modern America* (Albany, NY: SUNY Press, 2001), ix.

11 This is discussed in J. Nauright and T. Magdalinski, '"A Hapless Attempt at Swimming": Representations of Eric Moussambani', *Critical Arts* 17, 1–2 (2003), 106–22; and D. Booth and J. Nauright, 'Embodied Identities: Sport and Race', in J. Nauright, A. Cobley, and D. Wiggins, eds, *Beyond C.L.R. James: Race and Ethnicity in Sport* (Fayetteville, AR: University of Arkansas Press, 2014), 41–62.

12 See J. Hoberman, *Darwin's Athletes: How Sport Has Damaged Black America and Preserved the Myth of Race* (New York, NY: Mariner Books, 1997); and the many reviews and debates this text evoked. More controversial is J. Entine, *Taboo: Why Black Athletes Dominate Sports and Why We're Afraid to Talk about It* (New York, NY: Public Affairs, 2001).

13 See D. Booth, *The Field* (London: Routledge, 2006).

14 For example, W.H. Boulware, 'Black Urban Leisure Pursuits and Cultural Identity in Eighteenth Century South Carolina and Georgia', *International Journal of Regional and Local Studies* Series 2, 1, 1 (2005), 83–106.

15 Nauright, *Long Run to Freedom*; A. Odendaal, *Cricket in Isolation: The Politics of Race and Cricket in South Africa* (Cape Town: The Author, 1977); C. Merrett and J. Nauright, 'South Africa', in B. Stoddart and K. Sandiford, eds, *The Imperial Game: Cricket and Cultural Power* (Manchester: Manchester University Press, 1998), 55–78.

16 J. Mulvaney and R. Harcourt, *Cricket Walkabout: The Australian Aborigines in England* (Melbourne: Macmillan, 1988).

17 G. Ryan, *Forerunners of the All Blacks: The 1888–89 New Zealand Native Football Team in Britain, Australia and New Zealand* (Christchurch: Canterbury University Press, 1993).

18 P. Vasili, *The First Black Footballer, Arthur Wharton 1865–1930: An Absence of Memory* (London: Routledge, 1998).

19 See J. Bale, *Imagined Olympians* (Minneapolis, MN: University of Minnesota Press, 2002); Booth and Nauright, 'Embodied Identities'; Nauright and Magdalinski, 'Hapless Attempt at Swimming'. Excellent

historical context on embodiment, race, and sport appears in D.L. Andrews, 'The Fact(s) of Michael Jordan's Blackness: Excavating a Floating Racial Signifier', in D.L. Andrews, ed., *Michael Jordan Inc.: Corporate Sport, Media Culture, and Late Modern America* (Albany, NY: SUNY Press, 2001), 107–52; and J. Schultz, 'Reading the Catsuit: Serena Williams and the Production of Blackness at the 2002 U.S. Open', *Journal of Sport and Social Issues* 29, 3 (2005), 338–57.

20 See Booth and Nauright, 'Embodied Identities'; K. Sandiford, *The Cricket Nurseries of Colonial Barbados: The Elite Schools 1865–1966* (Kingston: University Press of the West Indies, 1998).

21 J. Nauright, 'Race, Rugby and Popular Culture: "Coloured" Rugby in Cape Town, South Africa', in T. Chandler and J. Nauright, *Making the Rugby World: Race, Gender, Commerce* (London: Routledge, 1999), 27–42.

22 Booth and Nauright, 'Embodied Identities', 58.

23 A. Odendaal, 'South Africa's Black Victorians: Sport and Society in South Africa in the Nineteenth Century', in J.A. Mangan, ed., *Pleasure, Profit, Proselytism: British Culture and Sport at Home and Abroad 1700–1914* (London: Frank Cass, 1988), 193–214.

24 K. Sandiford, *Cricket Nurseries of Colonial Barbados*, 147.

25 M. Lomax, *Black Baseball Entrepreneurs, 1860–1901: Operating by Any Means Necessary* (Syracuse, NY: Syracuse University Press, 2001); D. Wiggins, *Glory Bound: Black Athletes in a White America* (Syracuse, NY: Syracuse University Press, 1997).

26 J. Coakley, *Sports in Society: Issues and Controversies*, 12th edn (Boston, MA: McGraw-Hill, 2014).

27 B. Carrington and I. McDonald, 'Introduction', in B. Carrington and I. McDonald, eds, *'Race', Sport and British Society* (London: Routledge, 2001), 4–10.

28 See L. Davis, 'The Articulation of Difference: White Preoccupation with the Question of Racially Linked Genetic Differences Among Athletes', *Sociology of Sport Journal* 7 (1990), 179–87; D. Wiggins, 'Great Speed but Little Stamina: The Historical Debate Over Black Athletic Superiority', *Journal of Sport History* 16 (1989), 158–85; S. Fleming, 'Racial Science and South Asia and Black Physicality', in B. Carrington and I. McDonald, eds, *'Race', Sport and British Society* (London: Routledge, 2001), 105–20. Fleming cites several 'scientific' studies of race and sport, including: M.J. Berry, T.J. Zehnder, C.B. Berry, S.E. Davis and S.K. Anderson, 'Cardiovascular Responses in Black and White Males During Exercise', *Journal of Applied Physiology* 74, 2 (1993), 755–60; J. Samson and M. Yerles, 'Racial Differences in Sports Performance', *Canadian Journal of Sports Science* 13, 2 (1988), 109–16; as well as the popular reaction: M. Gladwell, 'Why are Blacks So Good at Sport?', *Sunday Telegraph Review*, 20 July 1997, 1–2; S. Conner, 'Bannister Says Blacks Were Born to Run', *Independent*, 14 September 1995, 3; and S.L. Price, 'Is it in the Genes?', *Sports Illustrated* 87, 23 (1997), 53–5.

29 Wiggins, 'Great Speed but Little Stamina', 161, citing W.M. Cobb, 'Race and Runners', *Journal of Health and Physical Education* (January 1936), 3–7, 52–6.

30 E. Gorn, *The Manly Art: The Lives and Times of the Great Bare-Knuckle Champions* (London: Robson Books, 1986), 35–6.

31 D. Wiggins, 'Peter Jackson and the Elusive Heavyweight Championship: A Black Athlete's Struggle Against the Late Nineteenth Century Color-line', *Journal of Sport History* 12 (1985), 155; Gorn, *The Manly Art*, 227, 238.

32 R. Roberts, *Papa Jack: Jack Johnson and the Era of White Hopes* (New York, NY: The Free Press, 1985); G. Ward, *Unforgiveable Blackness: The Rise and Fall of Jack Johnson* (New York, NY: Vintage Press, 2006); T. Runstedtler, *Jack Johnson, Rebel Sojourner: Boxing in the Shadow of the Global Color Line* (Berkeley and Los Angeles, CA: University of California Press, 2013).

33 See M. Stokes, *D.W. Griffith's the Birth of a Nation: A History of the Most Controversial Motion Picture of All Time* (New York, NY: Oxford University Press, 2008).

34 T. Runstedtler, 'In Sports the Best Man Wins: How Joe Louis Whupped Jim Crow', in A. Bass, ed., *In the Game: Race, Identity, and Sports in the Twentieth Century* (New York, NY: Palgrave Macmillan, 2005), 48.

35 Runstedtler, 'In Sports the Best Man Wins', 64–7.

36 Hoberman, *Darwin's Athletes*.

37 C. Martin, 'The Color Line in Midwestern College Sports, 1890–1960', *Indiana Magazine of History* 98 (2002), 85–112; J. Nauright, 'The First African-American Football Captain: Theatrece Gibbs and Iowa Football in the 1930s', *Gridiron Greats: Magazine of Football History* 3, 6 (2004), 20–3; D. McMahon, 'Remembering the Black and Gold: African-Americans, Sport Memory, and the University of Iowa', in S.G. Whiting, ed., *Sport and Memory in North America* (London: Frank Cass, 2001), 63–98; Jamie Schultz, *Moments of Impact: Injury, Racialized Memory, and Reconciliation in College Football* (Lincoln, NE: University of Nebraska Press, 2016).

38 S. Cahn, *Coming on Strong: Gender and Sexuality in Twentieth-Century Women's Sport* (Cambridge, MA: Harvard University Press, 1994).

39 Ibid., 112.

40 J. Hargreaves, *Heroines of Sport: The Politics of Difference and Identity* (London: Routledge, 2000).

41 N. Lanctot, *Negro League Baseball: The Rise and Ruin of a Black Institution* (Philadelphia, PA: University of Pennsylvania Press, 2004); Lomax, *Black Baseball Entrepreneurs*; Ruck, *Sandlot Seasons*; R. Peterson, *Only the Ball Was White* (New York, NY: Oxford University Press, 1992).

42 Lomax, *Black Baseball Entrepreneurs*; Peterson, *Only the Ball Was White*.

43 Lanctot, *Negro League Baseball*; Peterson, *Only the Ball Was White*.

44 See Nauright, *Long Run to Freedom*.

45 See discussion on sub-Saharan Africa by Nauright (319–29) in. S.W. Pope and J. Nauright, eds, *The Routledge Companion to Sports History* (London: Routledge, 2010).

46 J. Tygiel, *Baseball's Great Experiment: Jackie Robinson and His Legacy* (New York, NY: Oxford University Press, 1983; 25th anniversary edn 2008).

47 M. Lomax, 'The African-American Experience in Professional Football', *Journal of Social History* 33, 1 (1999), 163–75; T.G. Smith, 'Outside the Pale: The Exclusion of Blacks from the National Football League, 1934–1946', *Journal of Social History* 15 (1988), 255–81.

48 For an interesting discussion of the role of students and student athletes in the ending of segregation in NCAA football, see L. Demas, 'Beyond Jackie Robinson: Racial Integration in American College Football and New Directions in Sport History', *History Compass* 5, 2 (2007), 675–90.

49 For more on this, see J. Nauright, '"Like Fleas on a Dog": New Zealand and Emerging Protest Against South African Sport, 1965–74', *Sporting Traditions* 10, 1 (1993), 54–77.

50 For example: C. de Broglio, *South Africa: Racism in Sport* (London: International Defense Aid Fund, 1970); R. Lapchick, *The Politics of Race and International Sport: The Case of South Africa* (Westport, CT: Greenwood Press, 1975); R. Thompson, *Retreat from Apartheid: New Zealand's Sporting Contacts with South Africa* (Oxford: Oxford University Press, 1975); R. Archer and A. Bouillon, *The South African Game: Sport and Racism* (London: Zed Books, 1982).

51 See H. Edwards, *The Revolt of the Black Athlete* (New York, NY: Macmillan, 1969); D. Hartmann, *Race, Culture and the Revolt of the Black Athlete: The 1968 Olympic Protests and their Aftermath* (Chicago, IL: University of Chicago Press, 2004); for race and radical politics in global football, see G. Kuhn, *Soccer vs. State: Tackling Football and Radical Politics* (Oakland, CA: PM Press, 2011).

52 For more detailed discussion of these campaigns and their role in sports history, see Booth, *The Race Game*; Nauright, *Long Run to Freedom*.

53 F. Foer, *How Soccer Explains the World: An Unlikely Theory of Globalization* (London: HarperCollins, 2005); also see S. Agergaard and N. Tiesler, eds, *Women, Soccer and Transnational Migration* (London: Routledge, 2014); R. Elliott and J. Harris, eds, *Football and Migration: Perspectives, Places, Players* (London: Routledge, 2014). For baseball, see R. Ruck, *Raceball: How the Major Leagues Colonized the Black and Latin Game* (Boston, MA: Beacon Press, 2012); A. Klein, *Growing the Game: The Globalization of Major League Baseball* (New Haven, CT: Yale University Press, 2008); for ice hockey, see D. Whitson and R. Gruneau, eds, *Artificial Ice: Hockey, Culture and Commerce* (Toronto: Garamond Press, 2006).

2

THE ANTHROPOLOGY OF RACE AND ETHNICITY IN SPORT

Unfolding the map

Meghan Ferriter

In the first decade of the 2000s, I embarked upon fieldwork with the intent of exploring the ways people in the USA and Scotland talked about, played, and integrated sport into their daily lives. I was particularly interested in the ways hybridization and globalization intersected with professional sport, its labor flows, and the media–sports complex in the public understanding of sport in society. Were these forces eliciting a unified understanding of sport at local, professional, and global levels as individuals increasingly consumed mediated representations of sport? Was the collective being transcended in favor of a global or temporal connection? Or was it all about keeping it local and individual? There was a feeling that it was a big, wide world ripe for comparison and exchange at the close, local level of similarities and pulling back to find the difference in ever-expanding space and time. It seemed it would be very easy to get lost; I sought guides for my quest.

As I started to situate myself, I pursued anthropological guideposts that might help mark the way. The American experience of mediated sport – and secondary and collegiate sport with which I was most familiar – is colored by the intersections of gender, age, and race. The professional sporting spectacles are built through contests and reify inequality; the additional layers of stratification are defined at the points at which these factors of social identity intersect. I was confident anthropological projects that had preceded me would help me surface questions and perhaps refine my decision-making.

Instead, I was surprised to find limited focus with fieldwork on the anthropology of sport; there were starting points with ethnographies of supporter groups, which often finished with calls to action around sport based on its integration in the lives of people around the world. There seemed to be few resources for me to plan an unfolding journey. To help me make my way, I borrowed and became traveling companions with the definitions, markers, and poles of my disciplinary cousins in sociology. Since that point, anthropological inquiry in the sporting space has continued to grow.

Yet, the still loosely articulated anthropology of sport retains the ability – and holds the responsibility – to expand by exploring the experiences and consequences of race in sport. If direct investigations of sport and race and its effects have remained at the periphery of anthropological inquiry, are anthropological lenses appropriate for understanding the sites at which race and ethnicity converge with sport?

In this chapter, I affirm that anthropology is prepared to grapple with the varied terrain of lived experiences, representations, and the changing fields of sport. I add that it is a set of methods and epistemology that is just as capable of handling the consequences of race in this space. Anthropology's occasionally fuzzy focus on these intersections presents opportunities to sharpen the picture, while using the tools anthropologists wield to map out understanding.

This chapter encounters anthropology's history with and challenges of defining race and sport. It then tackles useful means of conceptualizing race and ethnicity and their consequences in defining social worlds. Then, after offering some starting points for the ways anthropologists and other social researchers have engaged with sport, I suggest several ways in which anthropology is suited to critically interrogating the consequences of racism and racialization in the context of sport. The intersections of these topics remain under-explored and, therefore, full of opportunity for researchers.

This chapter briefly touches on ethnicity, but focuses on the opportunities and transferable approaches from anthropology where race and sport meet. It also emphasizes research from cultural and social anthropological approaches, as discussed further below. I highlight these studies to serve as signposts as you keep this chapter in your hip pocket when undertaking explorations in the grounded contexts of local, amateur, national, professional, and global sport.

Getting bearings: exploring the field of anthropology

Before charting a course, it may be useful to pinpoint a few definitions. What is anthropology? Anthropology is the study of humans and culture. Consisting of four fields, anthropology includes a range of techniques and positioning for exploring humans and culture. In the USA, the four fields of anthropology are physical anthropology, archaeology, linguistics, and cultural anthropology. In the British tradition, social anthropology also evolved to study social actors and actions. Anthropologists share a desire to understand the world around them, to test and apply scientific theory to social settings, and to determine the structures of human interaction. They also interpret and tell the stories of social, political, and international relationships as they emerge: geographically, as embodied experiences, and with what symbolic properties.

Applying the four fields, you might elect to explore the ways particular groups of people communicate displeasure around officiating (linguistics) or compare the artifacts of leisure practice in Mexico to those in Afghanistan (archaeology). The concepts and procedures of physical anthropology may be easily applied to actively analyze sporting bodies and the limits of their experiences. Since physical anthropologists study growth and the way it is affected by activity, athletic enterprises are an appropriate vehicle for inquiry. The techniques of physical anthropology, including measuring and classifying body types, have direct and indirect use for exploration of sport behavior.[1] The four fields offer a holistic, encompassing approach to understand culture and social organization in current or historical contexts.

A hallmark of anthropology is fieldwork, and specifically for cultural anthropology, ethnography. While not an exclusively anthropological practice, ethnography remains a prominent methodology for undertaking social and cultural enquiry and understanding the situated experiences of social actors. Examples of ethnographic work are included below as one of the vehicles through which race has been explored. Anthropology is a discipline primed to unpack the intersecting manifestations of culture and social values in sport, as well as race and ethnicity: as inscribed upon physical movement, self-presentation, rituals and rites of passage, and political relationships.

Comparative approaches are also one of the strengths of anthropological research. The discipline of anthropology emerged and grew in a period of "contact" between Western cultures and indigenous populations. Combined with other scientific beliefs and social hierarchies, early anthropologists – individuals representing an educated, elite class – sought to understand the world around them by taking to the field.[2] Furthermore, cultural anthropologists concern themselves with expressions including rituals: the patterns of activity that are explored as signifying basic social messages relating to the group's organization and cohesion. Sport may be explored as both a ritual and a game – and can be read as a cultural construction that carries symbolic communication of meanings and values between participants.

Anthropology was, even in its infancy, a battleground of definitions and theoretical positioning. In particular, the practices of colonialism and scientific inquiry meshed with a desire to chart the physical world. Unilineal evolutionists, for example, believed anthropology should mirror the natural sciences in a pursuit of the general laws that dictate cultural development. Franz Boas is remembered as resisting racial typologies in favor of interpretations grounded in the local, specific contexts of culture. The Boasian tradition led early resistance against racism and its effects.[3]

Early anthropological projects included ethnological studies whose financial and political support demanded an understanding of the difference between populations; in the USA this included the classification work of the Bureau of (American) Ethnology, heavily influenced by theories of cultural evolution.[4] In these projects, the physical, economic, political, social, as well as leisure activities of populations were documented, along with language and other cultural practices. Anthropology, then, is tightly tied to the development of the concept of race(s); the discipline has remained a product of the political, economic, social, and cultural moments in which it is occurring.

Ericksen and Murphy have observed that anthropologists "have been able to discuss theory without always having to articulate just what it means to themselves or to others."[5] In many ways, the elusive nature of concrete definitions spills over into the anthropology of sport, as well as the ways anthropology has been challenged to articulate "race." Since the end of the twentieth century, anthropologists have been catalyzed internally by provocations from Michael Omi and Howard Winant (1994) and Carol Mukhopadhyay and Yolanda Moses (1997), and evaluated as still excluding race as a foundational concept.[6]

Culture defines, evolves, and reinforces concepts and practices of race and racialization; anthropology is designed to understand the cultural practices that condition members to perceive socially constructed categories as natural. Developing an understanding of the historical contexts of the discipline support moves forward into enquiries of our own with reflexivity and an ability to critically question our own origins, status, and privilege to understand the world into which we are entering as researchers.

Mapping race and ethnicity

Race is a system of classification that is socially defined and culturally constructed. Lacking a biological or genetic basis, race is a social category whose effect creates local inequalities and global differences and is applied to then justify those conditions as natural. In this chapter, I engage with the concept of "race" rather than exclusively racism and racialization. I take this position in this context because race remains more than a salient feature of sport and the lives of those who engage in and with sporting practices. Race is real; a categorization that packs a punch even while it floats like a bee. A formidable illusion, race and its effects stratify and impact the lives of athletes, fans, administrators, coaches, venue managers, sports journalists, and more. As Douglas Hartmann observes, "sport is one of the most powerful and important institutions in the production, legitimation and (at least potentially) contestation of contemporary racial formations."[7] It must be stated explicitly that – at the risk of giving the term authority – race requires anthropological focus to deal with constantly shifting forms of classification. Race and sport are equally enmeshed with lives in evident and invisible ways, and anthropology can help provide real examples to move beyond theoretical discussions of racism and racialization in sport.

While social inequality is written across the historical record, race is a modern concept. Created as a mode of classification, race thus remains divisive. The American Anthropological Association's 1998 statement on race states:

> How people have been accepted and treated within the context of a given society or culture has a direct impact on how they perform in that society. The "racial" worldview was invented to assign some groups to perpetual low status, while others were permitted access to privilege, power, and wealth.[8]

Race-based world-views are enacted through racism and racialization. The power of this social category is that the many cultural practices that it supports and informs are perceived as inevitable. As a constructed social category, race dictates access to specific economic and social resources and political power. It is a concept that is deployed in such a way as to enable and constrain practices and social interactions. Race is, therefore, a complex manifestation of intersecting systems of inequality.

Race is also a "floating signifier" that is used to mark boundaries and dictate the rules of inclusion and exclusion based on historically specific circumstances.[9] Race is not fixed and is always in flux as a process of negotiating interaction. Banton and Harwood explain "as a way of categorizing people, race is based upon a delusion because popular ideas about racial classification lack scientific validity and are moulded by political pressures rather than by the evidence from biology."[10] Yet, in sport, biological distinctions are consistently reinforced through racialized discourse regarding sporting performances.

Anthropology has over the last century and a half shifted constellations of definitions from a focus on perceived biological race, to culture, to ethnicity; indeed, Eric Wolf identified the "special responsibility" of anthropology to carefully interrogate the language wielded and definitions at play in its disciplinary discourse.[11] Ethnicity is about differentiation and pertains to boundary maintenance, a part of a process of exchange and interaction.[12] Ethnic groups share common cultural characteristics based on a shared history. While race is defined through difference and boundaries, ethnicity is articulated through similarities and boundaries. Anthropology is well placed to survey contours and layered contexts of these boundaries with ethnography.

Steve Fenton situates ethnicity, like race, as a socially constructed concept and offers the following as a starting point: "that ethnicity refers to the social construction of descent and culture, the social mobilization of descent and culture, and the meanings and implications of classification systems built around them."[13] Exploring definitions of ethnic groups and ethnicity in context also demonstrates the need to observe which group(s) constructs the category, thus implicating relations of power and discourses in the development of ethnicity.[14]

The concept of the "boundary" is essential to understandings of "race" as well as "ethnicity." Cornell and Hartmann have argued that race continues to be viewed as the most powerful and persistent group boundary.[15] Certainly it is one in which the lines are constantly marked. Definitions of ethnicity and "race" are defined through opposition, with categorizations varying as needed to serve the interests of power. In this way, race remains an illusion rather than a scientific reality; its impact, however, remains more than a nod to power.

Race and ethnicity have varied in their definitions over time based on cultural meanings and ideological stances; what has constituted the definitions of race at one time may become a marker of ethnicity at a later date. For example, Jews have been historically defined as a race but are now considered an ethnic group.[16] Similarly, in the nineteenth century, the Irish were framed within British media as a distinct race.[17] It is necessary that explorations of race, even in a contemporary sense, keep closely in mind the context of its historical framing since "race categories and meanings attached to them are not static."[18] The aspects that have been used to define these social categories have changed with time in relation to cultural conditions, historical processes, and interaction between groups of people.

To underscore once more: race is a myth *and* a reality. Anthropology's experiences in exploring and extrapolating from myth, then, would be an appropriate fit for detailing the serious nature of the concept with specific cases. Race is a process; something that is learned through interaction and reproduced by institutions.[19]

While discussing race and physical anthropology in 1997, Alan Goodman forecasted that "Race, or rather a rethinking of the terms and constructs of human variation, may paradoxically be a place where biological and cultural anthropologists might fruitfully come together again." If one extends this line of thinking to the intersections of sport, one might see where anthropological approaches and methods may rendezvous to articulate the consequences of racialization.[20] If the effect of race has been to categorize and stratify and the impact of ethnicity to define at the boundaries and borders, now there are opportunities for anthropology to use sport as the field of vision to blur, read between, and surface the meaning written across the lines.

With what latitude: sport in anthropology

Explorations of sport, leisure, and play have featured in anthropological accounts from the start of the discipline, from the work of Bronislaw Malinowski to Franz Boas, and Stewart Culin's and James Mooney's explorations of the sport of Native Americans.[21] A movement toward anthropology of sport, however, did not clearly emerge until the 1960s. Even then, sport and games were seen as expressing other conditions and meanings. The late Eduardo Archetti suggested that anthropology with a focus on the primitive and the past has largely turned away from the investigation of sport based on sport's role as a modernizing force.[22]

Bronislaw Malinowski's time with the Trobriand Islanders in the second decade of the twentieth century allowed him to theorize that social activities, including sport, which he observed as having been changed from its original code to an adapted version, functioned to meet the needs of individuals rather than society. In particular, Malinowski focused on the religious and ritualized dimensions of social activities, including cricket, and the ways they served to meet the needs of the people in performing violence, debate, and gambling.[23]

Even while some anthropologists detailed engagement with games, anthropology as a discipline regarded these sports as exotic activities and contrasts with modern culture. Sport was not yet a subject of sustained, comparative research.[24] In 1973, Clifford Geertz applied Jeremy Bentham's concept of deep play to Balinese cockfights and connected expressions of masculinity to competition. Soon after in 1976 Jerry Leach released a documentary film that detailed the lives and leisure of Trobriand Islanders; it highlighted participation and adaptation of a sport introduced as part of the colonizing process. In 1982, G. Whitney Azoy traced the politics and performance in the play of the equestrian sport buzkashi.[25]

These studies from Geertz, Leach, and Azoy demonstrated that sport is a valuable site at which one might study the culture and society in which it is performed; here, sport is approached as a vehicle for expressing or communicating cultural values, performing meaningful social activity, and making sense of one's world. Geertz's focus on interpreting social discourse and expressions of personality, and his richly detailed ethnographic writing and influence in the anthropology of sport, is also surfaced by his work beyond the Balinese and can be seen in other readings of sport as social activity and ritual in sport. Leach's 1976 film crafted a view into Trobriander cricket with a window into this culture as it had evolved since Malinowsi's study. The film was read as dynamically displaying the variations of play and cricket's functions at the local level – in colorful contrast to traditional (English) cricket. No one element is the creative response to colonizing influences for Leach, yet the complexity of the way sport is played in total by all serves as the contrast. This adaptation of sport, according to Leach, is what becomes a "creative adaptation of tradition to contemporary circumstances" and is, therefore, a window on culture at the intersections of space, time, and values.[26] In other contexts and two decades later, Arjun Appadurai investigated cricket as a means of enacting values removed from the contexts of colonialism tied to the origins of the sport in India.[27]

More comprehensive overviews and situating of sport in the disciplinary history of anthropology will detail the interactions between the founding perspectives of anthropology and the place of sport in cultures with which anthropologists came into contact.[28] Susan Brownell's edited volume surfacing the multifaceted interpretations and results of the 1904 Anthropology Days at the World's Fair in St. Louis further pinpoints turns in the disciplinary discourse through the lens of sport. The showcase of "savage" pitted against. "modern" in 1904 led to strong critical responses and a movement from a racial pseudoscience to more relativist approach; the perspectives in Brownell's volume expanded analyses of the enduring relevance of the event and the ideas it manifested.[29] Indeed, anthropology has continued to encounter sport, athleticism, and competition in many settings. Kendall Blanchard, in collaboration with Alyce Cheska in 1985, created the first general text providing an overview of the anthropology of sport. Emphasizing the role of cultural anthropology, their presentation of the anthropology of sport is organized to parallel an introduction to anthropology by focusing on theory, method, and ethnographic insights. Blanchard's revised edition matches the function of sports in levels of society (culture): bands, chiefdoms, primitive states, and archaic civilizations.[30] Throughout the text, the many ways in which anthropology may be useful in understanding the role, experiences, rituals, and purposes of sport are emphasized. The message is clear here, as similarly voiced by Noel Dyck and Hans Hognestad, and with Thomas Carter: the anthropology of sport has powerful potential for applied research and more is necessary.[31]

For the context of this chapter, however, Blanchard's text is lacking – it fails to directly discuss studies that have grappled with race, instead focusing on social organization and arrangements, gender, age, and history in the anthropology of sport. Additionally, though sport is an entrenched feature of contemporary societies, there are few considerations of the dimensions of sport participation and increasingly organized sporting infrastructure and professionalization of sport. The same lack of focus on race is seen in the very useful reflections on the utility of and need for more anthropology of sport from Allen Guttmann, Noel Dyck and Eduard Archetti, Roberts Sands, and Thomas Carter.[32] However, it should be noted that these works speak broadly to the need to understand the consequences of social categorization that constrains or stratifies social interaction.

Sport, particularly as practiced at the local level, is frequently perceived as a tool of integrating groups and assimilation. Explorations of community, identity, gender, economic transition, and language acquisition have selected local sporting spaces and groups as their foundation. However, by its nature and enactment in Western contexts, sport is also, as a project, generally both hierarchical and exposes divisive beliefs including racism and other exclusionary practices.

Sport in Western contexts may also be viewed as an agent of specific meanings determined as a result of exclusionary practices.

Anthropologists offer value to the study of sport and race as their training encourages them to look deeply at popular sports, as well as those that have less participation but may be locally preferred. With activities and passions that cut across class position, ethnic status, or regional affiliations, sport is particularly suited to carry simultaneous markers of individual and collective identities – think: "the nation."[33] Anthropology can provide insight on the way the constructed national identity is interpreted and applied at the local level when negotiating daily and mundane activities.

The disciplinary boundaries of anthropology have at times shifted, expanding to include new methodologies and technologies, and integrate analytical lenses including feminism and other critical theories. Race and sport continue to be defined by oscillating terms and contexts, through a range of examples in varying locales. Perspectives about "race" and "ethnicity" can be explored as historically rooted phases of scholarly enquiry. Even racism itself "differs across time and space as a result of intersecting and historical differences that individuals have and develop over their life cycles."[34] Racism also shifts to support the demands and goals of power. The historical use of racial categories has been "arbitrary and changeable and they have been employed in such a way as to convenience and privilege the dominant (White) population."[35] Picking apart race as a cultural construct reveals the change it has presented as a social category over time; how that category's impact has been interrogated is the discussion that follows.

Charting the terrain

What are the signposts for the anthropology of race in sport? Anthropology's methods, fields, and subjects of inquiry have successfully explored elements of social and cultural interaction in sites around the world. The resulting analyses offer valuable insights, as well as approaches to research. The studies are organized below in relation to several ways in which anthropological methods and lenses have approached anthropology of sport, race, and ethnicity. This is by no means an exhaustive list; for example, I do not detail the ways studies have explored sport as a vehicle for symbolic status or wealth. Also prominent in sport studies, but beyond the scope of this chapter, are engagements with and resistance to the nation.

To start, ethnography and methodological considerations and the organization and cohesion of small groups through and around sport. Then a look at the use of boundaries and drawing difference and the ways sport has been interpreted as a vehicle for meaning making and establishing status. Finally, I close this overview by looking at the ways anthropologists and others have encountered the political, economic, and social flows of the local to the global and colonialism and racism in relation to sport. While not all of these studies are explicitly anthropological, each offers valuable starting points and methods of investigating race and sport that can be adapted for anthropological research.

Ethnography and cultural contexts

The majority of anthropological forays with sport have touched on ethnographic and methodological considerations. Sport has been a physical site, a site of discourse and knowledge exchange; a space of contest over prowess, identity, and boundaries.

Ethnographies offer firsthand accounts of behaviors for those that derive community or identity from supporting the sporting competition of others. This may include appropriate sets of behaviors for particular places, contests, or interactions, whether supporting baseball or other sports.[36] Ethnographic work, again, is not the exclusive domain of anthropology. Sociological research and other ethnographic accounts of fan and supporter communities offer excellent starting points for grappling with constructed, and sometimes temporal, identities.[37] Existing ethnographies of sport often close with appeals for more grounded analyses to derive greater insights and observations, and distill latent meaning.[38] Recent work by Marc Fletcher emphasizes the shifting complexity of race and ethnicity in sport settings.[39] Fletcher explores the constant flux in negotiating identity among soccer fans in South Africa through ethnographic work, and offers a counterpoint to fandom and supporter research conducted in Europe. George Gmelch's work with professional baseball players provides insight into the dimensions, infrastructure, rituals, and constraints of sport enmeshed in complexes of media and entertainment in highly industrialized societies.[40]

Anthropology has detailed the expressions and utility of ethnic identity in political and social contexts, as well as surfaced nuanced accounts of the effects of racism. Paul Richards has employed ethnography to understand the ways soccer has been a mechanism for reintegrating adolescents into society following extreme violence and ethnic and political divisions.[41] Eduardo Archetti considers fieldwork in Latin American sport, focusing on meaning making. Here, there are starting points to understand identities, their changes in connection with sporting spaces, shared regional and national interpretations of teams and athletes as they conveyed constellations of values relating to region, class, masculinity, and race.

Ramón Spaaj's work with Somali refugee communities in Australia offers insights into the ways ethnicity may remain stable while other identities are porous; here, ethnicity is claimed through engagement with a sporting community.[42] And Juliane Müller has probed sporting spaces as sites for the development of community and post-migrant identities in Spain. Her findings question the integrative potential of sport, but highlight the constant negotiation of affiliations for Bolivian and Ecuadorian migrants.[43] Here, sport is revealed as a site generating inclusion, as well as exclusion; some of these processes are apparent in the studies below in which identities are delineated.

Marking the boundaries: creating, changing, and reinforcing identity

One of anthropology's strengths is applying comparative perspectives; race is a categorization constructed through comparison and creating difference. Therefore, it is reasonable that we would locate the anthropology and investigations of the effects of racism and race-based inequality in sport. In particular, studies have explored where and how identities have been constructed.

Thangaraj employed ethnographic methods to understand the negotiation of race, gender, and class in basketball courts by pulling apart the ways South Asian Americans navigate a space strongly marked by black–white racial dichotomies. The men in his study constantly defined minority identities by consuming dominant racializations in this specific site of sporting performance.[44] Fletcher explored the prominence of race in the experiences of South African football fans; specifically the racial discourses relating to fandom of professional football – Manchester United's 2008 pre-season tour of South Africa provided a space to surface the hierarchies and experiences of fandom. With an ethnographic approach, Fletcher investigated the intersections of socioeconomic status, leisure time, and resources for the expression of fandom – plus the dangers inherent in passionate support of sports in racialized settings. Additionally Fletcher's study demonstrates that professional football, as well as fandom, at the local and regional level is more racially and ethnically diverse than media and political discourses acknowledge, based on extensive ethnographic fieldwork.[45] Fletcher's research in South African football fandom reveals the ways race may be used as a lens for understanding and exploring the effects of racial classification. Furthermore, Fletcher's fieldwork challenges fixed notions of race to explore the way everyday interactions impact understandings of racial categorization in the demographic arrangement of cities like Johannesburg.[46]

Also in South Africa, Connie Anderson, Troy Bielert, and Ryan Jones have shown the ways sports such as soccer, cricket, and rugby have represented and resisted White supremacy.[47] As a result, these sports have both articulated the boundaries of individual identities in relation to sets of dominant values and redefined a collective history of the nation. Thus, sport remains a complex social enterprise, whether played or consumed as a spectator. The next way studies of sport have engaged with aspects of race, ethnicity, and nation is with a sense of nation.

Colonialism, race, resistance, and power

The structures of power inherent in colonialism are readily connected to the sport within those colonial contexts. Sport was enacted as a tool for enculturation of colonial values and a means of disciplining the bodies of local populations – and particularly through cricket and association football in the British imperial context. As a result of sporting codes being adopted at local levels, populations were exposed to both Western ideals and adapted sports to mesh with their values. The results included hybridization of sporting codes and forms of performance that were distinct to these regions. While not exclusively anthropological lenses, studies have specifically explored diffusion, acculturation, and adoption of Western ideals.[48] The ways in which these ideals were integrated brought particular sets of social behavior, standards, relations, and conformity through sport; the organization and ceremony, patterns of participation as well as exclusion, and increasingly hierarchical competition brought forward ways of thinking about the world through sport that aligned with an imperial project.[49]

Adaptations of sporting codes reveal intersections with other social relations that are dictated and guided by race-based inequalities. For example, Leite Lopes traces how the history of class identities and racial divisions guided the boundaries of professionalization of football in Brazil from the 1930s onward. As "white" Brazilians began transnational migration and sporting success in Europe, "black" athletes remained condemned to domestic, even local, success – or in the case of the 1950 World Cup defeat, to serve as the targets of blame for lack of sporting victory. Through these exchanges, an evolving hybrid form of play is believed to have emerged, along with a celebrated "multi-racial" team. Further connecting history with ethnographic work could unpack this nationalist discourse to understand the ways local experiences resists this narrative of the collective.[50]

Sport is, of course, also integrated at lived and local levels while referencing the national and global. Thus, for each site and study of sport, there are economic and political flows at play that can intersect with racial identities, class, gender, and age. Exploring interpretations of the performance of Cameroon's national football team in global competition, Vidacs delineates the effects of racism and intersections with national government policy as it is experienced at the local level.[51] Vidacs also captured the ways population flows are perceived as tied to sport and celebrating national identity across class lines with France's 1998 FIFA World Cup victory with a team composed of "immigrants" in the Cameroonian perspective.[52] Returning to the benefit of an anthropological lens, the ability to draw out the cultural, social, and political impacts of global flows on local sport will become increasingly useful.

Uncharted territory: what lies on the horizon?

If we've sketched the routes of the distances anthropologists and other social researchers have traveled so far with regard to race, racism, ethnicity, and more, what uncharted territory remains? Some issues to which anthropological lenses might be applied include:

- Exploring the intersections of race and ethnicity, and even nationalism with gender, class, and sexuality.[53] In particular, ethnographic work with the fans of women's sport and the impact of racism and racialization on their interpretations of sport.[54] Physical anthropology may serve as an embodied site for these social categories as well.[55]
- Undertaking an ethnographic inquiry into racialization and identity that surpasses the restrictions of space and time or are modeled on previous spaces, places, and times. Anthropological focus might turn toward the performance of sport and athlete identities as resistance to racism and racialization; or the adoption of ethnic identities through learning and exposure to specific sporting cultures, which may support or exclude participation by certain groups. These explorations would push at the permeability of boundaries in comparative contexts and draw out discussion of global flows.
- Unpacking the codification and professionalization of traditional sports, once perceived to be rituals, enculturation; also their role as vehicles for the diffusion of specific cultural, religious, or political values.
- Defining the contours of racism and racialization in projects of development instigated or promoted through sport, as well as their levels of success and failure in local contexts.[56] Anthropological approaches would also be useful for investigating the shifting social relationships as power is reorganized in the implementation and maintenance of community-based programs, such as those focusing on health.
- Extending comparative forays into understanding contemporary expressions of community and the constellation of the self in the midst of global flows and ascriptions of hybridization. This approach could be extended to unpack the layers of the local, grounded experiences as they are built through exchange with the complex and even contradictory of the global: whether imagined, spectacle, or mediated.
- Launching ethnographic studies of the racialization and divisions of physical spaces and structures of sport, such as shared-use recreational facilities, and the ways meaning is made in relation to the infrastructure that supports rotating large-scale entertainment events and the experiences of racism and inequalities of the labor supporting and the people consuming these events.

Additionally, opportunity abounds to interrogate the impact of the political economy of sport. This could be investigated at the regional, national, and international levels in activities of industrialization, team, and working conditions, and class- and race-based identities and demarcations.[57] This should particularly call to research in postcolonial contexts that are simultaneously experiencing sport as an agent of development and their people's sporting labor undervalued in a wider system of professional sport.[58] Existing ethnographies would serve as points of comparison for additional research that analyzes the structures of inequality that unfold from race and are evidenced in experiences of immigration.

The value of anthropological inquiry lies in its infinite arrangement of questions and close contextual investigation of experiences in sport: physical, social, symbolic, and cultural, and particularly in relation to the consequences of race. Taking leads from the analyses above provides coordinates with which one might start an exploration of race and its consequences.

Conclusion

This chapter was crafted to map the value of anthropological lenses for reading the prism of race and the fracturing effects of racism in sport. That includes a focus on the ways the varied components of the human experience in sport are explored with anthropological approaches, rather than merely discussing *what* has been studied. As suggested with the topics above, anthropology can do much to derive insights around the consequences of race in sport. Now is the time to better match this discipline to the questions, observations, and spaces demanding further analysis, while continuing to problematize the categorizations that naturalize difference and bolster inequality. Therefore, this trip around the topics of anthropology of sport and race inevitably echoes the calls from anthropologists for more study of sporting spaces, rituals, and embodied practices.

Anthropology continues to meld ethnography with comparative approaches – global and locally situated – and a desire to understand the effects of socially and culturally constructed identities. This allows anthropologists to find the intersections at which categorizations are established, and where they are negotiated. Sundry are the possible paths for anthropological enquiry into race and its effects in sport. The end of this journey now marks the start of a new adventure in qualitative inquiry.

Notes

1 Kendall Blanchard, *The Anthropology of Sport: An Introduction*, revised edition (Westport, CT: Bergin & Garvey, 1995).
2 See the following for summaries of the anthropological history and theory: R. Jon McGee and Richard L. Warms, *Anthropological Theory: An Introductory History* (New York, NY: McGraw-Hill, 2003); Paul A. Erickson and Liam D. Murphy, *A History of Anthropological Theory*, 4th edition (Toronto: University of Toronto Press, 2013); Thomas Hylland Eriksen and Finn Sivert Nielsen, *A History of Anthropology*, 2nd edition (London: Pluto Press, 2013).
3 James Peoples and Garrick Bailey, *Humanity: An Introduction to Cultural Anthropology* (Belmont, CA: Wadworth Cengage Learning, 2011), 103.
4 Richard B. Woodbury and Nathalie F.S. Woodbury, "The Rise and Fall of the Bureau of American Ethnology," *Journal of the Southwest* 41, 3 (1999), 283–96, 284.
5 Erickson and Murphy, *A History of Anthropological Theory*, 18.
6 Michael Omi and Howard Winant, *Racial Formation in the United States: From the 1960s to the 1990s*, 2nd edition (New York, NY: Routledge, 1994); Carol Mukhopadhyay and Yolanda Moses, "Re-establishing Race in Anthropological Discourse," *American Anthropologist* 99, 3 (1997), 517–33. See also Audrey Smedley and Brian D. Smedley, "Race as Biology is Fiction, Racism as a Social Problem is Real: Anthropological and Historical Perspectives on the Social Construction of Race," *American Psychologist* 60, 1 (2005), 16–26. For anthropology failing to discuss race, see Eugenia Shanklin, "Representations of Race and Racism in American Anthropology," *Current Anthropology* 41, 1 (2000), 99–103.
7 Douglas Hartmann, "Beyond the Sporting Boundary: The Racial Significance of Sport Through Midnight Basketball," *Ethnic and Racial Studies* 35, 6 (2012), 1007–22.
8 Executive Board of the American Anthropological Association on 17 May 1998, www.americananthro.org/ConnectWithAAA/Content.aspx?ItemNumber=2583, accessed 27 January 2016.
9 Sut Jhally and Stuart Hall, *Race: The Floating Signifier* (Northampton, MA: Media Education Foundation, 1996).
10 In John Downing and Charles Husband, *Representing Race: Racisms, Ethnicity and the Media* (London: Sage, 2005), 2.
11 Eric R. Wolf, Joel S. Kahn, William Roseberry, and Immanuel Wallerstein, "Perilous Ideas: Race, Culture, People," Sidney W. Mintz Lecture for 1992, *Current Anthropology* 35, 1 (1994), 1–12.
12 Richard Jenkins, *Rethinking Ethnicity: Arguments and Explorations*, 2nd edition (London: Sage, 2008).
13 Steve Fenton, *Ethnicity* (Oxford: Polity Press, 2003).

14 Fenton, *Ethnicity*; see also Lyton Ncube's ethnographic exploration of fan communities in Zimbabwe and the relationships of power manifested during the negotiation of identities. Lyton Ncube, "The Interface Between Football and Ethnic Identity Discourses in Zimbabwe," *Critical African Studies* 6, 2–3 (2014), 192–210.

15 In Kevin Hylton, *"Race" and Sport: Critical Race Theory* (New York: Routledge, 2009), 5.

16 Miri Song, *Choosing Ethnic Identity* (Oxford: Polity Press, 2003).

17 Meghan M. Ferriter, "Bringing Irish Nationalist Identity into Focus, 1880–1923" (unpublished Master's thesis, Old Dominion University, 2005).

18 Downing and Husband, *Representing Race*, 3.

19 See discussion of AAA and ASA statements on race in John Hartigan, "Conclusion: Anthropology of Race," *Anthropology of Race: Genes, Biology, and Culture* (Sante Fe, NM: School for Advanced Research Press, 2013), 187–98.

20 Alan H. Goodman, "Race and Anthropology: A Fatal Attraction?," *Reviews in Anthropology* 26, 4, (1997), 203–20.

21 See Stewart Culin, "Games of the North American Indians," in *Games of Skill*, vol. 2. (Lincoln, NE: University of Nebraska Press, 1907, reprinted 1992); James Mooney, "The Cherokee Ball Game," *American Anthropologist* 3 (1890), 105–32.

22 Eduardo Archetti, "The Meaning of Sport in Anthropology: A View from Latin America," *European Review of Latin American and Caribbean Studies/Revista Europea de Estudios Latinoamericanos y del Caribe* 65 (1998), 91–103, 93.

23 Blanchard, *The Anthropology of Sport*, 68.

24 Noel Dyck, "Getting into the Game: Anthropological Perspectives on Sport: Introduction," *Anthropologica* 46, 1 (2004), 3–8.

25 Clifford Geertz, *The Interpretation of Cultures: Selected Essays* (New York, NY: Basic Books, 1973); Jerry Leach, dir., *Trobriand Cricket: An Ingenious Response to Colonialism*, 54 min., Media Resources Center, University of California, Berkeley, CA (1976); G. Whitney Azoy, *Buzkashi: Game & Power in Afghanistan*, 3rd edition (Long Grove, IL: Waveland Press, Inc., 2012).

26 Jerry Leach, "Structure and Message in Trobriand Cricket," in Jack R. Rollwagen, ed., *Anthropological Filmmaking: Anthropological Perspectives on the Production of Film and Video for General Public Audiences*, reprint (New York, NY: Routledge, 2014), 237–52.

27 Arjun Appadurai, *Modernity at Large: Cultural Dimensions of Globalization* (Minneapolis, MN: University of Minnesota Press, 1997), 89–113.

28 E.g. Kendall Blanchard, "The Anthropology of Sport," in J. Coakley and Eric Dunning (eds), *Handbook of Sports Studies* (London: Sage, 2002), 144–57.

29 Susan Brownell (ed.), *The 1904 Anthropology Days and Olympic Games: Sport, Race, and American Imperialism* (Lincoln, NE: University of Nebraska Press, 2008).

30 Ibid.

31 Thomas Carter, "On the Need for an Anthropological Approach to Sport," *Identities*, 9, 3 (2002), 405–22.

32 See Blanchard, "The Anthropology of Sport"; Hans Hognestad, "Long-distance Football Support and Liminal Activities Among Norwegian Fans," in Noel Dyck and Eduardo P. Archetti, eds., *Sport, Dance and Embodied Identities* (New York: Berg, 2003), 97–113.

33 Archetti, "The Meaning of Sport in Anthropology."

34 Jeanette Armstrong and Roxana Ng, "Deconstructing Race, Deconstructing Racism," in Jo-Anne Lee and John Lutz, eds., *Situating "Race" and Racisms in Time, Space and Theory: Critical Essays for Activists and Scholars* (Montreal: McGill-Queen's University Press, 2005), 30–45, 37.

35 Miri Song, *Choosing Ethnic Identity* (Oxford: Polity Press, 2003), 13.

36 See Alan M. Klein, *Baseball on the Border: A Tale of Two Laredos* (Princeton, NJ: Princeton University Press, 1999); Holly Swyers, *Wrigley Regulars: Finding Community in the Bleachers* (Champaign, IL: University of Illinois Press, 2010).

37 Richard Giulianotti, "Football and the Politics of Carnival: An Ethnographic Study of Scottish Fans in Sweden," *International Review for the Sociology of Sport* 30, 2 (1995), 191–219; Hans Hognestad, "The Jambo Experience: An Anthropological Study of Hearts Fans," in Gary Armstrong and Richard Giulianotti, eds., *Entering the Field: New Perspectives in World Football* (Oxford: Berg, 1997), 193–210.

38 Bea Vidacs, "Through the Prism of Sports: Why Should Africanists Study Sports?" *Africa Spectrum*, 41, 3 (2006), 331–49.

39 Marc Fletcher, "More than Vuvuzelas? Towards an Understanding of Soccer Fandom in Johannesburg," *Critical African Studies*, 6, 2–3 (2014), 176–91.

40 George Gmelch, *Inside Pitch: Life in Professional Baseball*, 2nd edition (Lincoln, NE: Bison Books, 2006).

41 Paul Richards, "Soccer and Violence in War-Torn Africa: Soccer and Social Rehabilitation in Sierra Leone," in Gary Armstrong and Richard Giulianotti, eds., *Entering the Field: New Perspectives in World Football* (Oxford: Berg, 1997), 141–57.

42 Ramón Spaaj, "Beyond the Playing Field: Experiences of Sport, Social Capital, and Integration among Somalis in Australia," *Ethnic and Racial Studies* 35, 9 (2012), 1519–38.

43 Juliane Müller, "Local Relations and Transnational Imaginaries: Football Practices of Migrant Men and Women from Andean Countries in Spain," *Soccer & Society* 15, 4 (2014), 596–617.

44 Stanley Thangaraj, "Playing Through Differences: Black–White Racial Logic and Interrogating South Asian American Identity," *Ethnic and Racial Studies* 35, 6 (2012), 988–1006.

45 Marc Fletcher, "'You Must Support Chiefs; Pirates Already Have Two White Fans!': Race and Racial Discourse in South African Football Fandom," *Soccer & Society* 11, 1–2 (2010), 79–94.

46 Marc Fletcher, "'These Whites Never Come to our Game: What Do They Know About Our Soccer?' Soccer Fandom, Race, and the Rainbow Nation in South Africa" (unpublished doctoral thesis, University of Edinburgh, 2012).

47 Connie M. Anderson, Troy A. Bielert, and Ryan P. Jones, "One Country, One Sport, Endless Knowledge: The Anthropological Study of Sports in South Africa," *Anthropologica* 46, 1 (2004), 47–55.

48 John Bale and Joe Sang, *Kenyan Running: Movement Culture, Geography, and Global Change* (London: Frank Cass, 1996); Allen Guttmann, *Games and Empires: Modern Sports and Cultural Imperialism* (New York: Columbia University Press, 1994); Brian Stoddart, "Sport, Cultural Imperialism, and Colonial Response in the British Empire," *Comparative Studies in Society and History* 30, 4 (1988), 649–73.

49 Stoddart, "Sport, Cultural Imperialism."

50 José Sergio Leite Lopes, "Successes and Contradictions in 'Multiracial' Brazilian Football," in Gary Armstrong and Richard Giulianotti, eds., *Entering the Field: New Perspectives in World Football* (Oxford: Berg, 1997), 53–86. See also José Sergio Leite Lopes, "Class, Ethnicity, and Color in the Making of Brazilian Football," *Daedalus* 129, 2 (2000), 239–70.

51 Vidacs, "Through the Prism of Sports."

52 Bea Vidacs, "France in the Cameroonian Football Imagination," in Gary Armstrong and Richard Guilianotti, eds., *Football in Africa: Conflict, Conciliation and Community* (New York: Palgrave Macmillan, 2004), 169–82.

53 Fletcher and Bisschoff acknowledge the bulk of ethnographic work exploring fandom has focused on masculine supporter cultures and call for wider exploration as well. Marc Fletcher and Lizelle Bisschoff, "African Sport in the Global Arena: Contemporary Approaches and Analyses," *Critical African Studies* 6, 2–3 (2014), 123–33, 124.

54 My ongoing ethnographic work with online US women's soccer fans offers particularly revealing silences around race and ongoing negotiation of identities as fans intersecting with ethnicity and nationalism.

55 Physical anthropology has not been the focus of this chapter, but useful studies of embodied sporting experiences and the technologies of the body include two edited volumes: Robert R. Sands and Linda R. Sands, eds., *The Anthropology of Sport and Human Movement: A Biocultural Perspective* (Lanham, MD: Lexington Books, 2010); Noel Dyck and Eduardo P. Archetti, eds., *Sport, Dance and Embodied Identities* (New York: Berg, 2003). See also Marcel Mauss, "Techniques of the Body," *Economy and Society*, 2, 1 (1973), 70–88; Bale and Sang, *Kenyan Running*; P. David Howe, "Impairment: Sporting Bodies – Sensuous, Lived, and Impaired," in Frances E. Mascia-Lees, ed., *A Companion to the Anthropology of the Body and Embodiment* (Oxford: Wiley-Blackwell, 2011), 276–91; and Greg Downey, "Educating the Eyes: Biocultural Anthropology and Physical Education," *Anthropology in Action* 12, 2 (2005), 56–71.

56 One starting point, applying sociological perspectives: Simon C. Darnell, "Playing with Race: *Right to Play* and the Production of Whiteness in 'Development through Sport'," *Sport in Society* 10, 4 (2007), 560–79. Here, Darnell suggests that difference is drawn out through the development of sport into a series of contrasting values written across "white" bodies and bodies of color.

57 See, for example, Sikes and Jarvie's work with Kenyan women runners. Grant Jarvie and Michelle Sikes, "Running as a Resource of Hope? Voices from Eldoret," *Review of African Political Economy* 39, 134 (2012), 629–44; Michelle Sikes and Grant Jarvie, "Women's Running as Freedom: Development and Choice," *Sport in Society* 17, 4 (2014), 507–22. See the discussion in Mario Bick, "Review: The Anthropology of Sport – An Introduction," *American Ethnologist* 15, 2 (1988), 400–1.

58 For example, John Nauright applies a physical cultural studies approach and explores the ways pursuit of participation in a global economic system of inequalities intersects with sport in the specific contexts of South Africa; here, race and inequalities continue to be written onto black bodies symbolically, see John Nauright, "On Neoliberal Global Sport and African Bodies," *Critical African Studies* 6, 2–3 (2014), 134–43; also see Arjun Appadurai, *Modernity at Large: Cultural Dimensions of Globalization* (Minneapolis, MN: University of Minnesota Press, 1997), 89–113; and Wycliffe W. Simiyu Njororai, "Distance Running in Kenya: Athletics Labour Migration and its Consequences," *Leisure/Loisir* 36, 2 (2012), 187–209.

3

PHILOSOPHY, RACE AND SPORT

Rasmus Bysted Møller and Verner Møller

Introduction

Since Harry Edwards wrote his pioneering book *The Revolt of the Black Athlete* (1968), literature pertaining to sport and race has grown significantly. Impressive works such as John Bale and Joe Sang's *Kenyan Running: Movement Culture, Geography and Global Change* (1996) which explores the famous African running culture in the context of tradition and colonialism and thus opposes biological determinist explanations of the highly successful Kenyan running athletes, and John Hoberman's *Darwin's Athletes: How Sport has Damaged Black America and Preserved the Myth of Race* (1997), which exposes the detrimental effects that the celebration of black athleticism has had on America's general perception of black people as essentially different from white people, have been lauded, criticized and much debated. Anthologies such as: Grant Jarvie's *Sport, Racism and Ethnicity* (1991); Daryl Adair's *Sport, Race and Ethnicity: Narratives of Difference and Diversity* (2011); and John Nauright, Alan Cobley and David Wiggins', *Beyond C.L.R. James: Race and Ethnicity in Sport* (2014) have offered valuable contributions to the understanding of the pervasiveness of the problem in multiple sporting disciplines and contexts around the world. Kevin Hylton's *'Race' and Sport: Critical Race Theory* (2009) offers theoretical insights into the complexities and shifting nature of racism in and outside sport while Neil Farrington, Daniel Kilvington, John Price and Amir Saeed's *Race, Racism and Sports Journalism* (2012) examines the historical, social and cultural context in which the terms race and racism have been formed and addresses the media's contribution to shaping and maintaining stereotypical thoughts and opinions regarding these issues. The books mentioned are merely a select number of the works published on the topic within the social sciences and humanities in recent decades.[1] In light of this, it is remarkable that the subject has been largely neglected in the scholarly literature on the philosophy of sport. To the best of our knowledge, no monographs or anthologies devoted to philosophical analyses of the relationship between sport and race from an international perspective has yet been written.

The *Routledge Handbook of the Philosophy of Sport* (2015) – a comprehensive overview of the discipline's state of the art – consists of 29 thematic chapters, none of which are devoted to the relationship between race and sport. Jan Boxill's *Sport Ethics: An Anthology* (2003) contains a section comprising three chapters that focus on 'Sport and Racial Issues'. However, the first of these chapters is a critical review of journalist Jon Entine's book *Taboo: Why Black Athletes Dominate Sports and Why We Are Afraid to Talk About It* (2000), and the other two chapters are sociohistorical rather than philosophical in nature. In William Morgan's influential compilation *Ethics in Sport* (2007), the sport and race issue is addressed in two chapters in the final section, 'Select Issues in the Social Ethics of Sport: Violence, Exploitation, Race, Spectatorship, and Disability'; the first of these chapters is a review of John Hoberman's *Darwin's Athletes*, while the second chapter takes a history-of-ideas approach and offers a political-philosophical analysis of the relationship between sport and African-Americans very much in line with Hoberman's analysis. In light of this, it seems safe to say that issues of race have received scant attention within the philosophy of sport.[2]

The fact that philosophical inquiries into racism are few and far between may appear odd in comparison to other disciplines' interest in the topic, but is perhaps not surprising as the philosophy of sport in this regard mirrors philosophy in general. As pointed out by African-American philosopher Arnold Farr: 'Any cursory glance at the history of philosophy would seem to indicate that race has no place in philosophy.'[3] Farr explains this omission by pointing to the rationale of the discipline: 'Philosophy's goal of universality forces it to dismiss the particulars of one's existence. The possibility of introducing "perspective" into philosophy undermines philosophy's claim to the privileged view from nowhere.'[4] However, mainstream philosophy and the philosophy of sport differ in that the latter has a socially constructed particular as its object of inquiry. Sport is a social activity that involves culturally and historically situated human beings, and is therefore an arena in which racial conflicts in wider society are reflected.

The purpose of this chapter is to investigate how sport could be used as an educational tool in relation to race and racism because the inner logic of sport opposes racism and therefore implicitly functions as an antidote against it. This view has intuitive appeal. Fairness and equality are often mentioned as the cornerstones of sport's value system. Robert L. Simon and Drew A. Hyland have argued in favour of such a position, but before we present and explore their arguments we must review the fundamental concepts of race and racism.[5]

The concepts of race and racism

Most scholars agree that racist ideas originated in the eighteenth and nineteenth centuries.[6] The term race was used to differentiate human populations on the basis of phenotypes. It was believed that environmental factors had led to different physical and mental hereditary traits. In *La degeneration des animaux*, the natural historian George-Louis Buffon developed a race theory based on environmental ideas that profoundly influenced the understanding of human evolution at the time.[7] Buffon's line of thinking is clearly presented in the following passage:

> Ever since man began to settle under different skies and to move out of one climate into another, his nature has undergone changes … these changes became so great and so evident that one might think that the Negro, the Laplander, and the White are different species.[8]

Buffon considered whiteness as the norm and other races as degenerate. Today, there is almost universal agreement that race is a social construct that has no biological basis.[9] Analyses of human DNA have shown that there is much more genetic variation within 'racial' groups (approximately 94 per cent) than between them. Race, therefore, can hardly be defined in biological terms.[10] Since attempts to ground the notion of race on biology has proven futile, race is commonly believed to lack ontological foundation.[11] In spite of this, ideas about race have had a devastating societal influence. As John McClendon III writes: 'Somehow we are still faced with the nagging fact that "Race Matters", then we are obliged to ask, how do we account for its presence? Does not the social presence of race indicate its reality?'[12]

Whether race refers to something real or not, it still negatively influences modern humans even though many are sensitive towards racism and support race-neutralism or 'colour-blindness' as ideals. Even Buffon's naive idea of the normativity of whiteness still plays a role in Western societies. According to Lewis Gordon, the following example illustrates the way whiteness is still seen as the norm of what it means to be human:

> Consider, for example, the use of supposedly race-neutral terms such as 'woman', 'man', 'girl', 'boy', 'child', and 'one'. The impact of white normativity is readily apparent in that these terms … stand for white exemplars wherever there is the absence of an adjective designating color. There is, in other words, a parenthetical 'white' before each of these terms…. How often is 'the reader' in literature expected to be, if not white, at least a white perspective?[13]

Gordon's aim is to uncover how 'whiteness' continues to racialize non-whites by tacitly presenting itself as the norm 'others' deviate from. In light of this, one could argue that since society is far from colour-blind as it is, it will only hurt the endeavour to eradicate racism if we pretend that race does not exist. Advocates of affirmative action argue that we need to take into account the notion of race in order to compensate for the unjust distribution of wealth that has historical roots in slavery and imperialism. Simply making sure that our society is based on institutions and legal principles that are essentially colour-blind is not enough, since earlier injustices by whites has given them a head-start in competition-driven capitalist societies that ensures the continuation of their material and cultural privileges. According to Kelly Oliver, 'the rhetoric of equal treatment and color blindness operates to normalize whiteness. White is not considered a color, and equal treatment is used to cover up important and relevant differences between people, a cover-up that leads to unjust treatment.'[14]

In keeping with this term, 'race' appears to be an important tool to identify more subtle forms of racism so we cannot do away with the concept. Admittedly, it seems paradoxical to insist on the preservation of a concept that is widely understood as a fallacy in order to make up for social injustices justified by this antiquated concept. The problem facing those who want to preserve the term is that logically racism is dependent on an understanding of race as something real. If race cannot be defined as universal, racism has no real underpinning. In other words, if the reality of race is taken out of the equation, what is referred to as racism is qualitatively indistinguishable from other kinds of bullying, hostility and prejudice among people.

Racism is commonly understood as malicious prejudices concerning *races* standing in an inferior–superior relationship with each other. But if 'races' refers only to uneducated people's misperception of various human beings based on arbitrary features, we find ourselves facing the conundrum of how to define racism without any presupposition of existing races. We have not come across any dictionary that has succeeded in defining racism without reference to race. The problem of adequately defining racism without presupposing the existence of race encouraged the Norwegian government to remove the word race and racism from national laws altogether. Instead, their *Anti-Discrimination Act*, which came into being in January 2006, outlaws discrimination based on ethnicity, national origin, descent, skin colour, language, religion or belief.[15]

Although recognizing the paradoxical nature of the concept of race, we have chosen to use it as a necessary means to address and deal with racial issues in the real world. We do so because any attempt to overcome the connotations attached to race by replacing references to race with those to skin colour or national origin are doomed to fail. Why? Because if, indeed, the replacement of 'race' with 'skin colour' would correct the misperception of race as really existing, those who discarded the concept of 'race' and adopted the usage of 'skin colour' should truly perceive that Michael Jackson ceased to be black when his skin colour turned white. By the same token, people who discarded 'race' and replaced it with 'national origin' would be led to think of any black or white person as African-American if his ancestors immigrated to America from South Africa. Based on these examples, it should be obvious that meaningful debates about ethnicity and racism would no longer be possible if race were not used. Moreover, it would immediately change the meaning of African-American identity. One might argue that these would all be positive consequences because it would once and for all do away with racism. And we agree. However, it should be equally obvious that it is a utopian idea that policing language can eliminate racism. In order to oppose racism, it is important to know what it is, and clearly it is not just an arbitrary aversion, for example, against a certain skin colour. Feelings of antipathy towards blacks by white supremacists are more correctly described as racist than simply as 'discrimination based on skin colour', because it entails an ideology of cognitive or intellectual superiority based upon biological characteristics of race.

However, modern versions of racism are not just about any kind of superiority and inferiority. The belief that black people are physically superior to other races is based to a great extent on black athletes' domination in many physically demanding sports, but this does not mean that the sporting arena is one where blacks are merely celebrated and not abused. On the contrary, black people who excel in sport are – despite being lauded for their sporting achievements – still seen as inferior by racists as a consequence of biological characteristics pertaining to imagined racial characteristics. Removing the word race from the dictionary or even criminalizing the use of it will accomplish nothing since the mind always finds a way to express its thoughts and feelings, and therefore policing language is like herding cats.[16] It is too simplistic and superficial to target language and verbal expressions when dealing with racism. Expressions that have clear racist overtones to the English ear due to England's postcolonial history might be regarded as harmless, friendly or even affectionate in other cultural contexts. And even within the same cultural context there are other things to take into account, as McNamee maintains:

> Consider a circumstance in which a player or official has told a racist joke, used racial abuse or made a decision on the basis of some racial presumption. Interpretation of the significance of that might vary depending upon whether the perpetrator: says sorry (then or later) or shakes hands with a 'Well played mate' at the end of the game, insists it was 'just in the heat of the moment'; does so in a team founded on the principles of cultural pluralism; or elsewhere engages in actions to counter racism.[17]

It is important not to panic in an attempt to stamp out racism. To be racist 'it must be part of one's character; one's relatively settled dispositions to think, feel and act in regular and interrelated ways'.[18] If we widen the concept of racism so that it entails so-called one-off, temporary or situational racists, and even what Joel Kovel has called meta-racism, which is an unconscious form of racism that consists in an unawareness of, for example, structural racism, we end up with a blunt conceptual instrument that hurts many.[19]

In what follows we will try to analyse whether and to what extent the belief that sport has the potential to overcome racism is true. Whereas sport sociologists tend to see sporting values as a reflection of societal values, sport philosophers usually regard sport as a phenomenon that produces its own values. According to this view, often referred to as the internalist position, sport can form the basis of social change by making evident its values of fairness and equality.

Sport and race according to an idealistic interpretation of sports' educational value

Philosopher Robert L. Simon explores the relationship between sport and moral values in order to defend the educative potential of sport, and coins the term *broad internalism* for his favoured position: 'that there are values internal to sport and these values are supported by a broad understanding of the purposes and point of athletic competition'.[20] Broad internalism is, according to Simon, in opposition to the view that sports values merely reflect values in society. The 'mirror thesis' of sport that Simon calls externalism claims that sport serves a conservative social function by mirroring the dominant values of wider society. In line with this view, problems of racism in sport are to be expected as long as these problems are widespread in society. Sport has potential to ignite strong feelings and tensions in society that are normally subdued and can cause a crowd mentality to emerge in the sports arena as frustrations are vocally expressed. Consequently, it is not surprising that racial tensions found in society at large sometimes spill over into the world of sport. An example of an externalist theory of sport can be found in Jean-Marie Brohm's radical critique in which he depicts sport as a reflection of fundamental values in capitalist industrial societies.[21]

In contrast to externalism, broad internalism asserts that there are moral values that flow from the internal logic of sport. Prominent values that sport teaches are fairness and equality. According to broad internalism these values are not imported from outside but are genuine products of sport itself. They are independent values that sport has in common with democracy.[22] Simon provides the following example:

> equality and fairness are guaranteed not only by the commitment to following the rules, but also because the rules themselves must be equitable and not favour competitors on grounds irrelevant to the basic skills and virtues called forth by the challenges of the sport.[23]

Since racial injustices would be impossible in an ideal society in which equality and fairness was truly actualized, sport might contribute in this direction if it really does promote these values. Simon and others seem at first glance correct in asserting that equality and fairness are core values in both democracy and sport, but if we delve deeper we find that they play completely different roles in these areas, which in turn makes them entirely different values. The reason why we deem freedom and equality so important in well-developed democratic societies is that they are preconditions for the autonomous pursuit of happiness by society's 'weaker' people and therefore they ideally guarantee a just distribution of well-being. They protect all persons who might be seen as inferior, be it because of race, gender, sexual orientation, handicaps, etc., and ensure that they are not discriminated against and that there is no constraints of their movement, speech, thought and so on. Normally, the ruler does not need protection from the Universal Declaration of Human Rights and these rights were not formulated with the protection of the ruling classes in mind. Rights of freedom and equality guard the weak against morally corrupt ideas and acts of the powerful. In sport, freedom and equality serve the opposite purpose. Here, freedom and equality are thought important because they guard the strong against the weak. To understand why this is so, we need to take broad internalism seriously and examine closer 'the purposes and point of athletic competition'.

According to philosopher Scott Kretchmar, a sporting contest is a test of abilities, and since the concept of a test is logically primary to the concept of a con-test, a contest does not occur until 'two or more individuals (or groups of people) adopt the same or comparable tests and then commit themselves to producing higher individual scores than another'.[24] Because of this inherent logic of contests, the purpose of sport is 'to test the skill of one individual, or group of individuals, against the skill of another individual, or group of individuals, in order to determine who is more skilful in a particular, well-defined activity'.[25] If the result of a sporting contest is not representative of superior athletic abilities, the particular contest has lost its *raison d'être*. What is considered fair in sport is nothing more than a set of rules and actions in which victory is considered to be a designator of athletic superiority. As philosopher James Keating suggests: 'Fairness or fair play, the pivotal virtue in athletics, emphasizes the need for an impartial and equal application of the rules, if the victory is to signify, as it should, athletic excellence.'[26]

Consequently, as philosopher Pieter Bonte notes, the level playing field is 'rigged in favor of the talented'.[27] Equality and fairness in sport are only valued because they are preconditions for establishing *inequality* at the finish line. They are designed to rob the loser of any excuse other than the lack of talent or willpower to achieve victory. It protects the 'strong' athlete with a natural capacity to produce high levels of erythropoietin against EPO use by the naturally 'weaker' athletes, or the abled athletes against competition from the disabled who might rob them of victory if given a head-start.

To sum up: in democracies, equality and fairness protect the weak from the tyranny of the strong, whereas the sports version of these values protects the strong from the corruptive influence of the weak. Since the sports version of equality and fairness does not possess the moral qualities these values represent in democracy, it is far from obvious that sport can help transcend racism. Still, there might be other arguments within broad internalism that will work to this effect.

Philosopher Drew Hyland argues that the competitive nature of sport works against racism:

> Imagine yourself at a playground basketball court. You know that the conventions of the court are that the winning team gets to keep on playing, while the losing team must sit until their next turn comes around. Imagine as well that this is a popular court with a large number of participants waiting to play, so that losing the game will more or less assure that you will be sitting for an hour or two. Typically for a sporting situation, this puts a considerable stake on winning. Now imagine further that the teams are being picked. You are one of those choosing sides. You happen to be white. Obviously, you want to pick the best team possible so as to maximize your chances of continuing to play. The best player waiting to be chosen when your turn comes is black. But you are racist; you much prefer not to have blacks on your team. So you pass over the superior black player to choose an inferior player, but one who is white. In this situation, the preservation of your racism has a clear price, the likelihood that you will lose and have to sit.[28]

According to Simon's broad internalism, the independent ethical values of sport can come into conflict with unethical values in society and in such cases sport has the educational potential to improve society by transferring its values via its global media coverage. Hyland strikes the same chord when he writes:

> the 'direction' of movement between values in society and sport might be two ways, that while it is certainly true that values originating in society (the case of racism), there might be other values intrinsic to the very structure of the sporting situation itself, values which one might want to see reflected in the society at large.[29]

What, then, are the lessons society can learn from sport in relation to racism? With reference to the above-mentioned basketball example Hyland explains:

> A closer look at this fairly typical athletic situation suggests that the very structure of the situation – the choosing of sides and a clear stake in winning – carries implicit in it a set of values, or at least, quite clear lessons. For example, one maximizes one's chances of doing well if one acts according to the following principle: 'Judge people according to their ability' (In this example, their basketball ability, but the principle is obviously transferable). If one takes this principle to heart more generally, it might be a small step towards the overcoming of racism.[30]

In the following section we will critically examine the idealistic idea Hyland presents of sport as a fertile ground for a moral education in anti-racism.

The educational value of sport

No evidence suggests that judging people according to their ability will help overcome racism. On the contrary, ideas about differences in abilities among different races and ethnicities has been part of racist thinking and the success of black athletes has done nothing to remedy this to the benefit of the black community.[31] According to Hoberman, the athletic success of African-Americans has lured them away from intellectual pursuits towards sport, which has led to a form of physicalized anti-intellectualism among blacks that reinforce old widespread stereotypes of blacks being physically superior but intellectually inferior.

Within mainstream philosophy there are two baffling examples of overt racism emanating from two of the most respected philosophers of all time, David Hume and Immanuel Kant. In both cases, stereotypes of racial differences in abilities play a key role. Following Hume, Kant's otherwise enlightened reasoning breaks down in the following passage where he presents racist ideas concerning differences in abilities along racist lines:

> The Negroes of Africa have by nature no feelings that rise above the trifling. Mr. Hume challenges anyone to cite a single example in which a Negro has shown talents, and asserts that among the hundreds of thousands of blacks who are transported elsewhere from their countries, although many of them have even been set free, still not a single one was ever found who presented anything great in art or science or any other praiseworthy quality, even though among the whites some continually rise aloft from the lowest rabble, and through superior gifts earn respect in the world. So fundamental is the difference between these two races of man, and it appears to be as great in regard to mental capacities as in colour.[32]

There is a clear value judgement attached to superior abilities in Kant's claims, and it is not difficult to see how such expressions could help legitimize calamities such as slavery and later apartheid. One might argue that for two reasons Kant is not 'judging people according to their ability' as Hyland asks us to do. First, Kant is obviously wrong in his judgement of black people's abilities and it could be argued that this is what makes his judgement morally reprehensible, not that he is presenting a value judgement on account of capabilities. Second, one could argue that Hyland's principle requires that we judge *individuals* on account of abilities not groups of people. Let us look at these two objections in turn.

It is immediately clear that the first argument does not hold up to scrutiny, since Kant's value judgement would not be less reprehensible if he were right concerning the abilities of black people. There are indeed groups of people that can be identified on account of common characteristics, for example those who are mentally challenged to a degree that will in fact prevent them from presenting 'anything great in art or science', but we would normally not consider this group of less value on account of that fact alone. People may have a psychological tendency to make that value judgement, but that is a tendency we ought to resist. If we rationally legitimize it, we have taken the first step towards a fascist form of eugenics that few would wish to see resurface. In his article 'Is Our Admiration for Sport Heroes Fascistoid?', philosopher Torbjörn Tannsjö provides arguments to support this fear in a way that also attacks the second objection that demands that our judgement focuses on individuals and not groups, so let us now turn to this.

According to Tannsjö, our admiration for sport heroes 'springs from the very core of fascist ideology'.[33] Following the argument of Harald Ofstad, Tannsjö claims that 'the hard core of Nazism was a contempt for weakness'.[34] The problem involved in admiring sport heroes is the fact that 'When we celebrate the winner, we cannot help but feel contempt for those who do not win. Admiration for the winner and contempt for the loser are only two sides of the same Olympic medal.'[35] For the sake of argument, Tannsjö is obviously neglecting expressions of sympathy and pity for the losers witnessed time and again in sporting contests. Notwithstanding that fact, he presents a convincing argument to support his claim that also explains why judging individuals as well as groups on account of abilities is morally problematic:

> To see why this is so we ought to think critically about *why* we admire those who excel in the Olympics. Our feeling is based on a value judgment. Those who win the game, if the competition is fair, are excellent, and their excellence makes them *valuable*; that is why we admire them.... But our value terms are comparative. So if we see a person as especially valuable, because of his excellence … then this must mean that other people … those who are comparatively weak, are *less* valuable. The most natural feeling associated with *this* value judgement is – contempt.[36]

Tannsjö is aware of the seeming paradox involved in the thesis that our admiration for sporting excellence involves a contempt for the lack thereof, since most of us are far from excellent at any sport, which seems to imply that our contempt must be partly self-contempt. He therefore goes on to assert:

> We admire Carl Lewis for his excellence, and we feel some contempt for those who fall behind him. However, we know that we would never stand a chance of beating Carl Lewis. Does this mean that we realize we are among those who are weak? It means, probably, that we fear this. But many of us believe we have other skills that compensate for those Carl Lewis possesses. Even if we are not physically as strong as he is, we may possess other kinds of strength. We may excel in respects that are (in our own opinion) more valuable than 'strength' in the literal sense of the word.[37]

If it is true, as we maintained at the beginning of this chapter, that racism is an ideology of cognitive superiority based upon biological characteristics of race, it is not difficult to see how Tannsjö's analysis might relate (on the group level) to the well-known thesis among white racist folklorists who believe that black physical superiority is somehow related to intellectual inferiority. As Harry Edwards has pointed out, it does not hurt whites' sense of self-worth to grant physical superiority to blacks since athletic prowess counts for little outside sport and:

a multitude of even lower animals are physically superior to whites, not only to whites, but to mankind as a whole.... So by asserting that blacks are physically superior, whites at best reinforce some old stereotypes long held about Afro-Americans – to wit, that they are little removed from the apes in evolutionary development.[38]

Hyland asserts that sport demands that we judge people according to their abilities, and this may be true; but his second claim about the merit of that principle in overcoming racism is not convincing. Actually, the opposite claim seems more credible since it involves a celebration of perceived supremacy and contempt for perceived inferiority that has, in its aggressive form, been historically linked to malicious racist outcomes such as slavery and holocaust. Thus, it seems that ignoring this lesson taught to us by sport is the better option as Tannsjö implies: 'If we want to be sure that we do not get carried away by our admiration for winners, we ought to resist the very idea of moral excellence and betterness.'[39] Of course, this is no easy task. The predisposition to judge people on account of their capabilities has deep evolutionary roots. But the following claim by Tannsjö is more interesting:

To be sure, the idea of moral excellence in general and of moral excellence as (at least partly) a matter of strength of some kind, is an idea with deep roots in the history of philosophy, playing a crucial role for example in the ethical thinking of Aristotle.[40]

Virtue ethics

Tannsjö's critical remark directed at Aristotle's virtue ethics deserves attention since almost all sport philosophers who believe in the educational potential of sport direct their attention towards virtue ethical ideas in their attempt to instil the positive relationship between morality and sport. This is not surprising since the connection between athletics and virtue was strong in antiquity. In Homeric times, virtue was attached to a functionalist anthropology. The virtuous person was one who excelled at some specific task necessary for the community. The virtuous blacksmith gained status and respect as a result of his ability to create, for example, efficient and useful weapons, and the virtuous soldier was one who made excellent use of such weapons in war. Virtues were intricately related to honour, respect and status, because virtues were perceived as publicly displayed excellences. The ancient Olympic Games were demonstrations of virtue through excellence since superior skills were best demonstrated in comparison to the skills of others. There was an element of competition and efficiency in the Homeric understanding of virtues that fits hand in glove with the logic of sport. The idea of hidden virtues in one's character did not make sense in antiquity. Virtues had to be displayed for all to see through virtuous actions if they were to be recognized as virtues and therefore they were inextricably bound up with social recognition.

Aristotle's contribution to virtue ethics partly consisted in relating the functional aspect of virtues to more abstract anthropological ideas about the nature (eidos) of a human being.[41] According to Aristotle, the proper end (telos) of a human being is to live in accordance with their nature, which is reason or practical rationality that demands a well-balanced virtuous life as the basis for a good and successful life (eudaimonia). Virtues are internalized behavioural dispositions acting appropriately under the given circumstances. They are the result of a social practice where virtuous behaviour is acquired and practised so often that it becomes a habit (hexis).[42] Virtues are internalized by a repetition of actions that represents virtues. One becomes courageous by acting courageously etc.[43] Since the good life is a virtuous life and virtues cannot be explained without reference to the good life, there is an interdependent relationship between them that makes an explanation of either circular. The two concepts are interdependent. A virtuous person expresses his or her moral worth in public by displaying excellence that leads to esteem. The connection between moral worth (consisting in the possession of virtues) and the ability to excel in a publicly recognized way is so strong with Aristotle that it makes sense to equate virtues with various forms of excellences that enable a person to lead a good life. To put it differently, the idea of a publicly discredited but deeply moral person did not make sense to Aristotle because morality and esteem was inseparable.

After many years out of grace, Alasdair MacIntyre restored virtue ethics to glory in his book *After Virtue*. MacIntyre's effort to rehabilitate the ethical thinking of Aristotle is an attempt to steer moral philosophy out of the dead end it had been driven into by the futile search for the foundation of morality in the constituents of an individual that had been exercised since the age of Enlightenment.[44] According to MacIntyre, Aristotle was right in believing that morality was connected to social practice and he defines a practice as follows:

> By a 'practice' I am going to mean any coherent and complex form of socially established co-operative human activity through which goods internal to the form of activity are realized in the course of trying to achieve those standards of excellence which are appropriate to and partly definitive of that form of activity, with the result that human powers to achieve excellence, and human conceptions of the ends and goods involved, are systematically extended.[45]

MacIntyre mentions chess as an example. If one wants to know what internal values the game of chess has to offer, one has to learn how to play the game by learning its rules and play it long enough to understand the standards of excellence pertaining to it. The chess novice will soon learn that the standard of excellence pertaining to chess is only obtainable within the confinement of the rules of chess. As MacIntyre writes:

> A practice involves standards of excellence and obedience to rules as well as achievement of goods. To enter a practice is to accept those standards and the inadequacy of my own performance as judged by them. It is to submit my own attitudes, choices, preferences and tastes to the standards which currently partially define the practice.[46]

By accepting the rules of chess and its standard of excellence it becomes possible to learn the game by, for example, studying games of grand masters and thereby acquiring the skills necessary to appreciate the values of the game and obtain respect and status within the chess community. In order to reach that stage, one needs to process the virtues of chess. Virtue is defined by MacIntyre as 'an acquired human quality the possession and exercise of which tends to enable us to achieve those goods which are internal to practices and the lack of which effectively prevent us from achieving any such goods'.[47]

Since all sports are practices, they all contain values that are specifically related to the different forms of sport that exists. These values can only be obtained if one engages in a specific sport, as described above. Only then is it possible to internalize the virtues that have value both inside and outside of sport (for example: temperance, courage, cool-headedness, perseverance) and in that way a social practice such as sport contributes to the good life (eudemonia).

MacIntyre downplayed the importance of external values, crucial to Aristotle, such as esteem, status and respect, in acquiring a good life. Nevertheless, they are certainly part of today's elite sport and important constituents of elite athletes' notion of happiness; and if they are justly conferred in proportion to the excellence involved, McNamee sides with John Kekes, who allows external goods a role in the good life alongside internal goods as it appears in the following: 'The ultimate test of the goodness of our lives is whether they involve lasting possession of external and internal goods and whether the satisfactions derived from possession outweigh, in quantity and quality, such hardship and suffering as we experience.'[48]

Again, it is easy to see how virtue ethics' emphasis on the connection between excellence, moral worth and social recognition fits well with elite sport. As McNamee writes, 'esteem is tied to the internal logic of practices such as sport since they are public celebrations of ludic capacity'.[49]

Conclusion

Virtue ethicists have shown that sport does produce values of its own, as claimed by broad internalists. Unfortunately, these values are far from noble. Equating moral worth with excellence is to enter a morally problematic zone as we have seen, because it implies a fascist contempt for the genetically and socially weak and unsuccessful. If a group of persons identified by race, colour, ethnicity, nationality, etc. are ascribed less moral value because they are on average perceived to – or in fact do – perform at a lower level within highly valued social practices like art or science, aversive feelings towards this group are likely to occur. In modern, knowledge-based societies, the anti-intellectualism found within black culture has severe socioeconomic consequences that make it difficult for blacks to succeed in other valued social practices that require cultural capital. Learning from sport's internal logic and its affiliation with the teachings of virtue ethics that people should be *morally* judged according to their abilities, black and other non-white peoples might come to see sport as the one area where they can excel and gain some moral worth. It is, as John Valentine wrote in his review of Hoberman's *Darwin's Athletes*, as if:

> African-Americans had heeded the advice of Charles Murray and Richard Hernstein, authors of *The Bell Curve*, who argue that the 'wise' cultural response to residence at the bottom of the mental ability scale would be to develop a 'clannish self-esteem' based on the demonstrated aptitudes of one's group.[50]

The primary problem is not that black people are fixated on sport. It is rather that the world has been seduced by the idea of competition as a way to expose moral goodness by way of various forms of excellence in a hierarchical order from physical excellence at the bottom to intellectual excellence at the top. Of course, sport plays absolutely no positive role in this debacle as it promotes exactly those morally reprehensible ideas of virtues and vices being connected to excellence. This way, sport also serves a conservative function in collaboration with virtue ethical ideas. This is so because the ability to reach a level of excellence in adulthood is largely due to genetic and environmental factors outside an individual's control. It is much easier to excel within academia if one's genetic makeup and upbringing support the development of advanced cognitive abilities and the acquisition of cultural capital. Since important pre-conditions for achieving excellence are transferable from one generation to the next, it is, in a virtue ethical perspective, reasonable to speak of *moral capital* being to some extent transferred from one generation to the next. The value system in sport and virtue ethics serves a conservative function by making sure that moral worth is likely to stick with certain successful groups within society. The same is unfortunately true *mutatis mutandis* with regard to moral condemnation. Virtue ethics and sports' moral education are valuable for any person or any group of persons who are (thought to be) in possession of superior abilities, since such teachings add moral superiority to the long list of positive elements already constituting their good lives. For the less fortunate, they are a source of low self-esteem, stigma and possible discrimination. Sport holds the power to enrich people's lives in various ways, both as participants and spectators, but as a means to moral education and a vehicle for the promotion of a colour-blind society it is utterly impotent.

Notes

1 D. Adair (ed.), *Sport, Race and Ethnicity: Narratives of Difference and Diversity* (Morgantown, WV: Fitness Information Technology, 2011); J. Bale and J. Sang, *Kenyan Running: Movement Culture, Geography and Global Change* (London: Routledge, 1996); H. Edwards, *The Revolt of the Black Athlete* (New York, NY: Free Press, 1968); N. Farrington, D. Kilvington, J. Price and A. Saeed, *Race, Racism and Sports Journalism* (London: Routledge, 2012); J. Hoberman, *Darwin's Athletes* (New York: Houghton Mifflin, 1997); K. Hylton, *'Race' and Sport: Critical Race Theory* (London: Routledge, 2009); G. Jarvie, *Sport, Racism and Ethnicity* (London: Routledge, 1991); J. Nauright, A. Cobley and D. Wiggins, eds, *Beyond C.L.R. James: Race and Ethnicity in Sport* (Fayetteville, AR: University of Arkansas Press, 2014); G. Early, 'Sports, Political Philosophy, and the African American', in T.L. Lott and J.P. Pittman (eds), *A Companion to African-American Philosophy* (Oxford: Blackwell Publishers, 2003), 436–49.

2 Jan Boxill, ed., *Sport Ethics: An Anthology* (Oxford: Blackwell, 2003); Jon Entine, *Taboo: Why Black Athletes Dominate Sports and Why We Are Afraid to Talk About It* (New York, NY: Public Affairs, 2000); William Morgan's, *Ethics in Sport* (Champaign, IL: Human Kinetics, 2007).

3 A. Farr, 'Whiteness Visible', in G. Yancy, ed., *What Whites Look Like: African-American Philosophers on the Whiteness Question* (London: Routledge, 2004), 145.

4 Ibid., 146.

5 Drew A. Hyland, *Philosophy of Sport* (Minneapolis, MN: Paragon House, 1990); R.L. Simon, 'Sports, Relativism, and Moral Education', in J. Boxill, ed., *Sport Ethics: An Anthology* (Oxford: Blackwell, 2003).

6 Some believe that it has deeper historical roots. Benjamin Isaac, for example, argues that early forms of racism were common in classical antiquity and that 'those early forms served as prototype for modern racism'. B. Issac, *The Invention of Racism in Classical Antiquity* (Princeton, NJ: Princeton University Press, 2004), 1.

7 J. Pivetau, ed., *Oeuvres Philosophiques de Buffon* (Paris: Presses Univ. de France, 1954).

8 Quoted in Issac, *The Invention of Racism in Classical Antiquity*, 10.

9 K.N. Maglo, 'The Case against Biological Realism about Race: From Darwin to the Post-Genomic Era', *Perspectives on Science* 19, 4 (2011); J. Marks, *What It Means to be 98% Chimpanzee: Apes, People, and their Genes* (Berkeley, CA: University of California Press, 2003); S.M. Williams and A.R. Templeton, 'Race and Genomics', *New England Journal of Medicine*, 348, 25 (2003), 2581–2.

10 There is still some debate concerning the issue. See Maglo, 'The Case Against Biological Realism about Race'.

11 V. Anderson, *Beyond Ontological Blackness* (New York: Continuum Publishing Company, 1993); K.A. Appiah, *In My Father's House* (New York: Oxford University Press, 1992); N. Zack, *Race and Mixed Race* (Philadelphia, PA: Temple University Press, 1993).

12 J.H. McClarendon III, 'On the Nature of Whiteness and the Ontology of Race: Toward a Dialectical Materialist Analysis', in G. Yancy, ed., *What White Looks Like: African-American Philosophers on the Whiteness Question* (London: Routledge, 2004).

13 L.R. Gordon, 'Critical Reflections on Three Popular Tropes in the Study of Whiteness', in G. Yancy, ed., *What White Looks Like: African-American Philosophers on the Whiteness Question* (London: Routledge, 2004), 181.

14 K. Oliver, *Witnessing: Beyond Recognition* (Minneapolis, MN: University of Minnesota Press, 2001).

15 www.regjeringen.no/en/dokumenter/the-anti-discrimination-act/id420606, accessed October 2015.

16 V. Møller, 'Beyond Black and White: A Study of the Luis Suarez–Patrice Evra Controversy', in J. Nauright, A.G. Cobley and D.K. Wiggins, eds, *Beyond C.L.R. James: Shifting Boundaries of Race and Ethnicity in Sport* (Fayetteville, AR: University of Arkansas Press, 2014), 77–92.

17 M. McNamee, *Sports, Virtues and Vices: Morality Plays* (London: Routledge, 2008), 121.

18 Ibid.

19 J. Kovel, *White Racism: A Psychohistory* (New York: Columbia University Press, 1984).
20 Simon, 'Sports, Relativism, and Moral Education', 18.
21 J.-M. Brohm, *Sport: A Prison of Measured Time* (London: Ink Links, 1978).
22 P. Arnold, *Sport, Ethics and Education* (London: Cassell, 1997); H. Reid, *Introduction to the Philosophy of Sport* (Lanham, MD: Rowman & Littlefield, 2012).
23 Simon, 'Sports, Relativism, and Moral Education', 19.
24 R.S. Kretchmar, 'Soft Metaphysics: A Precursor to Good Sports Ethics', in M. McNamee and J. Parry, eds, *Ethics & Sport* (New York, NY: Taylor & Francis), 26.
25 K.M. Pearson, 'Deception, Sportsmanship, and Ethics', in William J. Morgan and Klaus V. Meier, eds, *Philosophical Inquiry in Sport* (Champaign, IL: Human Kinetics Publishers, 1995).
26 J. Keating, *Competition and Playful Activities* (Washington, DC: Rowman & Littlefield, 1978), 52.
27 P. Bonte, 'Anti-Doping Absolutism: A Darwinian Demasque', retrieved from: http://ph.au.dk/en/about-the-department-of-public-health/sections/sektion-for-idraet/forskning/forskningsenheden-sport-og-kropskultur/international-network-of-humanistic-doping-research/newsletters/march-2015/inhdr-commentary-pieter-bonde, accessed 15 May 2015.
28 Hyland, *Philosophy of Sport*, 11–12.
29 Ibid.
30 Ibid., 12.
31 Hoberman, *Darwin's Athletes*; A. Mosley, 'Racial Differences in Sports: What's Ethics Got to Do With It?', in J. Boxill, ed., *Sport Ethics: An Anthology* (Oxford, Blackwell, 2003); R. Williams and Y. Youssef, 'Division of Labor in College Football Along Racial Lines', *International Journal of Sports Psychology*, 6 (1975), 3–13.
32 I. Kant, *Observations on the Feeling of the Beautiful and Sublime*, trans. John T. Goldthwait (Berkeley, CA: University of California Press, [1763] 1960), 110.
33 T. Tannsjö, 'Is Our Admiration for Sport Heroes Fascistoid?', *Journal of the Philosophy of Sport*, 25 (1998), 24.
34 Ibid., 26; H. Ofstad, *Our Contempt for Weakness: Nazi Norms and Values – And Our Own* (Stockholm: Almqvist and Wiksell, 1998).
35 Ibid.
36 Ibid., 27.
37 Ibid.
38 H. Edwards, 'The Myth of the Racially Superior Athlete', *Intellectual Digest* 2 (1972), 58–60.
39 Tannsjö, 'Is Our Admiration for Sport Heroes Fascistoid?', 28.
40 Ibid.
41 Aristotle, *Nichomachean Ethics*, trans. T. Irwin, 2nd edition (London: Hackett Publishing, 1999).
42 Ibid., 1103a14.
43 Ibid.
44 A. MacIntyre, *After Virtue: A Study in Moral Theory* (London: Duckworth, 1981).
45 Ibid., 187.
46 Ibid., 190.
47 Ibid., 191.
48 Quoted in McNamee, *Sports, Virtues and Vices*, 67.
49 Ibid., 67.
50 J. Valentine, 'Darwin's Athletes: A Review Essay', *Journal of the Philosophy of Sport*, 26 (1999), 107.

4

INTERSECTIONS OF RACE AND GENDER IN SPORT

Sasha Sutherland

Sport is considered one of the largest and most popular global industries. Dominated primarily by white men and privileging white women, sports like football (soccer), gymnastics, tennis, and boxing have received much attention over the last century with the inflow of black sporting bodies into these traditionally white spaces. That influx has also catalysed a media sensation, albeit Americanized, favouring discourses on race and gender as social categories of analysis instead of earlier biological categories in the social world of sport. It has encouraged, incurred, and presented an outpouring of dialogues on racial stereotyping and gender marking in sports, especially pitting the black male and female sport personalities against the idealized white male and female bodies.[1] Discourses on race and gender have, therefore, moved beyond the biological to social categories of analysis steeped in relations of power where race and gender converge.

This chapter employs a cultural studies framework and interdisciplinary feminist analytical approach to interrogate race and gender in sports that are linked to material and ideological relations of power. It seeks to demonstrate the contemporary categories of analysis in sport as subjectively built upon precepts of racialized and gendered ideals in society. Those edicts prove disparaging for men of colour who are vilified against their white counterparts and for white women who are not considered legitimate heirs to sporting practices by virtue of not being male. The precepts are twice as contemptuous for women of colour who are removed from the sporting centre based on social categories, race, and gender.

Race and gender as socially constructed categories have always been rooted in systemic, economic, and social relations of power and white (male) privilege. The result of that privilege has been a disconcerting appraisal, primarily of the estranged black athlete whose success is supposedly based on genetic traits and innate physical talent, compared to the white male athlete who is seen as a good student and hard worker.[2] Very few images portray black athletes, male or female, as achieving success through hard work in spite of the systemic challenges pitted against them. This is especially troublesome in light of the universal belief in sport discourse that being a great athlete depends on hard work and training as well as talent. Consequently, this chapter will explore the importance of agency among athletes of colour in a social world perpetuating the ideology that 'white is right' against challenges to the very foundation of this paradigm.

Within academia, discourses on race and gender have privileged 'othered' (minority) social groups in an attempt to advocate for equality and social justice in the midst of white privilege.[3]

Research has primarily focused on white–black discrepancies and sex discrimination where men and women have been categorized by gendered constructions.[4] Recently, there has been more scholarly work completed on Latin and Asian sport personalities, exposing the inapplicability of universal or essentialist discourses about their participation in sport.[5] Recent research has also paid more attention to transgender athletes as 'othered' within gender and sport discourse.[6]

For the purposes of this chapter, which addresses race in relation to power, I refer to Booth and Nauright's discussion on race as a biological category encompassing different physical characteristics such as skin colour and texture; body shape and size; nasal, eye, and hair forms. However, where racial groups are socially constructed with little or no relationship to physical features, lighter skin tones were believed to reflect higher levels of intelligence, civility, and superiority.[7] I refer to sex as biological categories of male and female, but reference Eudine Barriteau's definition of gender, which sees those biological categories as hinging on social and cultural ideologies of what it means to be masculine and feminine – that is, social constructions of gender identity related to biological sex categories. Barriteau refers to gender as 'complex systems of personal and social relations through which women and men are socially created and maintained and through which they gain access to, or are allocated status, power and material resources within society'.[8] Kamala Kempadoo's conceptual distinction of sexuality from gender suggests that sexuality is 'a derivative of gender relations and identities but as constituting a distinct culture and set of social relations and identities that interact with, yet can be studied separately from, gender'.[9] These definitions are not exhaustive, but help to conceptualize what is intended when addressing race and gender, or rather the performance of gender in sport.

Race and (male) sport

The entry of black athletes into previously segregated sports initially unlocked a dialogue on race representation and embodiment in postcolonial Africa, Caribbean, and Europe. In these societies, exclusion from sport was tied to race, but the independence era and end of apartheid, as well as the Second World War, resulted in the entry of 'coloured' men in societal institutions, including sport. Race relations in the USA has always been contentious where individual and institutionalized racism has created antagonisms yet to be resolved, while Latin America and Asia have, until recently, been relegated to the margins of race discussions regarding mainstream sport. The discourse on race was primarily centred on black athletes and based on the belief that their innate physiological skills led to their success in sports like track and field, basketball, and American football. Steeped in histories of colonialism and racism, athletes like Jesse Owens, Arthur Ashe, and Jackie Robinson in the USA, cricketers like Frank Worrell and his West Indies cricket team, and footballers John Barnes and Pelé faced racial prejudice amidst their success and popularity in sports. Similarly, their contemporaries in basketball and American football, European football leagues, and boxing have been subjected to racial stereotyping.

The deep-seated stereotype that black athletes possess natural physical talents takes precedence over mental aptitude and encourages a hegemonic symbolism about that principle. It encourages athletic achievement over scholastic prowess and suggests the former is the primary, and perhaps only, means of social mobility among African descendants in the USA and Europe, despite evidence to the contrary.[10] The literature on black scholars in science, technology, medicine, and other academic fields is not privileged in mainstream media as is the spectacle of black performance in sport. As a consequence to the limited presentation of black academics in the mainstream media, there is a perpetuation of existing stereotypes that athletic achievement is the main avenue for social mobility among African descendants. That athletic success does not go beyond the field to the board room, furthering the view that black athletes are primitive, ill-disciplined, violent, aggressive and uneducated; characteristics suited to the playing field but not the more civilized board room.[11]

Conversely, representations of white athletes have largely promoted the idea that a positive work ethic and intelligence were and still are the determinants of white success in sport. Asian athletes have always maintained a unique but similarly marginalized position in the most popular Western sports, owing to perceptions about their niche in martial arts. In the USA, Latin American migrants have been positioned as baseball or soccer players and are less encouraged in other sports.[12] Rooted in power over access and privilege, race discrimination is often reproduced through hegemony in sport.[13]

While biological and physiological arguments over black prominence in sport have been largely discounted, the myth of the physically superior, as opposed to the hard working, black athlete has prevailed in white Western sports science discourse.[14] Popular representations of the black male athlete have perpetuated the jumping gene myth to explain the athletic success of black athletes. These racialized assumptions have largely ignored environmental factors that account for athletic success among black and white athletes in much the same way they magnified presumed hard work and intelligence among white athletes as precursors for their success in other sports. Over- and under-representations of minorities or 'othered' groups in sport continue, even as new research centres 'coloured' athletes with exhaustive work ethics negating traditional beliefs about race in sport.[15]

Very few black or othered athletes in the USA and Europe have eclipsed race dialogues until basketball legend Michael Jordan, golfer Tiger Woods, and track sensation Usain Bolt. These sport personalities transcended the pervasive stereotype often associated with black athletes in sport because their success and personalities surpassed race, age, and class barriers in an unthreatening way, though not gendered ones. Despite these images of success, racial prejudice in sport continues to disempower many athletes. One needs only to look at recent controversies in English and Italian football, which demonstrate the deep-rooted entrenchment of racial stereotyping and discrimination against non-white athletes like Boateng, Okore, and Brazil's 'Hulk'.[16] Participation in sport is premised on equality of opportunity and not on an individual's physiological makeup. However, it is widely accepted that there remains a racially constructed hierarchy in many sports based on a participant's perceived biological features.[17] Those biological features are stereotyped, with particular behaviours ascribed to them, resulting in anticipated performances for participants in sport with differing physical appearance.

While issues of race in sport have received much attention in the USA, many examples of race and sport challenges exist around the world. Australia's treatment of Aboriginal athletes is one example of postcolonial racial stratification. Nova Peris and Cathy Freeman have both described in interviews how the colour of their skin was always subject to scrutiny and racial prejudice while competing on behalf of Australia in the Olympics. Peris acknowledged being called a 'nigger' by opposing players, indicating 'it takes a thick skin to be black skinned'.[18] Adam Goodes, Lewis Jetta, and Nicky Winmar have also made clear that race relations are steeped in colour stratification in the land down under, rendering 'black' people othered within the society. Binary categories of race are perpetuated, as are the invincibility of 'whiteness' to the racial discourse and subjugation of indigenous people in Australia.[19] Race becomes an issue of 'white' versus 'other', where non-whites are disadvantaged within the spectrum of race relations and social privilege.

In the Caribbean, however, race is not experienced the way it is in the USA or Europe. The region has recently produced many outstanding athletes at the Olympic level who have not confronted the racialist thinking and discrimination experienced by their contemporaries elsewhere. Their examples point to the fallacy of the universality of any essentialist dialogue on race or gender. Although the Caribbean population exists as a result of colonialism and slavery, where blacks were considered the subordinated group, and where racism was reflected in sport through segregation of clubs and teams, the independence era and Civil Rights movement catalysed a consciousness among blacks that would eventually lead to their governing the political landscape in most territories.[20]

The result is the domination of the political landscape by African descendants, although economically the region is heavily reliant on white business owners. Importantly, the quest for athletic success among black Caribbeans does not take precedence over educational achievement. Sport is also not viewed as an alternative for individuals with poor academic records. Quite the contrary, many of the region's athletic champions are well educated, reinforcing the athlete–scholar aphorism that has become popular in many Caribbean islands. Race may be considered subversive in Caribbean society, but where race and sport meet, national identity and nationhood are reinforced.

Race is not simply an issue of colour or its associated connotations. It is symptomatic of struggles within society that aim to maintain the status quo in relations of power to the changing means of production, that is white privilege and disempowerment among other 'races'. Sensitizing disempowered groups to the opportunities of not simply being on display on the basketball court, football field, or athletic track, but owning the display challenges who governs, manages, and administrates sports. It questions who are the team owners, managers, and elite coaches in sport beyond singular athletes such as Michael Jordan, the legendary basketball player turned businessman and the first and only African-American to own an NBA team by 2015. Maintaining a focus on the debate over athletic aptitude in sport ensures a limited conversation regarding the ability to affect change in the economic and social relations of power in sport, while the media's popular presentations of athletes with cash money motifs subliminally perpetuates the idea that black athletes are merely on display for a consumer culture infatuated with sport.

Gender and sport: the male–female divide

Sport is considered a male-centred, male-dominated, and male-identified domain in which masculine hegemony, patriarchy, and domination are core tenets.[21] Gender, then, becomes a dichotomous engagement over women's right to be included, respected, and earn (positions of) power in sport. The dialogue has also included suggestions about changing the premise on which sport is built to recognize that difference should not result in inequity between men and women, and among masculinities and femininities in sport. Sport, instead, should embrace difference and offer inclusionary practices according to its posited philosophy for being.[22]

Bryson identified four barriers to women's participation in sport – specifically, male definitions of sport, male control of women's sport, men ignoring women's sport, and men trivializing women's sport.[23] These barriers to women's participation prevail in spite of the health and fitness and other movements that have encouraged increased participation in physical movement and sport for women, and more recently witnessed the movement of women into positions of power and authority in sport. I discuss three of the four barriers, contending it is difficult to ignore the prevalence of women's sport in contemporary media and sport dialogue.

Many sports continue to yield universal white male standards of participation that continually discount women as accepted members of the sporting world.[24] Despite increasing opportunities for women to compete in sport at the national and international levels of competition, definitions of sport continue to privilege men in a way that relegates even the most acclaimed female athletes to the margins. Even though victories by women are celebrated at the time of national or international prominence, research has revealed pervasive stereotypes about men and women's sport that still exist today.[25] The discourse on gender and sport still maintains that those who hold the power are men who created sport for their own use. Men maintain power in spite of the agency of women in some societies to coerce power from men.

The administrative control that men hold over many sports played by women is another limiting factor for the advancement of women's sport. The control of international sport federations is dominated by men and so are executive committees, ensuring that decision-making power in sport remains in the hands of men. Control over women's sport is also demonstrated in the allocation of resources and ways of speaking about women's sport. In 1991, for example, FIFA President Joseph 'Sepp' Blatter proclaimed that the future of football was feminine.[26] Blatter, in his awkward manner, was attempting to proclaim women's football as the major area for growth potential around the world. In 2004 this leader suggested that women play in shorter shorts, but in 2014 he declared FIFA was not ready for female leadership.[27] What is interesting is that in Blatter's 17 years at the helm of football, women's football did progress greatly. The 2011 World Cup was considered ESPN's most viewed and highest rated (soccer) football match in the USA ever, with 13.5 million viewers, and also setting viewership records in Germany and France.[28] The 2015 edition of the World Cup in Canada recorded the highest total attendance record in any FIFA tournaments other than the Men's World Cup.[29] Still, gender marking and sexual stereotypes that trivialize female athletes continue to exist, reminding women of their marginal place in sport.

Media coverage of women's sport is another debilitating barrier in the gender and sport discourse. It is in the media that the trivializing of women's sport through gender marking and focusing on non-sport-related aspects of competition is reflected.[30] Until recently, women's sport coverage was almost non-existent in the media. However, with record-breaking performances by female athletes, fans around the world were forced to recognize the contributions by and successes of women in their respective sports. Coverage in the media acknowledged outstanding performances, but generally veered towards non-sport-related topics. Media coverage typically commences with gender marking – for example, Women's Tennis versus Tennis – and is invariably accompanied by an emphasis on the physical features rather than the athletic ability of women. This emphasis on beauty and non-athletic performance is evidenced by internet searches on the 'best', 'fastest', or 'greatest' female athletes of all time, which has revealed lists of the 'hottest' or 'sexiest' female athletes among search results.[31] Women in sport often engage in 'apologetic' behaviours such as beautification before competition to appear more feminine, downplaying their strength and aggression or emphasizing their heterosexuality[32] so they are not perceived as lesbian, a negative stereotype in the hyper hetero-sexualized sport world. Hardy posits that this behaviour exists to reinforce gender hierarchies and the performance of gender among female athletes. Using Butler's theoretical approach to society's binary conceptions of gender, Hardy suggests that in performing gender identity in the female apologetic, what is masculine is not feminine and vice versa, reinforcing Butler's position that gender is an embodying performance for men and women.[33]

Athletic recognition has improved for women in sport in recent times, ensuring women are respected for their competitiveness in sport, and is decreasing slowly the need for female apologetic behaviours. Now the concept of beautification in sport hinges on agency as much as it does on the female apologetic; but not all women have had that privilege when one considers the descriptions of women of different races or ethnic backgrounds. This has resulted in competing femininities in sport.

Competing femininities: where race and gender meet

When women in sport are not compared to men for their lack of aggression, force, and violence, or for their overly compassionate nature, timing, and skill, they are compared to each other. Race and gender are shrouded in preferred images of femininity even for women in sport, the result being blatant disregard for female athletes who contravene accepted preferences. The preferred standard privileges a heterosexual female that has 'light skin and long, straight hair'[34] and who is extremely feminine. Bonnie Berry in *The Power of Looks* suggests racial features 'speak, incorrectly, to social dictates of attractiveness. Given that Caucasian features, including light skin tones, are more socially prized than non-white features',[35] they are preferred images of beauty and attractiveness. These features subliminally dictate that white women are more feminine than black women, reinforcing their preference as mates and role models, and white privilege within an 'othered' grouping.[36]

The discourse situates black and white representations hierarchically, with the norms of beauty, and within sports particularly, having Caucasian women at the top, with mixed race females and Asians next, and black women at the bottom.[37] Contemporary images in magazines and advertisements reinforce and perpetuate these beliefs when advertisements promoting skin lightening products render black skin as unwanted, shameful, and a sign of losing.[38] Herring *et al.* suggests that skin colour, hair texture, eye shape, lip thickness, eye colour, and nose shape are stratified, and African-Americans with European features (light skin, 'good' hair) are subjectively ranked higher than those with dark complexions and 'kinky' hair. He further suggests that this stratification is not endemic to the black community, but to Asian and other racial groupings as well.[39]

Examples of this beauty stratification exists in sport. The successes of female athletes like Venus and Serena Williams have done little to quell the racialized lens through which they are seen, especially in relation to spectator favourites of the early 2000s such as Maria Sharapova and Anna Kournikova. Serena is consistently racialized in tennis, representative of the black community that is seen as undesirable. Both she and her sister have been referenced as the 'Williams brothers' by Russian Tennis Federation president Shamil Tarpischev, who was also an International Olympic Committee (IOC) member in 2014. When Serena Williams earned in 2015 the first calendar tennis Grand Slam in 27 years, many were focused on her presumed muscularity and rumours she used performance enhancing drugs rather than the historical significance of her accomplishment. When Gabrielle Douglas became the first African-American to win a gold medal in both single and team events in the 2012 Olympic Games, many spectators were focused on her hair and its representation of a particular standard of beauty, even in the black community.[40] In 2013, Simone Biles became gymnastics' first 'black' world champion, which resulted in racially charged comments by Italian gymnast Carlotta Ferlito and Italian gymnastics official David Ciaralli.[41] When questioned in an interview about Simone Biles' success at the World Championship, Ferlito responded 'I told Vanny (Ferrari) that next time we should also paint our skin black, so then we could win too.' Ferlito subsequently apologized on Twitter for the comment. David Ciaralli, who is also an IOC member, in defending Ferlito, stated 'Carlotta was referring to a trend in gymnastics at this moment, which is going towards a technique that opens up new chances to athletes of colour (well-known for power)' while penalizing the more artistic Eastern European style that allowed Russians and Romanians to dominate the sport for years. He further commented 'why aren't there blacks in swimming? Because the sport doesn't suit their physical characteristics. Is gymnastics becoming the same thing, to the point of wanting to be colored?'[42] Both comments resulted in controversy about racial stereotyping, reinforcing earlier assumptions that black athletes are never praised for working harder to be victorious. Theirs is always a victory based on genetics and connotations about athletic superiority. At the same time that black athletes were 'body shamed' on social networks, Caitlyn Jenner, a white transgender athlete (former 1976 Olympic decathlon gold medallist competing as Bruce Jenner) received the Arthur Ashe courage award for her transgender change. Jenner's celebration in the media was not without backlash, but it did reinforce perceptions that standards of beauty are continually privileged in relation to white communities, while other/othered races are subjected to institutionalized prejudice for not measuring up to those standards.

Race and gender: the transgender and intersexed athlete

One of the most recent discourses in sport is apprehension towards accepting transgender athletes in male–female competition. Although discussions regarding transgender athletes surfaced as far back as the early twenty-first century over individuals like Renée Richards and Mianne Bagger, recent media coverage of Santhi Soundararajan of India, Caster Semenya of South Africa, and Fallon Fox of the USA revived the dialogue about the place of transgender and intersexed athletes in sport and gender equality in sport beyond the male–female dichotomy.[43] The rules of most sports declare male and female categories for participation and do not account specifically for the inclusion of transgender or intersexed athletes. Questions surrounding sex identification, unfair advantage, and good governance in sex identification practices engulfed the sports world as discussion on policies such as the Stockholm consensus (2004) adopted by the IOC ensued.

The Stockholm consensus allows for transgender athletes to compete in sport at the international level, having met particular criteria including 'surgical anatomical changes … legal recognition of their assigned sex … by the appropriate authorities and hormonal therapy … administered in a verifiable manner and for a sufficient length of time to minimize gender-related advantages in competitions; and the recognized eligibility period being two years after gonadectomy'.[44] The consensus also allows that 'the medical delegate (or equivalent) of the relevant sporting body shall have the authority to take all appropriate measures for the determination of the gender of a competitor', granting sport federations autonomy to verify the sex of athletes competing under their auspices.[45] However, the consensus received criticism for not making allowances for non-surgical cases and for implementing legal recognition parameters, which were not always possible.[46] Furthermore, there were no parameters set for intersexed athletes, meaning sport federations retained the right to allow or refuse participation of transgender and intersexed athletes, clinched as their ultimate right to act according to what they determined to be in the best interest of the sport. This was the case of the 800-metre race in the Asian Games. Soundararajan of India, after being examined in 2006, was identified as a man and stripped of the silver medal. A similar incident occurred with Semenya of South Africa in 2009 when Semenya failed a gender test administered by the International Amateur Athletic Federation (IAAF) after winning the 800-metre gold medal at the World Athletics Championships in Berlin. Semenya was initially banned, but subsequently cleared by the IAAF in 2010 to return to competition and compete as a woman. Soundararajan was not so fortunate.

These two incidents demonstrate the strength of biological categories in determining participation and segregation in sport and also illuminate the social indifference to categories not conforming to traditional classifications of male or female. The inherent need to categorize athletes as male or female represents the ease with which separation occurs in sport, even at the risk of excluding competent participants, and the uneasiness with which transgender athletes are considered by many others in the sport community; as a direct contravention to biological sex categories and associated social roles, thereby rendering them 'other'. Indeed, the reaction to athletes of colour and gender has raised the spectre of further unfair advantage such as that levelled at East Germans and others during the Cold War, as Anaïs Bohoun demonstrates.[47] Thus 'natural' notions of physical 'superiority' of black male bodies combine to label these 'others' as 'freaks' of nature who should not be allowed to compete.

The resulting significance is the role transgender athletes play in challenging or reinforcing relations of gender linked to exclusion, when men undergo the male to female change, but not when women undergo the female to male change. One of the key considerations becomes 'unfair advantage', reinforcing the perception that men in sport are automatically stronger and more powerful than women. It is reinforced not simply by these assumptions, but also by the responses of athletes who refuse to compete against transgender athletes in female sports such as boxing.[48] Here, sex reassignment, the biological question, is a non-issue because it maintains the male–female dichotomy. It is the ensuing conflict with male–female advantage that becomes problematic, as it reinforces the stereotype that men are naturally stronger and more powerful than women, and are therefore better suited to sport. Women cannot and should not play sport because their physical attributes are not conducive to sport.

Agency: an emerging trend not suited to all participants

Agency or empowerment among athletes emerge as a direct result of the conflicts over race and gender in sport. Athletes, once disadvantaged, find their causes in the media (an inherent double standard or simple news reporting) and obtain support from fellow athletes and organizations committed to combating injustice and inequity experienced through social responses to their participation in sport. With an inherent sense of ownership in each case, these athletes, once 'othered' in their sport communities, promote equity and defy stereotypes by returning to each tournament amidst the challenges they face. That sense of ownership traditionally existed among athletes who participated in sport on the basis of their white privilege and encouraged by its mainstreaming in Western societies. As athletes of 'colour' emerged as key players in their own spaces and later on the international sporting circuit, there arose a sense of ownership among them as well. Sport was no longer seen as an activity for white men by white men. What was theorized as white privilege is evidenced less among athletes in contemporary sport, if not among sport administrators and managers. The race and gender lines blurred with the presence of black and female bodies in sport even as the subliminal messages and undercurrents of the predominant race and gender dialogues remained largely unquestioned.

Female emergence and accommodation in sport has not changed the unequal relations of gender. His-stories are still privileged over her-stories, and sport history has primarily focused on men's histories, reducing the impact of and focus on women's contribution to and successes in sport. Women have therefore fought first for inclusion and recognition, and now equity and justice in sport. For transgender athletes, a more neutral approach to gender in sport is apparent, although that empowerment is typically more evidenced among white women and men than it is among their 'coloured' counterparts. The most recent and notable example of this is former decathlete Bruce Jenner's transition to his transgendered Caitlyn and the subsequent recognition and rewards she received for her brave decision. Jenner is still recognized as the Olympic gold medallist that competed as a man at the 1976 Games. Jenner transitioned to female without major ridicule, but that was not the case for intersexed athletes such as Semenya and Soundararajan. While empowerment and agency can often lead to a breaking of racial and gendered barriers in sport, a similar capacity at higher levels of coaching, managing, and administrating sport have been slower to materialize.

Race and gender: will things ever change?

Race and gender as contentious categories in sport are built upon racialized and gendered ideals in society that are difficult to overturn. These categories maintain a hegemonic influence over how we think about and do sport, and prescribe social responses to individuals who are different from the established status quo. Race and gender dictate privilege for a particular category of people, while excluding and sometimes humiliating others. When challenged or examined, race and gender reveal relations of power that pervade all institutions in society, including sport, and reveal few avenues for successfully challenging or changing existing stereotypes, behaviours, and institutionalized practices. However, the challenge situates both the 'victim' and 'victimizer' as shaped by their social and political realities, whether from the position of privilege or the position of disadvantage. The only difference is that their positioning guarantees vastly different outcomes for each group. The result of challenging racialized and gendered ideals are either outright confrontation with those exclusionary practices or agency to encourage a change in perceptions about 'othered' groups within the boundaries of sport.

The additional categories of transgender and intersexed athletes present another challenge to already contentious gender categories in sport, equity, and social justice, culture with power becoming centred in sport discourse relating to inclusion, exclusion, and governance. Relations of power become situated in race and gender relations and the more powerful groups in society assert their advantage in maintaining the status quo. Pervasive beliefs about race and gender encourage an unquestioned acceptance about race and gender ideologies. These beliefs also reinforce race and gender ideologies by perpetuating discriminatory practices in sport without question or weighted sanctions beyond verbal utterances of non-compliance by guilty parties and petty fines. When leaders engage in prejudicial behaviours and receive nominal sanctions, it conveys the subliminal message that others can engage in similar behaviours and fear little sanction. The consequence is that the athletes and/or administrator being ridiculed for their biological or physiological difference based on a flawed hierarchy of beauty remains unsupported by the very institution that encourages participation by all who wish to engage in contests.

With sport's increasingly global expansion, encouraged by the migration of athletes around the world, traditional conceptions about race and gender will be increasingly challenged and perhaps changed. Racial groupings, once considered distinct, will fade, meaning essentialist descriptions and stereotypes about race and gender in sport must be altered to include and accommodate, but ultimately represent the realities that currently exist in sport. Those realities include a sporting world where iconic figures are no longer all Caucasian, but include African-American, Samoan, Latin American, African, and Caribbean peoples, all replete with varied experiences that contribute to their success as individuals and alter the sport landscape. The realities also include increasing sensitivity to the political, economic, and social realities of race and gender relations among spectators, administrators, and governing bodies regarding racial tolerance in sport. The gender hierarchy must be altered to reflect a changing paradigm between and among men and women, and the race hierarchy must also be dissolved to shape a truly level playing field for all in sport.

This potential reality demonstrates that race and gender are therefore not mutually exclusive categories. They are interrelated categories that affect and are affected by culture and power economics in sport. They affect how sport is governed, spectated, and considered. Exclusion based on either category represents a limited awareness of race and gender issues and a failure to recognize the ideology of sport as a promoter of social inclusion for all peoples regardless of race, religion, sexuality, social, or political status. Ultimately, sport has the transformative power to (re)construct, (re)present, and (re)organize discourses on race and gender so that no one group is othered based on social ideas about who should play sport and why. These categories of analysis can shift the boundaries of sport beyond dichotomous representations to frame how othered categories are factored in discourse, rendering gender and race as antiquated representations of legitimate categories. Until such time, however, we continue to hope and work for changes in attitudes and opportunities.

Notes

1 Gina Daddario and Brian J. Wigley, 'Gender Marking and Racial Stereotyping at the 2004 Athens Games', *Journal of Sports Media* 2, 1 (2007), 29–51. See also Kevin Hylton, *Race and Sport: Critical Race Theory* (London: Routledge, 2009); Susan Tyler-Eastman and Andrew C. Billings, 'Biased Voices of Sports: Racial and Gender Stereotyping in College Basketball Announcing', *Howard Journal of Communication* 12, 4 (2001), 183–201; Margaret Carlisle Duncan and Michael A. Messner, 'The Media Image of Sport and Gender', in Lawrence A. Wenner, ed., *Media Sport* (New York: Routledge, 1998), 170–85; Judith Butler, *Bodies That Matter: On the Discursive Limits of Sex* (New York: Routledge, 1993); Judith Butler, *Gender Trouble: Feminism and the Subversion of Identity* (London: Routledge, 1990); George Yancy, *Black Bodies, White Gazes: The Continuing Significance of Race* (Lanham, MD: Rowman & Littlefield, 2008); also see Abby L. Ferber, 'The Construction of Black Masculinity: White Supremacy Now and Then', *Journal of Sport & Social Issues* 31, 1 (2007), 11–24; Marie Hardin, Julie E. Dodd, Jean Chance, and Kristie Walsdorf, 'Sporting Images in Black and White: Race in Newspaper Coverage of the 2000 Olympic Games', *Howard Journal of Communications* 15, 4 (2004), 211–27.
2 Hylton, *Race and Sport*, 2.
3 Jonathan Long, Paul Robinson, and Karl Spracklen, 'Promoting Racial Equality Within Sports Organizations', *Journal of Sport & Social Issues* 29, 1 (2005), 41–59; also, see Rodney K. Smith, 'When Ignorance is Not Bliss: In Search of Racial and Gender Equity in Intercollegiate Athletics', *Mizzour Law Review* 61 (1996), 329.
4 Timothy Davis, 'Race and Sports in America: An Historical Overview', *Virginia Sports & Entertainment Law Journal* 7 (2007), 291.
5 Arbena Joseph, 'Dimensions of International Talent Migration in Latin American Sports', in J. Bale and J. Maguire, eds, *The Global Sports Arena: Athletic Talent Migration in an Interdependent World* (London: Frank Cass, 2013), 99–111. See also J. Entine, *Taboo: Why Black Athletes Dominate Sports and Why We're Afraid to Talk About It* (New York, NY: Public Affairs, 2008); Jonathan Long, Ben Carrington, and Karl Spracklen, 'Asians Cannot Wear Turbans in the Scrum: Explorations of Racist Discourse Within Professional Rugby League', *Leisure Studies* 16, 4 (1997), 249–59.
6 Pat Griffin, 'LGBT Equality in Sports: Celebrating Our Successes and Facing Our Challenges', in G.B. Cunningham, ed., *Sexual Orientation and Gender Identity in Sport: Essays From Activists, Coaches, and Scholars* (College Station, TX: Texas A&M University, 2012), 1–12. See also Jennifer V. Sinisi, 'Gender Non-Conformity as a Foundation for Sex Discrimination: Why Title IX May Be an Appropriate Remedy for the NCAA's Transgender Student-Athletes', *Jeffrey S. Moorad Sports Law Journal* 19, 1 (2012), 343; Bal Singh, Kanwaljeet Singh, and Narinder Sharma, 'Equality, Equity and Inclusion: Transgender Athletes' Participation in Competitive Sports – A New Era', *Physical Culture and Sport Studies and Research* 49, 1 (2010), 85–8.
7 John Nauright and Douglas Booth, 'Embodied Identities: Sport and Race in South Africa', in John Nauright, Alan Cobley, and David K. Wiggins, eds, *Beyond C.L.R. James: Shifting Boundaries of Race and Ethnicity in Sport* (Fayetteville, AR: University of Arkansas Press, 2014), 43.
8 Eudine Barriteau, *The Political Economy of Gender in the 21st Century Caribbean* (New York: Palgrave, 2001), 26.
9 Kamala Kempadoo, 'Caribbean Sexuality: Mapping the Field', *Caribbean Review of Gender Studies: A Journal of Caribbean Perspectives on Gender and Feminism*, 3 (2009), 12.
10 Ellis Cashmore, *Making Sense of Sports* (London: Routledge, 2010).
11 Harry Edwards, 'The Black "Dumb Jock": An American Sports Tragedy', *College Board Review* 131 (1984), 8–13.
12 Tim Wendell, *The New Face of Baseball: The One-Hundred Year Rise and Triumph of Latinos in America's Favorite Sport* (New York, NY: Rayo, 2003).
13 Martti Siisiainen, 'Two Concepts of Social Capital: Bourdieu vs. Putnam', *International Journal of Contemporary Sociology* 40, 2 (2003), 183–204.

14 Harry Edwards, 'The Sources of the Black Athlete's Superiority', in Eric Dunning and Malcolm Dominic, eds, *Sport: Critical Concepts in Sociology – Volume III Sport and Power Relations* (London: Routledge, 2003), 5–18. See also John Hoberman, *Darwin's Athletes* (Boston, MA: Houghton Mifflin, 1997).

15 G.W. Whiting, 'From at Risk to at Promise: Developing Scholar Identities Among Black Males', *Prufrock Journal*, 17, 4 (2006), 222–9.

16 Jamie Cleland and Ellis Cashmore, 'Fans, Racism and British Football in the Twenty-First Century: The Existence of a "Colour-Blind" Ideology', *Journal of Ethnic and Migration Studies* 40, 4 (2014), 638–54.

17 Cheryl L. Cole, Michael D. Giardina, and David L. Andrews. 'Michel Foucault: Studies of Power and Sport', in R. Giulianotti, ed., *Sport and Modern Social Theorists* (New York, NY: Palgrave, 2004), 207–23. See also Brendan Hokowhitu, 'Race Tactics: The Racialised Athletic Body', *Junctures: The Journal for Thematic Dialogue* 1 (2011).

18 Jordan Baker, 'Nova Peris and Cathy Freeman Compared Racist Letters', *Sunday Telegraph*, 12 May 2013.

19 Damien Riggs, *Taking Up the Challenge: Critical Race and Whiteness Studies in a Postcolonising Nation* (Belair, SA: Crawford House Publishing, 2007). See also Aileen Moreton-Robinson, ed., *Whitening Race: Essays in Social and Cultural Criticism* (Canberra: Aboriginal Studies Press, 2004); Damien W. Riggs and Jane M. Selby, 'Setting the Seen: Whiteness as Unmarked Category in Psychologists' Writings on Race in Australia', in *Proceedings of the 38th APS Annual Conference* (2003), 190–4.

20 John Nauright and David K. Wiggins, 'Race', in S.W. Pope and John Nauright, eds, *Routledge Companion to Sports History* (London: Routledge, 2010), 148–61.

21 Jay Coakley, *Sports in Society* (New York, NY: McGraw-Hill, 2009). See also Lois Bryson, 'Sport and the Maintenance of Masculine Hegemony', *Women's Studies International Forum*, 10, 4 (1987) 349–60.

22 Heather Reid, *Introduction to the Philosophy of Sport* (Lanham, MD: Rowman & Littlefield Publishers, 2012), 167–77.

23 Robert Lake, 'Gender and Etiquette in British Lawn Tennis 1870–1939: A Case Study of "Mixed Doubles"', *The International Journal of the History of Sport* 29, 5 (2012), 691–710. See also Samantha Nanayakkara, 'Trivialisation of Women's Sports in Sri Lanka: Overcoming Invisible Barriers', *Sri Lanka Journal of Humanities* 37, 1–2 (2011), 149–55; Claire Knowles, 'A Critically Reflective Study into How Far Sports Broadcasting and Print Media Reflects and Confirms the Role of Women in Reported Sport', PhD dissertation (Cardiff Metropolitan University, 2004).

24 J. Hargreaves, *Sporting Females* (London: Routledge, 1994), 286.

25 Jayne Caudwell, 'Gender, Feminism and Football Studies', *Soccer & Society* 12, 3 (2011), 330–44. See also John Harris, 'Doing Gender On and Off the Pitch: The World of Female Football Players', *Sociological Research Online* 12, 1 (2007).

26 Gertrud Pfister, 'The Future of Football is Female!?', in A. Tomlinson and C. Young, eds, *German Football: History, Culture, Society* (London: Routledge, 2006), 93.

27 Marcus Christenson and Paul Kelso, 'Soccer Chief's Plan to Boost Women's Game? Hotpants', *Guardian*, 16 January 2004.

28 Robert Seidman, '2011 Women's World Cup Finals: ESPN's Most-Viewed and Highest-Rated Soccer Match Ever Averaging 13.5 Million Viewers', *TV by the Numbers* (2011), http://tvbythenumbers. zap2it.com/2011/07/18/2011-womens-world-cup-finals-espns-most-viewed-and-highest-rated-soccer-match-ever-averaging-13-5-million-viewers, accessed 31 July 2015; FIFA.com, 'FIFA Women's World Cup Germany 2011 Sets New TV Viewing Records', www.fifa.com/womensworldcup/news/y=2011/m=7/news=fifa-women-world-cup-germany-2011-sets-new-viewing-records-1477957.html, accessed 20 July 2011.

29 FIFA.com, 'Key Figures From the FIFA Women's World Cup Canada 2015', www.fifa.com/womensworldcup/news/y=2015/m=7/news=key-figures-from-the-fifa-women-s-world-cup-canada-2015tm-2661648.html, accessed 27 July 2015.

30 Michael A. Messner, Margaret Carlisle Duncan, and Kerry Jensen, 'Separating the Men From the Girls: The Gendered Language of Televised Sports', *Gender & Society* 7, 1 (1993), 121–37.

31 'Top 50 Hottest Athletes of 2016', Athletic Build: Home of the Athletic Body, http://theathleticbuild. com/the-top-50-hottest-female-athletes-of-2016, accessed 22 February 2016. See also 'Ultimate List of Hottest Female Athletes in the World' Total Sportek, www.totalsportek.com/list/hottest-female-athletes, accessed 22 February 2016.

32 Laurel R. Davis-Delano, April Pollock, and Jennifer Ellsworth Vose, 'Apologetic Behavior Among Female Athletes: A New Questionnaire and Initial Results', *International Review for the Sociology of Sport* 44, 2–3 (2009), 131–50.

33 Elizabeth Hardy, 'The Female "Apologetic" Behaviour Within Canadian Women's Rugby: Athlete Perceptions and Media Influences', *Sport in Society* 18, 2 (2014), 160.

34 Cheryl Thompson, 'Black Women, Beauty, and Hair as a Matter of *Being*', in *Women's Studies* 38 (2009), 831–56. See also Dwight E. Brooks and Lisa P. Hébert, 'Gender, Race and Media Representation', in Bonnie J. Dow and Julia T. Wood, eds, *The SAGE Handbook of Gender and Communication* (Thousand Oaks, CA: Sage, 2006), 297–317.

35 Berry, Bonnie, 'The Power of Looks: An Historical Analysis of Social Aesthetics and Status Gain'. Paper for the Society for the Study of Social Problems, San Francisco, Gig Harbor (2004).

36 Aia Hurtado and Abigail J. Stewart, 'Through the Looking Glass: Implications of Studying Whiteness for Feminist Methods', in Michelle Fine, Lois Weis, Linda Powell Pruitt, and April Burns, eds, *Off White: Readings on Power, Privilege, and Resistance* (New York: Routledge, 2004), 315.

37 Berry, 'The Power of Looks', 30.

38 BBC.com, '"Racist" Thailand Skin-Whitening Advert is Withdrawn'. 'Racist Ads: Seoul Secret Uses Cris Horwang in Blackface to Promote Skin-Whitening Pill', www.youtube.com/watch?v=4okNUKMHy1s, accessed 8 January 2016.

39 Cedric Herring, Verna Keith, and Hayward Derrick Horton, *Skin Deep: How Race and Complexion Matter in the 'Colour-Blind' Era* (Urbana, IL: University of Illinois Press, 2004).

40 Julee Wilson, 'Gabby Douglas' Hair: How Did Olympic History Turn into a Hair Debate?', *Huffington Post*, 8 August 2012.

41 *Mail Online*, '"Maybe Next Time We'll Paint Our Skin Black So We Can Win": Italian Gymnast Sparks Fury With Racist Jibe at 16-Year-Old New World Champion', 14 October 2013.

42 Philip Hersh, '"Italian Gymnastics Federation Calls Racially Charged Words a "Misunderstanding"', *Chicago Tribune*, 10 October 2013 (accessed 15 October 2015).

43 Susan Birrell and Cheryl L. Cole, 'Renee Richards and the Construction and Naturalization of Difference', *Sport: Sport and Power Relations* 3 (2003), 174. See also Ann Travers, 'Queering Sport: Lesbian Softball Leagues and the Transgender Challenge', *International Review for the Sociology of Sport* 41, 3–4 (2006), 431–46.

44 Sheila L. Cavanagh and Heather Sykes, 'Transsexual Bodies at the Olympics: The International Olympic Committee's Policy on Transsexual Athletes at the 2004 Athens Summer Games', *Body & Society* 12, 3 (2006), 75–102.

45 Ibid.

46 Lance Wahlert and Autumn Fiester, 'Gender Transports: Privileging the "Natural" in Gender Testing Debates for Intersex and Transgender Athletes', *The American Journal of Bioethics* 12, 7 (2012), 19–21. See also Juliet Jacques, 'Trans People and Sport: The Stockholm Consensus, Ten Years On', (blog) *Leap Sports*, 30 May 2014.

47 Michal Raz and Anaïs Bohuon, 'The Femininity Test in Sporting Competitions: A Classified History X', *CLIO Women, Gender and History* 37 (2013), 257–9. See also Anaïs Bohuon, 'Gender Verifications in Sport: From an East/West Antagonism to a North/South Antagonism', *The International Journal of the History of Sport* 32, 7 (2015), 965–79.

48 Loretta Hunt, 'How Fallon Fox Became the First Known Transgender Athlete in MMA', *Sports Illustrated* (2013). See also Tara Q. Mahoney, Mark A. Dodds, and Katherine M. Polasek, 'Progress for Transgender Athletes: Analysis of the School Success and Opportunity Act', *Journal of Physical Education, Recreation & Dance* 86, 6 (2015), 45–7.

5

POLICY AND MANAGEMENT

Marc Keech

Until the early 1960s there was little interest in developing domestic sport policies in any country. For all governments, developed and developing, non-aligned and postcolonial, modern international sport presented problems (spectator violence, defection of athletes, and drug abuse, for example) and opportunities (health benefits associated with sports participation, the promotion of foreign policy goals) for achieving political objectives.[1] Sport is of strong cultural significance to most developed nations, demonstrated by the amount of media attention devoted to national team success and the support for the construction of major stadiums and other sporting infrastructure with public funds. The phenomenon of developing sport policy filtered into the fabric of nascent sport policies of emerging nations from the 1960s to the 1980s. Sport is a resource available to help deliver non-sport policy objectives, demonstrating political power, combating social exclusion, reducing childhood obesity, improving economic development, and facilitating urban regeneration. Sport is a malleable and multidimensional tool of policy in that it is not only a public service, but also an important element welfare-related provision and a facet of economic activity. Thus, it can contribute in many ways to the achievement of governments' domestic objectives outside of sport policy as well as providing focus on instrumental aspects of sport, such as improving the performance of elite athletes and increasing participation in sport.[2] Issues of 'race' and ethnicity have become prominent elements of policies for the management of opportunities to participate in sport and the origins of the association between the phenomena are worth tracing briefly. As Bairner and Sugden noted:

> It is a truism that all societies are divided. There are divisions between racial and ethnic groupings, between the rich and the poor, the young and the old, between men and women, adults and children, the healthy and the sick and so on. All of these, and numerous other divisions besides, impact upon the world of sport. They are reflected in the ways in which sport is played, watched and organised. Sport may also reinforce, and in some instances, exacerbate the divisions.[3]

Law noted that although

> issues of racism and ethnicity remain topical and there is a steady growth in research
> and writing which engages with these issues across the varied fields of social policy,
> there is a noticeable underdevelopment in areas such as health and sport and leisure.[4]

Since that time, and in response to calls for more critical scholarship in the fields of sport and
race,[5] there has been a proliferation of writing on sport and race-related issues,[6] to the extent
that, while noting a degree of caution, the scope of scholarship on race and sport is impressive.[7]
While the scope is indeed impressive, policy and management issues continue to be redefined.
Following the publication of *Sporting Future: A New Strategy for an Active Nation*, the new
(Conservative) government sports strategy in the UK in December 2015, attention was drawn
to the priority placed upon, for example, the work required to tackle lack of diversity in senior
positions across the sport sector and a review of the barriers to women and minority groups
progressing into high-performance coaching roles.[8]

This chapter identifies key themes that have become prevalent within policy making for
sport and the associated management responsibilities inherent in increasing and managing sports
participation. It initially draws upon examples from predominantly 'white' nations, with more
established sport policy and sport management frameworks, to exemplify how, despite the
differences within individual nation states, consciously or unconsciously, the development of
sport policies and the associated sport management issues have exhibited similar patterns of
socio-political and historical development, despite the vastly different circumstances in each
individual country. Theoretically, the use of policy paradigms is particularly pertinent. Policy
paradigms are usually seen as attempts (by policy makers or other interest groups) to establish
causal relationships and to suggest how policy objectives might best be achieved. The
development of policy paradigms is implicit in much of the literature across the fields of sport
policy in sport management. For the purposes of this chapter, it is acknowledged that limitations
of space do not prevent a thorough theoretical engagement but that the overall frameworks
permit a much deeper analysis than available here. Responsibilities for managing participation
opportunities, particularly at a very local level, are often complex and require the application of
techniques and strategies evident in the majority of modern commercial, governmental, or
non-profit organisations.[9] Furthermore, the ability of either professionals and/or volunteers
working in sport to respond to the management issues identified is often reflected in their own
cultural or ethnic parameters. Sport, however, as a workforce, does not often replicate the
diversity required and presents considerable challenges to sports organisations.[10]

The historical and socio-political contexts

The historical and/or socio-political context of sport in not only each nation but, at times, sub-
regions or specific areas of each nation, illustrates the complexity of understanding required to
develop opportunities for sports participation. Policy developments, whether contemporary or
historical, almost without exceptions are shaped by the historical context within which they
take place. Yet, often, the reminder to take account of history often asks those working in sport
a series of complex questions that one may not have considered if the historical context has not
been provided. Furthermore, a question regarding 'whose' history is being provided and the
underlying power relations between the actors involved increases, rather than allays, fears about
understanding the environment in which one works. The emergence of sport not just in a
single country, but in countries with colonial history or in developing nations, often exhibits a

series of institutions which have come to define the emergence of sport. Indicatively, these may include: the emergence of and role of the state; educational systems; the growth of voluntary sports clubs, religions, the military, and the politics of identity and nationalism. More recently other influences would include labour organisations, political parties, and commercial organisations.[11]

The influence of the English public school system on the development of sporting opportunities and participation in the United Kingdom has been amply documented.[12] It is also evident in many other countries how the politics of participation has been defined through sport. For example, it has been illustrated how some of the first sports clubs in Montréal in the late nineteenth century became sites for a Canadian identity different from the British one,[13] since when there has been considerable study of the extent to which sport has contributed to the promotion of Québécois/Canadian national differences and different forms of nationalism in Canada as a whole. By 1978, sport and the distinctive forms of participation became an element of promoting Québécois identity and the 1994 electoral manifesto of Parti Québécois illustrated that leisure and sport were an expression of a community's cultural identity and that participation in sport was a strong tool for the promotion of a sense of belonging.[14] Echoing the latter point, Paraschak examined the role of participation and celebration of sports festivals in regard to race relations in the remote Northwest Territories of Canada, noting how practices in sport differed from the more populated south of the country.[15]

The notion that societies are inherently racist is difficult to argue against. A range of historical and contemporary discussions situate each country's socio–political context within structural inequalities that go beyond the scope of this chapter, but for sport, in particular, as Puwar argues, 'the systemic fantasy of imagined inclusiveness makes it difficult to see racism', for 'people are reluctant to confront the uncomfortable fact that racism is endemic to organisations and professions'.[16] Nevertheless, while there are copious examples of anti-racism and anti-discriminary platforms in sport, Carrington acutely summarises the systemic problem for sport in the title of his paper '"What I Said Was Racist – but I'm Not a Racist"'.[17] Systemic racism comprises 'a broad range of white–racist dimensions: the racist ideology, attitudes, emotions, habits, actions and institutions of whites'.[18] Writing about English men's football, Burdsey contends that

> this position emphasises the historical legacies of racial inequality and foregrounds the role of institutions and structures, recognising that racism is much more than a question of individual bigotry and prejudice. While racism is always specific temporally and spatially, and fluctuates in its manifestations – moving arguably towards more complex, subtle and nuanced forms – it has been an unceasing presence in English men's football over the last half-century.[19]

In Australia, the picture is little different despite the welcome generally of the rising number of Aboriginal rugby league stars. The inclusion and in whatever ways, however, of indigenous performers does not mean an absence of racism. It seems obvious to state, but without sport providing opportunities (and the associated aspirations), many young Aboriginal men would be in a worse position, and that debate is very male dominated. Michael Long, a regular figure on 'footy' coverage in Australia when 'homage' is paid to Aboriginal culture on Fox Sports, has always contended that sport has been the greatest ally of Aboriginal people in the fight against racism and in the quest for greater Aboriginal self-respect among the Australian community generally. Together, the examples presented above illustrate briefly the difficulty of tackling social inequalities around 'race', ethnicity and sport. Paradoxically, the difficulties in developing and managing participation opportunities in sport often take place in the context of more prevalent headlines, regardless of whether these headlines are historical or contemporary, which illustrates the darker, seedier, and shameful side of sport.[20]

Policy development 1982–2004: the UK experience and a focus on the 'need'

The development of policy in a wide range of countries is now articulated with great attention to detail,[21] but the particular elements of sport policy in individual countries are still being drawn out and analysed. In the UK, the first sport policy intervention on 'race' and ethnicity was expressed in the slogan of 'Sport for All'. Although always more an aspiration rather than a specific policy goal, Sport for All signalled a belief in the early 1970s that access to participation opportunities in sport was a right of citizenship.[22] Black and minority ethnic (BME) groups have been a target of national sport policy since 1982[23] and this emphasis gradually became reflected in the emergence of a community-development approach to local public policy, based on the principle of 'empowering' disadvantaged members of the local community. This revised strategic emphasis was confirmed with the publication of 'Sport in the Community: The Next Ten Years',[24] which argued for the need to 'target' recreationally disadvantaged groups, such as women, the disabled, the elderly, and ethnic minorities. The decision to 'target' population groups was the first, albeit somewhat tacit, acknowledgement that 'Sport for All' was flawed, as research evidence throughout the latter half of the 1970s increasingly indicated a failure on the part of the public sector services to attract ethnic minorities, the unemployed, the elderly, women, the disabled, and low-income groups. The Action Sport projects of the early 1980s were established as a response to urban unrest in inner-city areas highly populated by people from a variety of ethnic backgrounds,[25] but the focus on specific populations as perceived protagonists of disorder played an element in reinforcing stereotypes.

The problem with adopting the target-group approach is that it tended to misunderstand the cause of the estrangement felt by many black and Asian people towards sport. The emphasis on 'cultural constraint' or 'difference' led policy makers and sport development officers to problematise the target groups in question. In asking what it was about 'their culture', 'their religion' that needed to be understood in order for opportunities in sport to be made available, it allowed the traditional structures of British sport to be left unexamined. Therefore, the persistent 'problem' of relatively low levels of participation among many ethnic minority groups was inadvertently blamed on 'them', while at the same time legitimating a presumed normal level of sporting participation based on unacknowledged sporting practices of white, middle-class males. This approach persisted throughout the 1980s and for most of the 1990s,[26] and still remains a significant mechanism through which sports organisations address BME community needs.

In 1994 the Sports Council produced a series of documents highlighting key policy issues pertaining to their four priority target groups: young people, women and girls, participants with disabilities, and ethnic minorities. In a significant development, the Sports Council acknowledged that various initiatives were undertaken to increase their participation, but little was done to challenge the underlying causes of this inequity, reinforcing the point that a majority of decision makers illustrated little understanding of the sporting needs and aspirations of BMEs. Providers were not aware of how disadvantage and discrimination restrict access to sport.[27] By 2002, the development of the Active Sports programmes had seen integration of target groups within broader policy objectives. The national Active Sports targets identified that 10 per cent of young people and 5 per cent of coaches participating within the programme will be from BME groups. Despite these developments, it was evident that the target-group approach still exhibited a central feature of sport and the emphasis was and remains clearly on officers and managers at a local level to ensure equality of opportunity within local sporting communities.

Sport England published its own equity policy and operationalised it by also producing the Sports Equity Index.[28] The Sports Equity Index was formulated to provide the evidence base to underpin sports equity policy and initiatives in England and claimed to do this by providing an analysis of the relative propensity of different groups within the population to take part in sport.[29] A further development was exemplified by the production of the Racial Equality Charter for Sport. Governing bodies and sport organisations were required to make a public commitment to challenge and remove racial discrimination and to achieve racial equality in sport, encourage people from all communities to become involved in sport, welcome employees and spectators from all communities, and protect all employees and spectators from racial abuse and harassment. Furthermore, there were exhortations to encourage skilled and talented individuals from all communities to become involved at all levels of sports administration, management, and coaching, develop sports bodies so that they could develop the best possible racial equality policies and practices. All NGBs had to achieve the preliminary standard by March 2003 to receive Exchequer funding (88 per cent succeeded). Regional (county sports) partnerships (not linked to funding) fared much worse. Long *et al.* noted at the time of their publication that 87 per cent of organisations had racial equality policies but few had measures for staff to attend any form of training; 16 per cent of organisations did not recognise their responsibility for ensuring racial equality in sport. Sixty-two per cent carried out ethnic monitoring, but only 40 per cent had any BME staff. 'The key point at issue here is whether a procedure can change a culture.'[30] Thus, while there was consensus on need for equality and diversity, there remained an inability to implement it.

Community initiatives, in any nation, with any circumstance, tend to be tailored to policy criteria rather than the needs of the local community. It is apparent that local initiatives should take account of community need and attempt to ensure that the 'ownership' of any policy intervention designed to address issues of inequality be enacted with the cooperation of the specific community. With regard to local communities, as opposed to the work of sport organisations, Coalter *et al.* contended that the notion of 'community' inherent in many community sports initiatives often has implications of cultural homogeneity, stability, and consensus, a view which negates the practicalities of heterogeneous 'communities within communities'.[31] The nature and degree of social cohesion varies depending on the ethnic mix, the balance between long- and short-term residents, the age structure of the community and the gender balance. For example, via ties of religion, culture, and extended family networks, some minority ethnic communities, living within larger geographical 'neighbourhoods', may have a high degree of social cohesion – yet, in some ways, they may be separate from the larger community. Such communities raise complex issues relating to provision for sport, the balance between exclusive provision, integrated provision, and integrated participation and the nature of appropriate policy outcomes. Like other 'target' groups, BME communities have limited faith in the long-term commitment of local authorities. Development officers have to spend time with groups, identifying their needs and seeking to find ways to address these needs. A major element of any local strategy should augment existing cultural practices by assisting in the promotion of traditional cultural events, using them as an opportunity to raise the profile of sport and physical activity. The inclusion of physical activities at events such as the Mela festivals was seen as one way of building on the cultural practices of minority ethnic communities.[32]

The results of the first ever large-scale quantitative survey in the UK (mainly England) into the relationship between sports participation and ethnicity confirmed the existence of racial inequalities but also perpetuated discourse that reinforced notions of separation for individual ethnic communities.[33] The survey found that the overall participation rate for ethnic minority groups in sport was 40 per cent, compared with a national average of 46 per cent.[34] Further examination of the findings revealed differences in the levels of participation between minority population groups and marked differences in participation between males and females. The overall participation rate for male ethnic minorities was 49 per cent compared with a national average for men of 54 per cent; for female ethnic minorities it was 32 per cent compared with a national average for all women of 39 per cent. On average, Black Caribbean (39 per cent), Indian (39 per cent) and Pakistani (31 per cent) and Bangladeshi (30 per cent) populations illustrated rates of participation in sport below those of the national average (46 per cent). Only the 'Black Other' group (60 per cent) had participation rates higher than found in the population as a whole. National participation rates for women (39 per cent) were matched or exceeded by women from 'Black Other' (45 per cent), 'Other' (41 per cent), and Chinese (39 per cent) ethnic groups, while women who classified themselves as Black Caribbean (34 per cent), Black African (34 per cent), Indian (31 per cent), and Bangladeshi (19 per cent) had participation rates below the national average for all women. The gap between men and women's participation in sport is greater among some ethnic minority groups than it is in the population as a whole.[35]

Although some barriers to participation are common to both ethnic minority and white communities, there are specific issues relating to cultural/religious beliefs and perceived racist attitudes among both providers and other participants. There are three important points to be made here. First, there is a lack of understanding of inter- and intra-minority group differences and 'ghettoising' policy and practice often compounds this. Second, and as with other communities, 'bottom-up' initiatives which build on traditions, seek to address issues wider than sport, and use workers recruited from the relevant communities are those most likely to succeed. Third, as in other areas of provision, there is a need for greater clarity about the desired outcomes for such provision and these should be agreed in consultation with the relevant communities.[36] Nicholson *et al.* and Coalter contend that sports policy interventions can only have a minimal impact on aggregate levels of sports participation – either because such interventions are ill-informed or because the determinants of sports participation lie well beyond the realms of sport policy, descriptive market segmentation, or individualised theories of behaviour change. Challenges to identity, such as having to show others an unfit body, appearing incompetent at core skills and, for women, appearing overly masculine are regularly identified as barriers to participation by people from all backgrounds.[37]

Inherently, here, policy development looked at ascribed 'need'. What was wrong about this approach, other than mirroring, in some ways, the target-led approach, was that 'need' became conflated with 'demand'. As Long *et al.* ably summarised, a critical level of barriers remained steadfastly in place in the UK,[38] despite the funded and localised reportage available. Targets did not take into account the diversity of some communities and the different local circumstances. As a result, each Active Sports Partnership was able to set its own targets based on local demographic analyses and research projects. The approach was significant and locally led as it depended on which organisation decided to invest into which level of research.

The local research in the UK 2000–04: lessons that should have been learned

Research in Slough, a town situated approximately 20 miles to the west of London, suggested that feelings of exclusion and barriers determined by an individual's ethnicity contributed to irregular use of facilities. In addition, for 21 per cent of ethnic minorities, if a majority of members of a sports club were from a different ethnic group, this became a barrier to participation. In Slough, where a majority of clubs were 'white', this finding raised fundamental issues about access, inclusion, and participation. An important element of including minority ethnic participants was the need to consider the isolation of participants. Twenty-one per cent of respondents stated they would not participate alone, while there were numerous anecdotes of young Asians not participating after negative experiences. Thirteen per cent reported that the need to 'fit in' with the majority cultural practices was also a barrier. Specifically, post-participation alcohol-related activities were recognised as a problem for Muslim participants.[39] Research in the Uxbridge ward of East Staffordshire, in the West Midlands region of England,[40] found that cricket was the most played sport by boys and girls, with levels of participation being more than twice that of the next popular sport, which was swimming. The three main reasons which prevented minority ethnic young people playing their favourite sport more often were: no time or too busy doing other things (65 per cent); don't know where to play (52 per cent); and any provision is too far away to get to (44 per cent). Even so, the experiences of PE at school were positive, with 70 per cent stating that they enjoyed it and that the white PE teachers were their role models.

Among the surfeit of locally induced research projects in the UK between 2000 and 2004, studies indicated that approximately one-third of young people had experienced misunderstanding, discrimination, or abuse arising from their religion or culture while playing sport. It was also noted that work undertaken by East Staffordshire Sports Development Unit to empower people from ethnic minorities to become qualified practising sports coaches had been successful but was heavily reliant on officers working on a one-to-one basis, reinforcing the issue that the 'harder to reach' populations, which included empowering minority ethnic groups in community sport provision, was and remains a time- and labour-intensive component of any work, which must be factored in to any work programmes.[41] In terms of policy and management, the locally induced projects offer the most acute and sensitised versions of local work.

Keech and Harrison identified that in Sussex, a relatively affluent area of the south of the UK, there was a gap in the knowledge of sports practitioners on how to address the needs of minority ethnic communities, primarily because of the relatively low population density of residents in the county. In local authorities, barriers such as strategic priorities and time constraints hindered the majority of practitioners from developing skills and knowledge in this area. While all working in the sport development profession would readily acknowledge the importance of equal opportunities, and are anti-discriminatory in their work, there is little evidence of proactive engagement with communities and a lack of specific training to address issues of cultural understanding and other related areas of provision.[42] Cricket, dance, and fitness related activities were seen as popular activities among BME communities. Keech and Harrison also found that there was a sizeable amount of 'informal' participation (i.e. outside of school or club structures). The home, the 'garden', and local parks were all popular venues for activities and respondents reported greater participation at these 'informal' sites than in local sports or youth clubs. Women from minority communities participated more at schools and places of worship, whereas a greater number of males, particularly with South Asian heritage, participated at community centres. Keech and Harrison worked with the Crawley Ethnic Minority Partnership (CEMP), a collective organisation that brought together community groups, to introduce sport to many non-participants. Working with CEMP and specific community organisations, there was a chance to consult with community groups and ascertain further the extent to which members of the community wish to become further involved in sport and exercise not only as participants, but also as coaches, officials and volunteers. A small minority of young people noted that there were few role models that they could identify with either nationally or locally. At a local level, one young person thought adults and older children could provide 'a good example to the rest about why they could play sport and what they would enjoy about it'. Community centres and places of worship are venues at which public sector providers are more likely to reach minority communities. There continues to be a gap in policy in the UK and most other nations about the extent to which extending participation opportunities to consider alternative methods of engaging BME communities in sport and exercise, and partnerships with health, community, and cultural groups and agencies, are potential mechanisms through which to achieve this. Furthermore, the research notes that racism and perceptions of ethnocentrism will continue to affect participation. Organisations responsible for the provision of activities are now charged with adopting an approach which identifies, understands, and responds to the needs of the community as 'legitimate' concerns rather than targeted or specialised programmes. Improving the provision of information about the benefits of sport and exercise can be built upon through the increasing awareness of second- and third-generation young people to promote improved and sustainable opportunities in local communities. The project recognised the importance of CEMP and its local community contacts within 24 different BME groups as a way of marketing and promoting activities as well as consulting with these communities. The project gained credibility through working with community 'gatekeepers', who were identified through CEMP. The research resulted in an interest from the Gurjar Hindu Union to look at volleyball provision in terms of both training for teams/coaches and participation. Aswin Soni, secretary of Gurjar Hindu Union, said:

> I am absolutely thrilled by the approach of Sussex Sports Partnership, and the fact that they are very proactive in gaining the research by actually speaking to the community. I am looking forward to working with them in the future.[43]

Despite the amount of local research, nothing really changed in the UK. As Cleland more recently noted, there are still many opportunities for local authorities to work more closely with ethnic minorities to reduce racial inequalities and barriers to participation.[44] The development of programmes for minority communities should be part of a long-term strategy. Shorter-term, one-off discrete projects can be valuable with these communities, but are more effective when integrated into long-term strategy.

The Exercise Alliance recommended that programmes for health and physical activity should adhere to the following principles:

- Involve people from BME groups in an ongoing consultative process to develop and evaluate programmes.
- Develop and offer a range of approaches, interventions, and options which best suit the needs of people from BME groups.
- Involve respected and valued members from BME society as role models or alliances.
- Use a variety of settings that are appropriate to the targeted communities, e.g. community centres, gurawars, mandirs, mosques, churches, health centres, etc.
- Ensure advice givers are knowledgeable, skilled, consistent, and confident.
- Tailor programmes specifically to the group's circumstances, addressing the cultural, religious, and socioeconomic barriers which hinder the capacity for people from BME groups to participate in physical activity.
- Consider the provision of transport to and from the selected venue for participants.
- Create a climate which combines socialising with exercise.
- Celebrate successes and share with people from BME groups as well as all agencies involved.

Nothing has changed since then – either in terms of the principles, nor in terms of the analysis. It becomes frustrating to keep hearing that there are 'new' initiatives and projects when they almost always fail to take account of the history that sport policy and management has now accrued. Sports policy has evolved in the context of general equality legislation and a steadily growing BME population. Several sports bodies have contributed to the policy arena with initiatives both to challenge discrimination and inequality and to promote participation and inclusion.[45] The large-scale public surveys offered important insights into patterns of participation, but there has been no public funding for surveys since in the UK.

The current focus in the UK: ignoring participation but looking at representation?

The United Kingdom, and specifically England, has recognised that minority groups are under-represented in sports administration. Some groups are worse off than others. Mihir Warty, a trustee for Sporting Equals, recently presented the *Leaderboard Report*, a piece of research revealing that of the 449 board members of the UK's national sports governing bodies, only 14 (3 per cent) were from black, Asian, or ethnic minority (BAME) backgrounds in 2013. The government's *Sporting Future* strategy has placed an emphasis on making improvements at board level, and has tasked QUANGOs UK Sport and Sport England with tackling the lack of diversity in senior positions and working with governing bodies to break down the barriers to recruitment.

> UK Sport chair, Rod Carr, complimented the strategy's focus on 'encouraging both governing bodies and sports organisations to have more diverse leaders', but hints that UK Sport and Sport England's work won't result in quotas. 'It's a bit premature, and personally I'm against target-driven culture', he says. 'It's about knowing people and getting people to apply for board and committee roles.' 'More diversity is needed at senior level and it's time for an informed debate about the best way this can be achieved', said Sport England chief executive Jennie Price, adding that responding to the needs of different communities 'is not an add-on, it's a must-do'. Arun Kang, chief executive of Sporting Equals, claims that while the number of BAME professionals in high-profile roles had not increased since 2014, there was now a 'real commitment' from governing bodies to 'embrace this agenda'. But the figures don't lie. *Sporting Future* revealed that half of the national governing bodies haven't reached the 2017 target of having 25 per cent female representation on their boards – that's before even taking into account BAME representation. Former sports minister Helen Grant introduced the target in 2014, with the implication being that failure to adhere may affect funding decisions. However, Grant is unsure about implementing further quotas for BAME representation, telling *Sports Management*: 'It would be nice if we didn't have to talk about quotas – we want people from every section of society knocking on the doors of the top jobs and getting them.' [46]

This excellent summary reinforces two key points. First, the politics of equity remain an important priority for all those in sport. Second, and more negatively, it is evident that sports organisations are a long way from truly promoting racial equality through policies for, and the management of, opportunities for sport.

Conclusion

The chapter has offered some brief observations on issues of policy and management. It has noted that issues of 'race' and ethnicity are considered, but in varying ways and by different policy makers. Particularly in light of more recent social phenomena surrounding migration and Islamophobia, it is clear that issues regarding minority communities will never disappear from the discourse of developing and managing opportunities for participation in sport. The work of Carrington and McDonald and Long *et al.* remains the primary source of work in terms of race, ethnicity and sport policy in the UK. However, there are serious lessons to be learned from the research conducted in the UK between 2000 and 2004. There has never, since or before, been the funding for the localised studies which took place at that time. Few other countries are able to demonstrate the rich nature of that local research but, unfortunately and not surprisingly, while that research may not exist there will not be the chance again for such research to take place in the UK. The principles identified in the UK are almost certainly no different to any other nation. And yet, it's acknowledged globally that people from minority communities participate in sport less than others. There's no reason why that should continue to be the case.

Notes

1 B. Houlihan, *Sport, Policy and Politics* (Abingdon: Routledge, 1997).
2 M. Keech, 'Sport Policy in Developing Countries', in G. Bravo, R. Lopez de D'Amico, and C. Parrish, eds, *Sport in Latin America: Policy, Organization, and Management* (Abingdon: Routledge, 2016), 21–33.
3 A. Bairner and J. Sugden, 'Sport in Divided Societies', in J. Sugden and A. Bairner, eds, *Sport in Divided Societies*, 2nd edition (Oxford: Meyer and Meyer, 2000), 3.
4 I. Law, *Racism, Ethnicity and Social Policy* (Hemel Hempstead: Prentice Hall, 1996), x.
5 See B. Carrington and I. McDonald, eds, *'Race', Sport and British Society* (London: Routledge, 2001).
6 B. Carrington, T. Fletcher, and I. McDonald, 'The Politics of "Race" and Sports Policy in the United Kingdom', in B. Houlihan and D. Malcolm, eds, *Sport and Society*, 3rd edition (London: Sage, 2015), 223.
7 B. Carrington, 'The Critical Sociology of Race and Sport: The First 50 Years', *Annual Review of Sociology* 39 (2013), 389.
8 DCMS (Department for Culture, Media and Sport), *Sporting Future: A New Strategy for an Active Nation* (London: DCMS, 2015).
9 R. Hoye, A. Smith, M. Nicholson, and B. Stewart, *Sport Management: Principles and Applications*, 4th edition (Abingdon: Routledge, 2015), 15.
10 J.S. Fink and D.L. Pastore, 'Diversity in Sport? Utilising the Business Literature to Devise a Comprehensive Framework of Diversity Initiatives', *Quest*, 51 (1999), 310–27.
11 B. Houlihan, 'Introduction: The Constraints of History', in B. Houlihan and M. Green, eds, *Routledge Handbook of Sports Development* (Abingdon: Routledge, 2011), 5–6.
12 See, for example, T. Collins, *A Social History of English Rugby Union: Sport and the Making of the Middle Classes* (London: Routledge, 2009); R. Holt, *Sport and the British: A Modern History* (Oxford: Oxford University Press, 1989); M. Polley, *Moving the Goalposts: A History of Sport and Society Since 1945* (London: Routledge, 1998).
13 R.S. Gruneau, *Sport, Class and Social Development* (Amherst, MA: University of Massachusetts Press, 1983); A. Metcalfe, 'The Growth of Organised Sports and the Development of Amateurism in Canada, 1807–1914', in J. Harvey and H. Cantelon, eds, *Not Just a Game* (Ottawa: University of Ottawa Press, 1988), 33–69.
14 Parti Québecois, *Des idees pour un pays: programme du parti Québecois* (Montréal: parti Québecois, 1994).
15 V. Paraschak, 'Variations in Race Relations: Sporting Events for Native People in Canada', *Sociology of Sport Journal* 14, 1 (1997), 1–21.
16 N. Puwar, *Space Invaders: Race, Gender and Bodies Out of Place* (Oxford: Berg, 2005), 137.

17 B. Carrington, "'What I Said Was Racist – but I'm Not a Racist": Anti-Racism and the White Sports/ Media Complex', in J. Long and K. Spracklen, eds, *Sport and the Challenges to Racism* (Basingstoke: Palgrave, 2011), 83–99.

18 J. Feagin, *Systemic Racism: A Theory of Oppression* (London: Routledge, 2006).

19 D. Burdsey, 'One Week in October: Luis Suárez, John Terry and the Turn to Racial Neoliberalism in English Men's Professional Football', *Identities: Global Studies in Culture and Power* 21, 5 (2014), 432.

20 E. Cashmore and J. Cleland, *Football's Dark Side: Corruption, Homophobia, Violence and Racism in the Beautiful Game* (Basingstoke: Palgrave Macmillan, 2014).

21 See, for example, G. Bravo, R. Lopez de D'Amico, and C. Parrish, eds, *Sport in Latin America: Policy, Organization, and Management* (Abingdon: Routledge, 2016); P. Koski and J. Lämsä, 'Finland as a Small Sports Nation: Socio-historical Perspectives on the Development of National Sport Policy', *International Journal of Sport Policy and Politics* (2015), DOI: 10.1080/19406940.2015.1060714; E. Skille, 'Sport for All in Scandinavia: Sport Policy and Participation in Norway, Sweden and Denmark', *International Journal of Sport Policy and Politics* 3, 3 (2011), 327–39; M. Waardenburg and M. van Bottenburg, 'Sport Policy in the Netherlands', *International Journal of Sport Policy and Politics*, 5, 3 (2013), 465–75.

22 Carrington *et al.*, 'The Politics of "Race"'.

23 M. Collins, *Sport and Social Exclusion* (London: Routledge, 2003), 135.

24 Sports Council, *Sport in the Community: The Next Ten Years* (London: Sports Council, 1982).

25 M. Rigg, *Action Sport: An Evaluation* (London: Sports Council, 1986).

26 Carrington *et al.*, 'The Politics of "Race"'.

27 Sport England, *Annual Report* (London: Sport England, 1994).

28 Sport England, *No Limits: Sport England's Equity Policy* (London: Sport England, 2002); Sporting Equals, 'Achieving Racial Equality: A Standard for Sport', information sheet, Institute of Sport and Recreation Management (2001).

29 Sport England, *No Limits*.

30 J. Long, P. Robinson, and K. Spracklen, 'Promoting Racial Equality in Sports Organisations', *Journal of Sport and Social Issues*, 29, 1 (2005), 54.

31 F. Coalter with M. Allison and J. Taylor, *The Role of Sport in Regenerating Deprived Communities* (Edinburgh: Scottish Executive, 2000), 30.

32 Ibid., 68–9.

33 N. Rowe and R. Champion, *Sports Participation and Ethnicity in England: National Survey 1999–2000* (London: Sport England, 2000).

34 The methods through which participation in sport and exercise is calculated has changed a number of times since the publication of this report. The figures mentioned here are for participation once in the last four weeks.

35 Ibid., 2–5.

36 Coalter *et al.*, *The Role of Sport*.

37 F. Coalter, 'Game Plan and the Spirit Level: The Class Ceiling and the Limits of Sports Policy?', *International Journal of Sport Policy and Politics* 5, 1 (2013), 3–19; M. Nicholson, R. Hoye, and B. Houlihan, eds, *Participation in Sport: International Policy Perspectives* (Abingdon: Routledge, 2011).

38 J. Long, K. Hylton, K. Spracklen, A. Ratna, and S. Bailey, *Systematic Review of the Literature on Black and Minority Ethnic Communities in Sport and Physical Recreation*. Conducted for Sporting Equals and the Sports Councils by the Carnegie Research Institute, Leeds Metropolitan University (2009).

39 Centre for Ethnic Minority Studies, *Ethnic Minorities and Sports Participation: Report on the Participation of Ethnic Minorities in Sport in Slough* (London: Royal Holloway University, 2001).

40 C. Hudson with R. Coleman, *Maximising the Inclusion of Young People from Socially, Economically and Geographically Deprived Communities: A Report for the Staffordshire Sports Partnership* (LIRC: Sheffield Hallam University, 2001).

41 Centre for Ethnic Minority Studies, *Ethnic Minorities and Sports Participation*.

42 M. Keech and R. Harrison, *Black and Minority Ethnic Group Participation in Sport and Physical Activity: A Case Study in Crawley* (Brighton: Sports Development Unit, 2003).

43 Ibid., 38.

44 J. Cleland, 'Working Together Through Sport? Local Authority Provision for Ethnic Minorities in the UK?', *Sport and Society* 17, 1 (2014), 38–51.

45 Long *et al.*, *Systematic Review of the Literature*.

46 M. Campelli, 'Boardroom Diversity in the Spotlight', *Sports Management*, 114 (2016), 34–5.

6

RACE AND SPORTS JOURNALISM

Jed Novick and Rob Steen

When Robin Daniels was writing his 2009 memoir of his fellow Lancastrian Sir Neville Cardus, renowned music and cricket correspondent for the *Manchester Guardian* from the 1920s until his death in 1975, the subtitle he finally plumped for was nothing if not apt – *Celebrant of Beauty*. Sportswriting's priorities have undergone enormous changes since Cardus's heyday, due in good part to the expansion of newspaper pagination and the advent of the internet, but also to a wider awareness of the folly inherent in the time-dishonoured view that sport should be immune to political and social reality.

It says much for the distance covered by the sporting media that the player chosen to adorn the cover of the 2015 *Wisden Cricketers' Almanack* was Moeen Ali, the rising England all-rounder and a proud Muslim brave enough to play in a Test match wearing a 'Free Palestine' wristband. Never mind that some – and not exclusively Jews – saw this gesture as one-eyed and/or foolhardy: here was a British Asian whose racial origins and religious faith had proved no bar whatsoever to becoming a national hero. Amir Khan and Naseem Hamed had preceded Moeen into the British national consciousness, but both were boxers, paths eased by the individualism of their sport. That said, Nasser Hussain, the cricketer who in 1999 became the first Asian immigrant to captain the English national team, was unlucky: *Wisden* had yet to introduce cover photographs when he was at his peak at the turn of the century as the man who rid the England XI of defeatism.

Similar progress has been witnessed elsewhere this young century. Those journalists fortunate to cover New Zealand's all-conquering rugby union teams could not care less whether victory emanates from the skill of a white man, a Māori or a Pacific Islander. The same goes for those reporting the comings and goings of the England cricket team, with its revolving mix of English, Irish, Scottish, Welsh, Southern African, Australian, Anglo-Caribbean and British Asian constituents. More complex have been the cases of Mo Farah and Mudhasen 'Monty' Panesar. Farah, who left poverty in Somalia at the age of eight, was hailed unreservedly as a national hero in the media after winning the 2012 Olympic 5,000 m and 10,000 m in London; while a figure of fun owing to his lack of mobility and seemingly clueless batting, the spin bowler Panesar, a Sikh, became a folk hero without breaking a single significant record. In both cases, sadly, acclaim would be diluted: Farah's reputation was tarnished in 2015 by evidence that his coach, Alberto Salazar, had given his other clients performance-enhancing drugs; Panesar's painful divorce led to prolonged lapses in behaviour and form, and subsequent loss of employment. That the latter's precipitous decline may have been a consequence, at least in part, of trying to assimilate and adopt cultural norms, particularly in his consumption of alcohol, is a subtext that warrants further examination.

For far too long, the words 'sport', 'politics', and 'race' never occupied the same sentence in a newspaper. Sport, or so the implicit reasoning went, occupied a parallel universe, untouched by such unpleasant considerations. Rare exceptions indeed were Jack Johnson, who became the first black world heavyweight champion in 1908, and Jim Thorpe, the unfeasibly talented Native American who won the pentathlon and decathlon at the 1912 Stockholm Olympics, sufficient to be named 'The greatest sportsman of the 20th Century' by the *Wide World of Sports* TV show and 'America's greatest sportsman of the 20th Century' by the US Congress. Both, unsurprisingly, brought out the worst in racist reporters, Johnson especially. In spotlighting Nazism, anti-Semitism and the athletic virtuosity of an African-American, Jesse Owens, at the 1936 Berlin Olympics, aka the 'Propaganda Games', removed the first significant brick in a global, white-built wall. Moreover, as the Civil Rights and Anti-Apartheid movements gathered steam in the 25 years following the Second World War, it became ever harder for editors and reporters to keep their blinkers on.

Some of those praised, and properly so, for refusing to avert their gaze are those who identified most naturally with the cause: Shirley Povich, a Jewish reporter who covered the 1936 Games for the *Washington Post*; Wendell Smith, a black American sportswriter either side of the Second World War; C.L.R. James, the illustrious Trinidadian Marxist who in 1960 spearheaded the campaign to install the West Indies cricket team's first full-time black captain and wrote *Beyond a Boundary*, still, more than half a century since its publication, the most resonant, influential and widely lauded book about sport and race. Also important has been the work of a number of other cricket writers, including Sir Hilary Beckles, especially his two-volume *The Development of West Indies Cricket*,[1] *A History of West Indies Cricket* by his fellow Jamaican and former prime minister, Michael Manley,[2] *The Spirit of the Game, A Maidan View* and *A History of Indian Cricket* by Mihir Bose,[3] *Twenty-two Yards to Freedom*,[4] a history of the game in colonial India by Boria Majumdar, his fellow Anglo-Indian, and *The Unquiet Ones*,[5] a comparable volume about Pakistani cricket by Osman Samiuddin. Today we are further blessed with the likes of Howard Bryant, Smith's foremost heir, and by other Asian, African and Caribbean cricket writers such as Sharda Ugra, Vaneisa Baksh, Firdose Moonda, Osman Samiuddin and Rahul Bhattacharya.

Given the racial origins of those writing the most influential sports pages, however, it was inevitable that attention to racial inequities should have been drawn primarily by white reporters, however reluctantly and belatedly. One obvious contemporary example can be found in the paltry number of non-white coaches and managers at the elite levels of association football in Britain and in American football. Before it was introduced, the Rooney Rule, a nod to affirmative action requiring all interviews for leading coaching positions to include a black candidate, was advocated by white journalists. Similarly, by dint of their platform, white journalists were at the forefront in the clamour for change that persuaded the Football League to announce in 2015 that it would follow suit.

Meanwhile, there can be little doubt that the most persistent scourge of racists over the past decade has been Dave Zirin, an American Jew whose insightful, trenchant work in this area can be found to best advantage in *A People's History of Sports in the United States* and *The John Carlos Story*,[6] as well as his weekly columns in *The Nation* and edgeofsports.com. No account of this topic, moreover, would be complete without due mention of *Race, Racism and Sports Journalism*,[7] wherein a quartet of thoroughgoing journalist-scholars from the University of Sunderland –

Neil Farrington, Daniel Kilvington, John Price and Amir Saeed – conclude that contemporary coverage of race on British sports pages is a good deal more rounded and fair-minded than many other academics would have us believe.

This chapter, though, is concerned with those who fought a lonelier battle in less enlightened times. Through the prism of civil rights in the USA and apartheid in South Africa, it focuses on sportswriters without a natural vested interest who made a difference.

'Press Box Red'

All too often neglected in discussions of Jackie Robinson's signing by the Brooklyn Dodgers in 1946, which led to him becoming North American baseball's first black major leaguer of the twentieth century, is the role of the media. While Robinson was making his name with the Kansas City Monarchs in the Negro Leagues, Wendell Smith, his erstwhile roommate and confidant, now a campaigning and resourceful black reporter with the *Pittsburgh Courier*, discovered that Isadore Muchnik, a liberal councillor in Boston, was pushing the city's major league teams, the Red Sox and the Braves, to integrate. Smith arranged a trial for Robinson and two other leading black players with the former, but it was never more than window-dressing; all left empty-handed. It seems more than coincidental that, while the Red Sox could have become the first major league team to integrate, they ultimately became the last.

Smith broke his homeward journey in New York to speak to Branch Rickey, president of the Brooklyn Dodgers and the visionary who had invented the farm system as a means of nurturing talent, suspecting he might be the likeliest executive to integrate baseball. Few knew this at the time, but Rickey, a conservative lawyer, had been concocting his own plan to do precisely that. His role in Robinson's breakthrough can never be overstated. Nor, therefore, can Smith's.

Yet while black journalists such as Smith were prominent in campaigning for an end to the colour bar, the best-remembered now, both perversely and inevitably, is Lester Rodney. Perversely, because Lester was white; inevitably, because white newspapers commanded so much more financial investment, and so many more readers, than their black-owned counterparts.

Motivation is crucial. In terms of political and social issues, Rodney, the subject of Irwin Silber's *Press Box Red* (2004), was arguably the first important campaigning sportswriter. As sports editor for the US Communist Party newspaper, *The Daily Worker*, from 1936 to 1958 (he resigned from the party once the scale of Stalin's murderous regime began to emerge in 1958), he launched the fight to integrate baseball in the 1930s. He was also the first writer to espy the promise of a second baseman named Jackie Robinson. 'Lester Rodney was a communist', emphasized David Margolick, an author and, as we write, contributing editor of *Vanity Fair* magazine. 'Whether because of that or in spite of that, he was also one of the most independent and courageous sportswriters of his day.'[8]

One of his early priorities, though, was to change perceptions of sport as a fitting subject for the inquiring mind. 'When I met my wife's father for the first time', he told his spiritual heir, Dave Zirin, in 2004, 'he said, "What do you do?" I said, "I write sports." He laughed uneasily and asked "but what do you really do?" He couldn't grasp that his daughter was marrying someone who just wrote about games.'[9]

At first, he told Zirin, 'I didn't have a full realization of what the meaning of sports could be.' The 1938 heavyweight fight between Joe Louis and Max Schmeling in New York City was a turning point:

Abner Barry was a black columnist of the day and he … told how during the preparation for that fight and the fight itself, the streets were eerily deserted like a scene from after the atom bomb drops in a movie. The minute the fight was over the streets were teeming with people and young kids were laughing and giving the mock Hitler salute. And this was happening in every city in the country including Southern cities. In Knoxville [Tennessee] Blacks poured out into the streets and fought with the police who tried to keep them from marching. So you say there's no social meaning to Joe Louis? There was a young Black man being led to death row and he cried out 'Save me Joe Louis!' It sounds corny and hokey, but it's true.[10]

Having established a niche for sport at the *Daily Worker* (albeit only a solitary page), Rodney set about addressing what he saw as a void. 'It's amazing,' he told Zirin:

You go back and you read the great newspapers in the thirties, you'll find no editorials saying, 'What's going on here? This is America, land of the free and people with the wrong pigmentation of skin can't play baseball?' Nothing like that. No challenges to the league, to the commissioner, to league presidents, no interviewing the managers, no talking about Satchel Paige and Josh Gibson who were obviously of superstar caliber. So it was this tremendous vacuum waiting. Anybody who became Sports Editor of the *Daily Worker* would have gone into this. It was too obvious. And some of the white comrades who had never paid attention to sports before began saying, 'Is this an all-white sport?' People didn't think about it. It was the culture of the times and it was accepted.

While the major papers occasionally carried reports of Negro League games in 1936, recalled Rodney, there was

never a mention that these players were barred from advancing to the major or even the minor leagues. No incredulous editorials blasting this un-American discrimination, no investigative articles listing the qualified or over-qualified black players, no queries addressed to the commissioner, the league presidents, the team owners, the managers, and the white players. The conscience of American journalism on baseball's apartheid ban, sorry to say, was not in the hands of America's major daily newspapers.[11]

Satchel Paige – after whom Woody Allen named his first son – was one of those 'over-qualified' players. One of the most compelling 'what ifs' of American sporting history surrounds how Paige, a wily, virtually unhittable pitcher, would have fared against Babe Ruth. Sadly, by the time Paige finally signed a major league contract with the Cleveland Indians in 1948, he was 42, his best days behind him. Another over-qualified player was Josh Gibson, a troubled soul who didn't live long enough to follow Robinson into the major league. Gibson inspired the following tribute from one of the greatest major league pitchers of all time, Walter Johnson, published in the *Daily Worker* in 1939:

There is a catcher that any big league club would like to buy for $200,000 [an unthinkable fee at the time]. They call him 'Hoot' Gibson and he can do everything. He hits that ball a mile and he catches so easy he might just as well be in a rocking chair. Throws like a rocket.[12]

Either Paige or Gibson could have been the first player to break the colour bar, but Robinson's character exerted a more profound influence than his athletic ability.

'It was not as though the worth of these African American athletes was unknown to the baseball establishment', reasons Silber:

> Many a Big League manager knew but wouldn't say publicly that there were at least several players of major-league calibre in the Negro Leagues they would be willing to bring to their clubs if the team owners would allow them to. Most owners knew it as well. But, as the 'bible' of Big League baseball, the [weekly] *Sporting News*, freely acknowledged in 1923, organized baseball had a 'tacit understanding that a player of Ethiopian descent is ineligible.' That 'understanding' prevailed for another twenty-two years.[13]

Rodney launched his campaign on 13 August 1936 with a dramatic announcement headlined 'Outlawed by Baseball!' – followed by three subheadings worthy of *The Sun* on a good day:

> The Crime of the Big Leagues!
> The newspapers have carefully hushed it up!
> One of the most sordid stories in American sports!

Cue a call to arms:

> Though they win laurels for America in the Olympics – though they have proven themselves outstanding baseball stars – Negroes have been placed beyond the pale of the American and National Leagues.
> Read the truth about this carefully laid conspiracy.
> Beginning next Sunday, the *Sunday Worker* will rip the veil from the 'Crime of the Big Leagues' – mentioning names, giving facts, sparing none of the most sacred figures in baseball officialdom.[14]

For the next three weeks, the sports page was not alone in trumpeting the promised exposé. 'Fans Ask End of Jim Crow Baseball' was one front-page headline, under which Rodney – in an un-bylined piece – laid into what he characterized as

> the un-American ... [and] invisible barrier of race prejudice [that] keeps the Negro players on the sidelines. Fans, it's up to you. Tell the big league magnates that you're sick of the poor pitching in the American League. You want to see Satchel Paige out there on the mound. You're tired of a flop team in Boston, of the silly Brooklyn Dodgers, of the inept Philadelphia Phillies and the semi-pro Athletics.... Demand better ball. Demand Americanism in baseball, equal opportunities for Negro and white. Demand the end of Jim Crow baseball![15]

In the wake of these and other articles, letters streamed into the offices of the *Daily Worker* – overwhelmingly, notes Silber, in favour of removing the colour bar. Two of Rodney's aims were to 'shoot down the notion that the white players and managers wouldn't stand for it by directly putting the question to them' and to 'put the league presidents and the commissioner on the spot by challenging them to say whether there was an official ban, which they denied, of course'.

But maybe the most important was to generate fan participation in the campaign. Our biggest asset, though, was that the time was right. Black athletes had stolen the show at the 1936 Olympics in Berlin, especially Jesse Owens…. This was all over the newspapers, which had these marvellous pictures of black medal winners draped with the American flag. And Joe Louis was on his way to the heavyweight title, the first time there'd be a black heavyweight champion in more than twenty years. So it was a good time to say, 'Why not in baseball?'[16]

The first manager Rodney spoke to was Burleigh Grimes of the Brooklyn Dodgers, the club Rodney had supported as a boy, the club he was covering dutifully and avidly in the summer of 1937. The men knew each other; Rodney knew Grimes respected him 'because he knew I didn't sensationalize things'. The leading question was straightforward enough: 'Burleigh', wondered Rodney, 'how would you like to put a Dodger uniform on Satchel Paige and Josh Gibson?' The response was not altogether surprising. 'Well, he looks at me like I'd just hit him over the head with a club', Rodney would recall. 'You just didn't talk about those things then. He stops for a minute. And then he begins to talk to me, patiently, like a father to a child.' In relating the story 60 years after the fact, Rodney realized he couldn't quote Grimes exactly, but these, he insisted, were 'almost' his exact words:

> 'Lester', he says, 'you're wasting your time. This'll never happen. Just think about the trains in the south. Think about the hotels. Think about the restaurants. How could it happen? It'll never happen.' So I say, 'Do you know some of the good black ballplayers?' And he says, 'Of course I do. We all do. I know how good they are. But let's talk about something else. First, it's never going to happen. And I don't wanna talk any more about it.' 'Burleigh', I say. 'Can I at least write, "I know how good they are – [says] Burleigh Grimes?"' Now he's almost livid. 'No, no!' he says. 'I'm not gonna stick my neck out!' He didn't want to be the first.[17]

Nor did anyone else. Nor, for that matter, was any major newspaper remotely interested in sticking its neck out. To Rodney, the media's complicity in the prolonging of the colour bar was beyond dispute. Take a story about the young Joe Di Maggio from that same summer. 'We were in the dressing room at Yankee Stadium', recalled Rodney:

> and somebody asked [him], 'Joe, who's the best pitcher you've faced?' And without hesitation young Joe said, 'Satchel Paige.' He didn't say 'Satchel Paige who ought to be in the big leagues', he just said Satchel Paige. So that was a huge headline in the next day's Daily Worker sports page in the biggest type I had: 'Paige best pitcher ever faced – DiMaggio.' No other paper reported that…. If the other reporters would hand that in, their editor would say, 'Come on, you're not stirring this thing up.' But we didn't see it as a virtue that we were the only people reporting on this. We wanted to broaden this thing and end the damned ban.[18]

When Lester first met Paige, in the latter's Harlem hotel during a trip to New York with the Kansas City Monarchs in 1937, the pitcher needed no invitation to express his disgruntlement. 'He knew I was from the *Daily Worker*', remembered Rodney.

> He knew my face because I had covered Negro League games and chatted with players. He was also aware of our campaign and even mentioned that he had read

about it while playing in Puerto Rico… While we talked he began to come up with ideas. Why don't they have a poll? Every Big League fan going into a game next year, just ask them yes or no, do you want coloured players in the Big Leagues. But he also had prepared one biggie in his mind beforehand. 'Let the winners of the World Series play an all-star Negro team just one game at Yankee Stadium', he says, 'and if we don't beat them before a packed house they don't have to pay us a dime!'

'Can I print that?' I ask. 'Absolutely', [he replied]. He wanted this in the newspapers, but he hadn't gotten anywhere because the papers weren't paying any attention to him. He was an embarrassment to them. Like a bad conscience. How does somebody who works for a paper that doesn't mention the fact that blacks are banned interview Satchel Paige and come out with this challenge? He can't. But Satch knew that we would…. We played this up big. He loved it. He wanted ten copies. It created a stir. I mean, here was the most famous black player in the country challenging the ban publicly for the first time. The challenge was never accepted, of course. And none of the papers carried it.[19]

In June 1939, Wendell Smith began a series of eight articles in the *Pittsburgh Courier*, interviewing 40 players and, more illuminatingly and importantly, all but one of the nine National League managers in what the paper billed as 'The Most Exclusive, Startling and Revealing Expose of the Attitude of the Major League Players and Managers Themselves Ever Written'.[20] In virtually every case, the managers maintained the party line – there was no official ban – while shifting the responsibility, patronizingly, on to the white fans and the white players – it was they who were unready for such a revolution.

After digesting the start of the *Courier* series, Rodney rang Smith to congratulate him. From that arose an informal agreement whereby their papers could reprint each other's stories on the campaign. When the *Daily Worker* began giving space to his articles, Smith, in turn, wrote to Rodney, conveying his appreciation and solidarity. 'Unfortunately', wrote Silber, 'but undoubtedly in keeping with the times and the generally conservative views of his paper – and possibly in deference to the cooperation he was getting from the baseball establishment – Smith's admiration for Rodney's and the *Daily Worker*'s efforts did not find their way into the *Courier*'s own pages.'[21]

Nevertheless, tacit acknowledgement of the *Daily Worker*'s campaign … came from the baseball establishment itself. In a move reminiscent of charges by the defeated Confederates after the Civil War that northern 'carpetbaggers' were stirring up otherwise happy-go-lucky 'nigras', defenders of baseball's racial status quo argued [that] there would be no problem with the racial state of baseball if it weren't for outside 'agitators' who, in the words of the *Sporting News*, 'have sought to force Negro players on the big leagues, not because it would help the game but because it gives them a chance to thrust themselves into the limelight as great crusaders in the guise of democracy…. Some coloured people are not looking at the question from the broader point of view, or for the ultimate good of either the race or the individuals in it. They ought to concede their own people are now protected and that nothing is served by allowing agitators to make an issue of a question on which both sides prefer to be let alone.'[22]

Later in 1939 came the first chink of light for Rodney – the first even vaguely favourable comment he had gleaned from a club owner: William Benswanger of the Pittsburgh Pirates, mindful of Louis Armstrong, Duke Ellington and Billie Holliday, said he really didn't see why signing a black player 'wouldn't be the same as having black musicians'. Up to now, on this sensitive matter, even Leo 'The Lip' Durocher, the cocky, outspoken manager who had replaced Grimes at the Dodgers, had refrained from airing his views. Now Benswanger had come out of the closet, Durocher felt emboldened. As Rodney stressed, he was unusually 'sophisticated' for a manager. 'Hell, yes!' Durocher replied upon being asked whether he would sign Paige or Gibson. 'I'd sign them in a minute if I got permission from the big shots.'[23]

Yet not for another three years, by when the Japanese had bombed Pearl Harbor and Rodney was in the army, did the *Daily Worker*'s histrionic, sneering, anti-communist rival the *Daily News*, then boasting the largest circulation of any US newspaper, make even a passing reference to Durocher's comments – and much the nicest thing you could say about that reference is that it was patronizing. The even more influential *Herald-Tribune*, recalled Rodney, was even 'snottier'. As the tide began to turn, nonetheless, Durocher's bold statement would prove a significant milestone.

Arguably Rodney's most heartfelt, impassioned article was one that had no lasting impact whatsoever on its target, Judge Landis, the baseball commissioner who had so shrewdly maintained the strictly unofficial colour bar. It was published in the *Daily Worker* on 6 May 1942, in the form of an open letter, shortly before Rodney was drafted into the army, by when the major leagues, supported by President Roosevelt, had resolved that baseball should not be interrupted; amid such troubling times, it would serve an important function as a public diversion. 'There can no longer be any excuse for your silence, Judge Landis', asserted Rodney:

> You are the one who, by your silence, is maintaining a relic of the slave market long repudiated in other American sports. You are the one refusing to say the word which would do more to justify baseball's existence in this year of war than any other single thing…. It is a silence that hurts the war effort…. America is against discrimination…. There never was a greater ovation in America's greatest indoor sports arena than that which arose two months ago when Wendell Wilkie, standing in the middle of the Madison Square Garden ring, turned to Joe Louis and said: 'How can anyone looking at the example of this great American think in terms of discrimination for reasons of race, colour or creed? Dorie Miller, who manned a machine gun at Pearl Harbor when he might have stayed below deck, has been honoured by a grateful people. The President of our country has called for an end to discrimination in all jobs. Your position as big man in our National Pastime carries a much greater responsibility this year than ever before and you can't meet it with your silence. The temper of the worker who goes to the ball games is not one to tolerate discrimination against 13 million Americans in this year of the grim fight against the biggest Jim Crower of all – Adolf Hitler. You haven't a leg to stand on.[24]

For two more seasons Landis did nothing – bar, that is, passing the buck, and the onus, to the club owners. Then, in November 1944, he died of a sudden heart attack. Inside a year, Silber recounts, Sgt Lester Rodney, then stationed with the 52nd Field Hospital on a remote island in the South Pacific, received a cablegram from New York sent by Nat Low, a fellow baseball integrationist: 'Congratulations. Dodgers yesterday signed Jackie Robinson for [their] Montreal farm [team]. You did it!' Rodney was 'stunned and elated'.[25] As a childhood Dodgers fan, he was doubly delighted. 'It completely united me. And it wouldn't have been the same if Cleveland or some other team had been the first.'[26]

Not until 1997, however, did Rodney receive his due. 'Something wonderful happened in the world of sports in 1997'; thus, in his foreword to *Press Box Red*, exulted Jules Tygiel, author of *Baseball's Great Experiment: Jackie Robinson and His Legacy*, just one of the scores of eminent American scholars who have not only adored baseball but seen it as an insight into American life.

> Amid the hoopla and commercial sensationalism that characterized much of the fiftieth celebration of Jackie Robinson's historic debut with the Brooklyn Dodgers, Lester was rediscovered.... The *New York Times* praised his coverage of the Robinson story as among the most accurate of the era. Rodney even appeared on CNN ... and several times on ESPN.[27]

This, Tygiel reasoned, was partly on account of Rodney's age – he was now in his eighties and had outlived most of his contemporaries – but primarily because he had been 'a catalyst ... in the most significant sports story of the century'.

Apartheid and beyond

One of the neglected legacies of apartheid has been the fate of those who sought to emulate Basil D'Oliveira. Unlike black Africans, they have enjoyed conspicuous success in cricket: Ashwell Prince was South Africa's first non-white captain; Vernon Philander and J.P. Duminy are currently among the world's leading players. In 2015, Telford Vice wrote an intensely moving and compassionate article about Henry Williams, the coloured fast bowler whose late-blooming international career entered rapid decline as soon as he agreed to bowl badly for money, having accepted a bribe from his corrupt white captain, Hansie Cronje. In the event, injury prevented him from carrying out what became known variously as a 'micro-fix' or 'spot fix' – not engineering the result but, in his case, bowling wides. The King Commission into match-fixing did for him.[28]

'Williams had been that rare thing – the coloured man nobody could argue did not deserve the chances he had earned', wrote Vice.

> He worked hard, took his wickets graciously, did not let success go to his head, and knew that where he came from was where he was going back to, and he was happy with that. But now he had blown all that. As he sat there, he was, in the eyes of South African cricket, others like him and – most importantly – himself, just another scar of shame for coloured people. The slanting sun brought warmth into the room for most of us. For Henry Williams, it brought a cold, hard, ugly truth.
>
> In what must have seemed to him an aeon ago, he had been a proud and respected member of a community that is at once adored and distrusted in South Africa's cultural firmament. Coloured people, as they are called and call themselves, endure a slew of stereotypes – that their sense of humour is infallible, whatever the circumstances; that they are born soaked in alcohol and go through life topping themselves up; that every sentence they speak is shot through with profanities; that they are prone to being snared into criminal gangs whose currencies are drugs and knives.
>
> Closer to the truth is that coloureds were not white enough to enjoy the top tier of privilege in apartheid South Africa, and are not black enough to enjoy the sweetest fruits of democracy in the modern age. To be born coloured in South Africa is to be disregarded, except when someone needs to laugh or fancies a drink and a punch-up.[29]

Amid the difficulties of transition, no issue aroused more controversy than that of selection quotas, introduced in international and provincial cricket and rugby union to encourage black Africans to participate and hence undo the damage caused by the racist selection policies of the apartheid era. Tristan Holme and Luke Alfred addressed the complexities with due sensitivity:

> In a previous conversation, Thokozani Peter didn't want to talk about racial quotas in cricket. Asked for his thoughts on the subject, Peter, a 24-year-old fast bowler, shifted uncomfortably in his chair, drew air through his teeth, and said: 'I'm scared of answering that question.' Frankly, no one can blame him. Nothing divides the South African cricket community quite like quota policies because few issues define the country and its most pressing conversations quite like race.
>
> Rather than having open discussions that would encourage transparency, the issue is either forgotten or conveniently ignored – as it was in the debate around Ryan McLaren's exclusion from South Africa's World Cup squad. Commentators and journalists asked whether McLaren should have cracked the nod ahead of Farhaan Behardien or perhaps Wayne Parnell; the reality is that the selectors are committed to picking seven players of colour – including one black African – in a 15-man squad, and so McLaren's actual competition was among the eight white players selected.
>
> It was a symptom of confusion. The policies have changed many times over the years but have been hidden in phraseology, which created the quota debate's most public blowout in 2008. Mickey Arthur, the coach, was part of a selection committee that named just four players of colour in a 14-man squad; it was vetoed by Cricket South Africa's president Norman Arendse because the team was expected to have seven.[30]

South Africa's 2013–14 season, recorded the statistician Andrew Samson, brought 308 appearances by black Africans out of a total of 1,926 in franchise cricket, and 919 out of 3,610 in the provincial game. Some clubs struggled to meet the requirements; others, as Holme and Alfred put it, were 'positioned to take advantage of the financial incentives'. Appearances by black Africans in franchise cricket (15.99 per cent) exceeded the quota (9.09 per cent). 'Similarly, with some provincial sides already fielding a healthy number of black Africans, the percentage of appearances (25.45%) exceeded the requirement (18.18%).'[31]

The problem, conclude Holme and Alfred:

> is that the q-word has developed such a stigma that it is difficult to sit down and have an honest conversation about what it means for the players directly influenced by it and whether it is having the desired effect of uplifting a community that was deeply disadvantaged under apartheid…
>
> When the majority of black South Africa is growing up in poverty, it means that by the time most black players are exposed to a decent level of cricket they are profoundly disadvantaged compared to players from privileged schools. As much as CSA has tried through quota policies, no governing body can remould history into the ideal image of eight or nine black Proteas that easily, particularly after something as deeply divisive and traumatic as apartheid. On the one hand, the governing body deserves criticism because its attempts at transformation over the past two decades can be seen as nothing more than a design to show the country's politicians enough black faces in teams. This lack of spiritual commitment to genuine change is in turn played out at the franchises.

On the other hand, CSA's mandate is to spread cricket; it is not tasked with building functional schools and ensuring that every young child who wants to play the game is adequately fed. As much as the politicians like to hold CSA to account in parliament, so the cricket body should be able to hold South Africa's incompetent and corrupt government to account on service delivery. Because the sad fact is that until South African society can be genuinely transformed, cricket will continue to lag behind in its own evolution.[32]

Denial and complicity

Reporting a demonstration against South Africa's 1960 cricket tour of England, undertaken shortly after the Sharpeville massacre, Charles Fortune described protesters as 'no more than the cats-paws of certain churchmen who seized on the visit of the cricketers as an opportunity to gain for themselves some public notice'.[33] Later a long-serving secretary of the South African Cricket Association, Fortune is most prominently commemorated these days by the name of the media centre at The Wanderers ground in Johannesburg. 'Fortune was a conservative', declared his anonymous *Wisden* obituarist, 'and appeared to take South Africa's exclusion from world cricket as something of a personal affront' (*Wisden* 1995).

In 2015 we asked Archie Henderson, not long retired as news editor of the South African *Sunday Times*, whether he could recall any white South African journalists taking issue with the way apartheid impacted on sport in the 1950s and 1960s:

> I can't think of anyone! Certainly not white. Terry Barron, who died homeless on the streets of Simonstown, tried to give the Peter Hain group a voice during the 1969–70 South African rugby tour of the UK and was snubbed by the team. Marshall Lee, who was more a general news writer on the Rand Daily Mail in the 70s, would have fitted that category but he never wrote for the paper's sports pages.[34]

Nor did matters improve much.

> Like many white sportswriters in the 80s and onwards, the issue of segregated sport was anathema. But it took some of us longer to get round than others. Today of course I have many regrets. In my brief stint as sports editor of the Cape Times in the 70s I could have done more to publish the full scorecards of 'coloured' club cricket as we did religiously on a Monday with white cricket. I remember trying to assemble a network of stringers to do this, but without success. It seemed, too, there was a lot of politics behind this; if Hassan Howa [the founder member of the non-racial South African Cricket Board of Control who led the campaign to boycott apartheid sport] did not like a particular stringer, that person would be snubbed. The one big success was a bloke called Dickie Isaacs, who got around from club to club using the minibus taxi system. Sadly, he died in a taxi accident shortly before unification. One of the great unsung heroes of cricket journalism.
>
> There was another incident which I remember when I decided to lead the main sports (back) page with a thrilling tie in the SACBOC provincial championship between Western Province and Transvaal. I deliberately did not distinguish in the headline that it was the 'coloured' WP side as opposed to the white one, which got more prominent coverage. There was a complaint about 'misleading readers' from

one big advertiser, but the editor (Tony Heard) discussed it with me and then dismissed the complaint.

But you can safely say that, as there is no white person today who ever supported apartheid, there are no sports reporters in favour of segregated sport. Certainly it did not show in any of their reporting or commentaries until the 90s. Now everyone claims struggle credentials. If there was a pioneer in this field (among the white sports journalists) it was Telford Vice, but at the time his writing did not get much play beyond the Eastern Cape where he was with the Daily Dispatch of East London. There were black journalists who were pushing for greater freedom in sport but they were few too; some collaborated with the establishment, which used its financial muscle to co-opt them. Others like Mogamad [Mo] Allie, who now reports for the BBC, was always firm and principled about his opposition to apartheid sport.[35]

Allie's memories chime with Henderson's:

As far as I could ascertain, there were no white sports writers who railed against the Apartheid government. In fact, as late as the Mike Gatting rebel tour in 1990 the white media and sports journalists were still supporting tours like these while at the same time being scathing of the anti-apartheid movement's demonstrations and attempts to stop the tour. Not only did most of the white sportswriters do nothing, they were, in some cases, condescending of the activism of the non-racial movement.

As for black writers, bearing in mind they had limited platforms at that time in our history, there were people like Abe Adams, later to become president of the anti-Apartheid SA Council on Sport (Sacos), who had strong opinions against the regime. The late Dennis Brutus, a former Robben Island prisoner, although an academic, also campaigned strongly against the racist regime in the 50s and 60s to the extent that he was forced out of the country and in 1962 set up the SA Non-Racial Olympic Committee (Sanroc) with the aim of isolating white SA from the Olympic movement.[36]

Nor did many visiting journalists rock the boat. R.S. Whitington, an Australian former first-class cricketer who had recently lived there, dedicated his account of Australia's 1966–67 tour of South Africa to 'the lonely land', yet not until chapter 7 does he even mention the cause of the nation's isolation. Even then, forgivably, he takes on trust Prime Minister John Vorster's announcement, in April 1967, that 'South African sportsmen could compete against non-white sportsmen abroad and that non-white sportsmen could be included in international teams making visits to South Africa'. This proclamation seemingly cleared the way for Basil D'Oliveira, a Cape Coloured printer's assistant who had migrated to England in search of reward for his skills and a better life for his family, to tour his homeland with his new national team two winters later. Whitington trumpeted it as 'a triumph for quietly-conducted, well-reasoned argument and negotiation'.[37] History begs to disagree.

A very small number of cricket writers were less easily or wilfully deluded than Whitington, less complicit than Fortune. On his first visit to South Africa in 1958–59, John Arlott, a revered journalist and BBC radio broadcaster from Hampshire, stopped outside the Nationalist campaign HQ on the night Henrik Verwoerd came to power in 1958. Arlott's companion expressed his dismay, whereupon Afrikaner party supporters layered his car in spit.[38] Upon arrival in that benighted land, Arlott was asked what race he was; in silence, he completed the requisite form and, in the appropriate category, declared himself 'human'. A few days later he asked a taxi driver to take him to a township; the poverty never left him. In 1960 it was Arlott to whom

D'Oliveira wrote in search of employment in England, Arlott who befriended him and Arlott who recommended him to his first English club.

Eight years later, during the so-called 'D'Oliveira Affair', Arlott was angered by the all-rounder's exclusion from the party to tour the Republic: to him, and many others besides, the reason was wholly political, a conviction supported by the clear desire of the Marylebone Cricket Club, which governed tour selection until the mid-1970s, to maintain good relations with South Africa, by the many former Conservative politicians who had served as the club's president, and by the right-leaning former public schoolboys who dominated the selection committee. Some weeks earlier Arlott had informed the BBC he would on no account commentate on South Africa's scheduled 1970 tour of England. He explained his reasoning in the *Guardian*, inspiring the young Peter Hain, the mainspring behind the highly effective 'Stop the 70 Tour' campaign. According to his son Timothy, Arlott had not wanted his friends 'to wonder what side he was on':

> Apartheid is detestable to me, and I would always oppose it … a successful tour would offer comfort and confirmation to a completely evil regime…. Commentary on any game depends, in my professional belief, on the ingredient of pleasure; it can only be satisfactorily broadcast in terms of shared enjoyment. This series cannot, in my mind, be enjoyable.[39]

D'Oliveira's subsequent inclusion in that 1968–69 England party, which led the duplicitous Vorster to cancel the tour on the ground that this was 'the team of the Anti-Apartheid movement', and in turn to South Africa being exiled from international cricket from 1970 to 1992, owed much to the public outcry that followed D'Oliveira's original omission. It would be wrong to propose that Arlott was alone in assailing the original selection: Peter Wilson of the *Daily Mirror* was equally appalled; even E.W. Swanton changed his tune, the same *Daily Telegraph* correspondent entrusted by the South Africans only weeks earlier as a go-between in an attempt to dissuade D'Oliveira from making himself available to tour – satisfyingly in vain. It would be no less incorrect to deny that Arlott's stance was the key catalyst in reframing and transforming the debate.

When Marx met Muhammad

Up to now, to ward off accusations of bias, we have resisted mentioning a friend of ours, but omitting Mike Marqusee from this roll of honour would be entirely unjust: his death while we were researching this chapter supplied the saddest of justifications for a tribute.

Characterizing himself as a 'deracinated New York Marxist Jew', Mike moved to Sussex to study and never returned, his affection for England stirred in good part by a burgeoning love for cricket. As beautiful as he found the game's techniques and rhythms, conveyed memorably in his work for *The Hindu*, *Wisden Asia*, *Cricinfo Magazine*, the *Financial Times* and the *Guardian*, there was another irresistible attraction: here was a sport wherein racial divisions had long been entrenched – and occasionally healed. No other major team sport, furthermore, had seen black (in the guise of the West Indies teams from 1965 to 1995) repeatedly overtake white, on the field if not in the committee rooms. Instead, as he would chronicle with an enthusiasm that would gradually give way to considerable unease at the resulting corruption and greed, India would be the first nation to break the traditional Anglo-Australian stranglehold over how the game was run and monetized.

A co-founder of the pressure group Hit Racism For Six, Mike's immersion in the game of Empire can readily be appreciated in *War Minus the Shooting*, a wide-ranging, penetrating travelogue of the 1996 World Cup played in India, Pakistan and Sri Lanka, a volume that did much to combat racial stereotyping and promote the subcontinent as the epicentre of the game.[40] A few years later, such was the respect and affection with which he was regarded in India – in contrast with the ludicrous lack of both in England, where Marxist cricket writers occupy a rung on the ladder of sports editors' preferences almost as high as that occupied by women rugby reporters – the news that he had been mugged made the front page. In February 2015, moreover, we discovered he had died via an email from Gulu Ezekiel, a journalist friend living in Delhi.

Mike's memorial celebration in London's Conway Hall in May 2015, attended by Arthur Scargill, the controversial former leader of the National Union of Mineworkers and the much-admired and future Labour Party Leader MP Jeremy Corbyn, found our friend and colleague Sharda Ugra, formerly sports editor of *India Today* and now editor of the immensely popular Indian arm of ESPNCricinfo.com, rendering her heartfelt thanks:

> Mike's engagement with South Asian cricket took place at a time when our writing in these parts was grappling between confidence in who we were and the conventional aspiration of wanting to be something else. Something maybe like England, with its well-nurtured traditions, or Australia and its hard-but-fair game centred around the mythology of mateship. Or the West Indies with its fast bowlers. In the 1990s, the cricket journalists of the world were, also largely divided between the haves and have-nots, or the north and the south, the developed and developing world. They were distanced from each other with very few exceptions from among the haves, who wanted to engage across cultures. Mike took to this scattered cricketing world, with curiosity, openness and energy. Not with orientalist wonder, but with objective and acute enquiry. It is why he was appreciated and befriended here.[41]

Yet Sharda was galvanized less by *War Minus the Shooting* than by *Anyone But England: Cricket and the National Malaise*, Mike's first non-fiction cricket book (he had previously written a terrific cricket novel, *Slow Turn*).[42] The first half of the title was a nod to Denis Skinner, an admirably principled Labour MP who, when asked which sporting team he supported, replied 'Anyone but England.' Here, even more than Sir Derek Birley's myth-shattering *The Willow Wand*,[43] was the book that captured the so-called 'gentleman's game' in its truest, most vivid and jaundiced colours. Most of the author's wryly eloquent disapproval was reserved for the way it was still run in his adopted home by, and for, the upper echelons of English society – which might well explain the subsequent reluctance of national newspaper sports editors to employ him.

'When we first heard about *Anyone But England*, even before we read it', recalled Sharda,

> a younger generation of Indian cricket journalists wanted to run down the road, pumping fists. Mike had hacked through a jungle of cricket's historical fakery, kicked down the doors of its temple, challenged the game's conservative and controlled narrative, and given it a vital and largely ignored global context. It echoed what many of us felt at the time, giving us a loud and clear voice.[44]

Yet while Mike adored India, and never cheered a sporting triumph more resoundingly than when Sri Lanka overcame the odds in 1996, beating Australia to win the World Cup, he did not shrink from the geopolitical realities inherent in this relocation of the game's emotional and economic heartland. As journalist and scholar Huw Richards put it in another tribute: 'The secular internationalist in him disliked the growing evidence of Indian, in particular Hindu, nationalism, while the American anti-capitalist saw a growing affinity for becoming more like America.'[45]

'So extreme had been the reactions to victory and defeat [in 1996]', noted Mike, 'observers had dubbed the cricket craziness of the subcontinent a psychosis'.

> Here was a global television spectacle which all three host nations hoped would boost their standing in the eyes of the world's financiers and investors. But the deep crises in all three societies kept erupting from under the glamour and hype. All three countries were opening their economies and following the well-worn IMF-charted path of privatisation, deregulation, cuts in public spending and encouragement of foreign investors. All three were building consumer sub-cultures in the midst of mass poverty. All three were racked with ethnic intolerance, and in all three the question of national identity was hotly contested. Not surprisingly, the World Cup raised yet again C. L. R. James's ever-pertinent question.[46]

Marqusee also wrote *Redemption Song: Muhammad Ali and the Spirit of the Sixties* (1999), a monumental work whose achievement can perhaps best be conveyed by the fact that it drew widespread critical acclaim even though so many others had already sought to capture the essence and importance of Ali – and even despite being published nearly a decade after Thomas Hauser's purportedly definitive oral history-cum-biography, *Muhammad Ali: His Life and Times.*[47] For the 2005 reprint, Marqusee added an Afterword that captures better than anyone, we would argue, what made Ali the most important sporting figure of all:

> Ali's real heroism lies in actions we can all emulate: in placing solidarity with human beings in remote lands above loyalty to any national government, in setting conscience before personal convenience. In the era of the war on terror, his example remains pertinent and powerful, but only if we retrieve the challenging historical reality that lies behind the harmless icon.[48]

These snapshots of key moments and people reporting on pivotal moments in the history of sport journalism and race and sport illustrate the role which journalists have played in advocating for social and structural change in the name of a colour-blind level playing field. Many more sport journalists sadly toed the 'party line', refusing to risk their access to inside information from sporting clubs and officials, but thankfully there were also brave pioneers who worked tirelessly to expose racial injustices in sport and who were active in leading the fight to break down racial barriers in sport. This kind of critical reporting remains crucial in the twenty-first century as increased globalization and migration have led to new forms of injustice and tensions linked to race and ethnicity in many countries.

Notes

1 H. Beckles, *The Development of West Indies Cricket* (London: Pluto Press, 1998).
2 M. Manley, *A History of West Indies Cricket* (London: Deutsch, 1988).
3 M. Bose, The Spirit of the Game (London: Constable & Robinson, 2012); M. Bose, *A Maidan View* (New Delhi: Penguin, 2006); M. Bose, *A History of Indian Cricket* (Cambridge: Cambridge University Press, 1990).

4 B. Majumdar, *Twenty-two Yards to Freedom* (New Delhi: Viking, 2004).
5 S. Osman, *The Unquiet Ones* (Uttar Pradesh: Harper Collins India, 2014).
6 D. Zirin, *A People's History of Sports in the United States* (New York: New Press, 2009); J. Carlos and D. Zirin, *The John Carlos Story* (Chicago, IL: Haymarket Books, 2011).
7 N. Farrington, *Race, Racism and Sports Journalism* (London: Routledge, 2012).
8 David Margolick, quoted in I. Silber, *Press Box Red* (Philadelphia, PA: Temple University Press, 2003).
9 www.counterpunch.org/zirin04032004.html, accessed 20 March 2015.
10 Ibid.
11 Silber, *Press Box Red*, 50.
12 Ibid.
13 Ibid., 51.
14 Ibid., 53.
15 Ibid., 53–4.
16 Ibid., 55–6.
17 Ibid., 59.
18 www.counterpunch.org/2004/04/03/an-interview-with-quot-red-quot-rodney, accessed 12 March 2015.
19 Ibid., 61–2.
20 Wendell Smith, *Pittsburgh Courier*, 15 July 1939, quoted in Silber, *Press Box Red*, 67.
21 Silber, *Press Box Red*, 68.
22 Robert Peterson, *Only the Ball was White* (New York: Gramercy, 1970), quoted in Silber, *Press Box Red*, 69.
23 Silber, *Press Box Red*, 70.
24 Lester Rodney, *Daily Worker*, 6 May 1942, quoted in Silber, *Press Box Red*, 81–2.
25 Silber, *Press Box Red*, 90.
26 Ibid., 28.
27 Ibid., vii.
28 For a discussion of this scandal, see John Nauright, 'White Man's Burden Revisited: Race, Sport and Reporting the Hansie Cronje Cricket Crisis in South Africa and Beyond', *Sport History Review*, 35, 1 (2005), 61–75.
29 Telford Vice, 'The Coloured Lie', *The Cricket Monthly*, ESPNcricinfo, January 2015, www.thecricketmonthly.com/story/816361/the-coloured-lie, accessed 22 March 2015.
30 Tristan Horne and Luke Alfred, 'The faces of transition', *The Cricket Monthly*, ESPNcricinfo, May 2015, www.thecricketmonthly.com/story/863979/faces-of-transformation, accessed 22 March 2015.
31 Ibid.
32 Ibid.
33 John Nauright, *Long Run to Freedom: Sport, Cultures, and Identities in South Africa* (Morgantown, WV: Fitness Information Technology, 2010), 133.
34 Email to author, 9 April 2015.
35 Emails to author, 9 April 2015 and 16 April 2015.
36 Email to author, 27 April 2015.
37 R.S. Whitington, *Simpson's Safari* (London: Heinemann, 1967), 133.
38 Timothy Arlott, *John Arlott: A Memoir* (London: Andre Deutsch, 1994), 71.
39 Ibid., 166–7.
40 Mike Marqusee, *War Minus the Shooting: A Journey Through South Asia During Cricket's World Cup* (London: Heinemann, 1996).
41 Email to author, 14 May 2015.
42 M. Marqusee, *Anyone But England: Cricket and the National Malaise* (London: Verso, 1994); M. Marqusee, *Slow Turn* (London: Joseph, 1986).
43 D. Birley, *The Willow Wand* (London: Queen Anne Press, 1971).
44 Ibid.
45 Huw Richards, 'The Transatlantic Iconoclast', *The Nightwatchman* 10 (2015), 60.
46 Marqusee, *War Minus the Shooting*, 5–6.
47 T. Hauser, *Muhammad Ali: His Life and Times* (New York: Simon & Schuster, 1991).
48 Mike Marqusee, *Redemption Song: Muhammad Ali and the Spirit of the Sixties* (London: Verso, 2005), 314.

7

'RACE', WHITENESS AND SPORT

Thomas Fletcher and Kevin Hylton

Introduction

In this chapter we investigate the relationship between 'race', whiteness and sport. We do this by providing a critical review of published works on 'race', whiteness and sport over a five-year period (2009–15). We acknowledge that many significant and seminal works set the scene for the papers included here and sometimes we expand our search parameters to include some of them. We ask a number of questions regarding whiteness: What is it? How is it manifest? How is it performed? How are its privileges sustained? We adopt the view that white identity is not just phenotypic, but is also performative and contingent. We are also mindful that whiteness processes, while not always acknowledged, are omnipresent; permeating all facets of everyday life, including sport. Indeed, whiteness operates at a number of levels of sport – from grassroots to governance structures – and, as a result, sport is an appropriate lens through which to ask questions of the centrality of whiteness and its implications for how we experience sport.

We begin the chapter by delineating our own biographies and explaining how whiteness impacts our own lives. Next, we provide an overview of the concept of whiteness and how it has been applied to sport. We then move to a discussion of our methodology, specifically highlighting our literature search protocol and its return. Following this we map out our critical race theory framework, whose advocates have been vociferous in its naming of and resistance to racialized power relations; whiteness critiques are central to this.[1] Next, we present findings from our literature search in which critical race theory not only informs our critique but also seminal ideas in the way whiteness is considered in sport and related areas. The findings are divided into five themes: white as normal; Otherness; sport media; colour-blindness; and researching whiteness. In the final section of the chapter, we assess the state of research regarding 'race', whiteness and sport, and suggest future research directions.

Though there is no support in science for the notion of 'races', we recognize the paradox of our earnest, if paradoxical, engagement with 'race' to indicate that 'race' and racism are structuring factors in society. We do this by acknowledging the spurious scientific basis of 'race' while also recognizing it as a lived reality and everyday social construction.[2] According to Roberts, the purpose of understanding 'race' is to recognize the power of one's own mind and status, and derive from that power the impetus necessary to reach individual and/or collective goals. She concludes that we are all each responsible for what we do with what we inherit. Roberts' comments resonate strongly with both authors, given our very different backgrounds.[3]

Fletcher was born in the 1980s, in a mining town in northern England. While coming from working class upbringings, by the time his parents had started a family, they had experienced a degree of economic mobility through careers in management and self-employment, respectively. Fletcher experienced what he considers to be a privileged upbringing. Relative economic stability meant that he wanted for very little – especially in sport where he was supported unconditionally. This support (alongside some talent) enabled him to represent his county at cricket from the age of 15 to the age of 21. Never acknowledging it at the time, he is now able to see how the workings of whiteness and white privilege facilitated his entry and progression in cricket. There is a general belief in most sports that to progress to higher levels of play your face must 'fit'. Fortunately for Fletcher, his did. Fletcher's white identity was shared almost exclusively by the management, coaches and teammates, thus ensuring that cricket remained a white habitus, where associated habits and tastes were normal and unproblematic. These privileges were never acknowledged but they certainly existed. Fletcher's experiences no doubt mirror those of many other white men navigating their way through the structures of sport. However, while Fletcher is now in a position to see and problematize these privileges, many others continue not to see, or are unwilling to see.

Hylton was born in 1960s East London to Jamaican parents who were invited to the UK with other willing members of the Commonwealth to fulfil essential jobs in under-served industries. Transport and health were the starting points for this working class family, as job security, settlement, remittances home and navigating the overt racism of the era became their main priorities. None of this impacted the self-consciousness of Hylton as a youth, as the school curriculum did not dwell on any of these issues; yet in sport, patterns emerged that only more critical reflections in later years revealed what could be described as racialized behaviours. Assumptions of natural ability in football, athletics and cricket were flattering facilitators of insiderness and hegemonic masculinity, yet at the same time those assumptions based upon racial stereotypes were also inferring other things about intellectual capacity and propensies for success in academic as well as sporting domains. We should not be surprised that these subtle patterns retain a certain resilience today, given racism's ability to adapt and be reinvented over time.

Differences aside, we are united by our commitment to anti-racism and social justice, and in our beliefs that the multifarious ideological underpinnings of whiteness lie at the heart of this fight. It is important to stress here that a focus on social justice must be coupled with the belief in the existence of 'injustice' before change can occur. As we will identify in the next section, many of the privileges afforded to whiteness rely on its supposed invisibility, hegemony and supremacy. The first step in combating these privileges and their effect is in explicitly identifying whiteness and making it visible. We believe that sport has a role to play in this.

Sports are not benign, whimsical leisure pursuits, devoid of political meaning; rather, they are serious spaces that should encourage critical engagement with issues of ethnic and racial inequalities. Critical studies of sport reveal that, rather than being a passive mechanism for merely reflecting inequality, sport is actively involved in producing, reproducing, sustaining and, indeed, acts as a site for resistance.[4] In social terms, however, sport has often been considered the great social leveller. In fact, sport continues to be cited as an exemplar par excellence of an agent of personal and positive social change. Numerous studies articulate the possibility of sport acting as a legitimate space for political struggle, resistance and change, and as a modality for 'self-actualization and the reaffirmation of previously abject identities'.[5]

Until the mid-1990s, the literature on the interconnections between 'race', ethnicity, racism and sport lagged behind other areas, most notably gender and disability studies.[6] In response to a number of calls for more critical scholarship in the fields of sport and 'race', there has been a relative proliferation of writing on sport and 'race-related' issues since the mid-1990s and into the twenty-first century.[7] During this time there has been a marked shift towards thinking about sport more critically, that is, toward thinking of sport as a productive cultural activity and social institution that makes and remakes ideas about 'race' and not only a domain impacted by racist discourses and ideologies.[8] This has involved examining how 'race' intersects with other social identities and inequalities, locating media representation(s) as central in the (re)production of racial ideologies, and thinking more critically about whiteness.

Whiteness and sport

Studies of whiteness arguably lag behind other areas of ethnic and racial studies. This pattern is not isolated to the study of sport. As Frankenberg previously noted, meaningful conversations with white people about 'race' are muted due to a denial of seeing 'race' and/or the polite distancing of the topic.[9] Early studies of whiteness asserted that white people do not see themselves as 'raced', yet enjoy privileges as a result of their whiteness.[10] These ideas have been supplemented by the unconscious defence of white privilege through colour-blindness,[11] learned ignorance,[12] meritocracies and broader ideals of level playing fields,[13] and notions of racism's demise emerging in post-race discourses.[14] The result of conscious or unconscious ambivalence toward white privilege leads to a legacy of what has been described as white supremacy, where systematic insidious processes of privileging manifests itself across a plethora of arenas and are not restricted to, for example, housing, education, health, economics, media and sporting arenas.[15]

The term 'white' can be 'interpreted as encompassing non-material and fluid dominant norms and boundaries'.[16] To be white, however, does not mean one will be privileged in the same way, or to the same extent. Within the white racialized hierarchy there are a number of strata with varying degrees of acceptability[17] or, as Long and Hylton suggest, different 'shades of White'.[18] For instance, those who appear phenotypically white, including Irish, Jewish and new migrant communities, such as Eastern Europeans, continue to occupy marginal positions.[19] In this chapter we use the term whiteness to refer to everyday invisible and hegemonic processes that privilege (and normalize) the position of white identities in society.

By the early twenty-first century, sociology and the sociology of sport have begun to ask new questions about whiteness. Historically, whiteness has been viewed as normal, with many academics alluding to the invisibility of white ethnicities.[20] Of course, this view is demonstrative of academic white logic because white ethnicities are always visible to black and minoritized others in the way that W.E.B. Du Bois' idea of the colour line was emphasized.[21] Classic writers in racial and ethnic studies such as Du Bois and Fanon began to articulate such ideas later applied in critical race theory that began with the call for racialized subjectivities, racialized to inform the disruption of racialized social arrangements.[22] So convincing is the 'white as invisible' thesis that Nayak refers to white ethnicities as 'cultureless',[23] while Bonnett has termed white the 'Other of ethnicity'.[24] Leonardo suggests that whiteness gains a significant amount of its power by 'Othering' the very idea of ethnicity.[25] These views beg the question of how whiteness acts implicitly through routine and normalized practices on the field and within social environments surrounding sports as a consequence of a white-centred culture.

It is necessary to ask a number of questions of whiteness and the different ethnic groups who are 'touched' by it: (1) Where and with whom should the awareness and responsibility for whiteness lie? (2) How responsible and aware of whiteness should those with white identities be? (3) How should black and minoritized ethnic groups relate to whiteness? (4) How might white people become conscious and critical of the privileges of whiteness to the betterment of black and minoritized ethnic groups?[26] At the core of these questions is the supposition that 'rather than simply describing what whiteness is, it is more useful to explain what whiteness does'.[27] After outlining our methodology, we utilize a critical race theoretical framework for articulating the processes of whiteness.

Methodology

Once a field or sub-field of study has produced a critical mass of scholarly studies it becomes sensible to 'take stock' and consider whether the answers to our questions can be derived from existing research.[28] This process also allows us to assess what gaps exist and where researchers might usefully focus their attention. This chapter presents findings from a systematic review of research outputs in the areas of 'race', whiteness and sport over a five-year period. According to Long and Hylton, systematic review 'involves collating all the evidence within agreed boundaries and then imposing a research design hierarchy to make judgements about quality that will determine whether a study is admitted into the analysis'.[29] By analysing the content of research outputs over a particular period of time, it is possible to establish which topics, issues, theoretical and methodological frameworks are/were of interest/importance at specific periods in time.[30]

Our primary focus was academic journals, for as Tomlinson advocates, they are the 'lifeblood' of many disciplines.[31] However, we acknowledge that significant work on 'race', whiteness and sport exists elsewhere,[32] and so we have also included monographs, edited collections and research reports in our searches. Our research was guided by three questions:

1   What are the dominant topics and areas of enquiry?
2   How central was whiteness and iterations of it?
3   What are the current limitations of academic work completed on 'race', whiteness and sport?

The primary data were retrieved from online databases using key word searches covering a period of five years: 2009–15 (searches took place in early 2015). The following academic databases were searched: *Academic Search Premier* and *Academic Search Complete*, *Sport Discus*, *Leisure Tourism Database*, *Sociological Abstracts*, *Physical Education Index* and *Ingenta Connect*. We also searched via Leeds Beckett University's 'in house' database, *Discover*. Search terms used were:

White		Sport
		OR
Whiteness	**AND**	Physical Education
		OR
White privilege		Physical Activity
		OR
		Leisure

We were interested in whether any of these combinations were featured at any point in each source. Though acknowledging limitations, Dart argues that words appearing in titles and/or key word searches 'give a fairly accurate description of the likely content of the paper'.[33] He continues by noting that 'any non-identification in the title, or key word list is not to suggest that the paper did not engage with theory ... the absence of a clearly identified theoretical framework does suggest it was not a central feature in their paper'.[34] We do not dispute this, but would add that some themes/issues – whiteness included – are often drawn upon implicitly without being acknowledged explicitly. The absence of any specific reference to whiteness could be interpreted to mean that whiteness was unimportant in these sources. However, as we demonstrate below, even where whiteness is only implied, it was self-evidently an intersecting or epistemological factor. Our aim was never to analyse and critique each source individually. Rather, we wanted to know how popular and central to the scholarly literature that work on whiteness has been.

We acknowledge the limitations of searching via databases, so we also followed up references to additional work cited in the sources. Despite our best efforts, it is likely that some material has been missed. This notwithstanding, we are confident that our analysis does reflect the research conducted over the 2009–15 time period.

Our search found 76 articles, published in 31 different journals (Table 7.1). Given that most of the established work on 'race' and whiteness has emerged from the field of sociology, it was not surprising that the most popular outlets were what would be considered sociology of sport, leisure and education journals. It was encouraging to find that a number of non-sport-related journals published some of these works.[35]

Table 7.1 List of sources and number of publications in each source

Source	Number
Sport in Society	8
Soccer and Society	7
Leisure Studies	5
Sport, Education and Society	5
Journal of Sport and Social Issues	5
International Review for the Sociology of Sport	4
Journal of Leisure Research	4
Physical Education and Sport Pedagogy	4
Ethnic and Racial Studies	4
Sociology of Sport Journal	4
Identities: Global Studies in Culture and Power	3
Journal of Black Studies	2
Quest	2
Race, Ethnicity and Education	2
Journal of Policy Research in Leisure, Tourism and Events	1
International Journal of Sport and Exercise Psychology	1
Sport Management Review	1
Journal of Sport Management	1
Sport in History	1
The Contemporary Pacific	1
European Physical Education Review	1
The International Journal of Sport and Society	1
Journal of Popular Culture	1
Media, Culture and Society	1
Journal of Intercollegiate Sport	1
Journal of Research in Health, Physical Education, Recreation, Sport & Dance	1
Annual Review of Sociology	1
Journal of Ethnic and Migration Studies	1
International Journal of Sport Policy and Politics	1
Journal of Teaching in Physical Education	1
Journal of Issues in Intercollegiate Athletics	1

In the first instance we read the abstract for each and created codes based on the content. Coding identified six recurring themes: critical race theory (CRT); white as normal; Otherness; sport media; colour-blindness; and researching whiteness. Each source was assigned one (or where there was overlap, more than one) of these themes. We next outline the CRT informed theoretical framework before turning to present our findings.

Critical race theory

Though CRT underpins this chapter, it is also one of the key themes that emerged from this review of the literature. In this section we introduce fundamentals of CRT before focusing on the theme of CRT and sport in the findings. Where CRT has been used in sport, leisure and cognate disciplines, it has drawn from key authors such as Crenshaw, Gillborn, Delgado, Ladson-Billings, Mills and Bell.[36] Derek Bell, prominent critical race theorist and law professor to President Barack Obama, urged people to accept the reality of the permanence of racism in society.[37] This was neither a nihilistic statement nor a loose pejorative remark, but one that acts as a fundamental, ontological position for many that have approached CRT from a lived racialized experience. Critical race theory is often described as an emergent, liberatory, 'race' centred theoretical framework that sharpened its intellectual tools in the crucible of American 'race' relations and critical legal studies. Fundamental state-sponsored racialized inequalities were regularly the central agenda for their contestations and discourses of racial liberation. Not only was 'race' the central point of attention for critical race scholars, but so was its absence in what others would deem a meritocratic society and in particular the 'objectivity' of the law. For many, revealing processes that reified racialized inequalities and privileges for individuals and entities, supported through the law and other social institutions, including sport, helped to facilitate perspectives that acknowledged the fallibility of individuals and structures. Notions of merit, privilege, ahistoricism, counter storytelling, interest convergence, centring 'race', intersectionality and, more recently, whiteness have all, to varying degrees, populated strands of CRT critiques.[38]

Most importantly, though not to the exclusion of intersecting forms of social oppression, a CRT framework must always centre 'race' with a view to challenging racialized dynamics in society. Like other critical race theorists, Youdell argues that 'race' is a:

> Feature of our institutions, our social practices, our everyday life, our discourses and our unconscious investments and attachments. Together these produce and reproduce race and race hierarchy as well as the 'common sense' that racism is aberrant, in decline and something that can be legislated away.[39]

Youdell echoes the words of Bell and other critical race theorists who assert the 'everydayness' of racism while explaining how its processes and practices are systematically executed in a plethora of fashions.[40] On this note, CRT cautions against complacency in regards to claims of racism being an aberration, 'a one-off'; any such explanations reduce such behaviours to the level of the individual while ignoring broader, embedded institutional and structural processes and practices. So, ideologies that mask these racialized dynamics such as colour-blindness, meritocracy and racial equality, often deemed to be discourses of the Left, force critical race theorists to remain sceptical about ahistorical incrementalism in struggles for equality, and the idealism of colour-blindness and meritocracy. The *lived reality* of 'race' and racism is undeniable for critical race theorists, which is why a realist pragmatism underpins all iterations of the term 'race' as it retains little traction in science.[41] Warmington's *scare quotes* surrounding much use of the term is to acknowledge this paradox, problematize its everyday use in rudimentary and inchoate vocabularies, and prompt continued critical challenges to racism, drawing on a more complex and political lexicon.[42]

Bell's notion of the rules of racial standing emphasizes how 'race' permeates everyday social relations. Racial relations can be understood in Bell's terms as a form of 'standing' that can empower some while disempowering others. There are five rules of racial standing that Bell outlines. *Rule 1*: black people are often 'denied standing' when they discuss issues related to 'race' and racism. Their testimonies can often be denied standing when they stand alone and are more likely to be valued where triangulated with more valued others. Bell uses the term 'special pleading' to refer to how black people's expertise on these issues is sometimes perceived. This can be writ large in sport where claims of racialized wrongdoing by players, spectators and administrators are looked upon suspiciously. *Rule 2*: black witnesses to racism are less effective than those generally implicated in reinforcing racism. In such cases their views receive 'diminished standing', except when they are echoed by those privileged by whiteness, who themselves are not denied standing or viewed as engaged in special pleading. *Rule 3*: black people are less likely to have diminished racial standing where they criticize other black people acting to disparage/upset powerful elites. Here their voices are more likely to retain a higher level of gravitas and standing as they are privileged by those implicated by the charges. *Rule 4*: Where a black person acts in a controversial way against a dominant group, that group will actively recruit influential black others willing to refute the statement or condemn the action. At this point, when black people are recruited by a dominant group to condemn other black and minoritized communities, Bell argues that they receive super standing. *Rule 5* reflects a recognition of an increasing critical awareness and sensitivity to racialized processes; as Bell states:

> As an individual's understanding of these rules increases, there will be more and more instances where one can discern their workings. Using this knowledge, one gains the gift of prophecy about racism, its essence, its goals, even its remedies. The price of this knowledge is the frustration that follows recognition that no amount of public prophecy, no matter its accuracy, can either repeal the Rules of Racial Standing or prevent their operation.[43]

In sport there have been a number of instances of the rules of racial standing in action that in themselves may seem like 'one-off' incidents or issues, though viewed through a historical lens they speak to the recurring nature of the negative racial processes in play that elicits the fifth rule of racial standing. For example, consider Kevin Prince Boateng's position when he walked off the pitch for receiving racist abuse from spectators while playing association football for AC Milan against Pro Patria. It has been argued that had Boateng's colleagues not followed him off the pitch his decision would not have received the standing that it did. Television pundit and ex-Arsenal striker Ian Wright, commenting on CNN, remarked:

> As a Black player, being racially abused, people will listen to you but they'll say 'ahh look at him playing the race card'... I had to deal with that all my life, but if you have the top White players alongside you, like with Prince Boateng when they walked off with him ... that's fine. But if you walk off as a Black guy people will say he's got a chip on his shoulder, he's walked off and doesn't care about his team.

Not only do Wright's comments show an awareness of racism in sport and the subordinate position of the black voice, he implicitly refers to the racial order in football and the working of hegemonic whiteness in the game. His views can be explained by recourse to reflections on his own denied and diminished standing, which he uses as the ontological starting point to draw his expert assessment of racism in football and the reason for the success of this intervention by Prince Boateng and his AC Milan colleagues. It is important to note that whiteness is not mentioned by Wright, though its absence in his explanation demonstrates its potential to remain unremarked. Elsewhere, ex-Chelsea player Ashley Cole's support of ex-England and Chelsea captain John Terry received enhanced standing as he volunteered his support to Terry's claims that he did not racially abuse Patrice Evra.[44] In the past, African-American sprinter Jessie Owens received 'super standing' as he was publicly endorsed by IOC Chief Avery Brundage to challenge and pacify the threat of black Power advocates John Carlos and Tommie Smith.

hooks, like Gillborn, prefers to use the term 'white supremacy', rather than racism or simply whiteness, to more fully come to terms with the subtle subordination of black and minoritized ethnic communities.[45] In sport we see this in the clustering of black bodies in lower positions of administration and leadership, or even the highest levels of performance, without being able to consistently break through glass ceilings.[46] hooks' analysis identifies a hegemonic value structure that neutralizes diverse ways of thinking and doing for more established ones. In this way, glass ceilings are more likely to be breached by those who think in the same way as those closer to networks of power in institutions.[47] Bell's rules of racial standing is evoked here in the way white supremacy imbricates itself on our social structures as it explains the acquiescence and collusion of some of those it works against.

There has been a noticeable development in the application of CRT to sport, physical education and leisure – in particular the study of whiteness and white privilege. Critical race theory has been used by sport and leisure scholars to apply a new lexicon to the study of racialized relations in sport and leisure arenas. Its tenets include challenging established epistemologies and ideologies, liberation and the transformation of racialized power relations, and debunking notions of meritocracy, colour-blindness and objectivity. The ideas encourage scholars to consider their approaches to the sociology of sport and asks 'has "race" been considered in these issues?' and 'whose knowledge and experiences are valued in these exchanges?'[48] Critical race theory as a pragmatic framework informs as much as it is informed by substantive scholarship, therefore it is important to recognize that it draws many of its foundational ideas from a range of domains that include critical legal studies, race critical and critical sociological arenas. Thus, CRT encourages a transdisciplinary intellectual engagement to the application of its framework and as such its contributions to sport and leisure permeate disciplines not typically associated with these disciplinary domains. For example, Winograd's work on the sports biographies of African-American football players in the journal *Race, Ethnicity and Education* makes a contribution to the issues on how colour-blindness in literature is perpetuated with young people.[49] Others do this specifically in sport, leisure and PE domains.[50]

Findings

In many of the themes, we have found that ideas are often drawn from a range of sources. For example, each section below has instances that have drawn directly or implicitly from CRT without it necessarily being the focus of the study. Further, CRT is the only theoretical theme to emerge in this literature search, reflecting more its direct engagement with issues of 'race', racism and whiteness, which are central aspects of its core ideas. Where authors use a CRT lens explicitly in their analyses of whiteness, contributions vary from arguing the case for sport, PE and leisure scholars to engage more seriously with CRT and 'race',[51] to the commodification of blackness in the NBA,[52] critique of Olympic legacies,[53] 'race' talk in formal PE settings and the whiteness of sex segregation and class in women's ski jumping.[54] Drawing on the earlier work of Scraton and Watson, Long and Hylton, Singer, Hartmann, Hylton, and Arai and Kivel adopt a CRT lens to critique the notion of whiteness in the context of leisure research.[55] They present a loosely diachronic conceptualization of whiteness in leisure research, suggesting the idea of fourth-wave 'race' research in leisure studies. This fourth wave is characterized by attention to the ideological and discursive production of the workings of whiteness and racism. Hylton is more explicit in making the case for how CRT can be applied to sport and how CRT is a useful framework for destabilizing racial privilege in support of social justice.[56] Ultimately, CRT encourages an activist scholarship that confronts the complacencies of left-leaning intellectuals to force them to name 'race', racialization and the place of whiteness within what can be viewed as the oppressive arenas of sport and leisure. Disputes over how history, theory and action intersect (and inhibit) are at the heart of Hylton and Morpeth's examination of 'race' rhetoric and the London 2012 Summer Olympic Games. Amid popular rhetoric celebrating the UK's, London's and the Games' multiculturalism, the authors caution the capacity of single mega-events, such as an Olympic or Paralympic Games, to evoke change within institutions – e.g. sport – so historically entrenched with racial inequalities. Indeed, they label the very suggestion that 'single-mega-event policies are the answer to broader social issues that magically overtake entrenched racial inequalities' as 'futile'.[57]

Like Singer and Hylton, Roberts' application of a CRT framework builds an alternative view of the purpose of sport and leisure research based on the importance of fighting against injustice.[58] Accordingly, the key to a CRT-informed social justice paradigm is in putting theory and intention into action:

> We need to … engage in antiracism efforts, develop a change in organizational policy, and fully comprehend how critical race theory impacts our scholarship. In this way, both researchers and practitioners may effectively articulate how whiteness preserves social privilege, maintains its position in the hierarchy of power, and persists in its dominance [in sport and leisure] entitlements. Positive change is not possible without moving social justice postulates into action.[59]

White as normal

Contemporary research has revealed a widespread denial of the existence or prevalence of racism by participants, practitioners and policy makers alike. There is a tendency among those who hold sport dear to explain away racism as either (or both) inevitable (competition brings out the worst in people) or part of the game. These practices are demonstrative of how a culture of whiteness permeates sport at every level in respect to those with little or no experience of racism being ambivalent about its nature, extent and impact. We found these themes appearing from teaching and coaching, participation as a player, spectator or volunteer, to management and governance.

Many of the contributions in this theme questioned the commitment of sporting institutions to making positive and meaningful changes in how they tackle racial inequalities. Long and Spracklen's analysis of anti-racism legislation in sport suggests that impact has only been partial, in that commitment to racial equality does not routinely permeate the structures of organizations.[60] This reluctance to acknowledge racial inequality could also be seen in contributions focusing on the under-representation of minoritized ethnic communities in positions of influence (e.g. coaching and management) in sports organizations.[61] Trying to understand this problem, Bradbury seeks to explain the relationship between processes and practices of institutional racism and the continued under-representation of black and minoritized ethnic groups in leadership positions in football in Europe.[62] He, like Lusted and Cunningham *et al.*, argues that practices of institutional racism reproduce whiteness in sport and are underpinned by patterns of hegemonic white privilege embedded within the core structures of decision-making bodies at the highest levels of football.[63]

These issues are further reinforced by white coaches holding more negative perceptions of black and minoritized ethnic athletes than black and minoritized ethnic coaches do of white athletes.[64] Discussions of under-representation were also highly gendered. The vast majority focused on males, but some did present female experiences. Borland and Bruening's examination of the under-representation of black females as head coaches in collegiate basketball adopts an intersectional approach to exploring whiteness.[65] They argue that college athletic departments are hegemonically white and male.

Other studies in education identified how the Eurocentricity of pedagogies helped to maintain the whiteness of sporting spaces, while simultaneously Othering 'ethnic minorities'.[66] Flintoff's analyses of black and minoritized ethnic student–teacher experiences of PE teacher-training courses argues that PE teacher education is overwhelmingly white.[67] Via the use of individual narratives, Flintoff documents the experiences of black and minoritized ethnic students on these courses, highlighting how they feel excluded and Othered by, among other things, the white curriculum, white colleagues and white students.[68] Rossi, Rhynne and Nelson, and Darnell argue a similar case in Australian and Sport for Development contexts.[69]

A number of less prominent case studies emphasize how racial processes lead to racialized outcomes in terms of access and participation in sport. Harrison, for example, illustrates how processes of everyday racism work to secure skiing's social spaces as predominantly white, thereby restricting the participation and representation of black skiers.[70] Similarly, in Canada, Rich and Giles' research into the Canadian Red Cross Swim Programme identifies that the programme does not currently offer cultural diversity training for instructors – most of whom are white.[71] The programme perpetuated a racialized discourse on leadership that revealed: (1) all participants should perceive risk and demonstrate leadership like whites/Euro-Canadians; and (2) behaviours that reflect white/Euro-Canadian beliefs are normal alternative ways of behaving.[72]

Otherness

In this context, Otherness became synonymous with those revealed to be in the margins, occupying liminal spaces or removed from centres of influence characterized by whiteness. Resistance and blackness, Asianness and 'abnormality' were prominent themes.[73] A number of contributions in this theme discussed blackness as struggle, often in relation to colonial oppressors. However, Carrington warns that the inclusion of more black participants in sports in the West, coupled with wider political struggles for recognition, have not stopped sport from acting as a site for political struggle between black people and white elites. For example, Carrington further suggests that early public displays of black sporting prowess were highly influential in challenging Western racial logic, including that of black degeneracy, in what he terms 'the Myth of Modern Sport', a Eurocentric model of sport's global diffusion, which presupposes the physical, mental and emotional superiority of the white 'race' over other 'races'.[74]

The point of departure for other studies positions blackness as something to be managed by the superiority of white logic. Douglas explores the ways in which white people in tennis (fans, administrators and journalists) represent and objectify black tennis players.[75] McDonald and Toglia, and Griffin consider how blackness and black masculinity have been commodified by the NBA, where representations of blackness and whiteness are manipulated and reproduced by the NBA and media.[76] Lorenz and Murray also argue that the NBA's dress code is a mechanism whereby blackness is policed within a framework of white acceptability.[77]

The existence of South/British Asian communities in sport and leisure has become more commonplace over the last 15 years. Studies of South/British Asian males have focused mainly on football, cricket and boxing, and have examined issues related to racial stereotypes and conflict, regional and national identities, British citizenship, integration and assimilation, hybrid and diasporic identities, and experiences of playing sport, supporting national teams and attending sports stadia.[78] Studies examining South/British Asian females and sport have focused predominantly on football, but also include sports such as basketball and kabaddi.[79] Each notes how traditionally South/British Asian women were believed to be constrained from entering sporting spaces because of religious practices and cultural norms. They identify family and partner disapproval, fear of going out alone and community pressures as potential barriers. However, they also look beyond such barriers, instead stressing the relative agency of many South/British Asian females in accessing and progressing in sport.

Farooq-Samie's examination of Muslim female basketballers argues that much of the research has depicted Muslim females as victims of their religion and victims of 'the veil'.[80] She argues how, via sport, many Muslim women are exerting their agency to present their bodies in much the same way as white women. Similarly, Bains' study of kabaddi among members of the British Indian diaspora turns the idea of sporting participation on its head by arguing that it is their *non*-involvement in kabbadi that forms an important part of their identities as Punjabi women in the UK. Unlike much existing research into gender and sport, for Bains, kabbadi 'is an arena where patriarchal relations are negotiated and maintained but, unlike many other sporting spaces … it is not a contested site for women where they struggle for representation'.[81]

The supposition that leisure and sport spaces can support processes of social inclusion, yet may also serve to exclude certain groups, is continued in Long et al.'s analyses of new migrant communities in the UK.[82] They explore how leisure and sport spaces are encoded by new migrants, but how struggles over those spaces and the use of social and cultural capital are racialized. Moreover, Long et al. argue that white European migrants find it easier to access leisure and sport provision when compared to other migrants – e.g. black Africans.[83] Being phenotypically white affords some degree of privilege over black migrants, but their white appearance only gains them contingent inclusion.[84]

Davidson's account of the Gay Games adopts a completely different perspective. She argues that in moving beyond the celebration of gay and lesbian affirmation, the Games' push for normalization produces a biotechnology of whiteness, class privilege and racism. She suggests that the Gay Games movement is a political technology of white supremacy whereby a particular form of privileged gay pride has been commodified to present a corporate image of a normative, hegemonic form of whiteness.[85]

Sport media

The impact of the media on creating and reinforcing stereotypes and as a vehicle for everyday racism and oppression is well documented across many disciplinary areas. In their review of sport and physical activity participation among black and minoritized ethnic communities, Long and Hylton found that most studies challenge the notion of 'positive' stereotypes, instead highlighting the 'pernicious process of negative racialisation'.[86] The sport media are a key site in the construction of whiteness, but historically they have also been influential in challenging assumptions about white and Othered bodies.[87]

Spracklen dedicates a chapter on whiteness and the sport media, where he argues that sport and entertainment intersect to construct whiteness.[88] He suggests that sports media – whether traditional television programming or live sports events or modern media outlets such as online blogs and discussion forums – are places where whiteness is constructed, but rarely resisted. The view that the sport media are institutionally racist is developed further by Price *et al.*, and van Sterkenburg *et al.*[89] Price *et al.* identify three key areas in which elements of institutional racism are to be found. First, regulatory practices, in the form of the Press Complaints Commission, have downplayed and ignored problems of discriminatory content; second, recruitment practices have led to a chronic lack of diversity within the sports journalism profession; and third, damaging racial stereotypes persist in sports coverage.[90]

Other case studies include analyses of high-profile sports and sport stars – British long-distance runner Paula Radcliffe, association football player Cristiano Ronaldo and New Zealand rugby among them. In an analysis of Radcliffe, Walton argues that unlike representations of other female sporting 'heroes' (e.g. Cathy Freeman, Kelly Holmes), media representations tend not to centralize her ethnicity. Walton attributes this to Radcliffe's whiteness and therefore her 'racelessness'.[91] Similarly, Grainger *et al.* attempt to analyse how the growing presence of Polynesian players has led to the 'whitewashing' of rugby in New Zealand.[92] There is an assumption in rugby union and rugby league that Polynesians are suited to the sport because of their racial distinctiveness. Perceptions of such distinctiveness can, in many cases, be attributed to the sport–media complex, which, as Carrington argues, has been heavily influential in constructing a number of (damaging) racial tropes.[93] Grainger *et al.* argue that such tropes are not only influential on the rugby pitch but off it too. They observe that many white parents are discouraging their children from taking up the sport as they do not feel they will be able to compete on the same level as the bigger, stronger and faster Polynesians; thus demonstrating some of the complexities of the racialization of a sport and that racial ideologies can affect everyone. They also point, moreover, to the influence of these tropes on white coaches and administrators of the game who, with racist notions of biological difference in hand, routinely scout and sign a disproportionate number of Polynesian players. These patterns, they argue, are leading to a 'whitewashing' of rugby in New Zealand.[94] To reinforce this debate, Hylton and Lawrence in 2014 presented images of Ronaldo to white British men and asked them to reflect on this and their own bodies. Driven by a theoretical framework of contingent whiteness, they argue that white British men's interpretations of Ronaldo's whiteness are inextricably linked to discourses of 'race', masculinities and football.[95]

Colour-blindness

Linked to notions of 'racelessness' and 'invisibility', there has been a tendency within sport, physical education and leisure to consider racism as a thing of the past. Where it might exist, it is viewed at the level of the individual, not institutional or structural. Within this context, where racial inequalities do exist they are viewed as the result of the collective cultural inadequacies of those it affects in that they should adhere to the 'bootstraps' analogy to pull themselves up. Such 'colour-blindness', and the attendant disavowal of historical racialized inequalities and 'race' privilege, remains a significant mechanism in the maintenance of whiteness and white privilege. If one does not recognize racial inequalities, then racial hierarchies will be reified and remain unproblematized.

Conceding that white ethnicities and privileges are regularly unacknowledged, Harrison *et al.* tested the assumption that black and minoritized ethnic teachers are more culturally aware and competent in relation to understanding racial issues compared to white teachers. Their article indicates significant differences between white and minoritized ethnic teachers who score higher in both multicultural teaching knowledge (MTK) and multicultural teaching skills (MTS) than the white teachers.[96] This work was reinforced by Winograd regarding the prevalence of colour-blindness in children's sports literature, which uncovered discursive styles that centred whiteness, including the reinforcement of 'historically racist stereotypes and images of black men' that position them as animalistic, brutish and unintelligent.[97] Sport-specific case studies that highlight the complexities of these colour-blind arguments include Burdsey on microaggressions (everyday subtle racisms) and professional South Asian cricketers in England, and Merrett, Tatz and Adair on South African rugby and cricket.[98]

Researching whiteness

The majority of the sources on researching whiteness are written by white researchers who centralize their own identities to elucidate some of the challenges facing white researchers when conducting studies with minoritized ethnic participants. The sources address variously the complexities of conducting qualitative research across racial divides and white anxieties and white guilt. Flintoff and Webb, and later Flintoff *et al.*, examine the operation of whiteness within PE teacher education (PETE).[99] Flintoff and Webb note that 'race', ethnicity and whiteness are largely absent from PE literatures, and present some cautionary notes on the complexities of white researchers working with minoritized ethnic communities. The authors draw on their own deficiencies, reflecting how by drawing on a 'racialized other' deficit discourse in their pedagogy, and by ignoring 'race' in their own research on inequalities in PETE, they have failed to disrupt universalized discourses of 'white-as-norm', or addressed their own privileged racialized positioning. The latter is the focus of Fletcher's reflections on conducting research with both white British and British South Asian cricketers in England. Fletcher argues that reflecting critically on our biographies and positionality is the first step in recognizing how whiteness operates in order that we can begin to work to disrupt it. He warns how white researchers (of sport) are, at times, culpable of reinforcing dominant racial discourses rather than challenging them; and suggests that we must consider the racialized context(s) of our own experiences and not presume that 'race' is experienced only by black and minoritized ethnic individuals (see also Rossi *et al.*'s study of indigenous communities in Australia; and Spracklen *et al.*'s study of northernness, blackness and whiteness). Spracklen *et al.* argue that a researcher's own histories and identities are pivotal in how they are accepted as legitimate ethnographers and insiders, but those histories and identities also pose a critical challenge to researchers and those in the communities with whom researchers interact.[100]

Discussion

We have provided a thematic overview of the findings from our analysis. In the final section of this chapter we attempt to provide a critique of these sources and suggest future directions for research. We maintain that sport is an especially problematic institution from which to examine 'race' and whiteness because it is posited as an exemplar of colour-blindness, meritocracy and egalitarianism.[101] Indeed, the 'level playing field' metaphor has been justified through a range of public campaigns to eradicate inequalities from sport. For McDonald, while these programmes can be credited with successfully reducing some of the toxic nature of racialized language, they have simultaneously oversimplified racism to the behaviour of individuals.[102] To position racism as a set of individual prejudices and behaviours, which are now policed through 'unfettered social policy to equality and anti-racism' obscures and conceals the historical, institutional and structural nature of racism.[103]

The ability to disrupt normative hegemonic institutional thinking about 'race' (in)equalities is partly why academic researchers remain highly influential in prompting institutional change. However, as we identify above, there is a tendency for white researchers to apologize for being white; citing their white identity as an obstacle to successfully capturing minoritized experiences. Clearly, a white researcher's ethnic identity will influence how they engage with sport issues. However, our reflexivity should not get in the way of us doing innovative work. Berry and Clair, for instance, suggest that reflexivity can stifle project development. They argue that the tendency of researchers to reflect on their vulnerability while in the field means that many researchers will retreat away from complicated and controversial topics, reverting instead to 'common ground' where their positionality is felt less. In so doing, they lament the loss of knowledge and loss of ethnographic understanding likely resulting from researchers being 'blocked', or denied access, due in part to their white identities.[104] The very idea of white researchers attempting to access the life-worlds of black and ethnic minoritized populations could be interpreted in this way. However, researching across cultural divides should not be treated with such trepidation. Unless we push certain boundaries of acceptability, these boundaries will never be redefined and valuable data never created.[105]

Few of the sources attempted to develop existing theories of whiteness, or indeed, suggest any new theories of whiteness. As illustrated above, most involved white researchers reflecting on their own positions of power, while suggesting similar caution to others who are predominantly white in the cognate disciplines. However, Arai and Kivel conceived of a fourth wave theory of 'race' and whiteness underpinned by CRT in leisure research that mandated scholars to re-examine 'race' and racism, challenge white hegemony and how it is internalized.[106] Others attempted to shift thinking on whiteness toward a poststructural detangling of the homogenized experiences of white people in debates about whiteness. This is an important step taken that not only offers a more nuanced view of racialized power relations, but also offers a more theoretical view of how power and privilege work in contingent fashions.[107]

The other sources that did attempt some kind of critique of whiteness tended to advocate for movement towards a social justice paradigm, often underpinned by CRT. The reticence of sport, PE and leisure researchers to develop theory reflects a common criticism of the sociology of sport literature, in that much of this work rarely uses sport as *generative* of social theory and at best shows how concepts and ideas developed in other contexts can be *applied* to sport.[108] In so doing, sport scholars are making little effort to contribute theoretical outcomes that can benefit other fields, namely ethnic and racial studies, sociology and social policy.

There is a growing recognition among policy makers and others that a progressive policy framework for eradicating racial abuse and inequalities in sport represents the start of the process rather than being an end in itself. Long and Spracklen argue that if racisms are to be eradicated from sport, those involved in the process need to have a nuanced understanding of the racism(s) to be contested. Their argument is based on the assumption that 'anti-racism is essentially reactive' because 'it is defined by the racism it opposes'.[109] In other words, if the commitment to racial equality is to be more than a form of paying lip-service, then it is also necessary to engage with the deep-rooted cultural relations of power that sustain racially exclusive practices. Without such a shift, then the danger is that the campaign for racial equality in sport may become little more than a managerial response by bureaucratic organizations compelled by law to show they have policies on equality in place, but understand little and do less about the place of whiteness and the entrenched cultures of racialized exclusion. Getting policy makers and activist scholars en-masse to contemplate legislative change – particularly changes that might compromise their own claims to power – 'will need a systematic campaign of lobbying, raising awareness and offering solutions'.[110] Indeed, advocating that anti-racism is not solely for the benefit of black and minoritized ethnic people is unlikely to sit well among those whose position is currently hegemonic – i.e. white people.[111] Indeed, as we have seen throughout this chapter, whiteness can be manifest in a variety of privileges, such as in governance, the classroom, being scouted, entry to clubs and coaching, just as the outcomes of such racialized processes can result in predominantly white structures such as the constituency of clubs and organizational hierarchies.

Moving forward

The methodology for this study limits a definitive assessment of the treatment that whiteness has received in the work of sport scholars over five years. Yet what it does offer is a broad overview of approaches to whiteness and the main problems explored and explained. In many ways the work on 'race' in sport research remains under-researched and under-theorized, while the overwhelming focus of work on 'race' and racialization tends to focus on the presence of racism(s). This is not unimportant work, though its reiteration suggests that its nature and extent is continually a theme being mapped and remapped by and for those unfamiliar with its dynamics in the everyday. In some ways, this is reflective of a sector where 'race', racism and racialization are not realities for most and therefore requiring of explanation and validation.

Where CRT argues that a focus on 'race' often speaks to the lived experiences and understanding of activist scholars engaged in these issues, the marginalization of it in sport reflects more the lack of diversity in the academy and its higher echelons of governance. The knowledge formers and policy makers that would prosper from those ideas emerging, that embrace a reflexivity toward personal identities and the way whiteness privileges, can use these ideas in a positive way. As a result of this a focus on issues concerning whiteness remains a more challenging critical step for many academics and policy makers, who do not see themselves as 'raced' and are therefore 'raceless'. In such cases it is understandable why dominant paradigms, curricula, organizational environments and social justice agendas in sport and related areas reproduce epistemologies with blindspots regarding racialized power relations, hierarchies and intersecting forms of racialized oppression. Analogous to this, the work on heterogeneity, diaspora and contingencies offers immense potential to build upon the methodological reflexivities that some researchers have recently engaged with. They move our theoretical understanding forward in terms of not just naming whiteness, but also articulating how it plays out in the everyday realities of racialized people and therefore offering insights into how to disrupt it.

Notes

1 Delgado and J. Stefancic, eds, *Critical White Studies* (Philadelphia, PA: Temple University Press, 1997).

2 L. Guinier and G. Torres, *The Miner's Canary: Enlisting Race, Resisting Power, Transforming Democracy* (Cambridge: MA: Harvard University Press, 2003).

3 N.S. Roberts, 'Crossing the Color Line with a Different Perspective on Whiteness and (Anti)racism: A Response to Mary McDonald', *Journal of Leisure Research* 41, 4 (2009), 506.

4 K. Dashper and T. Fletcher, 'Introduction: Diversity, Equity and Inclusion in Sport and Management', *Sport in Society* 16, 10 (2013), 1–6.

5 B. Carrington, *Sport, Race and Politics: The Sporting Black Diaspora* (London: Sage, 2010), 36.

6 J. Long and K. Spracklen, eds, *Sport and Challenges to Racism* (Basingstoke: Palgrave Macmillan, 2011).

7   For example, see B. Carrington and I. McDonald, eds, *'Race', Sport and British Society* (London: Routledge, 2001); K. Hylton (2005) 'Race, Sport and Leisure: Lessons from Critical Race Theory', *Leisure Studies* 24, 1 (2005), 81–98.

8   B. Carrington, T. Fletcher and I. McDonald, 'The Politics of "Race" and Sports Policy in the United Kingdom', in B. Houlihan, ed., *Sport in Society*, 3rd edition (London: Sage, 2016).

9   R. Frankenburg, *White Women, Race Matters: The Social Construction of Whiteness* (London: Routledge, 1993).

10 C. Harris, 'Whiteness as Property', *Harvard Law Review* 106 (1993), 1707–91; J. Kincheloe, S. Steinberg and N. Rodriguez, *White Reign: Deploying Whiteness in America* (New York: St. Martin's Griffin, 1991); P. McIntosh, *White Privilege and Male Privilege: A Personal Account of Coming to See Correspondences Through Work in Women's Studies* (Wellesley, MA: Wellesley College Centre for Research on Women, 1988).

11 E. Bonilla-Silva, *Racism Without Racists: Color-blind Racism and the Persistence of Racial Inequality in the United States* (Lanham, MD: Rowman & Littlefield, 2010); M.A. Burke, *Racial Ambivalence in Diverse Communities: Whiteness and the Power of Color-Blind Ideologies* (Plymouth: Lexington Books, 2012); Z. Leonardo, *Race, Whiteness and Education* (London: Routledge, 2009).

12 C. Mills, *The Racial Contract* (Ithaca: Cornell University Press, 1997); S. Sullivan and N. Tuana, *Race and Epistemologies of Ignorance* (Albany, NY: State University of New York Press, 2007).

13 R. Delgado and J. Stenfancic, *Critical Race Theory: An Introduction* (New York: New York University Press, 2012); D. Gillborn, *Racism and Education: Coincidence or Conspiracy?* (London: Routledge, 2008).

14 P. Gilroy, 'Race Ends Here', *Ethnic and Racial Studies*, 21 (1998), 838–47; B. St. Louis, 'Post-race/Post-politics? Activist-intellectualism and the Reification of Race', *Ethnic and Racial Studies* 25 (2002), 652–75.

15 Gillborn, *Racism and Education*; Leonardo, *Race, Whiteness and Education*; C. Mills, 'White Ignorance', in S. Sullivan and N. Tuana, eds, *Race and Epistemologies of Ignorance* (Albany, NY: State University of New York Press, 2007), 12–38.

16 S. Garner, *Whiteness: An Introduction* (London: Routledge, 2007), 67; also see S. Garner, 'Whiteness Under Threat?', *Leisure Studies Association Newsletter* 94 (2013), 39–44.

17 N. Puwar, *Space Invaders* (Oxford: Berg, 2004).

18 J. Long and K. Hylton, 'Shades of White: An Examination of Whiteness in Sport', *Leisure Studies* 21, 1 (2002), 87–103.

19 J. Long, K. Hylton and K. Spracklen, 'Whiteness, Blackness and Settlement: Leisure and the Integration of New Migrants', *Journal of Ethnic and Migration Studies* (2014), DOI: 10.1080/1369183X.2014.893189.

20 Bonilla-Silva, *Racism Without Racists*; R. Dyer, *White: Essays on 'Race' and Culture* (London: Routledge, 1997); R. Frankenberg, 'On Unsteady Ground: Crafting and Engaging in the Critical Study of Whiteness', in M. Bulmer and J. Solomos, eds, *Researching Race and Racism* (London: Routledge, 2004); V. Ware and L. Back, *Out of Whiteness: Colour, Politics, and Culture* (London: University of Chicago Press, 2002).

21 W.E.B. Du Bois, *Black Reconstruction in America 1860–1880* (New York: The Free Press, 1998); F. Fanon, *Black Skin, White Masks* (London: Pluto, [1967] 1986); C. West, *Race Matters* (Boston, MA: Beacon Press, 2001).

22 K. Crenshaw, E. Taylor and D. Gillborn, *Foundations of Critical Race Theory in Education* (London: Routledge, 2009); b. hooks, *Talking Back: Thinking Feminist, Thinking Black* (Boston, MA: South End Press, 1989); P.J. Williams, *Seeing a Colour-Blind Future: The Paradox of Race* (London: Virago Press, 1997).

23 A. Nayak, '"Ivory Lives": Economic Restructuring and the Making of Whiteness in a Post-industrial Youth Community', *European Journal of Cultural Studies* 6, 3 (2003), 305–25.

24 A. Bonnett, *Anti-Racism* (London: Routledge, 2005).

25 Leonardo, *Race, Whiteness and Education*.

26 Adapted from Roberts, 'Crossing the Color Line', 497.

27 M.G. McDonald, 'Dialogues on Whiteness, Leisure and (Anti)racism', *Journal of Leisure Research* 41, 1 (2009), 9.

28 J. Long and K. Hylton, 'Reviewing Research Evidence and the Case of Participation in Sport and Physical Recreation by Black and Minority Ethnic Communities', *Leisure Studies* 33, 4 (2014), 379–99; J. Long, K. Hylton, K. Spracklen, A. Ratna and S. Bailey, *Systematic Review of the Literature on Black and Minority Ethnic Communities in Sport and Physical Recreation* (Sporting Equals and the Sports Council, 2009).

29 Long and Hylton, 'Reviewing Research Evidence', 379.
30 J. Dart, 'Sport Review: A Content Analysis of the *International Review for the Sociology of Sport*, the *Journal of Sport and Social Issues* and the *Sociology of Sport Journal* across 25 Years', *International Review for the Sociology of Sport* 49, 6 (2014), 645–68.
31 Tomlinson advocates they are the 'lifeblood' of many disciplines, cited in Dart, 'Sport Review', 646.
32 For example, K. Hylton, *'Race' and Sport: Critical Race Theory* (London: Routledge, 2009); B. Carrington, 'The Critical Sociology of Race and Sport: The First Fifty Years', *Annual Review of Sociology* 39 (2013), 379–98; A. Smith, *C.L.R. James and the Study of Culture* (Basingstoke: Palgrave Macmillan, 2010); Long and Spracklen, *Sport and Challenges to Racism*; D. Adair, ed., *Sport, Race, and Ethnicity: Narratives of Difference and Diversity* (Morgantown, WV: Fitness Information Technology, 2011); D. Adair, ed., *Sport: Race, Ethnicity and Identity: Building Global Understanding* (London: Routledge, 2015); D. Burdsey, ed., *Race, Ethnicity and Football* (London: Routledge, 2013); K. Spracklen, *Whiteness and Leisure* (Basingstoke: Palgrave Macmillan, 2013); J. Nauright, A.G. Cobley and D.K. Wiggins, eds, *Beyond C.L.R. James: Shifting Boundaries of Race and Ethnicity in Sport* (Fayetteville, AR: University of Arkansas Press, 2014).
33 Dart, 'Sport Review', 651.
34 Ibid., 660.
35 See Carrington, 'The Critical Sociology of Race and Sport', for further discussion.
36 K. Crenshaw, *Critical Race Theory: The Key Writings That Formed the Movement* (New York, NY: New Press, 1995); D. Gillborn, N. Rollock, C. Vincent, eds, *Race, Ethnicity & Education, Special Issue on Critical Race Theory in England* 15 (2012), 121.
37 D. Bell, *Faces at the Bottom of the Well: The Permanence of Racism* (New York, NY: Basic Books, 1992).
38 Crenshaw, *Critical Race Theory*; Crenshaw *et al.*, *Foundations of Critical Race Theory*; Delgado and Stenfancic, *Critical Race Theory*; Gillborn *et al.*, *Race, Ethnicity and Education*.
39 D. Youdell, 'Fabricating "Pacific Islander": Pedagogies of Expropriation, Return and Resistance and Other Lessons from a "Multicultural" Day', *Race, Ethnicity and Education* 15 (2012), 141–55.
40 Bonilla-Silva, *Racism Without Racists*; J. Feagin, *The White Racial Frame: Centuries of Racial Framing and Counter-Framing* (London: Routledge, 2010); M. Omi and H. Winant (2002) 'Racial Formation', in P. Essed and D.T. Goldberg, eds, *Race Critical Theories* (Oxford: Blackwell, 2002); M.M. Zamudio, C. Russell and F.A. Rios, *Critical Race Theory Matters: Education and Ideology* (London: Routledge, 2011); K. Hylton, A. Pilkington, P. Warmington and S. Housee (eds), *Atlantic Crossings: International Dialogues on Critical Race Theory* (Birmingham: CSAP/Higher Education Academy, 2011).
41 A. Pilkington, S. Housee and K. Hylton, *Race(ing) Forward: Transitions in Theorising 'Race' in Education* (Birmingham: CSAP/Higher Education Academy, 2009); UNESCO, *Declaration on Race and Racial Prejudice* (Paris: UNESCO, 1978).
42 P. Warmington, 'Taking Race Out of Scare Quotes: Race-Conscious Social Analysis in an Ostensibly Post-Racial World', *Race, Ethnicity & Education* 12 (2009), 281–96.
43 Bell, *Faces at the Bottom of the Well*, 125.
44 Cf. D. Burdsey, 'One Week in October: Luis Suárez, John Terry and the Turn to Racial Neoliberalism in English Men's Professional Football', *Identities: Global Studies in Culture and Power* 21, 5 (2014), 429–47.
45 hooks, *Talking Back*; Gillborn, *Racism and Education*.
46 S. Bradbury, J. van Sterkenburg and P. Mignon, 'The glass ceiling in European football: Levels of representation of visible ethnic minorities and women in leadership positions, and the experiences of elite level ethnic minority coaches', www.Farenet.org (2015).
47 C. King, *Offside Racism: Playing the White Man* (Oxford: Berg, 2004).
48 K. Hylton, 'This Way ... This Explains my Reality: Critical Race Theory in Sport and Leisure', in J. Fink, A. Doherty and G. Cunningham, eds, *Routledge Handbook of Theory in Sport Management* (London: Routledge, 2015).
49 K. Winograd, 'Sports Biographies of African American Football Players: the Racism of Colorblindness in Children's Literature', *Race, Ethnicity & Education* 14 (2011), 331–49.
50 K. Hylton, 'How a Turn to Critical Race Theory Can Contribute to Our Understanding of "Race", Racism and Anti-Racism in Sport', *International Review for the Sociology of Sport* 45 (2010), 335–44; K. Hylton, 'Race Talk! Tensions and Contradictions in Sport and PE', *Physical Education and Sport Pedagogy* 20, 5 (2015), 503–16; K. Fitzpatrick and L.J. Santamaría, 'Disrupting Racialization: Considering Critical Leadership in the Field of Physical Education', *Physical Education and Sport Pedagogy* 20, 1 (2015), 1–15; A. Flintoff, F. Dowling and H. Fitzgerald 'Working through Whiteness,

Race and (Anti) Racism in Physical Education Teacher Education', *Physical Education & Sport Pedagogy* (2014), DOI: 10.1080/17408989.2014.962017.

51 S. Arai and D.B. Kivel, 'Critical Race Theory and Social Justice Perspectives on Whiteness, Difference(s) and (Anti)racism: A Fourth Wave of Race Research in Leisure Studies', *Journal of Leisure Research* 41, 4 (2009), 459–70; Roberts, 'Crossing the Color Line'; Hylton, 'How a Turn to Critical Race Theory'.

52 R.A. Griffin, 'The Disgrace of Commodification and Shameful Convenience: A Critical Race Critique of the NBA', *Journal of Black Studies* 43, 2 (2012), 161–85.

53 K. Hylton and N.D. Morpeth, 'London 2012: "Race" Matters and the East End', *International Journal of Sport Policy and Politics* 4, 3 (2012), 379–96.

54 Hylton, 'This Way Explains My Reality'; A. Travers, 'Women's Ski Jumping, the 2010 Olympic Games, and the Deafening Silence of Sex Segregation, Whiteness, and Wealth', *Journal of Sport & Social Issues* 35 (2011), 126–45.

55 S. Scraton and R. Watson, 'Confronting Whiteness? Researching the Leisure Lives of South Asian Mothers', *Journal of Gender Studies* 10 (2001), 265–77; Long and Hylton, 'Shades of White'; J. Singer, 'Addressing Epistemological Racism in Sport Management Research', *Journal of Sport Management* 19 (2005), 464–79; D. Hartmann, 'Rush Limbaugh, Donovan McNabb, and "A Little Social Concern"', *Journal of Sport & Social Issues* 31, 1 (2007), 45–60; Hylton, *'Race' and Sport*; Arai and Kivel, 'Critical Race Theory'.

56 Hylton, *'Race' and Sport*; Hylton, 'How a Turn to Critical Race Theory'.

57 Hylton and Morpeth, 'London 2012', 382.

58 Singer, 'Addressing Epistemological Racism'; K. Hylton, 'Talk the Talk, Walk the Walk: Defining Critical Race Theory in Research', *Race, Ethnicity and Education* 15 (2012): 23–41; Hylton, 'This Way Explains My Reality'; Roberts' 'Crossing the Color Line' application of a CRT framework builds an alternative view of the purpose of sport and leisure research based on the importance of fighting against injustice.

59 Roberts, 'Crossing the Color Line', 507.

60 Long and Spracklen, *Sport and Challenges to Racism*.

61 K. Agyemang and J. DeLorme, 'Examining the Dearth of Black Head Coaches at the NCAA Football Bowl Subdivision Level: A Critical Race Theory and Social Dominance Theory Analysis', *Journal of Issues in Intercollegiate Athletics* 3 (2010), 35–52; J. Cleland, 'Working Together Through Sport? Local Authority Provision for Ethnic Minorities in the UK', *Sport in Society* 17, 1 (2014), 38–51.

62 S. Bradbury, 'From Racial Exclusions to New Inclusions: Black and Minority Ethnic Participation in Football Clubs in the East Midlands of England', *International Review for the Sociology of Sport* 46, 1 (2011), 23–44; S. Bradbury, 'Institutional Racism, Whiteness and the Underrepresentation of Minorities in Leadership Positions in Football in Europe', *Soccer & Society* 14, 3 (2013), 296–314.

63 J. Lusted, 'Playing Games with "Race": Understanding Resistance to "Race" Equality Initiatives in English Local Football Governance'. *Soccer & Society* 10, 6 (2009), 722–39; G. Cunningham, K. Miner and J. McDonald, 'Being Different and Suffering the Consequences: The Influence of Head Coach–Player Racial Dissimilarity on Experienced Incivility', *International Review for the Sociology of Sport* 48, 6 (2012), 689–705.

64 Ibid..

65 J.F. Borland and J.E. Bruening, 'Navigating Barriers: A Qualitative Examination of the Underrepresentation of Black Females as Head Coaches in Collegiate Basketball', *Sport Management Review* 13 (2010), 407–20.

66 See also Mowatt and French's comments on the underrepresentation of Black women in research: R.A. Mowatt and B.H. French, 'Black/Female/Body *Hypervisibility* and *Invisibility*: A Black Feminist Augmentation of Feminist Leisure Research', *Journal of Leisure Research* 45, 5 (2013), 644–60.

67 A. Flintoff, 'Playing the "Race" Card? Black and Minority Ethnic Students' Experiences of Physical Education Teacher Education', *Sport, Education and Society* 20, 2 (2012), 190–211; A. Flintoff, 'Tales from the Playing Field: Black and Minority Ethnic Students' Experiences of Physical Education Teacher Education', *Race Ethnicity and Education* 17, 3 (2014), 346–66.

68 Also see the following, who emphasize how the relationship between sport and education can also serve to (re)produce ideas about 'race'. L. Azzarito, 'The Panopticon of Physical Education: Pretty, Active and Ideally White', *Physical Education and Sport Pedagogy* 14, 1 (2009), 19–39; D.D. Douglas and J.M. Halas, 'The Wages of Whiteness: Confronting the Nature of Ivory Tower Racism and the Implications for Physical Education', *Sport, Education and Society* 18, 4 (2013), 453–74; D.K. Wiggins, '"Black Athletes in White Men's Games": Race, Sport and American National Pastimes', *The*

International Journal of the History of Sport 31, 1–2 (2014), 181–202; Hylton, 'This Way Explains My Reality'; B. McDonald, 'Coaching Whiteness: Stories of "Pacifica Exotica" in Australian High School Rugby', *Sport, Education and Society* (2014), DOI: 10.1080/13573322.2014.935318

69 A. Rossi, S. Rhynne and A. Nelson, 'Doing Whitefella Research in Blackfella Communities in Australia: Decolonizing Method in Sports Related Research', *Quest* 65 (2013), 116–31; S. Darnell, *Sport for Development and Peace* (London: Bloomsbury, 2012).

70 A.K. Harrison, 'Black Skiing, Everyday Racism, and the Racial Spatiality of Whiteness', *Journal of Sport and Social Issues* 37, 4 (2013), 315–39; Travers, 'Women's Ski Jumping'.

71 K.A. Rich and A.R. Giles, 'Examining Whiteness and Eurocanadian Discourses in the Canadian Red Cross' Swim Program', *Journal of Sport and Social Issues* 38, 5 (2014), 465–85.

72 For an alternative reading on 'race' and swimming, see J. Wiltse, 'The Black–White Swimming Disparity in America: A Deadly Legacy of Swimming Pool Discrimination', *Journal of Sport and Social Issues* 38, 4 (2014), 366–89.

73 J. Davidson, 'Racism Against the Abnormal? The Twentieth Century Gay Games, Bipower and the Emergence of Homonational Sport', *Leisure Studies* 33, 4 (2014), 357–78.

74 Carrington, *'Race' and Sport*, 25.

75 D.D. Douglas, 'Venus, Serena, and the Inconspicuous Consumption of Blackness: A Commentary on Surveillance, Race Talk, and New Racism(s)', *Journal of Black Studies* 43, 2 (2012), 127–45.

76 M.G. McDonald and J. Toglia, 'Dressed for Success? The NBA's Dress Code, the Workings of Whiteness and Corporate Culture', *Sport in Society* 13, 6 (2010), 970–83; Griffin, 'The Disgrace of Commodification'.

77 S.L. Lorenz and R. Murray, '"Goodbye to the Gangstas": The NBA Dress Code, Ray Emery, and the Policing of Blackness in Basketball and Hockey', *Journal of Sport and Social Issues* 38, 1 (2014), 23–50; also see McDonald and King's case study of the ambiguous relationship between Barack Obama's election campaign and sport: M.G. McDonald and S. King (2012) 'A Different Contender? Barack Obama, the 2008 Presidential Campaign and the Racial Politics of Sport', *Ethnic and Racial Studies* 35, 6 (2012), 1023–39.

78 D. Burdsey, *British Asians and Football: Culture, Identity and Exclusion* (London: Routledge, 2007); D. Burdsey, 'Role with the Punches: The Construction and Representation of Amir Khan as a Role Model for Multiethnic Britain', *The Sociological Review* 55, 3 (2007), 611–31; D. Burdsey, 'British Muslim Experiences in English First-Class Cricket', *International Review for the Sociology of Sport* 45, 3 (2010), 315–34; D. Burdsey and K. Randhawa, 'How Can Professional Football Clubs Create Welcoming and Inclusive Stadia for British Asian Fans?', *Journal of Policy Research in Tourism, Leisure and Events* 4, 1 (2012), 105–11; T. Fletcher, 'The Making of English Cricket Cultures: Empire, Globalisation and [Anti]Colonialism', *Sport in Society* 14, 1 (2011), 17–36; T. Fletcher, '"Who Do 'They' Cheer For?" Cricket, Diaspora, Hybridity and Divided Loyalties Amongst British Asians', *International Review for the Sociology of Sport*, 47, 5 (2012), 612–31; T. Fletcher, 'Cricket, Migration and Diasporic Communities', *Identities: Global Studies in Culture and Power* 22, 2 (2015), 141–53; T. Fletcher and K. Spracklen, 'Cricket, Drinking and Exclusion of British Pakistani Muslims?', *Ethnic and Racial Studies* 37, 8 (2014), 1310–27; T. Fletcher and T. Walle, 'Negotiating Their Right to Play: Asian-identified Cricket Teams and Leagues in Britain and Norway', *Identities: Global Studies in Culture and Power* 22, 2 (2015), 230–47; S. Johal, 'Playing Their Own Game: A South Asian Football Experience', in B. Carrington and I. McDonald, eds, *'Race', Sport and British Society* (London: Routledge, 2001); P. Raman, '"It's Because We're Indian, Innit?" Cricket and the South Asian Diaspora in Post-War Britain', *Identities: Global Studies in Culture and Power* 22, 2 (2015), 215–29; J. Williams, *Cricket and Race* (Oxford: Berg, 2001).

79 A. Ahmad, 'British Muslim Female Experiences in Football: Islam, Identity and the *Hijab*', in D. Burdsey, ed., *Race, Ethnicity and Football* (London: Routledge, 2013); S. Farooq, '"Tough Talk", Muscular Islam and Football', in D. Burdsey, ed., *Race, Ethnicity and Football* (London: Routledge, 2013); S. Farooq-Samie, 'Hetero-Sexy Self/Body Work and Basketball: The Invisible Sporting Women of British Pakistani Muslim Heritage', *South Asian Popular Culture* 11, 3 (2013), 257–70; A. Ratna, '"Who Are Ya?" The National Identities and Belongings of British Asian Football Fans', *Patterns of Prejudice* 48, 3 (2014), 286–308; H. Bains, 'Kabbadi Tournaments: Patriarchal Spaces and Women's Rejection of the Masculine Field', in K. Dashper, T. Fletcher and N. McCullough, eds, *Sports Events, Society and Culture* (London: Routledge, 2014).

80 Farooq-Samie, 'Hetero-Sexy Self/Body Work and Basketball'.

81 Bains, 'Kabbadi Tournaments', 155.

82 Long *et al.*, 'Whiteness, Blackness and Settlement'.

83 Ibid.
84 For more detail on contingent whiteness, see K. Hylton and S. Lawrence, 'Reading Ronaldo: Contingent Whiteness in the Football Media', *Soccer & Society* (2014), DOI:10.1080/14660970.2014 .963310.
85 Davidson, 'Racism Against the Abnormal'.
86 Long and Hylton, 'Reviewing Research Evidence', 10.
87 Spracklen, *Whiteness and Leisure*.
88 Also see Hylton, *'Race' and Sport*.
89 J. Price, N. Farrington, D. Kilvington and A. Saeed, 'Black, White, and Read All Over: Institutional Racism and the Sports Media', *The International Journal of Sport and Society* 3 (2013), 81–90; J. Van Sterkenburg, A. Knoppers and S. De Leeuw, 'Race, Ethnicity, and Content Analysis of the Sports Media: A Critical Reflection', *Media, Culture & Society* 32, 5 (2010), 819–39.
90 See Van Sterkenberg *et al.* 'Race, Ethnicity and Content Analysis'; McDonald and Toglia, 'Dressed for Success'; Lorenz and Murray, 'Goodbye to the Gangsta'.
91 T. Walton, 'Theorizing Paula Radcliffe: Representing a Nation', *Sociology of Sport Journal* 27 (2010), 285–300.
92 A.D. Grainger, M. Falcous and J.I. Newman, 'Postcolonial Anxieties and the Browning of New Zealand Rugby', *The Contemporary Pacific* 24, 2 (2012), 267–95.
93 Carrington, *Sport, Race and Politics*.
94 Grainger *et al.*, 'Postcolonial Anxieties'.
95 Hylton and Lawrence, 'Reading Ronaldo'.
96 L. Harrison, Jr., R.L. Carson and J. Burden, Jr., 'Physical Education Teachers' Cultural Competency', *Journal of Teaching in Physical Education* 29 (2010), 184–98.
97 Winograd, 'Sports Biographies'.
98 See D. Burdsey, 'That Joke Isn't Funny Anymore: Racial Microaggressions, Color-Blind Ideology and the Mitigation of Racism in English Men's First-Class Cricket', *Sociology of Sport Journal* 28 (2011), 261–83 on microaggressions (everyday subtle racisms) and professional South Asian cricketers in England; D. Rowe, 'The Televised Sport "Monkey Trial": "Race" and the Politics of Post-Colonial Cricket', *Sport in Society* 14, 6 (2011), 792–804; C. Merrett, C. Tatz and D. Adair, 'History and its Racial Legacies: Quotas in South African Rugby and Cricket', *Sport in Society* 14, 6 (2011), 754–77.
99 A. Flintoff and L. Webb, '"Just Open Your Eyes a Bit More": The Methodological Challenges of Researching Black and Minority Ethnic Students' Experiences of Physical Education Teacher Education', *Sport, Education and Society* 17, 5 (2012), 571–89; Flintoff *et al.*, 'Working through Whiteness'.
100 T. Fletcher, '"Does He Look Like a Paki?" An Exploration of 'Whiteness', Positionality and Reflexivity in Inter-racial Sports Research', *Qualitative Research in Sport, Exercise and Health* 6, 2 (2014), 244–60; also see Rossi *et al.*, 'Doing Whitefella Research'; K. Spraklen, T. Timmins and J. Long, 'Ethnographies of the Imagined, the Imaginary and the Critically Real: Blackness, Whiteness, the North of England and Rugby League', *Leisure Studies* 29, 4 (2010), 397–414.
101 Hylton, 'How a Turn to Critical Race Theory'.
102 McDonald, 'Coaching Whiteness'.
103 Hylton, 'How a Turn to Critical Race Theory', 341.
104 K. Berry and P. Clair, 'Reflecting on the Call to Ethnographic Reflexivity: A Collage of Responses to Questions of Contestation, *Cultural Studies/Critical Methodologies*, 11, 2 (2011), 199–209.
105 T. Fletcher, 'Does He Look Like a Paki?'.
106 Arai and Kivel, 'Critical Race Theory'.
107 Long *et al.*, 'Whiteness, Blackness and Settlement'; Hylton and Lawrence, 'Reading Ronaldo'.
108 Carrington, *Sport, Race and Politics*.
109 Long and Spracklen, *Sport and Challenges to Racism*, 7.
110 J. Long and K. Spracklen, 'So What Has Changed (and What Has to Change)?', in J. Long and K. Spracklen, eds, *Sport and Challenges to Racism* (Basingstoke: Palgrave Macmillan, 2011), 255.
111 P. Thomas, 'Marching Altogether? Football Fans Taking a Stand Against Racism', in J. Long and K. Spracklen, eds, *Sport and Challenges to Racism* (Basingstoke: Palgrave Macmillan, 2001).

8

GLOBALIZATION, MIGRATION AND RACIALIZATION IN SPORT

Sine Agergaard and Mari Haugaa Engh

Introduction

Although definitions of globalization are debated, most scholars agree with Roland Robertson's seminal definition: 'The compression of the world as a whole and the intensification of consciousness of the world as a whole.'[1] This increasing global connectedness in geographical and imaginary terms is evident in sports labour migration. Increasing numbers of athletes and sports personnel migrate across national and international borders and connect with places that were previously beyond their geographical reach.[2] Moreover, an increasing number of athletes imagine their career trajectories as transnational rather than bound to specific local and national settings and policies.[3]

Nevertheless, the perspective of figurational sociology reminds us that globalization is not merely about increasing interconnectedness; rather, in global sports figurations, groups and individuals are interdependent and they are bound up in a dynamic yet uneven balance of power.[4] Norbert Elias and John Scotson have argued that members of groups which hold power over other interdependent groups tend to think of themselves as being 'better'.[5] Thus the theory goes that established groups maintain their 'power surplus' by describing outsiders as being in subordinate positions. In other words, if established groups maintain their power surplus, sports labour migration may result in reinforcing the established groups' self-image while also maintaining the stereotypical images and stigma ascribed to the outsiders. In this, the outsiders themselves may also have the opportunity to partake.

The aim of this chapter is to analyse the ways in which processes of categorization are played out in relation to sports labour migration, as well as the role athletes themselves play therein. In focus are the ways in which club managers and coaches in the Global North as well as players from the Global South define 'us and them'. Particular attention will be given to processes through which African sports labour migrants are represented as national, cultural and racial Others, while the established group self-identifies with the white majority. The chapter draws on empirical material from case studies of Nigerian and South African women football (soccer) players' migration into Scandinavian clubs. Through applying the French sociologist Didier Fassin's perspective on racialization we will draw attention to the ways in which African players are identified and ascribed 'Otherness' in the Scandinavian context, but also the ways in which the migrant athletes themselves recognize and respond to these generalizations.

A perspective that draws attention to processes of racialization is important here, given the fact that Othering (not only in racial terms) is often found to be a part of competitive sports, e.g. in relation to opponents or rival teammates. Moreover, processes of ascribing racial Otherness are not innocent acts but are based in historical legacies and global power relations. European sports clubs and their managers and coaches are in the position to recruit players from the Global South and evaluate their characteristics. Further, references to the evolutionary and biological primitiveness of black athletes are consistently reproduced in sports.[6] These images may also be projected onto broader society as evidence of generalized characteristics of African 'Otherness'.[7]

Studies of sport and race

Sociological studies of sport have demonstrated clearly that sport contributes to racial categorization and ethnic identity making.[8] A number of other axes of social differentiation, such as gender, class, nationality, etc., form part of these processes, and are also defined, reasserted and negotiated through sports. In other words, 'intra-acting categorizations' shape processes of identifying others and self in sports.[9]

When examining the literature on sports, race and ethnicity it is evident that the issue of race has received more attention in North American scholarship than in the European context, where the focus seems to lie more with ethnicity. It has been suggested that the historical legacy of the racial persecution of Jews in the Second World War has led to a racial avoidance in Europe.[10] This contrasts with the history of engagement with race in the US context through which various strategies have been tried out to deal with racial differences.[11] Reflecting this contextual difference, the early literature on sport and race was mainly developed in the USA. Here, studies drew attention to racial stacking, the process through which generalized representations about the physical superiority of black athletes inform their assignation to positions in the field requiring physical skills and endurance, rather than intelligence and quick decision making.[12]

In the European countries race is seldom made explicit in studies of sport, yet remains present as an underlying assumption regarding differences between 'us and them' in terms such as integration, ethnicity and culture. This is, for example, reflected in studies that describe the various ways in which sport has become a vehicle for integration policy in various European countries.[13] In the Nordic countries in particular, race is rarely directly invoked, but finds subtle expression through references, for instance, to the underdevelopment of players and teams from the African region that are invited to participate in Scandinavian tournaments.[14] In a broader sense, the Nordic countries often present themselves as countries with high levels of equality, and as being key contributors to international solidarity.[15] In popular imaginations the Nordic countries often appear as essentially 'colour-blind' and 'innocent' as far as the history of colonial conquest and expansion goes.[16] However, research has indicated that despite public claims to the contrary, race remains a salient feature in Nordic sport.[17]

In existing literature a number of theoretical perspectives on sports and race have been deployed, ranging from critical race theory to postcolonial theory.[18] As described in a meta-review, studies of race and sport have mainly adhered to two main paradigms; the critical and the functionalist-evolutionary.[19] The critical paradigm takes the perspective of the Other and often points to racial discrimination, while also describing responses and resistance to racism as well as opportunities for transformation. Within the functionalist-evolutionary paradigm sports researchers tend to ignore structural as well as individual racism, referring instead to a melting-pot understanding of sport and society. Seen in relation to these general tendencies in the literature, the perspective on racialization processes appears relevant. First, it draws attention to the various ways in which racial difference is ascribed despite the increasing absence of explicitly racist language with anti-racism campaigns in sports. Second, processes of racial Othering are more complex than critical views on racial discrimination suggests. The suggested perspective on racialization processes will be elaborated and discussed in greater detail below.

Racialization

The concept of racialization is not new to studies of race. The concept pays attention to processes of categorization; the representational processes of defining a racial Other that also entails the definition of a sense of self.[20] Our understanding of racialization processes is greatly inspired by the work of the French professor of sociology, Didier Fassin, and the French professor of political science, Eric Fassin. The grounding of their work in French sociology and phenomenology is among others described in a chapter by Didier Fassin in the *Companion to the Anthropology of Body and Embodiment*.[21]

Fassin argues that rather than discussing whether racial discrimination occurred in specific events, we should think in terms of 'the processes through which races are embodied and bodies are racialized'.[22] Fassin draws attention to the fact that it is the accumulation and internalization of racial incidents and encounters over time that inform processes of racialization. He argues that the 'thickness of the body', its embodied experiences over time, is crucial here.[23] In other words, Fassin draws our attention to the fact that race and processes of racialization are experienced differentially depending on the racial identity of the subject.

According to Fassin, racialization involves three processes, and also three persons. Thus this perspective has the basic methodological implication of calling for identification of all involved parties: the ascriber, the ascribed and the observer. For all three persons racialization processes are to be interpreted as based in their accumulated experiences of 'race' over time; the body is the site for the embodiment of racial memory.

Thus the first part of the racialization process is ascription, the act of differentiating between self and other in racial terms.[24] When understanding that this process is based on embodied experiences of racial incidences over time rather than in particular encounters, processes of ascription are related to identifying certain groups and individuals as racial Others. Still, ascription is not merely about defining the racial Other; it also defines the racial norm. Ascription may be accompanied by a negative moral evaluation through disqualification and stigmatization of the racial Other, or a positive evaluation through a valorization of racial diversity, although this is often linked to paternalistic attitudes. Regardless of the kind of moral evaluation that is taking place, ascription is always a political act in that it emerges from power relations through which established groups hold the capacity to evaluate the characteristics of others.

The second element of racialization processes is recognition; the response to an experience of ascription, which involves identification with the ascription that is imposed.[25] This is when the racial Other recognizes that attention has been drawn to generalized racial differences. The degree to which an ascription is recognized as racial Othering is related to the second person's embodied experience of belonging (or being ascribed belonging) to a racial group that has been characterized not only in the specific incident, but through longer socio-historical processes. Processes of recognition can also range from the *reversal* of the stigma to the *reinforcement* of discrimination or even the *repudiation* of racialization. While Fassin remains open to the potential reversal of stigma through recognition, he emphasizes the socio-historically embodied power relations inherent in racial Othering. Hence, three attitudes are theoretically available to the ascribed; to ignore or pretend to ignore the ascription as racial Other, to reject the ascription and use the associated stigma in a resistant battle, or to internalize and possibly overplay the ascription. These choices are often tightly associated and do not always correspond to actual and practical choice.

The final element of racialization processes, Fassin argues, is objectification. Here a third party observes, comments on, narrates, analyses or measures the racial scene. Although often forgotten by most works on racialization, the witness (journalist, sociologist, statistician, politician) plays a crucial role in qualifying the process and giving it a public life.[26] Objectification is part of the process of producing a racial Other. It can impose categories on individuals and groups, but it can also reveal realities until then unseen by the ones who are ascribed racial stigma.[27] In other words, objectification is not a neutral process but a performative act that contributes to racialization in contradictory ways.

A critical case

To illustrate and discuss the potential of applying the above outlined perspective on racialization processes, we will draw on empirical material from case studies of African (Nigerian and South African) women soccer players who have migrated into Scandinavian clubs (in the years 2009–13). All three Scandinavian countries (Norway, Sweden and Denmark) relatively early started contributing to the development of women's soccer, and their national and club teams have been successful in international tournaments.[28] Today, all three countries have well-established women's soccer leagues, and clubs in all three countries have recruited international players from abroad at least since the early 1990s.[29] Particularly Swedish women's soccer clubs have recruited from abroad, to the extent that up to 50 per cent of top-level league players were international migrants in the 2008/09 season.[30] In 2013 Nigerian women soccer players made up the second largest group of international players in the Swedish top league.[31] Despite depictions of infrastructural and socio-cultural barriers to the development of women's soccer, research has illustrated that women's leagues were set up in Nigeria and South Africa already in the 1960s.[32] Meaning that while African teams have not received as much publicity as European and North American teams, there is a relatively long history of organized women's soccer on the continent. Internationally, Nigeria has been the most successful country on the continent, having participated in all six Women's World Cups and won the African Women's Championship eight out of ten times.

The case of Nigerian and South African women soccer players migrating into Scandinavian clubs appeared to us as so-called critical cases.[33] That is, as cases in which it is most likely for racialization processes to occur. As black women, Nigerian and South African sports labour migrants are visible others in white-majority Scandinavian provincial cities. Moreover, as women soccer players they are likely to appear as the gendered 'Other' in the football clubs. In our analysis, we will pay particular attention to the various ways in which the group of African women soccer players interviewed responded to experiences of racial Othering, ranging from denial to rejection and complicity. Because of the emerging professionalization of women's soccer in Scandinavia, it is mainly players from abroad that are recruited to work as full-time professionals. These international players have often undertaken long-distance migrations to clubs with barely institutionalized structures and sparse financial resources.

The material included in this chapter is drawn from the first author's studies of the broader phenomena of women's soccer migration.[34] In particular, we draw on interviews conducted with six Scandinavian club managers and coaches, and ten Nigerian and South African women soccer players that were playing in Scandinavian clubs between 2009 and 2012. Moreover, we also draw on interview material from the second author's PhD project.[35] This project examined the migratory route between Nigeria and Scandinavia, and consisted of multi-sited fieldwork according to the principle of 'following the people'.[36] In this, the second author lived with current and former migrants in their places of residence in Nigeria as well as in six different Scandinavian women's soccer clubs. Conducting fieldwork in multiple sites, the main research method became in-depth semi-structured interviews. Typically, three interviews were conducted with each of the available 11 current, and former, Nigerian women soccer migrants. As part of the PhD project, individual interviews were also conducted with 12 current and former sport managers and coaches. In total, 18 interviews with club managers and coaches, and 21 interviews with African women soccer players have been considered for this chapter.

Despite some variety, all of our interviews with club managers and coaches inquired into their considerations about and experiences with recruiting players from abroad, while the interviews with players focused on their migratory moves and experiences. When talking with club managers and coaches, we did not ask them about differences between domestic and African players, but about their experiences with international players. As will be apparent in the following, most of our informants promptly distinguished between 'us and other' and described national, cultural and racial differences. This chapter is the first to examine our shared material for references to the Othering of African players. In analysing we have re-read our own and each other's interview transcripts, marking the parts of the interviews where references were made to African players' Otherness or responses were given to experiences of being the Other in the Scandinavian context. The excerpts were then meaning-categorized in relation to Fassin's perspective on racialization. Working deductively from a specific perspective on racialization has allowed us to interpret excerpts that reject the presence of racial discrimination but still draw attention to fundamental processes of Othering that also entail references to racial differences. Working from this perspective we have not been interested in, nor capable of judging, whether particular experiences of racial Othering were sensed as racial discrimination.

Bearing on our position as white, middle-class Scandinavians, the club managers and coaches often appeared willing to share generalized understandings of Africans as 'the Other' with us, while the migrant players' experiences were not as readily accessible. Nevertheless, in particular, the second author accessed the field through particular African players and spent considerable time with all of the interviewees. Drawing on a large number of interviews with players as well as single interviews with their club managers and coaches, the analysis below will illustrate the complex ways in which Otherness was ascribed to sports labour migrants and recognized by them in the Scandinavian context.

Ascription of (racial) difference

In the interviews with club managers and coaches a general trait was that their considerations about recruiting players were tied to generalized differentiations between players from various nationalities. This is apparent in the following quote from a Scandinavian coach:

> There are different characters in different countries, but an American player you know they are really good to include in the group, they are strong, have endurance and they are really tough. So if you get a tip about one then you are alright. There are also very few American players that fail in the Swedish league. Finnish players all the Nordic players you also don't worry about, and in the Icelandic ones you really find the same things. We have both an Icelandic and a Finnish – they also speak Swedish so it is really simple they are like Swedes – good, loyal, hardworking, almost no difference.
>
> *(Morten, coach)*

What is noteworthy in this statement is not only the straightforward generalizations about national differences, but also the implicit way in which a sense of self is defined that only certain others are made part of. Players from various countries are evaluated for their capacity to relate most closely to the national characteristics of the Nordic players.

In several of the interviews, club managers and coaches included the interviewer in the identification of self. The mere presence of the interviewer seemed to encourage the informants to build alliances and to identify an 'us'. This is apparent in a quote from a Swedish club manager who did not only include himself and the second author who is Norwegian, but also players from North America and Germany as being part of a 'we' that is different from South Americans and Africans.

> I don't know but I think South American countries and African countries, if I can generalise a bit, I think they are more with the ball it is important to train soccer, whereas we others Americans, Norwegians, Germans understand that we also have to train the tough stuff.
>
> *(Niels, club manager)*

In the quote above, and a number of other interviews, reference is made to the idea that African players lack professional training when arriving in Scandinavia. Through these assertions, club coaches and managers draw attention to a generalized image of sports on the African continent as consisting of playful street games and amateur leisure activities.[37] This is remarkable given the fact that the players in front of them, the African players we have interviewed, played professional football in their home countries for several years before migrating. Thus, we are reminded that Otherness is ascribed together with a normative (often negative but also positive) evaluation of the characteristics of others. In this case, African players appear to be simultaneously playful and in need of training. Moreover, while race is not explicitly mentioned, the coaches and managers juxtapose characteristics of players from North American and Northern European countries with African and South American players. In this demarcation they invoke and reinforce a historically developed racial geography demarcating the characteristics of human beings in the Global South from those in the Global North, even if nationality functions as a symbol or code for racial Othering – a distinction in nationality terms that is indicative of the general racial avoidance that dominates European debates.[38]

Club managers and coaches also describe differences between African and Scandinavian players in utterances about the devotedness of African players. For instance:

> She is completely focused on soccer, she goes to training and then it is all about soccer, about performing the maximum.
>
> *(Karl, former club manager)*

The club managers and coaches often repeated this appreciative description of African players as devoted and goal-oriented. However, this characteristic was not linked to the sporting ambitions of African players, nor the fact that the African players tend to be the only full-time paid professionals in the clubs (Scandinavian and European players are mostly part-time soccer professionals who study or do other work in addition to playing soccer). Rather, African players' dedication and commitment is interpreted as being a result of poverty and underdevelopment in Africa. In this sense, the African players are perceived to 'need' football to find a way out of poverty and patriarchy.

Culture, upbringing, that is the reason. I think the African women are, first of all when they are born … [they] fetch food, clean up at home, if you are lucky you get to go to school. I don't think one understand what a big responsibility they are born with, a heritage that we have no idea about. Here it is natural that we get to go to school, it is natural that if I don't succeed in soccer then I can succeed in school.

(Pelle, former club manager)

Descriptions like this rely on an expansive generalization of a diverse group of girls and women, in which assumptions about subordination are often ascribed uncritically. This notion of 'poor and uneducated Africans' seems to form part of prevailing Scandinavian ideas about self and other.[39] In our interviews, the club managers and coaches tended to present South African and Nigerian players as generalized African Others, rather than a specific group of highly skilled individuals that are engaged in professional soccer.

Although the club managers and coaches also positively evaluated the players' African Otherness, this was often accompanied by paternalistic evaluations and attitudes. This is apparent when coaches and managers talk about the need to help African players develop into 'complete players', educating them as to the need for taking showers with the rest of the team after training, or helping them to do the laundry in a washing machine:

Try to imagine the opposite, how it must be for them to come up here. That you have to do laundry and use washing powder and such things. You must remember that there are many things they have to learn. Things that are obvious to us.

(Jane, club manager)

The club managers and coaches often referred to the need for African players to learn and become 'civilized' to adapt to the culture and way of life in Scandinavian countries. In this linear evolutionary logic, African players are presumed to need civilization in order to 'catch up' with the modernity and liberty that is seen to characterize Scandinavian societies.

A more explicitly negative evaluation of African players was apparent in coaches' and managers' frank utterances about their preference for African players due to their affordability. This was also linked to ideas about African players' inability to understand the European game:

The reason we have chosen [Nigerians] is because they are relatively cheap, they are good players good athletes like they are well-trained but they don't understand the game.

(Pelle, former club manager)

The quote above, and several other extracts from interviews, referred to the ambiguous cost of recruiting African Others when describing the resources needed to integrate players:

To put it this way from developing countries it becomes difficult. Yes, getting Americans, English, Swedes, Germans, Australians, it is a lot easier.

(Aron, club manager)

The club managers and coaches point to the difference in the effort needed to integrate players from what they term developed and developing countries into Scandinavian clubs and societies. They do this despite having described, in other parts of the interviews, that most of the players they have recruited from African countries are experienced international professionals who have travelled extensively with their national teams, and/or had previous experience with international employment.

The club managers and coaches mainly ascribe the African players' Otherness to their culture, nationality or a need for civilization and integration. In this, the racial Otherness of the 'primitive black athlete' is also hinted at. In the club managers' and coaches' descriptions, African players are portrayed as natural athletes who are extremely strong and muscular, but lack technical and tactical skills. In the interviews carried out by the first author, club managers and coaches suggested that the African players recruited to their clubs could have joined the circus or made a career as sprinters because of their impressive physiques. Such ideas about the 'natural' athletic superiority of black bodies are not merely descriptive. They are based in generalizations that support stigmatizing ideas of racial difference, in which white athletes are associated with intelligence and mind-work (brain) and black athletes with muscularity and strength (brawn).[40]

What was particularly apparent in our interviews was the ways in which club managers and coaches described the physical capacity of the African players not as a result of hard work and intensive training, but as a mere result of the natural capacities of black bodies. These assessments, however, were never linked to the fact that Scandinavian clubs tend to recruit African players who are offensive rather than defensive players:

> *Interviewer*: Does she play the centre-forward (offensive mid-fielder)?
> *Coach*: Yes, she plays the centre-forward. That is what she was created for. She does not do anything special (to get this position). She has such strong arms and such a strong stomach. She is created like that from nature, she's like a cat or something. She's crazy strong and explosive.
>
> *(Finn, coach)*

These stereotypes also have a particular gendered dimension. Ideas about the natural strength and power of the black athlete function to construct male and female black bodies as being (hyper)masculine, and hence raise concerns and suspicions as to the sex/gender of black female athletes. Carrington has argued that stereotyping of black athletic bodies has been more damaging for black women than for men as it positions them as 'mannish amazons', 'whereas black male athletes come to be seen as hyper-masculine, black female athletes [are] seen as not female at all'.[41] The presence of such concerns about the femaleness and femininity of black women athletes was made evident when one Scandinavian club manager suggested that the Nigerian players in his team were so naturally powerful that she was stronger even than him, a man. Although he did not make any explicit reference to this player being mannish or unwomanly, he nevertheless articulated an interpretive frame in which blackness suspends 'normal' gendered expectations. In this sense, the club coaches and managers articulated notions of race and gender in which black women are presented to fall outside of white gender normativity.

Recognition of racial ascription

In our interviews with mainly Nigerian, but also South African players, experiences of racial discrimination in Scandinavian clubs were seldom mentioned or elaborated. The players seemed mainly concerned with their own performance on the field rather than with their social integration and treatment off the field. While some said that their knowledge of Scandinavian language was insufficient for them to 'hear' racialized articulations, others said that they simply do not pay any attention to such attitudes. As professionals their primary concern lies with sustaining good relationships with teammates and coaches, and not with exposing or resisting racial prejudice. In this sense, identifying and resisting racial ascription was often not in the best interest of the players. Most of the players, at some point in the interviews, expressed such denialist responses to racialization, while they at other times would reinforce the stereotypes assigned to them.

Almost all of the informants described experiences that may be interpreted as them having recognized racial ascription. For instance:

> people just say whatever they have in their heads. Like 'you nigger' you know, they say it not because they want to hurt you, but because they don't see anything wrong in it.
>
> *(Mary)*

Here, Mary, a Nigerian player, suggests that Scandinavians lack knowledge and experience with the politics of racial terms and designations. She recognizes that although the intent is not necessarily malicious, ignorance as to the historical legacies of racial categorization lead Scandinavians to employ potentially offensive racial terms and expressions.

While reluctant to identify ascriptions as acts of racial discrimination, the African players we interviewed nevertheless exposed and engaged with paternalistic generalizations of Africa and Africans that they had come across:

> when you are black they will see you like maybe you are hungry or you don't have a home or you just come here because you're hungry. But they don't know because it's the game you choose to play because you love this game that's why you move and see all about the game what the game looks like.
>
> *(Chinedu)*

Above, one of the players refers to her experiences of being met in Scandinavia with generalized understandings of Africans as hungry and poor, and the perception that migration from Africa is fundamentally a result of despair. Chinedu feels that her love for football and her identification as a professional is not recognized, and that an identity involving migration-as-need gets imposed on her. While she does not object to being identified as racially Other, Chinedu in fact calls attention to the implicit racial categorization as black in general references to 'Africans', and she rejects the subsequent negative ascription.

While club representatives would consistently avoid race-language and refer instead to nationality (e.g. Nordic versus African), the players we interviewed were all comfortable naming and claiming race.

> They are different, their brain is different. In my heart our brain is not the same. I feel we are different. White people they are casual, they do not think that there is death. They are just living their life the way they want. Black people doesn't do like that.
>
> *(Florence)*

In Florence's experience, black and white people are different in their approach to life. In her reinforcement of racialized difference, Florence proceeds to place a negative stigma on whiteness and to valorize the black experience. As such, Florence recognizes racialized differentiation, but rejects the notion that blackness is subordinate or inferior.

Other players reinforced the racial Otherness that was ascribed to them, particularly in relation to notions of physiological and muscular difference. Cathy, for instance, suggested that Africans are 'blessed with a good physique':

> it is true that black players are stronger. It is natural. Black people from Africa is stronger and faster, maybe it is a gift from God. It is the time I came here that I saw. We are stronger than Scandinavian players, faster than white players.
>
> *(Cathy)*

In this statement, Cathy claims that black players are naturally stronger and faster than white players, a 'fact' that gives them an advantage as footballers. Our concern here is not with the truth-value of these claims, but rather with how these racial ascriptions are recognized and experienced by the African players themselves. Both Cathy and Mary, who is cited below, express unrestrained support for the ascription of muscular strength to blackness, but state that it was after arriving in Scandinavia that they came to recognize this racial difference.

> They tell me I'm different because I'm African. Because they are like, African muscles are different from their own. We have very good muscles, more than them, because you know everybody has muscle but I think we are more elastic than them.
>
> *(Mary)*

It was the evaluation by physiotherapists in Scandinavia that made Mary aware of what is presented as a muscular difference. This racial differentiation and ascription of Africans as stronger, faster and more flexible than white players appears to serve the players in reinforcing their value and worth as soccer professionals. By reinforcing a uniqueness vis-à-vis Europeans and North Americans, the African players support the reproduction of their own mobility. By insisting on their embodied and physical difference in relation to other players, they heighten their chances of being offered a prolonged and/or new contract.

However, while many of the African players we interviewed argued that black women are naturally stronger and faster, a few also commented on the continuous production of this stereotype. Uche, for instance, suggested that the ascription is an expectation that African players learn to perform so as to be successful:

> You have to be tough, you have to be like really strong. But, I think that's what gives African players edge over the Scandinavian players. Like if you're tough, if you're hard, you'll easily get noticed. I think that was one of the things that kept me moving.… I wasn't like the best player, but I think at the time everyone they always count on me like, you're strong, you're tough, you have to take this player out. So that was like a cool thing to me like, I mean it's a double work because like you have to just put the player out or your team will be like oh, you know? So you just have to be tough to play.
>
> *(Uche)*

In this statement, Uche reveals the ambiguity of ascription and recognition; African players have to work to reinforce their racial Otherness in order to maintain and/or produce new terms of employment. With her reference to double work, Uche describes that she has to work both on reinforcing her racial Otherness and her visibility as a capable player. Here, racial identification and ascription works as a positive asset, although it reinforces dominant racialized associations of blackness with 'brawn' and whiteness with 'brain'. The African players we interviewed expressed recognition of, and responses to, racialization that appeared to consist of quite strategic choices.

As precariously employed soccer players, which are often employed on short-term contracts and hold insecure career development paths, it is in the players' professional interest to overlook negative racial prejudice and discrimination, and to reinforce the racial differentiation that associates them with unique skills and capacities. This form of response illustrates Fassin's claim that 'Recognizing oneself as Black means resisting racial ascription.'[42] By recognizing the racial ascription in a manner that takes control of the stigma and redefines it as an asset, the 'sting' of the racial ascription is removed. By taking control over the terms of definition and racial ascription, initially imposed by Scandinavian coaches, managers and physiotherapists, the African players we interviewed appear to be variously resisting racial hierarchies and prejudice.

Yet, some of the quotes from the players also indicate a permanence in their embodied experiences; being embedded in historical legacies and power relations as black Africans no matter where you are situated:

> I don't know, just sometimes I just feel, that if you are black you are black. There is even people when you are with white people sometimes they pretend like they don't have that, that racism, but sometimes you tend to feel it you know. When things are happening, like getting an injury, it's going to take you time to go to the hospital, but thinking if it was a Danish player things was gonna happen so quickly, you know. Things are not coming that easy, like we struggle to get things. Like it's frustrating. You are black. We will always be black.
>
> *(Patricia)*

Patricia refers to her experience of being black in Scandinavia and draws attention to the 'impossibility' of changing her position as a racial Other. Still, the analysis above has shown that the players' recognition of their position ranges from attempts at reversing the stigma to ignoring and even reinforcing the racial differences in ways that are to their benefit.

Concluding discussion

As noted in the review, the perspective on racialization suggested in this chapter differs from the general tendency in sociological studies of sports and race towards stressing either the melting-pot understanding of sport and society in which racial and ethnic differences have disappeared, or focusing on racial discrimination and the victims of racism. This chapter has drawn attention to the processes of racialization in which African players are not only ascribed racial Otherness, but also how they recognize and respond to racialization. Through reinforcing certain racial ascriptions they heighten their own value and visibility as professionals. By exploring some of the complex processes of ascription and recognition of race, our analysis has demonstrated the relevance of applying Fassin's perspective on racialization. However, we have not been able to provide a detailed analysis of the informants' embodied experiences here, nor have we inquired into the third dimension of racialization – that of objectification.

A noteworthy piece of research that may discuss our perspective and findings is a forthcoming book by Carl-Gustaf Scott. Scott examines both overt and more hidden institutional forms of racism in Swedish soccer, paying special attention to the experiences of African (and other black) male soccer players at all levels of the sport.[43] This study, as well as studies of colonial complicity and the racial Othering of Africans in other social spheres, suggest that the Nordic countries are not as racially innocent and colour-blind as they would like to present themselves.[44] Moreover, the paternalistic approach to developing countries appears to not only contain implicit assumptions about racial differentiation and Othering, but contributes also to the self-identification of Scandinavians as providers of development aid.[45]

Another noteworthy piece of research to discuss the findings in this chapter is Christian Ungruhe's article on African male soccer migration to Germany. Ungruhe demonstrates a development from visible forms of racial discrimination in Germany taking place in the 1980s and 1990s, where African players were called monkeys and bananas were thrown on the field, to more subtle forms of racial Othering identified today.[46] Further, Ungruhe uses the concept of self-charismatization to describe the ways in which African players use processes of racial Othering to reinforce their unique characteristics in the soccer industry. This finding is in line with our argument that African women soccer players in Scandinavia exert agency in reinforcing and redefining ideas of racial differentiation and ascription. Other studies have shown that African women soccer migrants, like other highly skilled migrants, are intimately involved in processes of producing and reproducing their transnational mobility.[47]

The tendency observed by Ungruhe that overt forms for racial discrimination seem to disappear while more subtle forms of racialization still exist, may also apply to Scandinavian countries. Recently, collaborative efforts have been laid into developing programmes to fight racism in Danish, Norwegian and Swedish soccer.[48] However, celebrating that political efforts are made to combat racial discrimination in European countries may leave us blind to more subtle forms of racialization. Moreover, removing 'race' from language makes it more difficult to engage with, recognize and confront discriminatory practices and articulations. With academic ethnocentrism, this chapter has suggested that processes of racial Othering in sport may be better off being understood in their complex nature rather than being named and abolished as racial discrimination.

Notes

1   R. Robertson, *Globalization: Social Theory and Global Culture* (London: Sage, 1996), 8.
2   J. Maguire and M. Falcous, *Sport and Migration: Borders, Boundaries and Crossings* (London: Routledge, 2010).
3   S. Agergaard and T.V. Ryba, 'Migration and Career Transitions in Professional Sports: Transnational Athletic Careers in a Psychological and Sociological Perspective', *Sociology of Sport Journal* 31, 2 (2014), 228–47.
4   J. Maguire, *Global Sport: Identities, Societies, Civilizations* (Cambridge: Polity Press, 1999).
5   E. Eide and A.H. Simonssen, *Verden skapes hjemmefra: pressedekningen av den ikke-vestlige verden 1902–2002* (Oslo: Fakboglaget, 2008); N. Elias and J.L. Scotson, *The Established and the Outsiders: A Sociological Enquiry into Community Problems*, 2nd edition (London: Sage, 1994).
6   J.M. Hoberman, *Darwin's Athletes: How Sport has Damaged Black America and Preserved the Myth of Race* (Boston, MA: Houghton Mifflin Co., 1997).
7   C. Ungruhe, 'Natural Born Sportsmen: Processes of Othering and Self-Charismatization of African Professional Footballers in Germany', *African Diaspora* 6, 2 (2014), 196–217.
8   B. Carrington, *Race, Sport and Politics: The Sporting Black Diaspora* (London: Sage, 2010); B. Carrington, 'The Critical Sociology of Race and Sport: The First Fifty Years', *Annual Review of Sociology* 39 (2013), 379; K. Hylton, *'Race' and Sport: Critical Race Theory* (London: Routledge, 2009); G. Jarvie, *Sport, Racism and Ethnicity* (London: Falmer, 1995); J. MacClancy, ed., *Sport, Identity and Ethnicity* (Oxford: Berg, 1996).
9   K. Barad, 'Posthumanist Performativity: Toward an Understanding of How Matter Comes to Matter', *Signs* 28, 3, 801–31.
10 D.T. Goldberg, 'Racial Europeanization', *Ethnic and Racial Studies* 29, 2 (2006), 331–64.
11 D.T. Goldberg, *Racial Subjects: Writing on Race in America* (London: Routledge, 1997).

12 D.S. Eitzen and D. Furst, 'Racial Bias in Women's Collegiate Volleyball', *Journal of Sport & Social Issues* 13, 1 (1989), 46–51; B.D. Johnson and N.R. Johnson, 'Stacking and Stoppers: A Test of the Outcome Control Hypothesis', *Sociology of Sport Journal* 12, 1 (1995), 105; B. Margolis and J.A. Piliavin, '"Stacking" in Major League Baseball: A Multivariate Analysis', *Sociology of Sport Journal* 16, 1 (1999), 16; R.A. Stebbins, 'Stacking in Professional American Football: Implications from the Canadian Game', *International Review for the Sociology of Sport* 28, 1 (1993), 65–73.

13 S. Agergaard, 'Development and Appropriation of an Integration Policy for Sport: How Danish Sports Clubs have Become Arenas for Ethnic Integration', *International Journal of Sport Policy and Politics* 3, 3 (2011), 341; A. Elling, P. De Knop and A. Knoppers, 'The Social Integrative Meaning of Sport: A Critical and Comparative Analysis of Policy and Practice in the Netherlands', *Sociology of Sport Journal* 18, 4 (2001), 414–34; M. Theeboom, H. Schaillée and Z. Nols, 'Social Capital Development Among Ethnic Minorities in Mixed and Separate Sport Clubs', *International Journal of Sport Policy* 4, 1 (2012), 1–21.

14 M.H. Engh, S. Agergaard and J. Maguire, 'Established–Outsider Relations in Youth Football Tournaments: An Exploration of Transnational Power Figurations Between Scandinavian Organizers and African Teams', *Soccer and Society* 14, 6 (2013).

15 L. Sawyer and Y. Habel, 'Refracting African and Black Diaspora Through the Nordic Region', *African and Black Diaspora: An International Journal* 7, 1 (2014), 1–6.

16 S. Keskinen, *Complying with Colonialism: Gender, Race and Ethnicity in the Nordic Region* (Farnham: Ashgate, 2009), 276.

17 M. Andersson, *Flerfarget idrett: Nasjonalitet, migrasjon og minoritet* (Oslo: Bokforlaget, 2008); P.B. Massao and K. Fasting, 'Race and Racism: Experiences of Black Norwegian Athletes', *International Review for the Sociology of Sport* 45, 2 (2010), 147–162; P.B. Massao and K. Fasting, 'Mapping Race, Class and Gender: Experiences from Black Norwegian Athletes', *European Journal for Sport and Society* 11, 4 (2014), 331.

18 S.C. Darnell, 'Playing with Race: Right to Play and the Production of Whiteness in "Development through Sport"', *Sport in Society* 10, 4 (2007), 560; S.C. Darnell and L.M.C. Hayhurst, 'Sport for Decolonization: Exploring a New Praxis of Sport for Development', *Progress in Development Studies* 11, 3 (2011), 183–96; Hylton, *'Race' and Sport*; Massao and Fasting, 'Race and Racism'.

19 Carrington, *Race, Sport and Politics*.

20 R. Miles, *Racism* (London: Routledge, 1989).

21 D. Fassin, 'Racialization: How to Do Races with Bodies', in F.E. Mascia-Lees, ed., *A Companion to the Anthropology of the Body and Embodiment* (Malden, MA: Wiley-Blackwell, 2011), 421–34.

22 Fassin, 'Racialization', 421.

23 Ibid., 430.

24 Ibid., 420.

25 Ibid., 423.

26 Ibid., 425.

27 Ibid., 426.

28 J. Hjelm and E. Olofsson, 'A Breakthrough: Women's Football in Sweden', *Soccer & Society* 4, 2 (2003), 182–204; E. Skille, 'Biggest but Smallest: Female Football and the Case of Norway', *Soccer & Society* 9, 4 (2008), 520–31; E. Trangbæk and A. Brus, 'Asserting the Right to Play: Women's Football in Denmark', *Soccer & Society* 4, 2 (2003), 95–111.

29 V.L. Botelho and S. Agergaard, 'Moving for the Love of the Game? International Migration of Female Footballers into Scandinavian Countries', *Soccer and Society* 12, 6 (2011), 806–19.

30 S. Agergaard and N.C. Tiesler, eds, *Women, Soccer and Transnational Migration* (London: Routledge, 2014).

31 M.H. Engh, *Producing and Maintaining Mobility: A Migrant-Centred Analysis of Transnational Women's Sports Labour Migration*, PhD Dissertation, Aarhus University, Department of Public Health, Section for Sport, 2014.

32 C. Onwumechili, 'Urbanization and Female Football in Nigeria: History and Struggle in a "Man's Game"', *The International Journal of the History of Sport* 28, 15 (2011), 2206; C. Pelak, 'Women and Gender in South African Soccer: A Brief History', *Soccer & Society* 11, 1, (2010), 63–78; M. Saavedra, 'Football Feminine: Development of the African Game: Senegal, Nigeria and South Africa', *Soccer & Society* 4, 2–3 (2003), 225–53.

33 B. Flyvbjerg, 'Five Misunderstandings About Case-Study Research', *Qualitative Inquiry* 12, 2 (2006), 219–45.

34 Cf. Agergaard and Tiesler, *Women, Soccer and Transnational Migration*.

119

35 Engh, *Producing and Maintaining Mobility*.
36 G.E. Marcus, *Ethnography Through Thick and Thin* (Princeton, NJ: Princeton University Press, 1998).
37 B. Vidacs, 'Through the Prism of Sports: Why Should Africanists Study Sports?', *Africa Spectrum* 41, 3 (2006), 331–49.
38 Goldberg, *Racial Subjects*.
39 Keskinen, *Complying with Colonialism*.
40 Carrington, *Race, Sport and Politics*; Hoberman, *Darwin's Athletes*.
41 Carrington, *Race, Sport and Politics*, 80.
42 Fassin, 'Racialization', 424.
43 C.-G. Scott, *African Footballers in Sweden: Race, Immigration and Integration in the Age of Globalization* (London: Palgrave Macmillan, 2015).
44 Keskinen, *Complying with Colonialism*.
45 Eide and Simonssen, *Verden Skapes*; *hjemmefra*; M. Gullestad, 'Blind Slaves of Our Prejudices: Debating "Culture" and "Race" in Norway', *Ethnos* 69, 2 (2004), 177–203.
46 Ungruhe, 'Natural Born Sportsmen'.
47 Engh, *Producing and Maintaining Mobility*.
48 www.stopracismen.dk/sr/nyheder/page/11, accessed 7 May 2015.

9

SPORT FOR DEVELOPMENT AND PEACE

Neoliberal global sport and African bodies[1]

John Nauright

A new "hot topic" known as sport and international development emerged in the first two decades of the twenty-first century. Yet, even within this area originally conceived as a way to "do good" in and through sport, there is much debate as to what the aims and objectives are and should be. Rather than simply viewing sport and development as another area in which to train students for sporting careers, this area offers the potential for a re-centering of sport in the academy as a transformative practice. However, if ill-conceived, sport and international development/sport and youth development runs the risk of perpetuating the problem created by neoliberal capitalism and its associated sporting enterprises rather than offering alternatives that include strengthening democracy, enhancing quality of life through health and fitness, and contributing to community-based sustainable economic futures.

It is important to understand historical frameworks of global power and processes that began in the imperial/colonial era whereby Western (white) body culture practices were inscribed onto colonial bodies, replacing and subverting local physical cultural practices in order to understand better why contemporary sport development in the Global South is often viewed as a form of neocolonialism or neo-imperialism, and even paternalistic racism.

This critique is not intended as an indictment of sport and international development per se, but to suggest that understanding communities as they exist is an important first step to establishing what support might be useful. Indeed, few studies have engaged with communities where sport is played beyond official programming that has been externally introduced. Links to grassroots football in poor and specific African contexts have been analyzed, but many more case studies are needed across the continent and beyond.[2] Community-based projects are difficult to start, let alone to be spontaneous. In this context the need is often to facilitate participation. Facilitation encourages and diversifies approaches whereby each community can promote its own vision of development. The facilitation process should serve to promote genuine community empowerment. Thus, to empower people facilitation should provide resources, opportunities, vocabulary, knowledge and skills to capacity build in communities. My philosophy here follows the late Tanzanian leader Julius Nyerere: "[d]evelopment brings freedom, provided it is development of people. But people cannot be developed; they can only develop themselves."[3]

Over the past decade much has been written about the efficacy of sport in youth development around the world, though not without a measure of critical understanding.[4] In addition, a multitude of sport development programs have emerged in the Global South under the label of sport for international development and peace, or SDP. These initiatives have gained further legitimacy from global institutions such as the United Nations and global sports organizations such as the International Olympic Committee (IOC) and the International Federation of Football Associations (FIFA). Indeed, both of the latter organizations have actively sought to globalize their brands through increased engagement in the Global South and developing world by taking their showcase events of the Olympic Games and association football/soccer World Cup to previously untapped (or at least undertapped) regions such as South Africa, Brazil, southern Russia, China and Qatar. Indeed, the 2010 World Cup held in South Africa was promoted as a World Cup for all of Africa, and through bringing the world of football to the continent, FIFA argued it could make a difference not only to host cities and the host nation of South Africa, but other countries in Africa as well.

Yet, World Cup events were concentrated in and around the main urban areas in South Africa, particularly in the Johannesburg–Pretoria (Tshwane) region of Gauteng; Durban in KwaZulu-Natal; and Cape Town. Other large cities such as Port Elizabeth and Bloemfontain also hosted events. No matches were held in the entire (and geographically large) province of the Northern Cape and many other areas received little direct or indirect benefit from the World Cup being in South Africa. While numerous arguments can and have been made about who benefits and who loses from the hosting of large-scale events, many of these have not taken a long-term historical perspective.[5] This is particularly problematic when examining events as well as sport and international development in the Global South.

It is important to understand historical frameworks of global power and processes that began in the imperial/colonial era whereby Western body culture practices were inscribed onto colonial bodies, replacing and subverting local physical cultural practices. This allows for an understanding of contemporary sport development in the Global South as a form of neocolonialism or neo-imperialism.

In the latter part of the nineteenth century, precisely during the period when modern sports were codified and organized and new modern scientific disciplines were emerging, Western nations divided much of the rest of the world into colonial territories, and Africa in particular was completely allocated among European powers who drew arbitrary boundaries that had little to nothing to do with African state formation already in progress. Thus colonial territories such as "Kenya" were written onto the African landscape by Europeans.

European colonizers sought to conquer their new territories and compare and contrast what they found with their own societies. To fulfil their scientific mission, the spoils of Empire were shipped back to the colonial center, and, once interpreted, placed on public display in museums, zoos, and international and travelling exhibitions. Exhibiting colonial exotica allowed those at "home" to experience faraway places and mysterious cultures and peoples in a process David Cannadine has called "ornamentalism."[6] Displaying native peoples as exotic, primitive, or backward confirmed and legitimated Western colonial expansion and conquest as the "white man's burden" to bring "civilization" to the rest of the world. The civilizing mission was supported by a biological imperative and thus the body became the primary site where the construction of the exotic Other occurred.[7] As Z.S. Strother argues, "The body became the signifier of the real, the authentic. Its choreographed presence validated the colonial imagination."[8] The Western gaze over a long period of time was trained to see the African body as Other and different, labelled "wild" and "primitive."

Empire became a place where white men could seek adventure and profit. A literature of colonial adventure and fantasy emerged, including works by Rudyard Kipling, Joseph Conrad, H. Rider Haggard, and Edgar Rice Burroughs and other adventure stories aimed at boys. Indeed, in some colonial settings where whites had settled, physical prowess began to exceed that of British men as Australian cricketers in the late 1870s and 1880s and New Zealand, South African, and Australian rugby players in the first decade of the 1900s achieved sporting success against the "mother country."[9] Fictional characters such as Alan Quartermain and Tarzan demonstrated the power of the white man to dominate nature and the local population, while fantastic images of the wild and primitive warrior, most particularly the Zulu, created an Other against which such heroes could be read.[10] Tarzan first appeared in literature in 1912, but was translated onto the motion picture screen by the 1930s, played by American Olympic swimming champion Johnny Weismuller, who was the "Lord of the Jungle" in 12 movies. Zulu-themed toys appeared in the USA by this time and Africa became part of an American fantasy already framed by cowboy versus Indian "Westerns" which aided in legitimating an American world view little different from that of Western Europe.

What has all of this got to do with sport and international development? The construction of Africans and other Native peoples as "Other" remains potent in the twenty-first century. John Bale outlines in the opening of his book *Imagined Olympians* (which examines European framing of the Tutsi physical cultural practice of *gusimbuka urukiramende* in terms of Western high jumping), how in November 1995 then British Prime Minister John Major supported a scheme to send "sporting missionaries" to Africa. Major and others argued that the continent held a vast reserve army of athletic talent that could be used as sports labor in the global sports economy. In reporting on Major's idea, the London *Times* illustrated the story with a photograph of a Tutsi man jumping over the heads of two white men. As Bale states:

> The photograph represented part of what the author described as "plenty of treasure [that was] to be found" in late twentieth-century Africa. It communicated an image of African athleticism, and it was taken in 1907. The late twentieth-century article that accompanied the photo implied the need for the more civilized Europe to rescue African athletes from their primitive conditions by giving them the gift of Western sports. In this way they could be taken to a place where their skills could be appreciated and used.[11]

Bale argues that the representation of African body cultures by Europeans was as significant as actual colonial rule in generating perceptions of "Africa" both on the continent and globally. Bale refers to "Africanism," drawing upon Edward Said's concept of "Orientalism," to explain a Western style that makes statements about Africa: "representing Africa in a style for dominating, restructuring, and, often, having authority over it." Bale argues further that while there are a number of works that discuss sport and empire, "they are characterized by an unwillingness to attempt an excavation of colonial representations of pre-colonial movement cultures." In presenting a number of illustrations of *gusimbuka*, Bale states that these produced a variety of ways of seeing Africa and the African: "as *exotic, mysterious, powerful* – and as *athletic* [emphasis added]." However, Bale reminds us that within Rwanda itself, the result of representations of Tutsi body culture led to them being viewed as a super "race" of athletic bodies shaped in European discourse, and, by implication, the Hutu were different or inferior as they did not have a similar body culture tradition. Here, Bale touches on a crucial point that requires further analysis in the history of sport in Africa. We have to begin to unravel the impact of sport, colonialism and representation on different groups within various locales in Africa, as well as between "African" and "European."[12]

Through its early links to the global imperial project and the emergence of a sports science that has often been used to compare bodies against a white male norm, the modern Olympics has contributed to the cultural colonization of the world in the name of elitist achievement sport and Western capitalism. At the same time, the Olympic Movement has attempted to shroud this process in the ideologies of Olympism, "fair play" and global inclusivity and universalism. Like other transnational or global movements, the Olympic Movement has attempted to become a "world system." Projects including Olympic Aid and Olympic Solidarity, and other efforts to deliver sporting activities and technologies to non-Western nations, directly parallel efforts to produce an undifferentiated global consumer.

In Africa, the body was central to the imperial project, though as much through the ways in which class was read onto the colonial body as race. Participation in modern sport was viewed as part of "civilized" development and the "civilizing" project, which was centered on the adoption of Western styles of dress and bodily deportment.[13] Those Africans who adopted Western dress, attitudes and sports were accepted as junior partners in the colonial hierarchy, while those who remained uneducated or involved in "traditional" activities were viewed differently. The colonial project hinged on the support of traditional hierarchies and class and cultural distinctions, though it could by no means control the outcome once sport was unleashed on the rapidly increasing urban masses in Johannesburg, Brazzaville, Leopoldville, Lusaka, Nairobi or Lagos.[14]

The moralizing of leisure time and ideals of controlled development and capacity building still informs much of development discourse today and is still being written over the top of local physical cultures.[15] It has come, however, with the realization that "development" as sold to the Global South over the past half-century has not succeeded in reducing the gap between rich and poor nations. Indeed, the chasm has widened. Thus other means for achieving greater capacity and debates about growth versus sustainability have led to culture, environmental stewardship and sport as areas where "development" could best be promoted.

Since 2003, the United Nations (UN) has advocated for sport as a development tool. The UN declaration of 2005 as the Year of Sport and Physical Education provided an official endorsement of sport as a technology that could contribute, among other things, to development, peace, local development, cultural understanding and the achievement of the Millennium Development Goals (MDGs).[16]

Sport for development has been analyzed in different ways from large event impacts and legacy to local contexts and any correlation between the two.[17] For examples in the South African context, see Tomlinson *et al.*'s 2009 book *Development and Dreams*, which explored the likely development legacies of the 2010 World Cup.[18] With UN legitimation and an increasing awareness on the part of the IOC, FIFA, and leading clubs and leagues around the world, sport and international development has mushroomed as an area of both practice and study.

Ambiguity in the relationship between sport and development should, therefore, be examined. As such, "questions about how to understand the relationships between forms of sport, forms of organization, types of social capital and forms of development, or the extent to which such relationships can exist"[19] should be explored. Levermore states that:

> There is clearly potential for sport to be used as a new engine in advancing various dimensions of development, something grasped by a growing number of policy makers. However, more evaluation is required to determine the exact nature of its potential.[20]

The use of football as a development and humanitarian tool has been present for at least three decades.[21] Football can be exploited for various and diverse aims. Many NGOs specifically endorse football as a development tool (examples include: Grassroots Soccer, Streetfootballworld, Play Soccer, and Right to Play). Sport in development has been relevant in peace building (examples include: Football4Peace[22] and PeacePlayers International) and as a tool to fight racism and ease ethnic tensions.[23] Sport development to enhance life skills has also been widely touted.[24] In specific relation to football, studies have investigated the role of coaches in developing life skills among their players.[25] Authors have cautioned, however, that linking sports development with sports mega-events and transnational sporting organizations may not be sustainable and in fact may be detrimental or divert money into showpiece projects that have little use-value to local populations.[26] Two examples should suffice. In St. Lucia, FIFA provided the funding for a new soccer stadium complete with a FIFA-standard field. Unfortunately the stadium is now used as a hospital since it sits on the south of the island near the international airport, but is nearly two hours' drive from the major population centers of the impoverished island. In South Africa, many showpiece soccer initiatives were displayed in the two years leading up to the World Cup and during 2010. These were nearly all located in the metropolitan regions of the three largest cities of Johannesburg, Durban, and Cape Town, areas already receiving the bulk of aid and infrastructural inputs. The rest of the country, by contrast, has fallen further behind those regions, leading to increased in-migration and greater disparities between regions within the country.

Cautionary comments about race and the rush to do sport as "development"

In its current practice at elite professional and mega-event level and as promoted and sold as "development," sport(s) offers little that challenges neoliberal economics and, as operated in the developing world (mostly in what we would call the Global South), promotes a neo-imperialism that perpetuates inequalities generated in the era of imperialism/colonialism.[27] While I am skeptical about the possibility of real change in and through sport, I suggest that there are alternatives whereby sport can promote sustainable futures and challenge the status quo. In building on critiques by others as overviewed by Darnell and by Brian Wilson,[28] I hope to expand debate whereby challenges to the practice of accepted norms such as "Olympism," "development," and "character building" might be decoded and recast particularly in terms of how we view sport pedagogically and how we envisage sport as a vehicle for social and economic "development" in spaces of the Global South and marginalized spaces of the Global North.

My skepticism is largely shaped by the structural forces shaping the global economy. As deindustrialization practices have accelerated over the past 30 years, production has shifted from developed to less developed societies. This process has been explored in detail for the global sporting goods industry by George Sage.[29] Sage demonstrates how low-cost labor and poor working conditions shape an industry that has now become a global system where "they work while we play." Much more research on this topic should be an urgent priority and there is good work being done analyzing the use of migrant workers in international sports.

Playfair 2012, a group that monitored the labor conditions surrounding the London 2012 Olympic Summer Games, found evidence of child labor, poor working and living conditions, poverty wages, and draconian work discipline at the Chinese factories manufacturing pins, badges, and London 2012 mascot dolls. This led to some changes on the part of the London 2012 Organising Committee, though these came late in the day and made little difference to the lives of those producing these prized souvenirs.[30] However, sustained activism can make a difference. United Students Against Sweatshops (USAS) has partnered with Asian workers exploited and then abandoned by Adidas to campaign for their universities to end their athletic sponsorship contracts with the sporting goods giant. As of 20 April 2013, 15 universities had responded to the USAS "Badidas" campaign. Earlier campaigns highlighted sweatshop practices by Nike that violated Indonesian labor laws and some universities also ended their contracts with Nike. As a result, Nike eventually listened and amended some of their practices. These efforts are mere starting points in the campaign to promote health in and through sports and fitness around the world. It is impossible to suggest that sport and physical activity are social goods, if the only social good it serves are middle- and upper-class interests in advanced capitalist societies.[31] The political economy of global sport currently favors the global neoliberal status quo and should be challenged in terms of impact on human rights, anti-racism struggles, and to promote a more equitable world.

Constraints and opportunities

Discourses surrounding the African body remain potent.[32] Through early links to the European-led global imperial project which coincided with the appearance of a sports science at times obsessed with measuring "Other" bodies against the norm of white males, modern sporting organizations contributed significantly to the cultural colonization of the world as achievement sport and capitalism progressed to include nearly every nation on Earth. Eichberg suggests modern sport illustrates "Westernization" and the proliferation of "global cultural experiences, expressions and events," including the Olympic Games, have been homogenizing processes, a process Jules Boycoff calls "Celebration Capitalism" as the world gathers to experience the Olympics or the FIFA World Cup.[33]

Given the history of modern sport and associated physical cultural practices, practices firmly situated within the development of modern industrial and post-industrial capitalism and the supporting political regimes of imperialism and colonialism, what interventions can and should be made by those of us interested in fitness and sport? The first and fundamental principle is that the right to health and to participate in physical activities has to be promoted as a fundamental human right, as has been advocated by the UN and stated by transnational organizations including the European Union. Interjecting our voices into public debates about health care, safety in public space, and promotion of issues that enhance social justice are not only local issues, they are national and global ones. Africa needs to be recast from a place to do projects and where there are bodies to work on, and rather "develop" to a space where cultural exchanges and local knowledge teaches as much to outsiders as outsiders arrive hoping to teach local populations. A new Afrocentric approach is needed, however, whereby local institutions and stakeholders examine needs based on their own worldview rather than the worldview generated in the Global North. Perhaps then the mapping of the African body, as well as its racialization, will indeed be a thing of the past.

Notes

1 An earlier version of this chapter appeared as John Nauright, "On Neoliberal Global Sport and African Bodies," *Critical African Studies* 6, 2/3 (2015), 1–10.
2 K. Manzo, "Development Through Football in Africa: Neoliberal and Postcolonial Models of Community Development," *Geoforum* 43 (2011), 551–60; S. Mchombo, "Sports and Development in Malawi," *Soccer and Society* 7, 2–3 (2006), 318–38; N. Schulendorf, E. Sheery and K. Rowe, "Sport for Development: An Integrated Literature Review," *Journal of Sport Management*, 30 (2016), 22–39.
3 J. Nyerere, *Man and Development* (Oxford: Oxford University Press, 1974), 60.
4 For examples, see S. Darnell, *Sport for Development and Peace: A Critical Sociology* (London: Bloomsbury, 2011); R. Levermore and A. Beascom, *Sport for International Development and Peace* (Basingstoke:

Palgrave, 2009); J. Sugden and J. Wallis, eds., *Football for Peace? The Challenge of Using Sport for Co-Existence in Israel* (Aachen: Meyer & Meyer, 2007); B. Wilson, *Sport and Peace: A Sociological Perspective* (Toronto: Oxford University Press, 2012). In the US domestic urban context, see R. Pitter and D. Andrews, "Serving America's Underserved Youth: Reflections on Sport and Recreation in an Emerging Social Problems Industry," *Quest* 49, 1 (1997), 85–99.

5   For overview examples, see H. Lenskyj, *The Best Olympics Ever? Inside Sydney 2000* (Albany, NY: SUNY Press, 2002); H. Lenskyj, *Olympic Industry Resistance: Challenging Olympic Power and Propaganda* (Albany, NY: SUNY Press, 2008); J. Nauright, "Global Games: Culture, Political Economy, and Sport in the Globalized World of the Twenty-First Century," *Third World Quarterly* 25, 7 (2004), 1325–36.

6   D. Cannadine, *Ornamentalism: How the British Saw Their Empire* (London: Penguin, 2001).

7   C. Shilling, *The Body and Social Theory* (London: Sage, 1993), 57.

8   Z.S. Strother, "Display of the Body Hottentot," in B. Lindfors, ed., *Africans on Stage: Studies in Ethnological Show Business* (Bloomington, IN: University of Indiana, 1999), 37.

9   J. Nauright, "Colonial Manhood and Imperial Race Virility: British Responses to Colonial Rugby Tours," in J. Nauright and T.J.L. Chandler, eds., *Making Men: Rugby and Masculine Identity* (London: Frank Cass, 1996), 121–39.

10 B. Carton and J. Nauright, "'Last Zulu Warrior Standing': Cultural Legacies of Racial Stereotyping and Embodied Enthno-branding in Postcolonial South Africa," *International Journal of the History of Sport* 32, 7 (2015), 876–98; L. Vivanco and R. Gordon, eds., *Tarzan was an Eco-Tourist… and Other Tales in the Anthropology of Adventure* (New York, NY: Berghan Books, 2006).

11 J. Bale, *Imagined Olympians: Body Culture and Colonial Representation in Rwanda* (Minneapolis, MN: University of Minnesota Press, 2002), xvii.

12 Ibid.; also see E. Said, *Orientalism* (New York, NY: Pantheon Books, 1978).

13 D. Booth and J. Nauright, "Embodied Identities: Sport and Race in South Africa," in J. Nauright, A. Cobley, and D. Wiggins, eds., *Beyond C.L.R. James: Race and Ethnicity in Sport* (Fayetteville, AR: University of Arkansas Press), 41–62.

14 A.G. Cobley, *The Rules of the Game: Struggles in Black Recreation and Social Welfare Policy in South Africa* (Westport, CT: Greenwood Press, 1997); P. Martin, *Leisure and Society in Colonial Brazzaville* (Cambridge: Cambridge University Press, 1995).

15 See, T. Couzens, "'Moralizing Leisure Time': The Transatlantic Connection and Black Johannesburg, 1918–1936," in S. Marks and R. Rathbone, eds., *Industrialisation and Social Change in South Africa: African Class Formation, Culture and Consciousness, 1930* (London: Routledge, 1987), 314–37.

16 F. Coalter, "Sport-for-Development: Going Beyond the Boundary?" *Sport in Society* 13, 9 (2010), 1374–91.

17 D.R. Black, "The Ambiguities of Development: Implications for 'Development through Sport,'" *Sport in Society* 13, 1 (2010), 121–9.

18 U. Pillay, R. Tomlinson, and O. Bass, eds., *Development and Dreams: The Urban Legacy of the 2010 World Cup* (Pretoria: Human Sciences Research Council of South Africa, 2009); also see S. Cornelissen, "Crafting Legacies: The Changing Political Economy of Global Sport and the 2010 FIFA World Cup™," *Politikon* 34, 3 (2007), 241–59.

19 Coalter, "Sport-for-Development," 1386.

20 R. Levermore, "Sport: A New Engine of Development?" *Progress in Development Studies* 8, 2 (2008), 189.

21 One can argue that missionary promotion of sports for converts throughout the colonial world in the late nineteenth and twentieth centuries constitutes earlier attempts to use sport for development; however, in the contemporary sense of the term, we see renewed efforts at sports proselytism from the 1970s onward with significant development since the latter 1990s.

22 Football4Peace is an NGO housed at the University of Brighton with partner programs linked to the University of Ulster.

23 See Mchombo, "Sport and Development in Malawi," 320; Sugden and Wallis, *Football for Peace*.

24 M. Jones and D. Lavallee, "Exploring Perceived Life Skills Development and Participation in Sport," *Qualitative Research in Sport and Exercise* 1, 1 (2009), 36–50.

25 D. Gould, K. Collins, L. Lauer, and Y. Chung, "Coaching Life Skills Through Football: A Study of Award Winning High School Coaches," *Journal of Applied Sport Psychology* 19, 1 (2007), 16–37.

26 For example, see A. Giampiccoli, S. Lee, and J. Nauright, "Destination South Africa: Comparing Global Sports Mega Events and Recurring Localized Sports Events in South Africa for Tourism and Economic Development," *Current Issues in Tourism* 16, 3 (2015), 229–48.

27 Also see, Darnell, *Sport for Development and Peace*; S. Darnell, "Playing with Race: *Right to Play* and the Production of Whiteness in 'Development Through Sport,'" *Sport in Society* 10, 4 (2007), 560–79.
28 Wilson, *Sport and Peace*, 150–2.
29 G. Sage, *Globalizing Sport: How Organizations, Corporations and Media are Changing Sport* (Boulder, CO: Paradigm Publishers, 2010).
30 Playfair, *Campaign for a Sweat Free Olympics* (2012), www.playfair2012.org.uk/2012/07/campaign-progress-and-challenges, accessed 26 May 2015.
31 United Students Against Sweatshops, *Victory!* (2013), http://usas.org/2013/04/24/victory-badidas-campaign-forces-adidas-to-respect-indonesian-garment-worker-rights, accessed 23 May 2013.
32 Booth and Nauright, "Embodied Identities"; J. Nauright and T. Magdalinski, "'A Hapless Attempt at Swimming': Media Representations of Eric Moussambani," *Critical Arts: Journal of South–North Cultural and Media Studies* 17, 1/2 (2003), 106–22.
33 H. Eichberg, *Body Cultures: Essays on Sport, Space and Identity*, edited by J. Bale and C. Philo (London: Routledge, 1998); J. Boykoff, *Celebration Capitalism and the Olympic Games* (London: Routledge, 2014).

PART II

Race and ethnicity in sport

Case studies from around the world

10

AOTEAROA/NEW ZEALAND

Geoff Watson, Farah Palmer, and Greg Ryan

Introduction and overview

Sport has been linked to national and ethnic identity in Aotearoa/New Zealand since the second half of the nineteenth century.[1] It has given New Zealand its most recognizable national symbol – a silver fern on a black uniform. It is also linked to dominant narratives central to New Zealand's self-image, notably the notion that New Zealanders are an active, physical people blessed with an environment where sport and recreation are available to all and where anyone can achieve within an apparently egalitarian society.[2] There is a long history of engagement with sport and physical activity among all ethnicities in New Zealand, particularly between Māori (the name generally used to refer to the indigenous people of New Zealand) and Pākehā (the name by which New Zealanders of European/British ancestry are widely known); descendants of the signatories of the bicultural covenant in New Zealand known as the Treaty of Waitangi signed in 1840.[3]

Sport has retained its significance as a marker of race relations ideology as New Zealand society has become more multicultural since the late 1960s. Playing and supporting sport, particularly the national men's rugby team widely known as the All Blacks, is a central part of the pan-ethnic New Zealand identity connoted by the term 'kiwi' or 'kiwi culture' (the kiwi is a flightless bird, native to New Zealand which has become widely recognized as a national symbol).[4] While sport has often been credited with exercising a positive influence in promoting ethnic and pan-ethnic identities, there are more critical perspectives. Sport has been used to promote stereotypes of particular ethnic groups, such as the achievements of Māori and Pacific Island (a pan-ethnic term that refers to people with family and cultural connections to the South Pacific Islands) athletes being denied due recognition by assertions that their success is attributable to their supposedly 'natural' ability in sport.[5] Sport has also been a site of racial abuse, vilification, and discrimination, both on the field and in wider debates about the composition of teams.

This chapter provides an overview of the evolving relationship between sport and ethnicity in Aotearoa/New Zealand. It is divided into five sections, each representing a broad rather than strictly demarcated phase. The first section examines the role of sport in Māori society. The second investigates the role of sport in colonial society, in particular the way it represented an emerging national and bicultural identity. The third section discusses an emerging multiculturalism in sport during the interwar period. The fourth section discusses the increasingly contested nature of sport and biculturalism between 1945 and 1990 and an accompanying ethnic diversification of sport. The final section discusses the relationship between sport and ethnicity during the last quarter-century as New Zealand negotiates its status as a nation with a bicultural heritage and ever-increasing multicultural society.

Ngā Taonga Takaro: sport in Māori society

According to European ethnographer Elsdon Best, Māori people in pre-European times referred to all games and pastimes as 'the arts of pleasure' or *nga mahi a te rehia*.[6] More recently these treasured Māori forms of play and leisure are referred to as '*ngā taonga takaro*' by kaitiaki (guardians) of this type of traditional knowledge, such as Harko Brown.[7] These games and exercises were used as elementary training for battle, and required manual dexterity and agility, as well as calculation skills, mental alertness and the ability to memorize. Harko Brown also acknowledges *ngā taonga takaro* were a key component of the peace-making process between iwi (tribes) and hapū (sub-tribes) by means of regular inter-tribal sports competitions and feasting (hakari) which had a strong spiritual as well as physical element.

Popular games among Māori included wrestling (whatoto, nonoke, mamau), spinning tops (pōtaka tākiri), stick games (tī rākau, poi rākau), darts (teka), canoe races (waka), long-distance running races, knuckle bones (kōruru), hand games (tākaro-ā-ringa), string games (whai), performing arts and dance-related activities (kapa haka, including activities such as haka, waiata-a-ringa, moteatea, and poi), kite flying (manu tukutuku), and stilts (waewae rakau) to name a few.

Brendan Hokowhitu has argued that 'the philosophies underpinning Māori tribal physical activities ... were incomprehensible to European notions of physical activity or sport' because they were often imbued with accompanying narratives or *pūrākau* that passed on significant cultural knowledge regarding cosmology and genealogy (whakapapa) as well as multiple cultural concepts such as revenge (utu), protocol (kawa), integrity (mana tangata), as well as the power and importance of women (mana wahine), family (whanau), and the land (mana whenua).[8] Many cultural customs (tikanga-a-Māori, tikanga-a-iwi) were integrated into these games and pastimes and included spiritual as well as physical elements, but the missionary and colonial influence considered these practices as heathen or barbaric and therefore inappropriate to include in formal colonial institutions such as schools, which often led to their demise and discontinuation among Māori.[9]

Despite these challenges, ngā taonga takaro endured; indeed, they have experienced something of a resurgence. Some Māori games like *ki-o-rahi* (ball game) and *mu torero* (board game) were adopted enthusiastically overseas in elementary schools and universities.[10] There is also a World Indigenous Games, where a team from New Zealand share a number of *ngā taonga takaro* with other indigenous competitors. Today *ngā taonga takaro* are used by sports, health and education providers in mainstream New Zealand society for various outcomes, including cultural rejuvenation and pride, *whanaungatanga* (kinship), health and well-being, and education.[11]

Sport and biculturalism *c.*1835–1914

Between 1835 and 1914 New Zealand changed from an independent land predominantly populated and governed by Māori (only 1 per cent of New Zealand's population were Pākehā in 1840) to a settler colony and later self-governing Dominion of Britain in which Māori comprised approximately 5 per cent of the population.[12] This dramatic transformation was as much cultural as it was demographic. In terms of ethnicity, New Zealand changed from being a place where Māori and Europeans shared some commercial and religious interests, to a self-proclaimed 'Britain of the South Seas' which positioned itself as the most loyal member of the British Empire.[13] This process, which historian James Belich has referred to as 'recolonisation' was driven at a demographic level by mass British emigration to New Zealand, at an economic level by New Zealand directing virtually all of its agricultural exports to Britain, at a political level by repeated professions and demonstrations of loyalty, such as contributing more than 100,000 troops to the Great War, and also through ongoing cultural ties, particularly sporting connections.[14] The Treaty of Waitangi (the Treaty) was an important document in this process, as it paved the way for British recolonization and signalled the eclipse of Māori mana (prestige and power) by British sovereignty.[15] Historically, sport and war were one of the few areas in which Māori entered into the Pākehā domain on a level playing field. Hokowhitu argues Māori were allowed access to these arenas because the representation of the Māori athlete or the Māori warrior did not conflict with the trope of savagery that pervaded the social narrative on Māori men during this time.[16]

The transplantation of British sports reinforced both New Zealand's self-image as a British colony and an emerging narrative of biculturalism. New Zealand's first three decades as a British colony, between 1840 and 1870, coincided with a significant transformation of sport in Britain. Previously viewed largely as a recreation, sport became integral to the schooling of upper-class males, many of whom came to live in colonies such as New Zealand, because it was seen as a useful means of maintaining order in schools and encouraging the virtues of teamwork, honesty, and acceptance of authority.[17] Accordingly, playing sport in New Zealand was favourably viewed as demonstrating that the best features of British life were being practised in the new colony. Sport featured prominently in early celebrations of newly established European settlements.[18] Between 1870 and 1914 a variety of national sporting organizations were established and sport became an integral part of Pākehā culture, developing its own set of rites, rituals, symbols, and stories, many of which were discussed in newspapers and on social occasions. Such rituals were not unique to New Zealand, but they became invested with local meanings. One sport in particular, rugby union, became identified as an exemplar of New Zealand manhood because early international teams, including the 1888–89 Native Team and the 1910 Māori team, performed well in the sport and its unique requirements of physical strength allied to disciplined teamwork and pragmatic innovation closely reflected the idealized self-image of New Zealand society.[19] Yet while sport played an important role in the emergence of a distinct national identity in New Zealand, it also reinforced connections to Britain, reassuring European New Zealanders that culturally they remained closely connected to their ancestral homeland. The generic, implicitly Pākehā, New Zealand identity which emerged between 1890 and 1914 was, it must be noted, one that privileged purportedly male virtues of strength and resilience.[20] Women also played an active role in the pioneering of sport in New Zealand, especially in schools, but women's sport was not linked to cultural and national identity to the same extent.[21]

The participation of Māori in sport was particularly useful to the dominant narrative of race relations because it symbolized the racial equality New Zealand prided itself upon from the time of the signing of the Treaty. Māori participated in European sports from the earliest years of European settlement. They are recorded as playing cricket at mission settlements as early as 1835, and taking part in sporting events at early provincial anniversaries and being keen participants in horse racing. Māori were also active participants in golf and tennis. Kurepo Tareha won the New Zealand Amateur Golf Championship in 1903 and tennis was widely played among Māori communities, particularly on the east coast.[22] But above all it was rugby that was credited with integrating Māori and Pākehā. There is evidence of Māori participation in the game from the early 1870s and of dedicated Māori clubs by the early 1880s.[23] Māori participation in European sports provided evidence of Māori adopting European ways, something which was widely believed to be an inevitable consequence of colonization as Europeans became dominant by virtue of increased population, land acquisition by both purchase and confiscation following conflicts during the 1860s, and the consequent socio-economic marginalization of Māori.[24] Against this background, participation in sport was a symbolic reminder of the continued existence of Māori communities, yet it was also linked to the idea of racial amalgamation which held that in the long term Māori would be brown-skinned Pākehā, albeit a people still regarded as essentially 'primitive' and only selectively admitted to equal citizenship in areas such as sport and the armed forces, which did not threaten the authority of the dominant culture.[25]

Many Māori who became prominent in New Zealand sport attended missionary schools such as Te Aute College, which were established with a view to giving a small number of Māori an education modelled on British public schools so they could become leaders of their people and teach them to adopt European ways of thinking.[26] Sport, however, became a site where, because of their expertise and leadership, Māori could assert some influence. The New Zealand Native rugby team, comprising mainly Māori players, toured Australia and Britain in 1888–89, winning 78 of their 108 matches.[27] The symbolism of a Māori team touring Britain playing a British sport fitted well with notions of the 'civilizing mission' of the British Empire, but also provided a symbol of Māori resilience.[28] Tom Rangiwahia Ellison, who played in the 1888–89 team and captained the first New Zealand team to play under the auspices of the New Zealand Rugby Football Union (NZRFU) in 1893, moved that the Union adopt a black jersey with a silver fern as the uniform for its national team. But while some Māori players occupied prominent roles in New Zealand rugby, the NZRFU were, on the whole, ambivalent towards Māori participation, only assuming formal responsibility for the game in 1910 when they feared Māori might turn to the rival new rugby league code.[29]

Another barrier to Māori involvement in rugby and sport more generally arose from the fact that until the second half of the twentieth century the Māori population was almost entirely rural and frequently located in areas of limited Pākehā population – and therefore in precisely those areas where organized sport was least established. Contrary to a prevailing mythology, the greatest strength and continuity in New Zealand sport has always been in urban areas and especially the four main cities and larger provincial towns. While there were no particular obstacles to informal play or 'scratch' games within local communities, and teams and competitions did emerge in many rural areas, formal competition frequently struggled to survive as distance, limited population, and working conditions drained enthusiasm. Therefore most Māori were not well placed to access the publicly visible sporting infrastructure where players progressed from club to province to national team.[30]

Biculturalism and emerging multiculturalism: 1914–45

The period between 1914 and 1945 saw sport consolidate its position in New Zealand society through expanded provision in schools, shorter working hours, improved communications and other infrastructure, and limited government involvement. But sport, previously a symbol of racial equality and inclusion in New Zealand, also became a visible site of exclusion. In 1919 'Ranji' Wilson, a member of the New Zealand army rugby team and of Anglo-West Indian parentage, stayed on board the ship when the team arrived in Durban out of deference to South

Africa's racial policies.[31] When the South African rugby team played New Zealand Māori during their first tour of New Zealand in 1921, there was considerable controversy when a touring journalist was reported as saying that the South African team were 'disgusted' that white New Zealanders had cheered a Māori team against members of their own race.[32] In 1928 prominent Māori players George Nepia and Jimmy Mill were omitted from the All Black team that toured South Africa. When South Africa toured New Zealand again in 1937, they did not play against a New Zealand Māori team. Prior to their arrival, some members of Te Arawa iwi (tribe), citing the 1921 incident, questioned whether Māori ought to welcome the Springboks. Drawing on a nineteenth-century theory which asserted that Māori derived their ancestry from Aryan peoples in India, prominent Māori Scholar Sir Peter Buck (Te Rangi Hiroa) ironically argued Māori ought to be regarded as better than other coloured peoples.[33]

However, sport remained important in maintaining Māori communal identities at a time when they were economically and politically marginalized. Leaders such as Princes Te Puea Herangi, Apirana Ngata, and T.W. Ratana promoted sports as a means of maintaining connections between Māori, iwi, hapū, and whanau (family). During the 1920s and 1930s a number of Māori sports organizations were formed. Apirana Ngata took a keen interest in tennis and under his leadership the Māori Lawn Tennis Association was formed in 1926. The New Zealand Māori Golf Association was formed in 1931; the Māori Rugby League Board of Control was formed to administer Māori League in 1934; and the Tairawhiti Māori Hockey Federation was also operating by the mid-1930s. Overseas tours by Māori rugby teams, particularly the 1926–27 tour to Europe, also showcased the achievements of Māori on a world stage.[34] Māori sports women also featured internationally. The first international tour of a New Zealand netball team to Australia in 1938, for instance, was captained by Māori woman Meg Matangi.[35]

The interwar period also saw an emerging multiculturalism in New Zealand sport, although it was not framed in that manner at the time. New Zealand hosted its first teams representing Asian, Pacific, and African-American peoples. A football (soccer) team representing Chinese universities toured in 1924; Indian hockey teams toured in 1926, 1935, and 1938; a Fijian women's hockey team toured New Zealand in 1936 and the Fiji rugby team in 1939, and an African-American team from Le Moyne College, widely referred to as the 'Negro Debaters' visited New Zealand in 1938.[36] These teams attracted generally positive media coverage for their performances and the way they conducted themselves. Such a reception was in marked contrast to New Zealand's immigration policies of the period, which actively excluded Chinese and Indian peoples. One possible explanation for this contradiction is that the Chinese and Indian teams were generally drawn from Western-style educational institutions or from 'loyal' sections of these societies such as the army. Moreover, they did not pose any economic threat to society and by welcoming such teams New Zealand could reassert its self-image as a good host. A longer-term legacy of the tours was the formation of Indian Sports Clubs in New Zealand in Wellington in 1935 and Christchurch and Auckland in 1936. These clubs were formed with the purpose of promoting a collective Indian identity while also making connections with the dominant culture, and their formation was a significant achievement given that the Indian population in New Zealand was 1,200 in 1936.

Contested biculturalism and multiculturalism *c.*1945–90

The period between 1945 and 1990 saw both consolidation and contestation within New Zealand sport. On the one hand, existing beliefs were reinforced by significant expansion in sporting facilities and participation evident in the two decades following the Second World War. With most New Zealanders working a 40-hour week and trading restricted on weekends, sports clubs remained the focal point of community identity.[37] The success of athletes such as Peter Snell, Yvette Williams, and Murray Halberg at the Olympic Games; Ruia Morrison making the quarter-finals in Wimbledon tennis in 1957; the All Blacks recording their first-ever series victory against South Africa in 1956; and Edmund Hillary and Tenzing Norgay successfully ascending Mount Everest in 1953 further cemented sport as a marker of New Zealand identity because it gave concrete proof that New Zealanders could distinguish themselves on the world stage.[38] Sporting prowess was linked to a generic national identity rather than Māori and Pākehā specifically, but by virtue of the fact that Māori and Pākehā comprised virtually the entire population it implicitly became a marker of identity for both ethnicities.

Between 1960 and 1990, however, the bi-racial identity embodied by sport became increasingly contested, primarily because of the divisions created by sporting contacts with South Africa, but also because of the increasing questioning of sport by social movements such as second-wave feminism, Māori activism, and some within sport itself. Although there had been further protest against the exclusion of Māori from the 1949 All Blacks team to South Africa, it was not until Māori were excluded from the 1960 tour that there was significant Pākehā opposition, in the form of the Citizens All Black Tour Association, with more than 150,000 people signing a petition calling for the NZRFU to stop the tour if Māori were not included. Although Māori and Pacific Island players were included in the 1970 tour to South Africa, the focus of protest had now changed, with the anti-apartheid movement arguing that all sporting contact with South Africa ought to cease while apartheid was in place because there could be 'no normal sport in an abnormal society'.[39] The withdrawal of more than 20 nations from the 1976 Olympic Games in opposition to the All Blacks 1976 tour of South Africa and the extensive violence that occurred during the 1981 South African tour of New Zealand resulted in a reappraisal of the place of sport, especially rugby, in New Zealand society.[40] Sport was embarrassing, rather than distinguishing New Zealand on the world stage and the contacts Māori formed with indigenous activists and the anti-apartheid movement in opposing sporting ties with South Africa focused their attention on race relations within New Zealand, with many concluding that racism remained a significant problem.[41] It was not until South Africa was excluded from the 1987 Rugby World Cup, which New Zealand hosted and won, that rugby regained its position as a game which united New Zealanders rather than divided them.[42]

The presence of players of identifiably Pacific Island heritage, Joe Stanley and Michael Jones, in the 1987 World Cup rugby team – and Rita Fatialofa and Margaret Matenga in the world champion 1987 netball team – reflected an increasing multiculturalism within New Zealand sport.[43] To some degree, this reflected an increasing Pacific Island population within New Zealand. In 1951 the census recorded 3,624 Polynesians in New Zealand; by 1961 there were 14,340; by 1981 they numbered 94,000; and by 1991 175,000.[44] As the Pacific Island population increased, so too did their prominence in sport, particularly as first- and second-generation immigrants passed through the New Zealand school system where they began to be selected in age-group and then adult representative teams.[45] The Pacific Island communities, which tended to be concentrated in Auckland and Wellington, gravitated towards clubs with a reputation for being welcoming to Pacific Island communities, such as Ponsonby Rugby Club, or the Pacific Island Church netball club in Wellington, which was formed in 1953. By the 1970s, when players such as Bryan Williams and Bernie Fraser were regular selections in the All Blacks, the sporting prowess of Pacific people was being more widely acknowledged. Sporting connections between Pacific people, Pākehā, and Māori were, however, mediated through what Teresa Teaiwa and Sean Mallon refer to as an 'ambivalent kinship'. While recognized in some circles for their sporting ability, they were also criticized for their perceived inability to play the 'patterned' style of game favoured by predominantly Pākehā coaches and selectors. This tension reflected in microcosm the position of Pacific Island peoples within New Zealand society. While they were welcomed as a willing source of factory labour during the 1960s, when the New Zealand economy soured during the early 1970s Pacific Island immigrants who did not hold residency rights, particularly the Tongan community, were the focus of the infamous 'dawn raids' against 'overstayers'.[46]

New Zealand's Asian communities also became more visible in sport. By 1962 the Indian Sports Clubs had formed a New Zealand Indian Sports Association, which oversaw an annual tournament at Queen's Birthday Weekend and organized fixtures for New Zealand Indian representative teams in hockey and cricket. In 1967, Narotam (Tom) Puna became the first Indian selected for a New Zealand cricket team and by the early 1970s Ramesh Patel had represented New Zealand in hockey and Praven Jeram in soccer. By the early 1980s there were four Indian players in the New Zealand men's hockey team, a remarkable achievement given the Indian population numbered 11,244 in 1981.[47] The New Zealand Chinese Association has also run an annual sports tournament from 1948 with the principal aim of promoting and maintaining connections among the Chinese community.[48] The growing involvement of Chinese and Indian communities in sport reflected post-war changes in immigration policies that made it easier for these people to settle in New Zealand. Initially viewed as sojourner communities, they now became settler communities. The Chinese population increased from 4,940 in 1945 to 25,653 in 1986, and their participation in sport reflected their integration into the dominant culture.[49]

Embracing multiculturalism? Sport and the promotion of ethnic and pan-ethnic identities

The period from the 1980s to the early 2010s was one of both continuity and change in the relationship between sport and society in New Zealand. On the one hand, sport has remained central to national identity in New Zealand and the dominant team sports in 1945: rugby union, netball, and cricket have retained their privileged position, despite a complementary trend towards greater participation in individual and unstructured sports and activities.[50] A survey conducted between 2007 and 2008 found that 61.7 per cent of New Zealanders regularly participated in sport, which placed New Zealand third in the world.[51] Since the 'Graham Report' in 2001, successive governments have greatly increased their investment in sport, in part because success in sport is seen as generating a cohesive national identity.[52] On the other hand, New Zealand society has become much more ethnically diverse and the ethnic composition of many of New Zealand's national teams has changed significantly. In 1951 Europeans comprised 93.3 per cent of New Zealanders, Māori 5.96 per cent and 'other' peoples, including Asian and Pacific Peoples 0.74 per cent.[53] By 2013, Europeans were 74.9 per cent of the population, Māori 14.9 per cent, Pacific Peoples 7.4 per cent, and Asians 11.8 per cent.[54] This transformation was disproportionately evident in New Zealand's dominant team sports. By 2001, for example, Māori and Pacific Peoples comprised 56 per cent of players in Super Rugby franchises.[55]

At the grassroots/community level, Māori participation in sport and recreation activities is the highest of all ethnic groups in New Zealand, and Māori are more likely than Pākehā to participate in sport and recreation through regular club competitions (28.3 per cent compared to 22.9 per cent) and short-term organized sports.[56] Māori adults were also more likely than non-Māori to be involved in roles such as coach, referee/official, administrator, or parent helper.[57] The 2013/14 survey conducted by Sport New Zealand revealed that touch rugby (11.7 per cent) and netball (11.3 per cent) were organized sports that made the top ten most popular sport and recreation activities for Māori, while touch rugby (17.7 per cent), netball (14 per cent), volleyball (13.6 per cent), and rugby (13.5 per cent) made the top ten activities for Pacific Peoples surveyed. In some professional sports, such as rugby union, Māori and Pacific Peoples have the highest conversion rates from amateur to professional levels.[58] The number of Māori and Pacific Peoples representing New Zealand at the Olympic and Commonwealth Games was, however, minimal until the inclusion of sports in which Māori and Pacific Peoples are highly involved, such as netball, sevens rugby, basketball, volleyball, and hockey.[59] Eighteen of the 22 players (over 80 per cent) named in the New Zealand women's sevens squad in 2016 (the year of the Rio de Janeiro Olympics), for instance, were of Māori heritage.

Despite the high visibility and engagement of Māori and Pacific Peoples in some organized sports, Māori and Pacific participation at the executive level of sport leadership is limited.[60] In 2011, for instance, only 16.6 per cent of national team/athlete leaders (e.g. coaches, managers, medical staff) were identified as Māori, and only 33 (5.3 per cent) of all national sport organization (NSO) board members were Māori.[61] The limited opportunities for Māori and Pacific Peoples in decision making and leadership roles may also reflect the race-based logic that success of athletes of colour is attributed to innate and instinctive attributes rather than due to the influence of training, discipline, work ethic, and intellect.[62] As a result, opportunities for Māori and Pacific athletes in coaching, governance, and management are limited.

The increasing prominence of Pacific Peoples in representative teams has also been accompanied by racial stereotyping. In Tom Hyde's 1993 *Metro* magazine article, a well-known national netball selector and coach recalled how 'people had always looked at Polynesian players as "one offs". They had no stickability, so people weren't prepared to put their shirts on them.'[63] Interviewees in the same article also stated that Polynesian athletes had 'Polynesian flair', and were 'naturally superior to us in talent ... but they didn't have the discipline' while also asserting they were 'unpredictable and innovative'.[64] The rhetoric surrounding the browning of New Zealand sport since the 1990s conflates Māori and Pacific Peoples together as one group. This occurs despite brown athletes being influenced by diverse cultures (e.g. Samoan, Tongan, Niuean, Māori, Rarotongan, Fijian), tribal groups (e.g. Ngāti Porou, Tūwharetoa, Kai Tahu, Tainui, etc.), levels of assimilation, and cultural knowledge.[65]

Despite evidence that racist stereotypes and attitudes exist at the individual level, any frank or in-depth discussion about racism at the socio-cultural or structural level in New Zealand is met with 'considerable hostility and resistance'.[66] For example, when former All Black Andy Haden claimed in 2010 that a successful rugby franchise had long operated a racially based quota system of three Polynesian players, these comments were immediately dismissed by rugby authorities who re-directed attention away from what presented as institutional racism towards a personalized critique of Haden, who had used the term 'darkies' during the televised interview.[67] Hippolite and Bruce also refer to this scenario to highlight how conversations regarding racism in New Zealand tend to be shut down.[68]

Since the 1980s there has been a surge of Māori-led sport, recreation, and physical activity initiatives that have distinctive cultural elements embedded within them. Some initiatives are built around traditional Māori games and physical activities, while others are cultural adaptations of conventional modern sports and physical activities (e.g. IronMāori, TriMāori). The commonality among them is the use of distinctive Māori cultural elements and identity to mobilize wide Māori interest and support, the reliance on volunteerism and the goodwill of networks and benefactors. Leading Māori development scholar Professor Sir Mason Durie advocated for Māori leadership initiatives to enable Māori to live and advance as Māori and to participate fully as global citizens, while enjoying good health and a high standard of living.[69] He also called for Māori self-determination or *tino rangatiratanga* through 'economic self-sufficiency, social equity, cultural affirmation and political power'.[70] Sport has been used by Māori since the 1980s to advance these aspirations for full citizenship, good health, a high standard of living and self-determination through partnership with the state (Sport New Zealand's He Oranga Poutama programme), education initiatives (schools with a focus on Māori approaches to sport development such as Tū Toa and Manukura), health initiatives (IronMāori and Toi Tangata), a revival of *ngā taonga takaro* (ki-o-rahi, waka ama, kapa haka), as well as through national (Māori Sports Awards), regional (Māori rugby tournaments), and tribal initiatives (Waikato-Tainui Games). *Moving the Māori Nation*, a report prepared in 2013 for the Ministry of Māori Development (Te Puni Kōkiri), argued that sport can be a means to encourage *whānau ora* (family health) and engage *whānau* (family) in *te ao Māori* (the Māori world), in particular *te reo* (Māori language), *tikanga* (Māori culture), *whānaungatanga* (kinship), *manaakitanga* (caring) and *rangatiratanga* (sovereignty).[71] It found Māori-led sport, recreation, and physical activity programmes were achieving positive results across a broad range of outcomes, among whanau (family), hapū (sub-tribes), iwi (tribes), and Māori communities. Indeed, several initiatives are touching the lives of thousands of participants.

One example of the above is Te Timatanga Ararau Trust in Hastings, established in December 2007 to support Māori to make lifestyle changes through increased exercise and improved diet and nutrition. In December 2009, after running several small *hikoi*/fun run events, the Trust led by Heather Skipworth hosted its first Māori-based half-ironman event under the IronMāori brand. The event was designed to encourage *whānaungatanga* (kinship) with team entries, *tamariki* (children) events and a variety of distances provided. The Trust also promoted the benefits of being smoke-, drug-, and alcohol-free at all its events. The event attracted 304 participants (88 per cent Māori) in its first year, 560 (92 per cent Māori) in 2010, and in 2012 the number participating had to be capped at 1,550 for safety and logistical reasons.[72]

Hosting sport mega-events in New Zealand, such as the America's Cup (2000) and the Rugby World Cup (RWC) in 2011, provided opportunities to represent to the world a highly constructed form of national identity that often includes selective representations of indigenous culture and diversity. The significance of rugby union in the symbolic construction of nationhood in New Zealand has been recently acknowledged and researched since the British Lions Tour of New Zealand in 2005 and the hosting of the RWC in 2011.[73] Scholars have noted that Māori imagery was extensively deployed in the promotion of these events, partly because sponsors value the sense of 'authenticity' provided by such promotions as one way of addressing concerns about the increasing commercialism and corporatism evident in rugby union since it became professional in 1995. In his analysis of the 2005 Lions Tour of New Zealand, Mark Falcous suggested a 'boutique' construction of diversity occurred where the prominence and foregrounding of tikanga Māori (Māori culture) was prevalent. This, he suggested, provided a veneer of ethnic inclusiveness in New Zealand that masked underlying racial tensions in New Zealand society.[74]

The *haka*, a pre-match recitation now performed by many New Zealand sporting teams but popularly associated with the All Blacks, has featured prominently in advertising and popular culture. Falcous suggests the pervasive use of haka imagery in tour media was intended to reflect national unity among the All Black players who have Pākehā, Māori, and Pacific Island heritage because it provides the perfect way to reconcile the discourse of biculturalism and that of nationalist unity via rugby simultaneously.[75] Jackson and Hokowhitu also note that the haka, as performed by the All Blacks and other sports teams/athletes is symptomatic of *tikanga Māori* being misappropriated by the NZRFU and sponsors for commercial gain.[76] Hokowhitu notes that when the haka (like other *ngā taonga takaro*) are disembedded from any meaningful Māori framework, it provides an illusion of bicultural unity, multicultural harmony and nationalistic spectacle without addressing the ongoing marginalization of minority groups such as Māori.[77] The haka, along with other Māori imagery/tikanga (moko, facial gestures such as pukana and whatero), also provide corporate sponsors with an exotic cultural spectacle for global consumers, often void of deeper engagement with diversity or indigenous worldviews. As Jackson and Hokowhitu (2002) conclude, new global technologies are both the saviour and enemy of indigenous culture because they seek fresh cultural territory, thus providing opportunities for cultural development, but nothing is sacred.[78]

As New Zealand becomes more culturally diverse, sport and the imagery and practices associated with it are more important for promoting a collective and united identity on the world stage. Māori artefacts and symbolism in particular provide a point of difference as New Zealand tries to distinguish itself from its colonial sibling (Australia) and parent (Britain). An address to the New Zealand Olympic Committee (NZOC) on 19 June 2012, from the Honourable Dr Pita Sharples, then Minister of Māori Affairs, illustrates this:

> New Zealand indigenous Māori culture [is] not something that divides us it is something that brings our entire nation together. Our heritage, our courage, our culture, our ability to unite – many peoples as one: this is our unique edge we have over the rest of the world. This is who we are. This is what a New Zealander is.

The notion that New Zealanders are an active, united, and courageous people, shaped by their rugged terrain, has been further reinforced by recreational sport and adventure tourism. Perhaps the best-known example of this is the Coast to Coast Race, in which competitors run, kayak, and cycle from Kumara on the South Island's west coast to Sumner on the east coast, which has been running since 1983.[79] Although recent in origin, such events echo New Zealand's 'pioneering' heritage, in the way competitors pit themselves against nature. The idea of New Zealand as a natural paradise has been actively promoted in the '100% Pure New Zealand' advertising campaign which highlighted the possibilities of active recreation in New Zealand's outdoors.[80]

New Zealand's Asian communities have also become more prominent in sport. This is in part a reflection of the significant increase in New Zealand's Asian population since immigration regulations were liberalized in 1987. In 1986, there were 20,000 Chinese and 12,000 Indians in New Zealand. By 1996, 173,502 people identified as Asian, 4.8 per cent of the population.[81] In terms of public profile, Asian participation in sport has been particularly evident in golf, two golfers of Korean ancestry – Lydia Ko and Danny Lee – being New Zealand's top-ranked golfers at the time of writing. Lydia Ko's achievement in becoming the number-one ranked in women's golf in February 2015 was widely praised. Although their achievements resulted in some positive coverage for New Zealand's Korean community, such recognition could be quickly withdrawn, as evidenced by the criticism Ko received when she changed coaches shortly after turning professional.[82] Their experiences reinforce the arguments of scholars such as Brendan Hokowhitu that achievement in sport has an, at best, limited effect in influencing the ways ethnic minorities are perceived by the dominant culture. New Zealand's Asian communities are, however, becoming more prominent in community sport, particularly in Auckland where they comprised 23 per cent of the population in 2013. A 2009 report on the sporting participation of immigrants and ethnic minorities in Auckland recorded that table tennis and badminton have seen significant growth in participation from Asian communities, one regional sports organization's table tennis membership being 90 per cent Asian, while another recorded an increase in the Asian proportion of its membership from 25 per cent in 1999 to two-thirds of its 900 members.[83]

Conclusion

Sport has been closely linked to ethnic and national identity in New Zealand. With respect to race relations, it symbolized a bicultural covenant from the late nineteenth century until at least the middle of the twentieth century, before arriving at its present position as a perceived unifier of New Zealand's increasingly multicultural society. Rugby Union, the code perceived as New Zealand's national sport, has played a key role in generating symbols, practices, and memories which have become embedded in New Zealand identity, to the extent that supporting the All Blacks is widely seen as a core part of being a 'kiwi', the pan-ethnic term commonly used to identify New Zealanders as a people. As this chapter has hopefully demonstrated, however, the role of sport in shaping ethnic identity extends well beyond rugby union. It has been an important agent in shaping ethnic and gender identities in New Zealand. The influence of sport resonates well beyond what happens on the field. This is partly because New Zealanders have chosen to invest themselves emotionally in sport and attribute particular values and characteristics to sporting teams, and partly because sport has been actively supported by political, religious, media, and tribal leaders. Sometimes, albeit more by accident than design, sport has challenged dominant values about race relations in New Zealand, particularly in the case of sporting contacts with South Africa. Sport has proven to be a flexible agent in generating national and community identities. While sport has been most commonly used to assert a unified New Zealand identity, it has also provided spaces in which ethnic and gender minorities have been able to express their identities. In many respects it has had a positive role in promoting understanding and positive relations among and between ethnic groups, but there are still issues of racism that need to be acknowledged and explored.

Notes

1 See, for example, Keith Sinclair, *A Destiny Apart: New Zealand's Search for National Identity* (Wellington: Allen and Unwin, 1986), 143–55; Ron Palenski, *The Making of New Zealanders* (Auckland: Auckland University Press, 2012), 241–301.
2 Government of New Zealand, *New Zealand Official Year-Book 1947–49* (Wellington: Government Printer, 1950), 118.
3 Both of these terms are contested. The validity of using 'Māori' as an appellation for the indigenous people of New Zealand has been questioned by some on the grounds that prior to European contact 'Māori' simply meant ordinary and was not used by Māori in reference to themselves. Māori identified with their tribal grouping, rather than with a collective Māori identity. Similarly, some New Zealanders of European ancestry object to the term 'Pākehā' because they believe it has a pejorative connotation. Brendan Hokowhitu, 'Rugby and Tino Rangatiratanga: Early Māori Rugby and the Formation of "Traditional" Māori Masculinity', *Sporting Traditions* 21, 2 (2005), 76–8; Claudia Bell, *Inventing New Zealand: Everyday Myths of Pakeha Identity* (Auckland: Penguin, 1996), 26–7.
4 Bell, *Inventing New Zealand*, 3–27, 179–81.
5 Brendan Hokowhitu, '"Physical Beings": Stereotypes, Sport and the "Physical Education" of New Zealand Maori', *Sport in Society* 6, 2–3 (2003), 192–218; Brendan Hokowhitu, 'Tackling Maori Masculinity: A Colonial Genealogy of Savagery and Sport', *The Contemporary Pacific* 2 (2004), 259–84.
6 Elsdon Best, *Games and Pastimes of the Maori: An Account of the Various Exercises, Games and Pastimes of the Natives of New Zealand, as Practised in Former Times; Including Some Information Concerning Their Vocal and Instrumental Music* (Wellington: Whitcombe and Tombs, 1925), 1.
7 Harko Brown, *Ngā Taonga Takaro: Maori Sports and Games* (Auckland: Penguin, 2008).
8 Brendan Hokowhitu, 'Authenticating Māori Physicality: Translations of "Games" and "Pastimes" by Early Travellers and Missionaries to New Zealand', *International Journal of the History of Sport* 25, 10 (2008), 1356.
9 Brown, *Ngā Taonga Takaro*, 9.
10 Ibid., 104–5.

11   Kate McKegg, Nan Wehipeihana, Kataraina Pipi, and Veronica Thompson, *He Oranga Poutama: What We Have Learned: A Report on the Developmental Evaluation of He Oranga Poutama* (Wellington: Sport New Zealand, 2013).

12   J.V.T. Baker, 'Population', in A.H. McLintock, ed., *An Encyclopaedia of New Zealand* (Wellington: Government Printer, 1966), 821–33.

13   See, for example, *Wanganui Herald*, 13 May 1869, 2; *New Zealand Herald*, 22 October 1892, 2; *Star*, 14 December 1880, 2.

14   James Belich, *Paradise Reforged: A History of the New Zealanders from the 1880s to the Year 2000* (Auckland: Allen Lane, 2001), 29–30.

15   Ranginui Walker, *Ka Whawhai Tonu Mātou: Struggle Without End* (Auckland: Penguin, 2004), 90–7.

16   Malcolm MacLean, 'Maori Rugby and Masculinity in New Zealand', in T.J.L. Chandler and J. Nauright, eds, *Making the Rugby World: Race, Gender, Commerce* (London: Frank Cass, 1999), 1–26.

17   Richard Holt, *Sport and the British* (London: Oxford University Press, 1989), 74–134.

18   In 1852, New Zealand was formally divided into six provinces: Auckland, Taranaki, Wellington, Nelson, Canterbury, and Otago, each of which were based around early centres of European settlement and had their own government. After the provincial governments were abolished in 1876, sport was the principal expression by which their identities were maintained. Geoff Vincent, 'To Uphold the Honour of the Province', in Greg Ryan, ed., *Tackling Rugby Myths: Rugby and New Zealand Society 1854–2004* (Dunedin: Otago University Press, 2005), 13–30.

19   Jock Phillips, *A Man's Country? The Image of the Pakeha Male* (Auckland: Penguin, 1987), 82–130.

20   Keith Sinclair, *The Native Born: The Origins of New Zealand Nationalism. Massey Memorial Lecture* (Palmerston North: Massey University, 1986), 11–12.

21   Scott Crawford, 'An Emancipation of Sorts: Recreational and Sporting Opportunities for Women in 19th Century Colonial New Zealand', *Canadian Journal of the History of Sport* 16 (1985), 38–56; Scott A.G.M. Crawford, 'Recreational and Sporting Opportunities for Women in a Remote Colonial Setting', in J.A. Mangan and R.A. Park, eds, *From 'Fair Sex' to Feminism: Sport and the Socialization of Women in the Industrial and Post-Industrial Eras* (London: Frank Cass, 1987), 161–81; John Nauright and Jayne Broomhall, '"A Woman's Game": The Development of Netball and a Female Sporting Culture in New Zealand, 1906–70', *International Journal of the History of Sport* 11, 3 (1994), 387–407; Shona Thompson, 'Challenging the Hegemony: New Zealand Women's Opposition to Rugby and the Reproduction of a Capitalist Patriarchy', *International Review for Sociology of Sport* 23, 3 (1988), 205–11.

22   G.M. Kelly, *Golf in New Zealand: A Centennial History* (Wellington: New Zealand Golf Association, 1971), 238. Aotearoa Māori Tennis Association, *A History of Māori Tennis: He hītori o te tēnehi Māori* (Auckland: Aotearoa Māori Tennis Association, 2006).

23   See, for example, Terry McLean, *All Blacks Come Back: Terry McLean Looks at New Zealand and World Rugby* (Wellington: A.H. and A.W. Reed, 1975), 15; Michael King, *Penguin History of New Zealand* (Auckland: Penguin, 2003), 386–8.

24   James Belich, *Making Peoples: A History of the New Zealanders from Polynesian Settlement until the End of the Nineteenth Century* (Auckland: Allen Lane, 1996), 247–72.

25   Brendan Hokowhitu, 'Physical Beings'.

26   Greg Ryan, 'The Paradox of Maori Rugby', in G. Ryan, ed., *Tackling Rugby Myths: Rugby and New Zealand Society 1854–2004* (Dunedin: Otago University Press, 2005), 89–103.

27   Greg Ryan, *Forerunners of the All Blacks: The 1888–89 Native Team in Britain, Australia and New Zealand* (Christchurch: Canterbury University Press, 1993).

28   Brendan Hokowhitu, 'Rugby and Tino Rangatiratanga', 86–91.

29   Ryan, 'The Paradox of Maori Rugby', 92–4.

30   Ibid., 91–2.

31   Doug Booth, *The Race Game: Sport and Politics in South Africa* (London: Frank Cass, 1998), 23.

32   For more on this, see David R. Black and John Nauright, *Rugby and the South African Nation* (Manchester: Manchester University Press, 1998).

33   Greg Ryan, 'Anthropological Football', in G. Ryan, ed., *Tackling Rugby Myths: Rugby and New Zealand Society 1854–2004* (Dunedin: Otago University Press, 2005), 105–22.

34   Malcolm Mulholland, *Beneath the Maori Moon* (Wellington: Huia, 2009), 44–62.

35   Nauright and Broomhall, 'A Woman's Game', 401.

36   Geoff Watson, 'Gentlemen Both On and Off the Field: The 1924 Chinese Universities Soccer Team in New Zealand', *New Zealand Journal of Asian Studies* 13, 2 (2011), 1–17; Geoff Watson, 'Affirming

Indian Identities? An Analysis of Imperial Rhetoric and Orientalism in the Tours of Indian Hockey Teams to New Zealand in 1926, 1935 and 1938', *Sporting Traditions* 21 (2005), 119–40.

37 Charlotte Macdonald, 'Sporting Spaces', in Giselle Byrnes, ed., *The New Oxford History of New Zealand* (Melbourne: Oxford University Press, 2009), 284–90.

38 For example, Ruia Morrison, a tennis player of Māori ancestry who made the quarter finals at Wimbledon in 1957, was described by reporters as being an athlete with a charming personality who displayed grace, speed, and agility. She was also considered a great advertisement for New Zealand. Terry McLean, *Silver Fern: 150 Years of New Zealand Sport* (Auckland: Moa, 1990); Michael Romanos, 'Ruia Morrison', *Tū Tangata* 30, (1986), 46–8. Mark Taylor wrote that her 'cool temperament and infectious charm made her almost as popular as entertainer cousin Howard Morrison': Mark Taylor, *High Flying Kiwis: 100 Heroes of New Zealand* (Auckland: Sporting Press, 1988), 129.

39 Booth, *The Race Game*, 6.

40 Trevor Richards, *Dancing on our Bones: New Zealand, South Africa, Rugby and Racism* (Wellington: Bridget Williams, 1999); John Nauright, '"Like Fleas on a Dog": New Zealand and Emerging Protest Against South African sport, 1965–74', *Sporting Traditions* 10, 1 (1993), 54–77.

41 Donna Awatere, *Maori Sovereignty* (Auckland: Broadsheet, 1984).

42 Alex Veysey, Gary Caffell, and Ron Palenski, *Lochore: An Authorised Biography* (Auckland: Hodder Moa Beckett, 1997), 230–1.

43 Pacific Peoples in New Zealand are represented by at least 13 distinct languages and cultural groups. The Pacific population includes people born in the Pacific Islands and in New Zealand. The many Pacific ethnicities are represented primarily by Samoan, Cook Islands, Tongan, Niuean, Fijian, and Tokelauan groups, with smaller numbers from Tuvalu, Kiribati, Papua New Guinea, Vanuatu, the Solomon Islands, and the small island states of Micronesia.

44 Tapu Misa, 'The Pacific Comes to Auckland', *New Zealand Herald*, 27 August 2010, www.nzherald.co.nz/nz/news/article.cfm?c_id=1&objectid=10667079, accessed 20 November 2015.

45 Jacqueline Leckie has noted the importance of schools in promoting the participation of sport among the Indian community and her observation is relevant to other ethnic minorities. Jacqueline Leckie, *Indian Settlers: The Story of a New Zealand South Asian Community* (Dunedin: Otago University Press, 2007), 123, 127.

46 Teresia Teaiwa and Sean Mallon, 'Ambivalent Kinships? Pacific People in New Zealand', in James Liu, ed., *New Zealand Identities: Departures and Destinations* (Wellington: Victoria University Press, 2005), 207–18.

47 Geoff Watson, *Sporting Foundations of New Zealand Indians: A Fifty Year History of the New Zealand Indian Sports Association* (Wellington: New Zealand Indian Sports Association, 2012), 61, 63.

48 David Fung, *Turning Stone into Jade: The History of the New Zealand Chinese Association* (Wellington: New Zealand Chinese Association, 2014), 130–6.

49 Te Ara The Encyclopedia of New Zealand, *Settler and Migrant Peoples of New Zealand* (Wellington: David Bateman, 2006), 109, 167. Fung, *Turning Stone into Jade*, 27.

50 Alec Astle, 'Sport Development: Plan, Programme and Practice – A Case Study of the Planned Intervention by New Zealand Cricket into Cricket in New Zealand', unpublished PhD Thesis, Massey University, 2014, 85–8.

51 Brad Humphreys, Katerina Maresova, and Jane Ruseski, *National Sport Policy, Sporting Success, and Individual Sport Participation: An International Comparison* (Public Choice Society, 2010), cited in Paul Christesen, *Sport and Democracy in the Ancient and Modern Worlds* (New York, NY: Cambridge University Press, 2012), 112.

52 Paul Dalziel, *Valuing Sport and Recreation in New Zealand* (Lincoln: AERU Research Unit, Lincoln University, 2011), http://nzae.org.nz/wp-content/uploads/2011/Session2/25_Dalziel.pdf, accessed 3 March 2016.

53 New Zealand Government, *Census, 1951* (Wellington: Government Printer, 1956), Vol. 8, 130.

54 Statistics New Zealand, *2013 Census: QuickStats About National Highlights* (Wellington: Statistics New Zealand, 2013). The trend towards ethnic diversification was particularly marked in Auckland, New Zealand's largest city, with 1.4 million people in 2013, where in 2013 Europeans comprised 59.3 per cent; Māori 10.7 per cent; Pacific Peoples 14.6 per cent; Asian 23.1 per cent, and Middle Eastern, Latin American, and African 1.9 per cent: www.stats.govt.nz/Census/2013-census/profile-and-summary-reports/quickstats-about-a-place.aspx?request_value=13170&tabname=Culturaldiversity, accessed 2 March 2016.

55 John Matheson, 'What's the White Answer?', *NZ Rugby World* 47, (2001) 20–38.

56 Sport New Zealand, *Sport and Active Research in the Lives of New Zealand Adults: 2013/2014 Active New Zealand Survey Results* (Wellington: Sport New Zealand, 2015).

57 Te Puni Kōkiri, *Ngā Māori i ngā mahi tākaro: Māori in Sport and Active Leisure. Fact Sheet 25* (Wellington: Te Puni Kōkiri, 2006).

58 Te Puni Kōkiri, *Te Māori i te whutupōro: Māori in Rugby. Fact Sheet 23* (Wellington: Te Puni Kōkiri, 2005). Email from NZRFU to Farah Palmer, 2014.

59 H. McGregor and M. McMath, 'Leisure: A Maori and Mangaian Perspective', in H.C. Perkins and G. Cushman, eds, *Leisure, Recreation and Tourism* (Auckland: Longman Paul, 1993), 44–57. Bevan Erueti and Farah Palmer, 'Te Whariki Tuakiri (The Identity Mat): Māori Elite Athletes and the Expression of Ethno-Cultural Identity in Global Sport', *Sport in Society: Cultures, Commerce, Media, Politics* 17, 8 (2014), 1061–75.

60 H.R. Hippolite, 'Towards an Equal Playing Field: Māori Women in Sport', *MAI Review: Intern Research Report* 1 (2008), 1–12; Ryan Holland, 'Governance of New Zealand National Sport Organisations: Pasifika and Māori Voices', unpublished PhD thesis, Massey University, 2012.

61 Holland, 'Governance of New Zealand National Sport Organisations', 238, 325–6.

62 Hokowhitu, 'Physical Beings'.

63 Tom Hyde, 'White Men Can't Jump: The Polynesianisation of Sport', *Metro*, September 1993, 67.

64 Hyde, 'White Men Can't Jump', 68.

65 P. Hirini and R. Flett, 'Aspects of the Māori All Black Experience: The Value of Cultural Capital in the new Professional Era', *He Pukenga Kōrero* 5, 1 (1999), 18–24.

66 R. Consedine and J. Consedine, *Healing our History: The Challenge of the Treaty of Waitangi*, 2nd edition (Auckland: Penguin Books, 2005), 158.

67 Tracy Watkins, 'Haden Saved by Holmes' Cheeky Darkie', www.stuff.co.nz, 31 May 2010, www.stuff.co.nz/national/3759664/Haden-saved-by-Holmes-cheeky-darkie, accessed 20 September 2011.

68 H.R. Hippolite and T. Bruce, 'Speaking the Unspoken: Racism, Sport and Māori', *Cosmopolitan Civil Societies Journal* 2, 2 (2010), 31.

69 Mason Durie, 'A Framework for Considering Māori Educational Advancement', a paper prepared for *Hui Taumata Mātauranga: Māori Education Summit*, 23–25 February 2001, Turangi and Taupo, Palmerston North, Massey University, 2001.

70 Mason Durie, *Whaiora, Māori Health Development* (Victoria: Oxford University Press, 1998), 239.

71 D. Goodwin, K. McKegg, L. Were, and J. Mika, *Moving the Māori Nation: Final Report Prepared for Te Puni Kōkiri by Tuakana Teina Collective* (Wellington: Te Puni Kōkiri, 2013).

72 Anon, 'Takitimu. Ironmāori: Iron Futures', *Kōkiri-Takurua*, Winter 2013, 22.

73 Toni Bruce, '(Not) a Stadium of Four Million: Speaking Back to Dominant Discourses of the Rugby World Cup in New Zealand', *Sport in Society: Cultures, Commerce, Media, Politics* 16, 7 (2013), 899–911; Mark Falcous, 'The Decolonizing of National Imaginary: Promotional Media Constructions During the 2005 Lions Tour of Aotearoa New Zealand', *Journal of Sport and Social Issues* 31 (2007), 374–93; Brendan Hokowhitu and Jay Scherer, 'The Māori All Blacks and the Decentering of the White Subject: Hyperrace, Sport, and the Cultural Logic of Late Capitalism', *Sociology of Sport Journal* 25, 2 (2008), 243–62.

74 Falcous, 'The Decolonizing National Imaginary', 377–90.

75 Ibid., 382.

76 S.J. Jackson and B. Hokowhitu, 'Sport, Tribes, and Technology: The New Zealand All Blacks Haka and the Politics of Identity', *Journal of Sport & Social Issues*, 26, 2 (2002), 125–39.

77 Hokowhitu, 'Tackling Maori Masculinity'.

78 Jackson and Hokowhitu, 'Sport, Tribes, and Technology'.

79 Bob McKerrow and John Woods, *Coast to Coast: The Great New Zealand Race* (Christchurch: Shoal Bay Press, 1994).

80 Margaret McClure, *The Wonder Country: Making New Zealand Tourism* (Auckland: Auckland University Press, 2004), 269–91.

81 Statistics New Zealand, *New Zealand Now, Peoples and Places*, Series Two (Wellington: Statistics New Zealand, 1997), 37. www2.stats.govt.nz/domino/external/pasfull/pasfull.nsf/84bf91b1a7b5d7204c256809000460a4/4c2567ef00247c6acc256b03000936c4/$FILE/PEOPLEAN.PDF, accessed 15 December 2010.

82 See, for example, Kris Shannon, 'Golf: Lydia Ko's Coach Change Unfortunate But Inevitable', *New Zealand Herald*, 23 December 2013; Emily Kay, 'Steve Williams Calls Lydia Ko's Decision to Dump Long-time Coach "Unethical", Career Threatening', 23 December 2013, www.sbnation.com/

golf/2013/12/23/5238430/lydia-ko-fires-coach-steve-williams-responds, accessed 3 February 2015. Lydia Ko was also criticized for continuing to receive funding from Sport New Zealand after turning professional. In May 2014 she indicated she would not seek continued funding from Sport New Zealand. *New Zealand Herald*, 'Golf: Ko Rocked by Backlash', 13 April 2014; *New Zealand Herald*, 'Golf: Ko Turns Down Funding', 9 May 2014.

83 Paul Spoonley and Catherine Taiapa, *Sport and Cultural Diversity: Responding to the Sports and Leisure Needs of Immigrants and Ethnic Minorities in Auckland* (Auckland: Massey University, 2009), 27, 32, 38–9. The 2013/14 Active Recreation Survey found that 14.9 per cent of Asians participated in badminton. Sport New Zealand, *Sport and Recreation in the Lives of New Zealand Adults: 2013–2014 Active New Zealand Survey Results* (Wellington: Sport New Zealand, 2015), 27.

11

AUSTRALIA

Daryl Adair

Australia provides a fascinating context for discussion about the intersection among race, ethnicity, and sport. The Anglo-Celtic games ethic was part of the cultural baggage of colonisers who, whether as convicts or free settlers, annexed what was previously Aboriginal land. When Australia became a federated nation in 1901, parliament henceforth instituted the 'White Australia Policy' (WAP); this had the intent of further isolating Indigenous peoples and curtailing the immigration of non-whites. Little surprise, then, that for much of Australian history the Anglo-Celtic games ethic was more exclusive than inclusive.[1]

Fast-forward to the twenty-first century and Australian public policy pertaining to Indigenous communities and ethnic minorities has hallmarks of liberal intent. First, the Commonwealth government is committed to the 'Closing the Gap' initiative, which aims to reduce Indigenous disadvantage in a host of socioeconomic areas.[2] Second, since the 1970s the government has endorsed the policy of multiculturalism; this now involves a robust intake of skilled, economically self-sufficient migrants from various countries.[3] On the face of it, therefore, Australia has evolved into a nation that is proactive about Indigenous well-being; it has also discarded the ethno-racial exclusivity of the WAP. Yet, while there has been change, substantial problems and challenges remain: both Aboriginality and multiculturalism are lightning rods to political divides in Australia.[4] In the midst of this imbroglio, how does twenty-first-century sport provide opportunities and deal with obstacles around cultural diversity and community engagement?

This chapter provides a brief overview of public policies relevant to Aboriginal and other non-white groups, as well as the position of ethnic minority groups in a continent that, in the wake of colonial annexation, became dominated by Anglo-Celtic peoples. The chapter begins with a historical overview of inclusion, marginalisation, or exclusion in colonial society and then reflects on Aboriginality and multiculturalism in Australia in recent decades. This narrative is interweaved with discussion about the place of sport, past and present. Sport has, after all, been one of the defining cultural attributes of Australia.[5] But has it been for people of colour and those of non-English speaking backgrounds?

Indigenous subjugation

Aborigines and Torres Strait Islanders, the Indigenous peoples of Australia, have cultures that extend over 40,000 years. In 1788, when Europeans began to annex what explorers called *Terra Australis*, there were around 500 distinct language dialects and a vast array of clan groups.[6] Aboriginal people hunted, fished, and traded with each other. They had traditional games requiring dexterity and athleticism.[7] Sometimes the clan groups fought. But all of them lived in harmony with the land and were exemplary custodians.[8]

From the late eighteenth century, however, the traditional way of Aboriginal life was eroded by colonial annexation of land, frontier violence, and the spread of foreign diseases. The oppression of Aborigines was accelerated during the nineteenth century by the imposition of laws and practices that subjugated and ostracised the original inhabitants, who attempted to resist these incursions.[9] The British Colonial Office called for 'protection' of Aborigines, but many of the settlers had genocidal intentions. By the mid-nineteenth century the colonies had been granted self-government; they deemed Aborigines to be a 'problem' and swiftly developed policies to promote separation. Many Aboriginal people were institutionalised on government reserves or Christian missions – almost always in rural or remote parts of the country, out of public sight and mind.[10] Indigenous people were none the less under local surveillance; their movements were curtailed as was their cohabitation. So-called 'mixed race' relationships were of particular concern to colonial authorities; coloured offspring provided a further complication to their efforts to keep the races apart.[11]

Because of this diminution of Aboriginal culture, Indigenous sports and games began to lose their functional relevance. Concurrently, Aboriginal confinement on reserves and missions introduced Indigenous people to the language, religion, and customs of Britain and Ireland. That process of colonial acculturation included male-focused sport – most notably cricket and boxing – as a means of instilling in Aboriginal boys and men agreement on rules and respect for the decisions of those in authority.[12] It seems remarkable, at first glance, that the first cricket team from Australia to tour England (1868) consisted almost entirely of Aborigines. However, this was an entrepreneurial initiative on the part of non-Indigenous sponsors and management, who saw an opportunity to draw big crowds and revenue for themselves from a series of exhibitions abroad – involving both cricket and displays of Indigenous physical culture. The Aboriginal cricketers performed ably, winning as many games as they lost.[13] However, there were no further Aboriginal cricket ventures abroad. During the 1870s colonial governments began to impose laws by which to officially distance Aborigines from white society. Colonial policies had become more punitive, moving from 'protection' via geographic isolation to 'segregation' via subjugated status. Racially specific measures included restrictions on Aboriginal freedom of movement outside of reserves, outlawing of mixed-race marriages, and territorial segregation of races – black, 'half-caste', and white.[14]

Immigration control

The Australian colonies had begun as settlements for convicts; only later did free settlers outnumber felons.[15] Discovery of gold was a catalyst for change. The gold rushes of the mid-nineteenth century were a stimulus to economic immigrants from places as varied as the USA and East Asia.[16] Among this cohort, Chinese arrivals were significant. By the late 1850s/early 1860s, Chinese men constituted nearly 20 per cent of all males in Victoria (though only 4.5 per cent of the colony's total population, since there were just eight Chinese females compared with nearly 25,000 Chinese males).[17] The Chinese had an ambivalent place on gold fields. They were reviled by whites as economic competitors and, in many cases, labelled as racial 'vermin'; yet Chinese entrepreneurs provided services that some locals appreciated, most notably illicit gaming houses. Both European and Chinese patrons could be found among the throngs of gamblers, since in houses of chance the colour of one's money was more important than the colour of one's skin. The Chinese were also active in colonial horse racing, not only as gamblers, but as owners of horse flesh.[18]

The Intercolonial Premiers' conferences of 1880–88 discussed a need for uniform legislation in terms of non-white immigration. By 1888 each of the colonies had agreed to exclude Chinese immigrants, though Queensland successfully pleaded a case to continue importing Pacific Islander labourers (for the sugar industry), but their overall numbers were to be strictly limited by Act of Parliament. Hence, there was now consensus to exclude virtually all non-white immigrants and to refuse British citizenship to non-white residents.[19] As will be seen, the WAP was fundamental to the vision for a newly federated Commonwealth of Australia, inaugurated in 1901.

Fortifying whiteness

By the turn of the twentieth century it was presumed by authorities that Aborigines were a 'dying race'. This view did not simply stem from an inane interpretation of divine providence or social Darwinism; it was reflected in the actions of government. State-sanctioned policies allowed the removal of Aboriginal children from their parents and relocation with white families.[20] As Phillip Knightley has described it: 'White welfare officers, often supported by police, would descend on Aboriginal camps, round up all the children ... bundle them into trucks and take them away. If their parents protested they were held at bay by police.'[21] These were deliberate efforts, under the guise of child welfare, to try to eliminate new generations of Aboriginal families.

Given the substantial difficulties for Aboriginal people in the wake of European annexation and the exercise of colonial authority in the interests of white supremacy, it is difficult to contemplate Indigenous engagement in sport as equals.[22] Historian Colin Tatz is the ideal guide: for decades he has surveyed discrimination against Aboriginal people in Australian sport, past and present.[23] Too often, he argues, sport has been a vehicle through which racial prejudice has thrived. For example, in the early 1900s the Queensland Amateur Athletics Association tried to ban all Aborigines from taking part in its competitions by complaining 'that they either "lacked moral character", "had insufficient intelligence" or "couldn't resist white vice"'. Thankfully, Tatz concludes, these 'appalling excuses were rejected by the national athletics body'.[24] However, the Queensland Amateur Athletics Association responded defiantly by declaring that all Aboriginal runners would now be classed as professionals, and were thus made ineligible to race under the banner of an amateur organisation.[25]

Racist opposition to Aboriginal sportsmen could also have been a result of their athletic ability. Matthew Stephen's research is replete with examples of this. When an Aboriginal athlete won the Pine Creek Handicap in the Northern Territory in 1895, the organisers made the ruling that 'no Aborigines or other coloured races be allowed to compete in European events'.[26] Australian Rules football, played locally in Darwin from 1916, featured a similar scenario. Aborigines and non-white migrants, such as the Chinese, established a team for all-comers, Vesteys, which dominated the Northern Territory Football League (NTFL) in the 1920s. However, in 1926 the white-administered NTFL changed its constitution to exclude non-white players. A colour bar was thus put into effect: only after the Second World War was Darwin's football league again fully integrated.[27]

Blurring of colours

The prospect of denying Aboriginality suited the politicians who, in 1901, proclaimed an Australian nation. The Constitution failed to mention Indigenous people, and one of the first pieces of legislation to pass the Federal Parliament was the WAP.[28] The prime focus of this law was to dissuade people of 'colour' and non-English-speaking immigrants from seeking residency in Australia. Short-term visitors could, with the support of a local sponsor and the consent of immigration authorities, be provided with an 'exemption certificate' that temporarily overlooked their 'alien' or 'coloured' status.[29] This loophole allowed occasional visits by non-white, 'foreign' athletes. Notwithstanding the racial separation underpinning the WAP, local sport fans typically flocked to see the skills and 'exotic' appearance of these performers. For example, the ubiquitous boxing entrepreneur Jimmy Sharman imported black pugilists from overseas – principally Americans and Pacific Islanders – to complement his rolling troupe of Aboriginal fighters. Boxing historian Peter Corris writes that 'race and colour played a large part in Sharman's approach' to promoting fights to white contestants, challenging them to 'measure up'. Paradoxically, the wily promoter was able to claim no colour discrimination in his boxing tents: 'black fought black, white fought white and white fought black'.[30]

Not surprisingly, there were differences of opinion and reaction to the participation of non-white and/or non-English-speaking athlete visitors in Australia. African-American boxer Jack Johnson was admired for his boxing prowess, but hated by many for defeating a white (Canadian) title holder (Tommy Burns) in Sydney in 1908.[31] He was a controversial figure who defiantly broke the so-called 'colour bar' in American boxing through his defeat of the white champion.[32] Yet only two years earlier, African-American cyclist Marshall 'Major' Taylor had beaten all comers in Sydney and was widely coveted by local sport fans. He was a charming figure who, despite suffering rough-house tactics from cycling opponents, was dignified in victory or defeat, not 'rocking the boat'.[33]

While Australia has a reputation for great beaches, there were conservative ideas about bathing in public, and thus limited aquatic skill sets among locals. Intriguingly, it was Tommy Tana, a dark-skinned visitor from the Marshall Islands, who inspired Manly beachgoers to try to emulate his feats of body-surfing. Australians were so taken with this new pastime that it become central to a local campaign which, by 1907, helped to overturn ultra-conservative laws that deemed bathing in the surf during daylight hours as indecent and hence illegal.[34] Subsequently, Alick Wickham, a Solomon Islander in Australia, became a renowned exponent of the overarm 'crawl' stroke, which eventually became famous.[35] The physical prowess of these non-Indigenous black men was not only observed, it was emulated. At a time when Aborigines were either barred or marginalised from public swimming pools (most notably in rural areas), another black-skinned athlete, the Hawaiian Duke Kahanamoku, was given special dispensation by the New South Wales Swimming Association to officially compete in local championships. His status as an Olympic champion overshadowed any issue with the colour of his skin.[36]

Kahanamoku was, however, best known in Australia for promoting surfing. His example was crucial because no one in Australia had ever been able to ride the waves with such aplomb. A few locals had tried to surf – whether on imported or homemade boards – but they had little success prior to the example set by Kahanamoku. In a magnanimous gesture, the Hawaiian offered his board to a local enthusiast, 15-year-old Claude West, who inspired by this gesture, went on to become Australia's first surfboard champion. Kahanamoku's visit was also significant because he surfed tandem with a local girl, Isabel Letham. She soon became a leading female board-rider, thus helping to pave the way for women to gain public acceptance (though this was slow in coming) as athletes of the surf.[37]

Visiting athletes of Asian origin were less renowned in Australia but, like Pacific Islander surfers and swimmers, were typically embraced by sports fans.[38] Despite well publicised local fears about an invasion by the so-called 'yellow peril' from East Asia, swimmers from Japan and footballers from China were received very hospitably during the 1920s.[39] There is plenty of irony about athletes of non-white appearance being accorded such status; not only because of the WAP, but because in the first half of the twentieth century Indigenous Australians had such a low profile in the nation's sporting culture.[40] For example, although a handful of Indigenous players did make it to first-class cricket, such as outstanding state-level bowlers Jack Marsh and Eddie Gilbert, they faced racist opposition from influential cricket officials; this in turn negated their opportunity to play for Australia.[41] Among all sports, boxing provided the most opportunities for Aboriginal athletes: they were managed by a white entrepreneur and, although their careers were mired by injury and pain, the ring was a place where Indigenous fighters met non-whites on a more-or-less equal basis.[42]

Assertive Aboriginality

In 1938, when New South Wales officials ostentatiously commemorated 150 years of British settlement in Sydney, Aboriginal activists declared a 'day of mourning'. For them there was nothing to celebrate and much to commiserate.[43] By the 1960s the American civil rights movement had helped to inform and radicalise Aboriginal activists and their supporters. The legendary Aboriginal leader Charlie Perkins led what was termed the 'freedom ride' into rural towns in New South Wales, where he and student activists reported on racism. In the outback town of Moree, for example, Aboriginal people were excluded from many public services, including the local school and the swimming baths.[44] Segregation was rife: the local cinema partitioned Aborigines at the front of the theatre, while at Moree Hospital there was a separate space for Aboriginal patients in the back of the facility. Even in death there was segregation. The town cemetery had an area where Aborigines were buried apart from whites.[45] This Australia looked very much like apartheid South Africa.

The late 1960s did, however, involve change. A national referendum in 1967 allowed the Federal government to make laws in respect of Aboriginal people, a role that the states had assumed previously.[46] The rise to power of the Whitlam Labor government in 1972 facilitated the prospect of reform in the interests of Aborigines; indeed, within a week of taking office, Whitlam had established a Royal Commission regarding land rights for Aborigines. However, it took another 20 years for the High Court to rule against *terra nullius*, which was the 1788 British colonial declaration that the Australian continent was unoccupied and belonged to no-one.[47] The outcome was the concept of native title, which recognises the continued ownership of land by local Indigenous Australians, though not to the exclusion of non-Indigenous proprietary rights. In some parts of rural Australia the principle of co-existence has been negotiated, whereby traditional Aboriginal land owners and pastoralists utilise the same territory.[48] However, the wealth that stems from the land, such as through corporate mining ventures in remote regions, has too rarely made its way into the hands of local Aborigines.[49]

Reconciliation

By the early twenty-first century, Aboriginal and Torres Strait Islander peoples, once the sole custodians of the Australian continent, constituted around 2.7 per cent of the national population. The raw number of Indigenous people – some 450,000 – is similar to most demographic estimates of the total Indigenous population before the arrival of Europeans.[50]

Although typecast as living in rural and remote regions, Aborigines are just as likely to be found in towns and major cities. There are, for example, more Aboriginal people residing in Sydney than in the entire Northern Territory. Common among this demographic is disadvantage – which is evident across virtually every socioeconomic indicator. Aboriginal people have, as examples, significantly lower life expectancy than other Australians,[51] much higher levels of unemployment,[52] considerably lower levels of education and income,[53] and are vastly over-represented in the nation's prisons.[54] Colonialism and subjugation have left a pernicious legacy of inequality and disempowerment in the lives of most Aboriginal people.

For most of the twentieth century, Indigenous Australians rarely rose to prominence in sport, largely because elite-level competitions in Australia only occasionally featured Aboriginal athletes. This made exceptions all the more novel and intriguing. When Aboriginal boxer Lionel Rose claimed the world bantamweight title in Japan in 1968, he was mobbed by hundreds of thousands of well-wishers upon his return to Australia. Not only was Rose the first Aborigine to win a world boxing title, he also became the first Indigenous person to be awarded the prestigious title of 'Australian of the Year'. A year later he reached the top of the music charts with the country and western song 'I Thank You'.[55] Along with tennis player Evonne Goolagong, who won seven grand slam singles finals between 1971 and 1980, Rose presented the image of an Aborigine who had 'made it' in white society. Both of these athletes appealed to non-Indigenous observers who ordinarily had little or no contact with Aboriginal people.[56] Unlike Aboriginal dissidents who established the Aboriginal Tent Embassy outside Parliament House in Canberra and used it to protest for land rights and a treaty with whites, these Aboriginal athletes were seen as non-threatening. In that respect, they had something in common with non-white athletes who visited Australia from 'exotic' places: they entertained without challenging the status quo.[57]

During the 1980s and 1990s, increased numbers of Aboriginal men participated at the elite level in the country's two largest football codes – Australian Rules and rugby league. As these sports became increasingly professional, the athleticism of footballers was more important than the colour of their skin, and there was an abundance of Indigenous talent waiting in the wings. By the early twenty-first century, players from Aboriginal or Torres Strait Islander heritage constituted around 10–13 per cent of all professional players in both the AFL and the NRL – a substantial proportion given that the Indigenous population of Australia is under 3 per cent of the national total.[58] However, Aboriginal athletes have battled long and hard against racism – both on and off the field. A turning point came in April 1993 when Aboriginal footballer Nicky Winmar raised his St. Kilda jumper to a group of bigoted Collingwood fans, proudly revealing to them his black skin. This was a dignified, symbolic retaliation.[59] However, Collingwood President Allan McAllister remarked that so long as Aborigines 'behaved themselves like white folks off the field, they would be admired and respected' on it.[60] There was much irony in this claim, for it seems unlikely Winmar would want to lower himself to behave like the Collingwood supporters who abused him. McAllister was persuaded by the football club to apologise for his comments and, in a transparent attempt to get himself 'off the hook', hastily organised a match between Collingwood and a team dubbed the Aboriginal All Stars – which promptly thrashed them.[61]

A debate had also taken place over whether on-field racial 'sledging' (taunting) was 'just' a tactic or, instead, a form of serious misconduct. This was not resolved properly until after 1995, when Essendon's Michael Long complained that a Collingwood ruckman had racially vilified him, and that this behaviour should be treated as an offence. The AFL, while slow to respond to this type of racism, has since become a national leader by introducing a wide-ranging anti-vilification code.[62] For the League it has been something of a win–win: Aboriginal footballers are now less likely to face on-field racism and the AFL brand has become associated positively with cultural diversity initiatives around the country. What is more, many Aboriginal athletes – whether in the AFL, NRL, boxing, or athletics – are now household names and often revered by both Indigenous and non-Indigenous fans.

Colin Tatz, however, argues that there are 'monumental contradictions' in the adulation by non-Indigenous Australians for so many Aboriginal stars of sport.[63] He believes that the affection is genuine, but most of these fans have little knowledge about where the Indigenous players come from, or the nature of their lives before coming to prominence as boxers, runners, or footballers. It can be all too easy – indeed convenient – for non-Aboriginal people to look to these athletes as examples of rising Indigenous circumstances generally. But it is hopelessly naive to imagine that deep-seated structural inequalities will be impacted upon in a substantive way by the individual success of 100 or so elite Aboriginal athletes.[64] Indeed, Tatz points to the absurdity of anyone appropriating Cathy Freeman's success at the 2000 Olympics 'as though she has single-handedly transformed the whole Aboriginal experience into the opposite of what it really is'.[65] Yet fantasies about such a connection exist, particularly when associated with simplistic ideas about 'opportunity for all'. The more that non-Indigenous Australians cheer for Aboriginal athletes, the more they can lay claim to championing Aboriginal advancement and 'fighting' racism.[66]

Of course, some Australians do not fit this mindset at all. Toni Bruce, in a study of letters to the editor of newspapers during the Sydney 2000 Olympics, found numerous examples of correspondents vehemently opposed to the notion that Cathy Freeman, as an Aboriginal Australian could embody the Australian nation. Several of these writers raged against what they saw as the 'political correctness' of having an Indigenous person light the flame at the opening ceremony of the Games.[67] Widespread hostility towards Aboriginal people remains nascent. It surfaced with a vengeance in the repeated booing, bullying, and heckling of the Aboriginal AFL icon and 2014 Australian of the Year, Adam Goodes. He has been an outspoken critic against racism in sport and society, but in the process has attracted trenchant critics. This imbroglio recently sparked a national debate about Goodes' views on race relations, the place of politics in sport, and the 'right' of people to 'express themselves' at a sporting event.[68] It has been an unedifying journey.

Ethnicity and multiculturalism

Issues of discrimination and stereotyping in sport have also been apparent among ethnic minority groups in Australia. While soccer, for example, was the most important sport for the great flood of European migrants after the Second World War, the game was typecast as 'foreign' by comparison to the existing staples of the rugby codes and Australian Rules.[69] Soccer was commonly ridiculed as 'wogball' and a game for 'poofters'; this derision not only impacted upon so-called New Australians playing soccer, but residents of British heritage with a passion for the sport.[70] Ethnicity has, of course, been part of Australian sport since the nineteenth century. Scots were particularly noticeable in golf and lawn bowls, Irish Catholics were prominent as bookmakers in the racing industry, while the English were especially zealous about cricket and fox hunting. These practices were basically extensions of migrant cultural baggage in the Antipodes.[71] But it would be misleading to speak of ethnic enclaves among the Australian population or within the sporting culture of the late nineteenth and early twentieth centuries. Indeed, despite protracted Anglo-Irish tensions, most notably after the Easter Rising of 1916, which had major impacts upon Australian society,[72] sport appears to have been less affected by sectarianism than education, party politics, and the public service.[73]

In Australia, historical research into sport and ethnicity has focused principally on the second half of the twentieth century.[74] It was given impetus as a subject for inquiry by the emergence of a Federal government policy of multiculturalism, first adopted by Labor in 1973.[75] Previously, New Australians were expected to assimilate into a dominant English-speaking, Anglo-Celtic culture. Now there was an emphasis on respect for group differences within a society that, as a consequence of mass migration – not only from Europe but increasingly Asia – had become more culturally diverse and ethnically cosmopolitan.[76] In terms of sport, however, little seemed to change. For example, although a promising 19-year-old fast bowler, Len Durtanovich, played junior representative cricket for New South Wales, it was the pragmatically renamed Len Pascoe who played for Australia between 1977 and 1982. His parents' Yugoslavian origins were, however, a source of derision for some cricket opponents.[77] Soccer, meanwhile, was still subject to discourses propounding it as a game for ethnic 'others' (so-called New Australians) and thus was not 'true-blue' Australian.[78] Sport was therefore primarily a culturally conservative institution within which traditional forms and norms of physical activity dominated.

During the past two decades, however, there has been a greater emphasis on social inclusion and the engagement of various communities into sport – with a particular focus on attracting males and females from culturally and linguistically diverse backgrounds (CALD), as well as refugees.[79] This commitment towards sport and social inclusion has coincided, ironically enough, with a move away from sports clubs dedicated to particular ethnic groups and has energised the 'cosmopolitanising' of Australian sport culture – within which people of all ancestries and skin colours are lured into sport en-masse. On the one hand this has opened new opportunities; on the other hand it has represented loss. For example, sports clubs organised by and for Jews have a long lineage in Australia.[80] This includes the Monash Golf Club in Sydney, named after Australia's renowned Jewish military commander of the First World War. Demographic and socioeconomic changes have in effect transformed Monash into a 'cosmopolitan' golf club, albeit with a Jewish past.[81]

This theme of loss has also been noticeable among soccer clubs that were originally formed to cater for the fraternal needs of ethnic groups from non-English-speaking backgrounds – Italians, Greeks, Serbs, Croats, and so on.[82] The profile and status of such clubs has been denuded since the mid-1990s by a National Soccer League (NSL) decision to in effect 'de-ethnicise' elite-level club competition in Australia.[83] A key expectation was that club names be revamped in an attempt to garner fan support from beyond an 'ethnic' base. Greek club West Adelaide Hellas, for example, changed its name to the West Adelaide Sharks. This was part of an explicit effort to reinvent soccer as a game intended to appeal to 'mainstream' Australia, not just particular ethnic communities that many of the clubs had historically represented.[84] At the elite level, club soccer faced protracted financial and administrative difficulties, as well as a perception (sometimes created by the media) that matches – for example between Serbs and Croats – were little more than occasions for historic, Europe-based inter-group hostilities played out in an Antipodean setting.[85]

The NSL has been supplanted by the A-League, which involves team franchises and single clubs representing cities or regions. The newly formed Football Federation Australia (FFA) was led by Jewish-Australian property magnate Frank Lowy, while the long overdue involvement of the Socceroos in the World Cup (2006) gave the sport – renamed football in Australia – unprecedented profile and public following. Although it is early days, the 'mainstreaming' of football via the A-League and the expectation of the Socceroos participating regularly in the World Cup appears to have the potential to put the game in a sounder financial position.[86] The fact that the Socceroos won the 2015 Asian Cup – on home soil – has also cemented the impression that the nation and the game of football are intertwined with the Asian region, quite a departure from Australia's fear of the 'yellow peril' and memories of war in the Pacific during the 1940s.[87]

On the home front, though, there remain tensions between what might be called 'old soccer' and 'new football'. The FFA's agenda is to mainstream football, in effect marginalising clubs with historical ethnic allegiances. Although Australia is multicultural and the FFA waxes lyrical that soccer represents Australian sport 'in all its diversity', this organisation bans ethnic/ national flags at games and prevents state league teams (who compete for the FFA Cup) from openly acknowledging their ethnic lineage or being sponsored by community organisations with ethnic affiliations. The FFA is nervous about ethnic enclaves in soccer; its vision for the future is a melting pot of ethnicities submerged beneath regional A-League teams – so much for a celebration of diversity.[88]

Conclusion

Unlike issues of health, poverty, and land rights, sport appears to be a 'good news' story for Aborigines. Despite a history of racism in sport, Indigenous people now feature as highly respected professionals in areas like athletics, boxing, Australian Rules football, and rugby league, though considerably less so in other sports. There is, one might say, less to feel 'guilty' about for whites when they gaze on professional sports as a means of engaging Indigenous people.[89] Beyond the playing field, though, Indigenous Australians are confronted with far greater challenges than they ever faced in sport.

Although multiculturalism has critics and opponents, it has entrenched bipartisan support in government, and sport organisations have a consistent aim of engaging participants and fans from diverse cultural backgrounds. In a pragmatic sense this is good business: a growing proportion of Australians were either born overseas or have parents who were migrants. But there is also a stronger sense of cross-cultural community engagement by sports themselves – for migrants, refugees, women, and Indigenous people.

Notes

1   Daryl Adair, 'Conformity, Diversity, and Difference in Antipodean Physical Culture: The Indelible Influence of Immigration, Ethnicity, and Race during the Formative Years of Organized Sport', *Immigrants & Minorities* 17, 1 (1998), 14–48.
2   Muhammad Azizul Islam, Ameeta Jain, and Shamima Haque, 'A Preliminary Analysis of Australian Government's Indigenous Reform Agenda "Closing the Gap" and Corporate Accountability', in S. Idowu, ed., *Key Initiatives in Corporate Social Responsibility* (Cham: Springer, 2016), 341–54; Kerrie Doyle, 'Australian Aboriginal Peoples and Evidence-Based Policies: Closing the Gap in Social Interventions', *Journal of Evidence-Informed Social Work* 12, 2 (2015), 166–74.
3   Geoffrey Levey, 'Multiculturalism and Citizenship: The Australian Experience', in Claudia Tazreiter and Siew Yean Tham, eds, *Globalization and Social Transformation in the Asia-Pacific: The Australian and Malaysian Experience* (London: Palgrave Macmillan, 2013), 132–46; Chris Wright, 'How Do States Implement Liberal Immigration Policies? Control Signals and Skilled Immigration Reform in Australia', *Governance* 27, 3 (2014), 397–421.
4   Jock Collins, 'Multiculturalism and Immigrant Integration in Australia', *Canadian Ethnic Studies* 45, 3 (2013), 133–49; Andrew Jakubowicz, '"In the Beginning All Is Chaos…": Roaming the Dystopic Realm in Australian Multiculturalism', in Stephen Castles, Derya Ozkul, and Magdalena Arias Cubas, eds, *Social Transformation and Migration: National and Local Experiences in South Korea, Turkey, Mexico and Australia* (Basingstoke: Palgrave Macmillan, 2015), 221–36.
5   Richard Cashman, *Paradise of Sport: A History of Australian Sport* (Petersham, NSW: Walla Walla Press, 2010).
6   William McGregor, ed., *Encountering Aboriginal Languages: Studies in the History of Australian Linguistics* (Canberra: Pacific Linguistics, 2008).

7 Reet Howell and Max Howell, *The Genesis of Sport in Queensland* (St Lucia, Qld: University of Queensland Press, 1992); Ken Edwards, 'Traditional Games of a Timeless Land: Play Cultures in Aboriginal and Torres Strait Islander Communities', *Australian Aboriginal Studies* 2 (2009), 32–43.

8 Geoffrey Blainey, *Triumph of the Nomads: A History of Ancient Australia* (South Melbourne: Sun Books, 1976).

9 Henry Reynolds, *With the White People* (Ringwood, Vic: Penguin, 1990); Henry Reynolds, *The Other Side of the Frontier: Aboriginal Resistance to the European Invasion of Australia* (Kensington, NSW: University of New South Wales Press, 2006).

10 Charles Rowley, *The Destruction of Aboriginal Society* (Canberra: Australian National University Press, 1970).

11 Katherine Ellinghaus, 'Absorbing the "Aboriginal Problem": Controlling Interracial Marriage in Australia in the Late 19th and Early 20th Centuries', *Aboriginal History* 27 (2003), 183–207; Colin Tatz, 'The Destruction of Aboriginal Society in Australia', in Samuel Totten and Robert Hitchcock, eds, *Genocide of Indigenous Peoples: A Critical Bibliographic Review*, vol. 8 (New Brunswick, NJ: Transaction Publisher, 2011), 87–116.

12 Colin Tatz, *Obstacle Race: Aborigines in Sport* (Kensington, NSW: University of New South Wales Press, 1995); Bernard Whimpress, *Passport to Nowhere Aborigines in Australian Cricket, 1850–1939* (Sydney: Walla Walla Press, 1999).

13 Derek Mulvaney, *Cricket Walkabout: The Australian Aboriginal Cricketers on Tour, 1867–8* (London: Melbourne University Press, 1967); David Sampson, 'Strangers in a Strange Land: The 1868 Aborigines and other Indigenous Performers in mid-Victorian Britain', unpublished PhD thesis, Faculty of Humanities and Social Sciences, University of Technology Sydney, 2000, https://opus.lib. uts.edu.au/handle/10453/20012, accessed 10 January 2016; David Sampson, 'Culture, "Race" and Discrimination in the 1868 Aboriginal Cricket Tour of England', *Australian Aboriginal Studies* 2 (2009), 44–60.

14 Daryl Adair, 'Declarations of Difference: Attempts to Exclude Non-Whites From Late Colonial Australia', *Flinders Journal of History and Politics*, 16 (1993), 16–26.

15 Robert Hughes, *The Fatal Shore* (New York: Knopf, 1987).

16 David Hill, *Gold: The Fever That Forever Changed Australia* (Sydney: William Heinemann, 2010).

17 Geoffrey Sherington, *Australia's Immigrants 1788–1988*, 2nd edition (Sydney: Allen & Unwin, 1990), 66; Charles Price, *Immigration and Ethnicity* (Canberra: Commonwealth Department of Immigration and Multicultural Affairs, 1996), 11; Sung-Wu Wang, 'Chinese Immigration, 1840s–1890s', in James Jupp, ed., *The Australian People: An Encylopaedia of the Nation, Its People, and Their Origins* (North Ryde, NSW: Angus and Robertson, 1988), 299.

18 Eric Rolls, *Sojourners: The Epic Story of China's Centuries-old Relationship with Australia* (St. Lucia, Qld: University of Queensland Press, 1992); John O'Hara, *A Mug's Game: A History of Gaming and Betting in Australia* (Kensington, NSW: University of New South Wales Press, 1988).

19 Marie de Lepervanche, 'Australian Immigrants, 1788–1940: Desired and Unwanted', in Edward Wheelwright and Ken Buckley, eds, *Essays in the Political Economy of Australian Capitalism*, vol. 1 (Sydney: Australia and New Zealand Book Co., 1975), 73–81; Alexander Yarwood, *Asian Migration to Australia: The Background to Exclusion, 1896–1923* (Melbourne: Melbourne University Press, 1964), 5–18.

20 Rowley, *The Destruction of Aboriginal Society*; Russel McGregor, *Imagined Destinies: Aboriginal Australians and the Doomed Race Theory, 1880–1939* (Carlton, Vic: Melbourne University Press, 1997).

21 Phillip Knightley, *Australia: A Biography of a Nation* (London: Jonathon Cape, 2000), 213.

22 Consistent with the patriarchal nature of high-performance sport, these athletes were almost exclusively male. See Daryl Adair and Wray Vamplew, *Sport in Australian History* (Melbourne: Oxford University Press, 1997).

23 Colin Tatz, 'Race, Politics and Sport', *Sporting Traditions* 1, 1 (1984), 2–36; Colin Tatz, *Aborigines in Sport* (Bedford Park, SA: Australian Society for Sports History, 1987); Tatz, *Obstacle Race: Aborigines in Sport*; Colin Tatz, 'Coming to Terms: "Race", Ethnicity, Identity and Aboriginality in Sport', *Australian Aboriginal Studies* 2 (2009), 15–31; Colin Tatz, 'Sport, Racism and Aboriginality: The Australian Experience', in Daryl Adair, ed., *Sport, Race and Ethnicity: Narratives of Difference and Diversity* (Morgantown, WV: FIT Press, 2011), 95–114; Colin Tatz, 'Race Matters in Australian Sport', in Jonathon Long and Karl Spracklen, eds, *Sport and Challenges to Racism* (Basingstoke: Palgrave, 2011), 100–16.

24 Tatz, 'Race Matters in Australian Sport', 109.

25 Ibid.

26 Matthew Stephen, 'Contact Zones: Sport and Race in the Northern Territory, 1869–1953', unpublished PhD thesis, Faculty of Law, Business and Arts, Charles Darwin University, 2009, 121.

27 Matthew Stephen, 'Football, "Race" and Resistance: The Darwin Football League, 1926–29', *Australian Aboriginal Studies* 2 (2009): 61–77; Matthew Stephen, *Contact Zones: Sport and Race in the Northern Territory, 1869–1953* (Darwin: Charles Darwin University Press, 2010).

28 Alexander Yarwood, *Asian Migration to Australia: The Background to Exclusion, 1896–1923* (Melbourne: Melbourne University Press, 1964).

29 Andrew Honey, 'Sport, Immigration Restriction and Race: the Operation of the White Australia Policy', in Richard Cashman, John O'Hara, and Andrew Honey, eds, *Sport, Federation, Nation* (Sydney: Walla Walla Press, 2001), 26–46.

30 Peter Corris, *Lords of the Ring* (North Ryde, NSW: Cassell Australia, 1980), 83–4.

31 Richard Broome, 'The Australian Reaction to Jack Johnson, Black Pugilist, 1907–09', in Richard Cashman and Michael McKernan, eds, *Sport in History: The Making of Sporting Traditions* (St. Lucia: University of Queensland Press, 1979), 343–63; David Headon, '"World's Fistanic History", Sydney 1908: "Flash Jack Johnson" vs "Sinking Tommy Burns"', *Sporting Traditions* 26, 2 (2009), 1–14.

32 Jeff Wells, *Boxing Day: The Fight that changed the World* (Sydney: Harper, 1998); Theresa Runstedtler, *Jack Johnson, Rebel Sojourner: Boxing in the Shadow of the Global Color Line* (Berkeley, CA: University of California Press, 2012).

33 Andrew Ritchie, *Major Taylor: The Extraordinary Career of a Champion Bicycle Racer* (Baltimore, MD: Johns Hopkins University Press, 1996); Andrew Ritchie, 'Major Taylor: Understanding the Complex Story of a Champion African-American Cyclist in White Australia, 1903–1904', in Daryl Adair, ed., *Sport, Race and Ethnicity: Narratives of Difference and Diversity* (Morgantown, WV: FIT Press, 2011), 77–94.

34 Gary Osmond, 'The Surfing Tommy Tanna: Performing Race at the Australian Beach', *The Journal of Pacific History* 46, 2 (2011), 177–95.

35 Gary Osmond and Murray Phillips, '"The Bloke with a Stroke": Alick Wickham, the "Crawl" and Social Memory', *The Journal of Pacific History* 39, 3 (2004), 309–24; Gary Osmond and Murray Phillips, '"Look at that Kid Crawling": Race, Myth and the "Crawl" stroke', *Australian Historical Studies* 37, 127 (2006), 43–62.

36 Ian Jobling, 'Duke Kahanomoku: Hawaiian Olympian – Outcomes of his Visit to Australia in 1914–15', unpublished paper presented to the ASSH-NASSH Conference, Hawaii, 1993.

37 Gary Osmond, 'Myth-making in Australian Sport History: Re-evaluating Duke Kahanamoku's Contribution to Surfing', *Australian Historical Studies* 42, 2 (2011), 260–76; Chris Gibson and Andrew Warren, 'Making Surfboards: Emergence of a Trans-Pacific Cultural Industry', *The Journal of Pacific History* 49, 1 (2014), 1–25; Douglas Booth, *Australian Beach Cultures: The History of Sun, Sand and Surf* (London: Routledge, 2012).

38 Gary Osmond and Marie-Louise McDermott, 'Mixing Race: The Kong Sing Brothers and Australian Sport', *Australian Historical Studies* 39, 3 (2008), 338–55.

39 Sean Brawley, '"They Came, They Saw, They Conquered": The Takaishi/Saito Tour of 1926/27 and Australian Perceptions of Japan', *Sporting Traditions* 26, 2 (2009), 49–66; Nick Guoth, 'A New China: Using Sport to Expose a Multi-Class Race through the 1923 Chinese Soccer Tour of Australia', *Sport in Society* 15, 4 (2012): 462–78; Gary Osmond, '"Lively Little Visitors" and "Peaceful Ambassadors": Reading Japanese Sporting Tours through the Australian Press – 1926 to 1935', *Sport in Society* 15, 4 (2012), 529–50.

40 Bernard Whimpress, 'Absent Aborigines: The Impact of Federation on Indigenous Sport', in Richard Cashman, John O'Hara, and Andrew Honey, eds, *Sport, Federation, Nation* (Sydney: Walla Walla Press, 2001), 47–54.

41 Bernard Whimpress, 'Few and Far Between: Prejudice and Discrimination Among Aborigines in Australian First Class Cricket 1869–1988', *Journal of the Anthropological Society of South Australia*, 30, 1–2 (1992), 57–70; Bernard Whimpress, 'The Marsh–Maclaren Dispute at Bathurst, 1902, and the Politics of Selection', *Sporting Traditions* 10, 2 (1994), 45–58; Whimpress, *Passport to Nowhere*; Mike Colman and Ken Edwards, *Eddie Gilbert: The True Story of an Aboriginal Cricket Legend* (Sydney: ABC Books, 2002); Max Bonnell, *How Many More Are Coming? The Short Life of Jack Marsh* (Sydney: Walla Walla Press, 2003).

42 Richard Broome, 'Professional Aboriginal Boxers in Eastern Australia', *Aboriginal History* 4 (1980), 49–72; Christopher Mooney and John Ramsland, 'Dave Sands as Local Hero and International Champion: Race, Family and Identity in an Industrial Working-class Suburb', *Sport in History* 28, 2 (2008), 299–312.

43 John Horner and Marcia Langton, 'The Day of Mourning', in Bill Gammage and Peter Spearritt, eds, *Australians: 1938* (Sydney: Fairfax, Syme and Weldon Associates, 1987), 29–35.

44 Ann Curthoys, *Freedom Ride: A Freedom Rider Remembers* (Sydney: Allen and Unwin, 2002), 117–18; Daryl Adair and Megan Stronach, 'Kwementyaye (Charles) Perkins: Indigenous Soccer Player and Australian Political Activist', *International Journal of the History of Sport* 31, 7 (2014), 778–94.

45 Noeline Briggs-Smith, *Moree Mob: Volume Two Burrul Wallaay (Big Camp)* (Moree: Northern Regional Library and Information Service, 2003), 12–13.

46 Bain Attwood and Andrew Markus, *The 1967 Referendum, or When Aborigines Didn't Get the Vote* (Canberra: Aboriginal Studies Press, 1997).

47 Larissa Behrendt, 'The Doctrine of Discovery in Australia', in Robert Miller, Jacinta Ruru, Larissa Behrendt and Tracey Lindberg, eds, *Discovering Indigenous Lands: The Doctrine of Discovery in the English Colonies*, vol. 1 (Oxford: Oxford University Press, 2010), 171–87.

48 Kalervo Gulson and Robert Parkes, 'From the Barrel of the Gun: Policy Incursions, Land, and Aboriginal Peoples in Australia', *Environment and Planning A* 42, 2 (2010), 300–13.

49 Marcia Langton and Odette Mazel, 'Poverty in the Midst of Plenty: Aboriginal People, the "Resource Curse" and Australia's Mining Boom', *Journal of Energy & Natural Resources Law* 26, 1 (2008), 31–65.

50 Australian Human Rights Commission, 'A Statistical Overview of Aboriginal and Torres Strait Islander Peoples in Australia: Social Justice Report 2008', www.hreoc.gov.au/social_justice/statistics/index.html#Heading34, accessed 10 July 2010; Australian Bureau of Statistics, *Year Book Australia* (Canberra: Australian Bureau of Statistics, 2002), www.abs.gov.au/ausstats/abs@. nsf/94713ad445ff1425ca25682000192af2/ bc28642d31c215cca256b350010b3f4!OpenDocument, accessed 10 July 2010.

51 Australian Bureau of Statistics figures for 2005–07 indicated that life expectancy of indigenous men was 11.5 years lower than for non-indigenous men, while life expectancy of indigenous women was 9.7 years lower than for non-indigenous women. Larine Statham, 'Aborigines Have "Worst" Life Expectancy', *Sydney Morning Herald*, 15 January 2010.

52 In 2001 the unemployment rate for indigenous Australians was 20.0 per cent, compared to 7.2 per cent for non-indigenous Australians. Australian Bureau of Statistics, *Year Book Australia* (Canberra: Australian Bureau of Statistics, 2004), www.abs.gov.au/Ausstats/abs@.nsf/0/ bc6a7187473c6fb6ca256dea00053a29, accessed 10 January 2016.

53 For example, 39 per cent of indigenous students stayed on to year 12 at high school, compared with 75 per cent for the total Australian population: Australian Bureau of Statistics, *Measures of Australia's Progress* (Canberra: Australian Bureau of Statistics, 2004), www.abs.gov.au/Ausstats/abs@.nsf/0/ A03CAD8F1C3F8 13BCA256E7D00002641, accessed 10 January 2016. Both high unemployment and low levels of education have impacted on the economic circumstances of indigenous people. In 2002, the average household income for indigenous Australian adults was 60 per cent of the non-indigenous average: Australian Bureau of Statistics, *Year Book Australia* (Canberra: Australian Bureau of Statistics, 2005), www.abs.gov.au/ausstats/abs@.nsf/00000000000000000000000000000000/ 294322bc5648ead8ca256f7200833040!OpenDocument, accessed 10 January 2016.

54 Australian Bureau of Statistics figures for 2004 indicate that 'Indigenous persons were 11 times more likely to be in prison compared with non-Indigenous persons', and that in 2003 some 20 per cent of prisoners self-identified as indigenous: Australian Bureau of Statistics, *Year Book Australia* (Canberra: Australian Bureau of Statistics, 2005), www.abs.gov.au/ausstats/abs@.nsf/000000000 000000 0000000000000000/294322bc5648ead8ca256f7200833040!OpenDocument, accessed 10 January 2016.

55 Lionel Rose and Rod Humphries, *Lionel Rose, Australian: The Life Story of a Champion* (Sydney: Angus and Robertson, 1969).

56 Tatz, 'Race Matters in Australian Sport'.

57 Kathy Lothian, 'Moving Blackwards: Black Power and the Aboriginal Tent Embassy', in Ingereth Macfarlane and Mark Hannah, eds, *Transgressions: Critical Australian Indigenous Histories* (Canberra: ANU E-Press and Aboriginal History Inc., 2007), 19–34.

58 Australian Football League, 'AFL Indigenous Round: Round Nine', 22 May 2007, www.afl.com.au/ Season2007/News/NewsArticle/tabid/208/Default.aspx?newsId=43746, accessed 31 March 2010; Roy Masters, 'League's Polynesian Powerplay Muscles in on Indigenous Numbers', *Sydney Morning Herald*, 24 April 2009.

59 Matthew Klugman and Gary Osmond, 'That Picture: Nicky Winmar and the History of an Image', *Australian Aboriginal Studies* 2 (2009), 78–89.

60 Adair and Vamplew, *Sport in Australian History*, 68.

61   Ibid.

62   Greg Gardiner, 'Racial Abuse and Football: The Australian Football League's Racial Vilification Rule in Review', *Sporting Traditions* 14, 1 (1997), 3–26; Ian Warren and Spiros Tsousis, 'Racism and the Law in Australian Rules Football: A Critical Analysis', *Sporting Traditions* 14, 1 (1997), 27–54.

63   Tatz, 'Race Matters in Australian Sport', 105.

64   Stella Coram, 'Performative Pedagogy and the Creation of Desire: The Indigenous Athlete/Role Model and Implications for Learning', *Australian Journal of Indigenous Education*, 36 (2007), 46–54.

65   Tatz, 'Race Matters in Australian Sport', 112.

66   Toni Bruce and Chris Hallinan, 'Cathy Freeman: The Quest for Australian Identity', in David L. Andrews and Steven J. Jackson, eds, *Sports Stars: The Cultural Politics of Sporting Celebrity* (London: Routledge, 2001), 257–70.

67   Toni Bruce and Emma Wensing, '"She's Not One of Us": Cathy Freeman and the Place of Aboriginal People in Australian National Culture', *Australian Aboriginal Studies* 2 (2009), 90–100.

68   Daryl Adair, 'Man Up? I See a Man Down: Booing and Being Adam Goodes', *The Conversation*, 1 August 2015, https://theconversation.com/man-up-i-see-a-man-down-booing-and-being-adam-goodes-45536, accessed 10 January 2016

69   Roy Hay, '"Our Wicked Foreign Game": Why has Association Football (Soccer) Not Become the Main Code of Football in Australia?', *Soccer and Society* 7, 2 (2006), 165–86.

70   John Warren, Andrew Harper and Josh Whittington, *Sheilas, Wogs and Poofters: An Incomplete Biography of Johnny Warren and Soccer in Australia* (Sydney: Random House Australia, 2002).

71   Adair, 'Conformity, Diversity and Difference'.

72   Mike Cronin and Daryl Adair, *The Wearing of the Green: A History of St Patrick's Day* (New York: Routledge, 2004).

73   Michael Hogan, *The Sectarian Strand: Religion in Australian History* (Ringwood Vic: Penguin Books, 1987); Jeff Kildea, *Tearing the Fabric: Sectarianism in Australia 1910 to 1925* (Sydney: Citadel Books, 2002).

74   Phillip Mosely, Richard Cashman, John O'Hara, and Hilary Weatherburn, *Sporting Immigrants: Sport and Ethnicity in Australia* (Sydney: Walla Walla Press, 1997).

75   Lois Foster and David Stockley, *Multiculturalism: The Changing Australian Paradigm* (Clevedon: Multilingual Matters, 1984).

76   James Jupp, 'One Among Many: The Relative Success of Australian Multiculturalism', in David Goodman, Chris Wallace-Crabbe, and Dinny O'Hearn, eds, *Multicultural Australia: The Challenge of Change* (Newham, Vic: Scribe, 1991), 119–33.

77   Geoff Lawson, *Henry: The Geoff Lawson Story* (Randwick, NSW: Ironbark Press, 1993); Gideon Haigh, 'Pascoe was Like a Bull at a Batsman', *The Age*, 21 February 2004.

78   John Hughson, 'Australian Soccer: "Ethni" or "Aussie" – The Search for an Image', *Current Affairs Bulletin* 68, 10 (2002), 12–16; Danforth Loring, 'Is the "World Game" an "Ethnic Game" or an "Aussie Game"? Narrating the Nation in Australian Soccer', *American Ethnologist* 28, 2 (2001), 363–87.

79   Tracy Taylor and Kristine Toohey, 'Negotiating Cultural Diversity for Women in Sport: From Assimilation to Multiculturalism', *Race, Ethnicity and Education* 1, 1 (1998), 75–90; Ramón Spaaij, 'Sport, Social Cohesion and Community Building: Managing the Nexus', in Peter Leisink, Paul Boselie, Maarten van Bottenburg, and Dian Marie Hosking, *Managing Social Issues: A Public Values Perspective* (Cheltenham: Edward Elgar, 2013), 107–25; Hazel Maxwell, Carmel Foley, Tracy Taylor, and Christine Burton, 'Social Inclusion in Community Sport: A Case Study of Muslim Women in Australia', *Journal of Sport Management* 27, 6 (2013), 467–81; Ramón Spaaij, 'Cultural Diversity in Community Sport: An Ethnographic Inquiry of Somali Australians' Experiences', *Sport Management Review* 16, 1 (2013), 29–40; Ramón Spaaij, Karen Farquharson, Jonathan Magee, Ruth Jeanes, Dean Lusher, and Sean Gorman, 'A Fair Game for All? How Community Sports Clubs in Australia Deal with Diversity', *Journal of Sport & Social Issues* 38, 4 (2014), 346–65.

80   Anthony Hughes, 'Muscular Judaism and the Jewish Rugby League Competition in Sydney, 1924 to 1927', *Sporting Traditions* 13, 1 (1996), 61–80; Anthony Hughes, 'Sport in the Australian Jewish Community', *Journal of Sport History* 26, 2 (1999), 376–91.

81   Colin Tatz, *A Course of History: Monash Country Club 1931–2001* (Sydney: Allen and Unwin, 2002).

82   Philip Mosely, *Ethnic Involvement in Australian Soccer: A History 1950–1990* (Canberra: National Sports Research Centre, 1995); Roy Hay, 'Croatia: Community, Conflict and Culture – The Role of Soccer Clubs in Migrant Identity', *Immigrants and Minorities* 17, 1 (1998), 49–66.

83 Christopher Hallinan, John Hughson, and Michael Burke, 'Supporting the "World Game" in Australia: A Case Study of Fandom at National and Club Level', *Soccer and Society* 8, 2–3 (2007), 283–297.

84 Hans Westerbeek, John Deane, and Aaron Smith, 'De-ethnicization and Australian Soccer: The Strategic Management Dilemma', *International Journal of Sport Management* 6, 3 (2005), 270–88.

85 John Hughson, 'The Boys are Back in Town: Soccer Support and the Social Reproduction of Masculinity', *Journal of Sport and Social Issues* 24, 1 (2000), 8–23; John Hughson, '"The Wogs are At It Again": The Media Reportage of Australian Soccer "Riots"', *Football Studies*, 1, 2 (2001), 40–50; Roy Hay, '"Those Bloody Croatians": Croatian Soccer Teams, Ethnicity and Violence in Australia, 1950–99', in Gary Armstrong and Richard Giulianotti, eds, *Fear and Loathing in World Football* (Oxford: Berg, 2001), 77–90.

86 Braham Dabscheck, 'Moving Beyond Ethnicity: Soccer's Evolutionary Progress', in Bob Stewart, ed., *The Games Are Not the Same: The Political Economy of Football in Australia* (Carlton, Vic: Melbourne University Press, 2007), 198–235; James Skinner, 'Coming in from the Margins: Ethnicity, Community Support and the Rebranding of Australian Soccer', *Soccer and Society* 9, 3 (2008): 394–404.

87 Alan Bairner, 'Asia's Land Down Under: The Socceroos and the 2015 Asian Cup', *Asia Pacific Journal of Sport and Social Science* 4, 1 (2015), 1–6.

88 James McGrath, 'True Multiculturalism isn't Ignoring Our Differences', *Huffington Post*, 26 February 2016, www.huffingtonpost.com.au/james-mcgrath2/true-multiculturalism-isn_b_9321570.html?ncid=edlinkauhpmg00000001, accessed 10 January 2016.

89 Daryl Adair, 'Shooting the Messenger: Australian History's Warmongers', *Sporting Traditions* 22, 2 (2006), 49–69.

12

BRITAIN

Luke J. Harris

Britain has been the home of modern sport and since its emergence in the nineteenth century it has been central to the nation's identity. Sport binds the nations of the United Kingdom together, but it also separates them and is perhaps the most prominent representation of the 'imagined nation'. Throughout the twenty-first century, Britain has become an ethnically diverse nation. The 2011 UK Census revealed that 'white British' was the largest ethnic group, with nearly 80 per cent of the population (45.1 million), with just over 20 per cent of the population being of a different ethnic background. This was a decrease from 2001, when 91.3 per cent of the population described itself as 'white British'.

The first major changes to the ethnic make-up of Britain came after the Second World War, with the first major influx of migrants to Britain appearing in 1948. This came with the arrival of the boat *Windrush*, which brought over 500 migrants from the Caribbean who came to help fill the labour shortage in war-torn Britain. Some believe the arrival of these men and women (and the 5,000 who came over the following four years) resulted in the spread of racism in Britain.[1] Following this initial migration, men, women and children from other parts of the British Empire followed, and Britain began to become the multicultural nation it is today.

Many of the migrants to Britain in the late 1940s onwards experienced both physical and verbal discrimination. For many migrants, it meant that despite their qualifications and skills, they found themselves unable to use them in jobs that were menial and low paid. This discrimination was recognised in 1967 by the government paper 'Political and Economic Planning Report: Racial Discrimination in England' (1967), describing racism against black workers in employment (and housing) as 'varying from the massive to the substantial'.[2] In 1976, the *Race Relations Act* outlawed such discrimination on the basis of 'colour, race, nationality or ethnic or national origins'. The racism and discrimination present across society from the Second World War to the present day are apparent within sport, demonstrating a close proximity between sport and wider British identity.

The migrants who arrived in Britain during the late 1940s were not the first immigrants to enter Britain, as there had been a long history of migration from other nations, primarily from Ireland and Jews from across Europe. Prior to 1945 it was these groups who faced racial discrimination, and sport was a prominent representation of these divisions within society. For example, Jews found themselves excluded from many sports clubs, particularly from the middle-class sports of rugby, tennis and golf.[3]

In his *Story of Sport in England*, historian Neil Wigglesworth (2007) states that exclusion is a 'recurring theme' in the history of English sport. He argues that 'these exclusions have been the result of petty snobbery, class selfishness, hypocrisy, religious bigotry, racism, sexism and xenophobia'.[4] Exclusion in sport, in which racism has continually been a major issue, has resulted in governmental involvement in an attempt to identify and counter them. Since 1965 official government policy has been one of inclusion and 'sport for all'. Nevertheless, many have continued to be excluded, 'including women, minority groups, school-aged children and the less well-off'.[5]

Modern sport began in the nineteenth century, and modern British racism emerged in the same period. During this period, small communities of ethnically different people emerged, particularly in the port towns of Liverpool, London, Cardiff and Bristol.[6] Subsequently, deep-seated stereotypical attitudes, particularly towards the black community 'in terms of political debate and domestic ideologies and policies towards "coloured workers" and their communities began to be formed'.[7] These attitudes have remained at the heart of racism and racially based discrimination for more than a century.

Comparable with other migrants, members of the black community became involved in both recreational and elite sport, with the Ghanaian goalkeeper Arthur Wharton being the first black professional footballer in England during the 1880s. Wharton was followed by the first professional outfield black footballer, Walter Tull, who played from 1908 to the outbreak of the First World War, when he joined the 'Footballers Battalion' and was killed in March 1918 during the German Spring Offensive in France. Prior to this, the Folkestone-born Tull, who had an English mother and Barbadian father, played for Tottenham Hotspur and Northampton Town, whom he represented over 100 times. Throughout his career, Tull endured racism from spectators, most prominently during his time at Tottenham.[8] This represents one of the earliest examples of racism inflicted by spectators of football. Such racism upon the basis of skin colour has continued throughout the twentieth century; as Scott Fleming and Alan Tomlinson argue:

> football can embody a popular aesthetic of collective endeavour, but it can also encourage prejudice, discrimination, stereotyping and ethnocentrism. It can bring different cultures together in common celebration, but it can also provide the basis for extreme, and very public, forms of xenophobia and racism.[9]

The abuse Tull encountered in the early part of the twentieth century became widespread during the 1970s and 1980s where 'football grounds have provided one of the largest public arenas in which racism can be openly expressed.'[10] Back *et al.* also explain the nature of racism within football grounds:

> Racist abuse in grounds occurs in an intermittent fashion, racist epithets and slogans are invoked in specific contexts and serve particular functions such that a series of fixtures may pass without any racist activity whilst a fixture with a heightened atmosphere or the appropriate circumstances can produce an explosion of racist activity. We have found that the perpetrators of racist activity are drawn from all age ranges and that racist activity is unevenly developed within the grounds as a whole.[11]

It was during the 1970s and 1980s that children of the post-war migrants became old enough to play professional football in significant numbers. A prime example of this is Laurie

Cunningham, Cyrille Regis and Brendan Batson, who played for West Bromwich Albion during the late 1970s. The men were nicknamed 'The Three Degrees' after a black singing group, and regularly encountered racism and stereotyping from spectators and fellow professional players alike. Batson stated that away fixtures could be an 'ordeal', as prior to the game he 'could see the National Front outside, handing out their racist literature', then during the game opposing fans would sing racist songs and throw bananas at the men.[12]

During this era right-wing groups became prominent among spectators and they attempted to use games for recruitment purposes. As sociologist Tim Crabbe comments: 'Groups such as the National Front were regularly seen distributing and selling their literature outside football grounds. But interest in the issue was partly related to the increasing presence of black players amongst the ranks of professional footballers.'[13] Tellingly, racism was not just limited to the stands. Cyrille Regis made his first of five international appearances for England against Northern Ireland in 1982, and prior to the game he received a bullet with his name on it in the post.

The throwing during a match of bananas towards black players was a sad but regular occurrence during the 1980s. This was often done by opposing supporters, but the players' own supporters are also believed to have thrown them, such as at the Jamaican-born John Barnes during his debut for Liverpool away at Arsenal.[14] Barnes, who represented England 79 times between 1983 and 1995, regularly encountered racism during the early part of his career, most prominently in November 1987 when he made his first appearances for Liverpool against Everton in the Merseyside derbies. In those matches, Barnes was the target of 'some of the most widespread radicalised chanting and barracking, by Everton supporters, ever witnessed in an English football ground'.[15] Despite the abuse in those games and many others, Barnes never reacted to it, which convinced some people that the incidents were not all that serious.[16]

Barnes' England debut in 1983 made him one of the first black players to represent England, although the first black player to take this honour was Viv Anderson, who played in a match versus Czechoslovakia in November 1978. This came over 50 years after the selection of striker Jack Leslie, who played for Plymouth Argyle in the 1920s and 1930s. He was initially selected by England in 1925, then later received a communication cancelling his call up to the England team, stating that they did not realise he was 'a man of colour'.

In the 1980s, black players who represented England also received abuse, such as that endured by Ian Wright when he made his debut for England 'B' in a match played at Millwall. This was an experience he does not remember fondly:

> The first time I pulled on an England shirt should have been one of the proudest days of my life. Instead it was spoilt for me in a terrible way by racism. The great memories I have of that night are overshadowed by the fact that I was targeted for abuse just because I was black, and the most sickening thing for me was that it happened virtually in my own back yard at Millwall.[17]

Comparable to the attitude across English football, players of all ethnicities have been well received in recent times when they have represented England. The national team has still encountered racism upon occasion when they have played overseas. In November 2004, England played Spain in a friendly match in Madrid and the team's five black members were constantly taunted by racist chanting. Then in October 2012, black members of the England Under-21 team were subjected to racist chanting and throwing of missiles in a Euro 2013 qualification match. Both of these matches resulted in negative responses from FIFA and UEFA and brought to the fore in the British media and press the issue of racism in football. This coverage has largely highlighted the belief that Britain is far more progressive than other nations in regards to racism in sport.

There is some evidence suggesting that, during the 1970s and 1980s, there was racial abuse in Scottish football. James Walvin argues that such incidents were more 'English than British. There were racial incidents in Scotland, but Scottish teams rarely attracted the virulent racism which so characterised the English game in the 1980s.'[18] In 1987 Mark Walters became the first Afro/Caribbean Briton to transfer from an English to a Scottish league club, when he joined Glasgow Rangers. He was also subject to racial abuse and bananas being thrown at him from the stands.

Writing in the late 1980s, Richard Holt indicated that although black players had to 'endure endless taunts' they were not the only group to suffer it: 'Pakistanis have the added stigma in the eyes of the white hooligan of tending to be better off, linguistically separate, less physical, and less interested in football.' He concluded that 'Racism seems to have become one of the most dangerous and distinctive aspects of contemporary football violence in comparison to earlier forms of juvenile disorder.'[19]

According to John Hargreaves, the problem was that the kinds of racial abuse explained here during this period were 'largely accepted in silence'.[20] Perhaps it was not dealt with because 'such sentiments struck a rich vein of popular racism which surfaced throughout society in those years'.[21] The racism present in society at large was exemplified by such comments as those made by Chief Superintendent David Polinghorne of Scotland Yard to a conference in 1981. He believed that the football stadium was 'a ground for racial harmony, where working-class blacks and whites stand side by side'.[22] Polinghorne, like so many others, believed that sport was immune to racism and was a place that brought people from all backgrounds together. The incidents revealed here, and many others, indicate otherwise.

During the 1980s racial discrimination in football came not just from the stands, but also from those within the game, as perceived physical attributes and negative character traits came to be associated with black players. These attributes were such as apparently having a dislike of the cold, a lack of bottle – lacking courage.[23] This was personified by the comment from Jim Smith during his time as a member of Queens Park Rangers during the late 1980s. He said that 'black players use very little intelligence; they get by on sheer natural ability'.[24] This argument fits into the larger debate on thoughts of black physical superiority but intellectual inferiority, which was common within society during this period and is a stigma that continues to be a common form of racism.

The need to challenge racism in football became a priority for the British government and Football Associations in the early 1990s. In 1991 the *Football (Offences) Act* was passed, making 'chanting of an indecent or racialist nature' illegal and providing a major step towards tackling issues that, while not as fierce or commonplace as they had been previously, were still present within the British game.

The 1990s also saw the launch of organisations dedicated to the eradication of racism within football. The first of these was the 1993 campaign 'Let's Kick Racism Out of Football', which was launched jointly by the Commission for Racial Equality and the Professional Footballers' Association. The organisation produced a ten-point plan which football clubs were expected to follow to challenge racism. The organisation changed its name to 'Kick It Out' in 1997 and in its first report 'criticized the football authorities, club and public, and private police, among others, for not doing enough to counter racism'.[25] This report demonstrated that despite the change in football culture during the late 1980s and early 1990s, racism was still an issue that needed to be challenged.

The establishment of 'Kick It Out' was followed by 'The Football Task Force', which was founded in 1998. Its founding statement included a seven-point remit, with one focused upon tackling the issue of racism within the game: 'Eliminate racism in football and encourage wider participation by ethnic minorities, both in playing and spectating.'[26]

Individual football clubs have also come up with their own plans to improve race relations within their communities. A prime example of this was Charlton Athletic, which created the 'bottom-up' 'Charlton Athletic Race Equality Partnership' (CARE). This was instigated by the London Borough of Greenwich and relocated to the club's stadium, 'The Valley' in 1992. Along with partners Greenwich University, Metropolitan Police and local multi-faith victim support groups, they undertook initiates which included:

- a newsletter, the *Equaliser*;
- home match tickets at less than half-price for CARE members;
- 'Show Racism the Red Card' and 'Roots of Racism' education packs;
- 'Face Value' project for 10–16-year-olds in school, exploring exclusion, peer pressure, prejudice, racist violence and mixed race relationships, carnival costumes and music for primary schoolchildren; PATH theatre and summer play-scheme for 16–21-year-olds;
- mini-soccer for primary girls;
- Plumstead Common sports festival;
- a study centre for 10–14-year-olds to help with homework, literacy, numeracy and computing.[27]

The change in football culture by the government, football associations, individual clubs and British society in general has ensured that the ugly scenes of racial discrimination once so commonplace within British football are now seemingly things of the past. This is not to state that racism has totally disappeared from the game; prominent incidents of racism within the game have occurred during the twenty-first century, with two high-profile events occurring during the 2011–12 season. These were incidents that brought racism in elite football 'back into the public eye and onto the political agenda'.[28]

The first of these incidents occurred when Uruguayan footballer Luis Suárez of Liverpool made racist comments towards Frenchman Patrice Evra of Manchester United in a Premier League match at Anfield on 15 October 2011. The comments made by Suárez resulted in him being fined £40,000, banned for eight games and a Football Association enquiry, which included a seven-day hearing. On 31 December 2011, the FA released the contents of their findings in a 115-page report which indicated that Suárez had 'damaged the image of English football around the world'.[29] Evra's testimony noted that Suárez had previously kicked him 'because you are black' and 'I don't speak to blacks' and used the word 'negro' five times as they argued. Suárez claimed that he only used the word 'negro' once and this was intended to be conciliatory and friendly.[30]

The second incident occurred between two English players: Chelsea and England captain, John Terry, a white footballer and Anton Ferdinand, a mixed race player representing Queens Park Rangers. In a Premier League match at Loftus Road, Terry made a racist comment towards Ferdinand, coming just eight days after the Suárez–Evra incident. The consequence of this was that Terry received a four-match ban and £220,000 fine, although it was not handed out until 11 months after the incident because Terry was taken to trial by the Crown Prosecution Service. Terry was acquitted of a racially aggravated public order offence by 'demonstrating a significant disjuncture between the law of the land and that of a self-regulating governing body (as well as the inconsistencies in the latter's own penalties)'.[31]

During the rest of the 2011–12 season the two men were constantly under the media spotlight and were the centre of attention for both the media and fans. A major part of both players' defences was that they should not be considered 'racist'. Terry commented that 'I have never aimed a racist remark at anyone and count people from all races and creeds among my closest friends.... I have campaigned against racism and believe there is no place for it in society.'[32] Suárez released a statement which said: '[Suárez] has played with black players and mixed with their families whilst with the Uruguay national side and was Captain of Ajax Amsterdam of a team with a proud multi-cultural profile, many of whom became good friends.'

Daniel Burdsey describes these two incidents and the fallout from them as a 'pivotal moment in relation to racism and anti-racism'.[33] He believes they represented the 'continuing presence of racism in the English game, the ineffectiveness of some current anti-racist procedures and the need for substantial penalties for racist acts'.[34] He also argues that many commentators viewed the incident as the 'return' of racism in football, which he believes indicates that 'prejudice and discrimination had gone away; or, perhaps more precisely, that they were being managed and suppressed effectively'.[35] The evidence utilised in this chapter demonstrates that racism in British football has been managed and reflects changes in society as a whole, but that the issue is still present.

Following these incidents, a House of Commons Culture, Media and Sport Committee undertook an enquiry into racism in football. It acknowledged that although racism had decreased significantly during the past quarter-century, fundamental problems still remained. It noted that 'football is not the source of racism', which Burdsey believes is 'illustrative of the dominant discourse, in that discrimination is seen as infiltrating the sport from external spheres'.[36]

Incidents such as the Suárez and Terry ones are not commonplace within British football, but they still do occur. Sometimes this can be mistaken for criticism of players, as such is the hostility of the game that 'from time to time and many, including some black players, do not distinguish between racist abuse and any other kind of criticism'.[37] For example, in the 2014–15 season Celtic's Aleksandar Tonev was given a seven match ban for 'using abusive language of a racist nature'[38] towards a fellow player, an incident which resulted in an outcry against racism within football and the offending player becoming unpopular among supporters.

In the 2010s many believe that the way racism demonstrates itself within professional British football is through the lack of representation of black and minority groups within the game, primarily through the opportunities given off the field, in coaching and the managing of teams. Jeffrey Webb, Head of FIFA's anti-racism committee, believes that racism within the English game was 'overt' and illustrated by the lack of black and ethnic minorities in boardrooms and dugouts. After Gordon Taylor of the Professional Footballers Association described it as a 'hidden problem', Webb stated: 'It's not hidden. It's hidden from a discussion standpoint. No-one wants to deal with it.'[39] The lack of ethnic minorities in coaching and upper-level administrative positions remains a major issue within British football and at the start of the 2015–16 season there were only three black managers within the Premier and Football League of 92 clubs. These were Chris Powell (Huddersfield), Keith Curle (Carlisle) and Jimmy Floyd Hasselbaink (Burton). In November 2015 Powell was sacked from his position after a number of poor results.

Another long-standing issue within British football is the attendance of minority groups at professional matches. Statistics state that minority groups make up 7.3 per cent of the total population, but just 1 per cent of spectators at Premier League matches. In 1996 the Sir Norman Chester for Football Research stated that black and Asian supporters were 'reluctant'[40] to attend matches, which still appears to be the case. Lack of attendance by members of the British Asian community can perhaps be linked to the lack of British Asian football players. Since it began in 1992, there has been just one British Asian player in the Premier League; Michael Chopra of Newcastle United. One problem facing British Asians is that they have suffered from stereotyping and notions of them not having either the interest or physique for the sport, and also being viewed as having a lack of stamina and poor coordination.[41] This has also been to the detriment of Asian women's involvement in sport, although other factors should be considered when considering this an entirely racial issue, as stated by Chappell *et al.*:

> The under-representation of Asian Women in British sport is partly the result of the patriarchal nature of Asian Family structures, and internalization of gender-specific roles and values that are historically rooted within Asian Culture. Sport is associated with masculinity, in which men are encouraged to participate, and women although not prohibited are neither expected nor encouraged to do so.[42]

British Asians of both sexes have continued to be heavily under-represented within British sport, excluding hockey, badminton and cricket.[43] Cricket's status as the game of Empire and its popularity within the indigenous people of the Indian subcontinent has ensured that it has a very different relationship and level of engagement with British Asians compared to football. According to the 2011 Census, those listed as either British Asian and from either an Indian, Pakistani, Bangladeshi or Sri Lankan background is 5.6 per cent of the population.

Although there is no evidence to suggest it was as widespread as in football, there is evidence that during the 1980s racial abuse from spectators was present at cricket matches. Gloucestershire fast bowler David Lawrence frequently experienced it when playing against Yorkshire during the 1980s. He stated: 'They called me nigger, black bastard, sambo, monkey, gorilla, they threw bananas and I had to take these insults.'[44] Burdsey states that Lawrence was not the only cricketer to suffer this abuse from the Yorkshire crowd, as during the 1980s and 1990s its infamous 'Western Terrace' gained a reputation for racist and Islamophobic comments by English supporters in matches versus the West Indies and the Indian subcontinent.[45]

The most famous issue of racism within English cricket occurred in 1990, when the former government Cabinet member, Norman Tebbit, suggested that a 'cricket test' should be used to measure migrants' loyalty to Britain.[46] He bemoaned that migrants were disloyal to Britain because they preferred to support their country of origin rather than England in cricket matches. He noted in an interview with the *Los Angeles Times*: 'A large proportion of Britain's Asian population fail to pass the cricket test.' He then went on to state: 'Which side do they cheer for? It's an interesting test. Are you still harking back to where you came from or where you are?'

This questioning of loyalty among British ethnic groups has been researched by academics and reveals aspects of racial exclusion within British society. Ratna *et al.* conducted research on the topic and one respondent answered that they did not support English national teams because of the way English people react 'because once they get a bit over the top, Rule Britannia and this nonsense starts coming out and then the English start coming out with the Tebbit test'.[47] For others, supporting the country of their ancestry has allowed them to keep a link with it and share a sense of identity with other members of their community.

References to the 'Tebbit Test' are occasionally made in summers when England plays against Asian opposition, such as in 2001 by the Indian-born captain of England, Nasser Hussain. After a match against Pakistan, he bemoaned that he 'cannot understand' why British-born Asians continue to support Pakistan or India.[48] Hussain's comments alienated him from many British Asians, who felt they were more accepted after Hussain was given the England captaincy in 1999.[49]

The support of British Asians for their country of ancestry has resulted in racist events in international matches. This most prominently occurred in 2006 when Sajid Mahmood, a Bolton-born fast bowler with Pakistani roots endured abuse from the crowd when he bowled against Pakistan in a test match in Manchester. He was dubbed a 'traitor' and was continually abused throughout the match. The incident occurred in a match where thousands of British citizens were present to support Pakistan; Werbner indicates: 'it is in the field of sport, through support of the [Pakistan] national team, that young British Pakistanis express their love of both Cricket and the home country, along with their sense of alienation and disaffection from British society.'[50]

The issue of alienation for British Asians within cricket has been an area of interest among sports authorities and academics. In 1997, a study by the Centre for Sport Development Research condemned England's cricket structure as overtly and institutionally racist. It stated that there was a two-tier structure within club cricket: one for whites and another for blacks and Asians. Two years later, Matthew Engel, the editor of the influential *Wisden Cricketers' Almanack*, suggested that black and Asian club players had become 'second-class' and that there was a 'cricketing apartheid' in operation.[51] The majority of research concerning the representation of British Asians within cricket has concentrated around the county of Yorkshire, a heartland of the game in England and the most successful of the English counties, winning 33 county championships in total.

At the highest level of the game within the county, the selection of Asian men has been a long-standing issue. In his article 'All Yorkshiremen are from Yorkshire, but some are more "Yorkshire" than others: British Asians and the myths of Yorkshire cricket', Thomas Fletcher argues that 'the long standing failure to field Asian and black players in the first team with any real consistency is demonstrative (for many) of ingrained racism within the club'.[52] He believes it was a result of the county's dislike of outsiders (which saw prior to 1992 only players who were born in Yorkshire able to represent the county): 'For many people in Yorkshire, minority ethnic communities (Asians included) were just not "Yorkshire" enough; in that, they did not imbue the famous sense of Yorkshire masculinity or possess the famous Yorkshire mentality.'[53] In another article, Fletcher wrote of identity and stereotyping impacting British Asian's opportunity to represent Yorkshire:

> Historically, Yorkshire cricketers are renowned for playing the game in a particular manner: in a Yorkshire-like way. Batsmen and bowlers alike should be hard, uncompromising and disciplined. Asian cricket has evolved with its own stereotypes attached to it (in Yorkshire at least), which constructed the way Asian people played the game as being incompatible with the Yorkshire way. Indeed, even in the present day, a number of insidious cultural racisms pertaining to Asian cricketers being irrational and unintelligent continue to exist at various levels of Yorkshire cricket.[54]

Despite the number of British Asians in Yorkshire, it was not until 2003 that a British Asian represented Yorkshire. The first player was Ismail Dawood, a wicketkeeper who had been born in Dewsbury. Dawood was followed by Ajmal Shahzad and Adil Rashid, who became the first British Asians from the Yorkshire Academy to play for the county, men who went on to become regulars in the Yorkshire team and represent England. The active pursuit of young British Asians by Yorkshire has had a negative impact for some who responded to Fletcher's research, believing it was having a negative impact on selection of white players.

The racial tension within league cricket has led many British Asians to form their own cricket clubs and leagues, rather than join established clubs. This can be attributed to long-standing tensions between the English and Asian populations, the racism which exists and how players who played for predominantly 'white'[55] teams felt excluded on the basis of such things as the drinking and social culture which existed at many clubs. Such is the divide that MacDonald *et al.* have argued that there are 'two separate and distinct cricket cultures in operation':

a white middle-aged, rural, county board-affiliated body of players and teams which play on good quality, privately rented cricket grounds in front of a handful of quiet and passive spectators; and a black and/or Asian cricket culture in which teams tend to be younger, urban, non affiliated and play on poor quality pitches, hired from local authorities, with relatively large groups of vociferous spectators in attendance.[56]

There have also been suggestions that racism in cricket is going beyond the field of play and that, like almost all British sporting associations, those running both English County Cricket and the England and Wales Cricket Board are racist. Comparable with those running other sporting associations, English cricket on the whole is run by men who can best be described as 'white British', although Wasim Khan, who was the first British Asian to play county cricket (when he played for Warwickshire in 1992) has led Chance to Shine, a charity which has attempted to increase the amount of cricket played in state schools. Since 2014 he has become chief executive of the Leicestershire County Cricket Club, one of the 18 county teams, making him one of the most influential men within the English professional game.

Rugby has a varied pattern within British culture. In England, the game has always enjoyed a strong middle-class following and this ensured that it remained amateur until 1988. Joseph Maguire argues that this was potentially part of the reason why in comparison to football it included relatively few ethnic minority players at elite level in the 1980s: 'maybe ... black working-class players "need" sponsored mobility to a greater extent than their middle-or upper-class counterparts'.[57] Although the game was amateur, top players were sponsored so that they could train and thus were essentially professional.

The first black player to represent England in rugby came a long time before Viv Anderson did so in football. In 1907, black player Jimmy Peters, who was known as 'Darkie Peters', played against Scotland. The *Yorkshire Post* commented that his selection was not popular on 'racial grounds'. Peters should have played against South Africa in 1906, but was withdrawn after the Springboks refused to play against him. Peters had played against the tourists earlier in the tour when they had visited Plymouth to play Devon. Initially, they refused to play against Peters because of his skin colour, but were persuaded to do so by the South African High Commissioner, who feared that the 20,000 fans present to watch the match might riot if the game was cancelled. Peters played one more test, against France where he scored a try. He was dropped for the next match against South Africa and did not represent England again.[58] Peters remained the only black player to represent England until Chris Oti won the first of his 13 caps against Scotland in 1988.[59]

In his research on the history of the English game, Tony Collins identified just one Jewish man to represent England in the amateur era (which ended in 1988). The man was John Raphael, an Oxford blue and first-class cricketer who played nine tests and was killed on the Western Front in 1917.[60] Equivalent to the England football team in the twenty-first century, the English national rugby team has been well represented by ethnic minority groups. The winning team from the 2003 World Cup had three players from an ethnic minority and for the 2015 World Cup five of the 31-man squad were from an ethnic group not described as 'white British'.

Along with elite footballers and cricketers, rugby players also suffered racial abuse from spectators during the 1980s. The following is a quote from an anonymous player who visited Gloucester during the 1980s as an opposition player:

> The worst incident I've had with any of the away supporters has got to be at Gloucester.... The first time I ran out there was probably about 7,000 in the ground, and as I've said there were the two wingers and myself, and as I ran out I heard

someone say 'Good God, there's three of them', and the chants as soon as I touched the ball, you know the chants would come out, and if the Gloucester forwards managed to get hold of me there was a big cheer.[61]

This type of abuse was similar to that experienced by professional footballers, as was the stereotyping which black players experienced during this period. In 1998, former union player Martin Offiah commented that there 'are some who still like to believe that although the black man may run like the wind, he'll crack under a bit of pressure'.[62] Other players also stated that they had suffered the same kind of stereotyping; 'you're black, you're quick, you're on the wing' and 'they say against black people is that they don't like being tackled, they don't like tackling, they haven't got good hands'.[63]

These examples are what Coakley considers to be part of the 'sports opportunity structure', which is the preservation of prejudices in sport, despite the excellence of black athletes and their over-representation in positions in team sports where they are deemed to require less intelligence.[64] This attitude is reflected on television and in the print media; racism can 'be seen to reflect a kind of nationalistic prioritization'.[65] There is also research that suggests that international success by black athletes gets played down in comparison with similar successes achieved by their white counterparts.[66]

Away from football and cricket, the biggest sport for the representation of ethnic minorities has been in track and field. In the 1980s the victories of black athletes Tessa Sanderson and Daley Thompson garnered them iconic status in Britain. In the view of Burdsey, their victories and those of boxer Frank Bruno, along with the success of many footballers, has changed the identity of black Britain:

> This sporting symbolism, alongside broader shifts in racial formation and achievements in popular culture, was indicative of an emerging, confident black Britishness. While by no means endorsed and validated by all – whether that be minority or majority communities – this positioning illuminated a changing politics of post-colonial nationhood and the influence of a (sporting) 'multicultural drift' (Hall, 2000). Elite sport has become subsequently a principal sphere in which minority ethnic people can emphasise their Britishness and attempt to subvert, temporarily racialized governmentalities of national belonging (Bruce & Hallinan, 2001, Burdsey, 2006; Carrington, 2013).[67]

Britain's most successful athlete in track and field is Mohamed Farah, who was born in Somalia and moved to Britain at the age of eight. He captured gold medals in the 5,000 and 10,000 metres during the London Olympics and is a five-time champion after victories at the 2011, 2013 and 2015 World Championships. Farah's success and popularity have seen him become a powerful symbol of a 'good'[68] migrant/Muslim in Britain. After his victories at the London Olympics there was an insinuation 'that public reception of Farah's athletic success might signify the wider integration and acceptance of Muslims in the UK'.[69] This coming after a decade of racial tension directed towards British Muslims.

The Great Britain and Northern Ireland team was enormously successful at both the Beijing 2008 and London 2012 Olympics, with the London Olympics 'Team GB' winning a record number of medals in the modern era of the Games. Success at both of these games came from athletes from privileged backgrounds. Daniel Burdsey states that the majority come from 'white sports',[70] such as in Beijing where Britain's 52 of 77 medals came in the sports of cycling (19), rowing (23) and sailing (10). All of the athletes who won medals in these events were white and in total there were only six British medallists in Beijing from minority ethnic backgrounds. At London in 2012 there were in total ten medals won by eight different medallists from minority ethnic backgrounds. This marked an improvement in number and in percentage as minority athletes took 6.5 per cent of the British medals, an improvement from 4.5 per cent in 2008, with gold medals won by Mo Farah (2), Nicola Adams and Anthony Joshua.

The administrations of the London 2012 Olympics and the British Olympic Association is not a reflection of the racial make-up of Britain and, like other sports, those at the top of British sports are predominantly 'white'. All 13 members of the British Olympic Association are white, while only one of the 18 members of the London Delivery Authority (LDA) board, one of the 18 members of the London Organising Committee of the Olympic Games and Paralympic Games (LOCOG) board, and two of the 17 members of the LOCOG senior team are from minority ethnic backgrounds.[71]

The history of anti-Semitism in British sport has been covered in detail by David Dee in his monograph *Sport and British Jewry: Integration, Ethnicity and Anti-Semitism, 1890–1970*.[72] It covers a range of sports in Britain, including golf, which saw such fierce anti-Semitism that Jewish golfers founded their own golf clubs.

The first of these clubs was formed in 1923 when Moor Allerton Golf Club was built north of Leeds. This club, like other Jewish clubs that followed, such as Whitefield in North Manchester (1932) and Shirley in Solihull (1958), were built with money that came from the local Jewish community. This was required because clubs were hostile to Jewish entry. Dee writes that Jewish golfers suffered from the 'blackball system' and a quota system, such as was in place at Hendon Golf Club, where the club stated 'we do accept them, but only in certain numbers'.[73] As was seen within other sports, the English Golf Union (EGU), the national ruling body for the sport, was insensitive to racial issues. Dee cites the *Jewish Chronicle* in 1960, which quotes the EGU's captain, W.G.L. Folkard, who defended a club's right to ban Jews by noting, 'a golf club is the extension of one's home, the election of new members is a purely domestic matter'.[74]

Anti-Semitism was also evident in tennis and the career of Angela Buxton, the Wimbledon Ladies Doubles Champion from 1956, and can be seen in the view of David Dee as 'typical'[75] of the Jewish experience in the sport during the mid-twentieth century. She was frequently turned down for membership at clubs and also was discriminated against in competition on account of being Jewish.

In more recent times, the association Tottenham Hotspur supporters have made with the Jewish religion has brought about discussion and controversy. Despite the claims of supporters, the club has no Jewish ancestry, although it was popular with Jewish immigrants who settled in London during the late nineteenth and early twentieth centuries. Some Tottenham supporters have branded themselves 'yids', a term which in 2013 the Metropolitan Police claimed was insulting to Jews and if heard could lead to criminal prosecution and/or a stadium ban.[76] Despite this, many supporters have continued to identify themselves by this term.

In 2014 West Bromwich Albion's French striker Nicolas Anelka, who celebrated scoring a goal by 'bending the elbow of his left arm and pointing his hand across his chest to his extended right bicep, in a gesture known as the quenelle'[77] was banned from competition. This gesture has strong anti-Semitic connotations in France, from where it originates. Despite Anelka's claim that it was an anti-establishment and not an anti-Semitic or racist statement, he was found guilty by an FA-appointed Independent Regulatory Commission of making a gesture that was 'abusive and/or indecent and/or insulting and/or improper (FA Rule E3[1]) and which 'included a reference to ethnic origin and/or race and/or religion or belief' (FA Rule E3 [2]).[78] The consequence of this was a five match ban, £8,000 fine and a requirement to attend an educational programme.

Away from elite sports, there is evidence to suggest there are still many racial issues in recreational and social sports. In 2003, Birmingham City Council catalogued barriers to leisure their black and minority ethnic groups (BMEs) faced, of which 'Overt Racism' was stated as being one of five issues, making up 17 per cent. It gave examples of the problems BMEs faced:

- abuse – called names (at swimming pool);
- people from other religious groups came to cause trouble so we Hindus never get to enjoy our events;
- there's always tension from teenagers in the park … they think they own the parks;
- I go out covered and you get nasty comments (park);
- English children (at Youth Centres) are racist.

Recreational sport is one area under constant scrutiny regarding inclusion. This was a major issue which the London 2012 Organising Committee attempted to address through its platform 'Inspire a Generation'.

Britain and British sport has had and will continue to face issues of racism. The immigration that Britain has experienced and will continue to experience through the migration of mainly EU nations faces new issues regarding race and racism. There can be little doubt that during the late 1970s and 1980s the atmosphere in British sport could be described as 'institutionally racist', with gestures commonplace from the terraces of many sporting stadiums. The issues commonplace in football have been largely eradicated and are no longer culturally acceptable as they once were.

Despite the steps taken, there are still many remaining issues across sport. Racial abuse of players playing elite and recreation sports remains. This primarily appears through discrimination and exclusion. Exclusion of ethnic minorities among those organising and coaching sports remains a prominent issue in the present day and one still in need of being addressed.

Notes

1 Peter Hennessey, *Never Again: Britain, 1945–51* (St Ives: Penguin, 2006), 442.
2 Cited in Paul I. Campbell, 'Cavaliers Made Us "United": Local Football, Identity Politics and Second-Generation African-Caribbean Youth in the East Midlands c.1970–9', *Sport in History* 33, 2, (2013), 176.
3 David Dee, '"There is No Discrimination Here, but the Committee Never Elects Jews": Anti-Semitism in British Golf, 1894–1970', *Patterns of Prejudice* 47, 12 (2013), 119.
4 Neil Wigglesworth, *The Story of Sport in England* (Abingdon: Routledge, 2007), 162.
5 Ibid.
6 John Solomons, *Race and Racism in Britain*, 3rd edition (Basingstoke: Palgrave, 2003), 44.
7 Ibid.
8 Phil Vasili, *Walter Tull (1888–1918): Officer, Footballer* (London: Raw, 2009), 16.
9 Scott Fleming and Alan Tomlinson, 'Football, Xenophobia and Racism-Europe and the Old Britain', in Udo Merkel and Walter Tokarski, eds, *Racism and Xenophobia in European Football* (Aachen: Meyer & Meyer, 1996), 2.
10 Les Back, Tim Crabble and John Solomons, 'Racism in Football: Patterns of Continuity and Change', in Adam Brown, ed., *Fanatics! Power Identity and Fandom in Football* (London: Routledge, 1998), 71.
11 Ibid., 84.
12 Dominic Sandbrook, *Seasons in the Sun: the Battle for Britain, 1974–1979* (London: Penguin, 2013), 575.
13 Tim Crabbe, 'From the Terraces to the Boardrooms: Reviewing Theories and Perspectives on Racism in Football', *International Review of Modern Sociology* 32, 2 (2006), 242.
14 Back *et al.*, 'Racism in Football', 79.
15 Ibid., 78.

16 John Barnes in *When Saturday Comes*, cited in John Garland and Michael Rowe, 'Field of Dreams? An Assessment of Antiracism in British Football', *Journal of Ethnic and Migration Studies* 25, 2 (1999), 340.

17 Ian Wright, *Mr Wright: The Explosive Autobiography of Ian Wright* (London: Willow, 1995), 104, cited in Ben Carrington, 'Ian Wright, "Race" and English identity', in *Sport Stars: Cultural Politics of Sporting Celebrity* (London: Routledge, 2001), 108.

18 James Walvin, *The People's Game: The History of Football Revisited* (Edinburgh: Mainstream, 1994), 194.

19 Richard Holt, *Sport and the British* (Oxford: Clarendon Press: 1989), 339.

20 John Hargreaves, *Sport, Power and Culture* (Cambridge: Polity, 1987), 113.

21 Walvin, *The People's Game*, 194.

22 *The Times*, 3 March 1981, quoted in Sandbrook, *Seasons in the Sun*, 575.

23 Garland and Rowe, 'Field of Dreams?', 342.

24 Ellis Cashmore, *Black Sportsmen* (London: Routledge & Kegan Paul, 1982), 45.

25 J. Garland and M. Rowe, 'Policing Racism at Football Matches: An Assessment of Recent Developments in Policing Strategies', *International Journal of the Sociology of the Law* 27 (2000), 251–66.

26 The Football Task Force, 'Eliminating Racism from Football', a report to the Minister for Sport, 30 March 1998.

27 Cited in Mike Collins, 'Social Exclusion and Sport in a Multicultural Society', in Mike Collins with Tess Kay, *Sport and Social Exclusion* (London: Routledge, 2003), 137.

28 Daniel Burdsey, 'One Week in October: Luis Suárez, John Terry and the Turn to Racial Neoliberalism in English Men's Professional Football', *Identities* 21, 5 (2014), 429.

29 'No Luis Suarez Appeal from Liverpool over Racism Ban', BBC Sport, 3 January 2012, www.bbc. co.uk/sport/0/football/16402384, accessed 29 November 2015.

30 For more on this issue, see Verner Møller, 'Racial Issues Beyond Black and White: The Luis Suarez Incident', in J. Nauright, A. Cobley, and D. Wiggins, eds, *Beyond C.L.R. James: Race and Ethnicity in Sport* (Fayetteville, AR: University of Arkansas Press, 2015).

31 Burdsey, 'One Week in October', 430.

32 Dominic Fifield, 'England Face Dilemma Over Racism', *Guardian*, 21 December 2011, www. theguardian.com/football/2011/dec/21/john-terry-charged-chelsea-racism, accessed 29 November 2015.

33 Burdsey 'One Week in October', 430.

34 Ibid., 431.

35 Ibid., 433.

36 Ibid.

37 Garland and Rowe, 'Field of Dreams?', 340.

38 'Celtic: Aleksandar Tonev Charged Over Alleged Racism', BBC Sport, 19 September 2014, www. bbc.co.uk/sport/0/football/29285903, accessed 12 September 2015.

39 'Racism in English Football Overt – FIFA Vice-President Jeffrey Webb', BBC Sport, 9 October 2014, www.bbc.co.uk/sport/0/football/29548003, accessed 3 September 2015.

40 Sir Norman Chester Centre for Football Research (1996) 'Carling Premiership Fan Surveys 1995/96', cited in Garland and Rowe, 'Field of Dreams?', 342.

41 J. Baines and R. Patel, *Asians Can't Play Football* (Birmingham: Asian Social Development Agency, 1996); T. Bayliss, 'PE and Racism: Making Changes', *Multicultural Teaching* 7, 5 (1998), 20.

42 Robert Chappell, Daniel Burdsey and Kate Collinson, '"Race" and Ethnicity in English Netball,' *Women in Sport and Physical Activity Journal* 13, 1 (2004), 58.

43 Frank Kew, *Sport, Social Problems and Issues* (London: Butterworth-Heinemann, 1997).

44 Chris Searle, *Pitch of Life: Writings on Cricket* (Manchester: The Parrs Wood Press, 2001), 15.

45 Daniel Burdsey, 'Midnight's Grandchildren at the MCC: British Asians, Identity and English First-class Cricket', in Chris Rumford and Stephen Wagg (eds), *Cricket and Globalization* (Cambridge: Cambridge Scholars Publishing, 2010), 261.

46 'Tebbit Proposes Cricket Test for Immigrants', *Daily Express*, 21 April 1990.

47 Ratna Aarti, Lawrence Stefan and Partington Janine, '"Getting Inside the Wicket": Strategies for the Social Inclusion of British Muslim Cricketers', *Journal of Policy Research in Tourism, Leisure and Events* 8, 1 (2016), 11.

48 Raj Kaushal, 'The Tebbit Test is Just Not Cricket', *Guardian*, 25 November 2001, www.theguardian. com/uk/2001/nov/25/race.world9, accessed 3 September 2015.

49 Kamran Abbasi, 'East or West, Nasser's Best', *Guardian*, 25 August 1999, www.theguardian.com/ sport/1999/aug/25/cricket5, accessed 3 August 2015.

50 Pnina Werbner, 'Our Blood is Green: Cricket, Identity and Social Empowerment Among British Pakistanis', in Jeremy McClancy, ed., *Sport, Identity and Ethnicity* (Oxford: Berg, 1996), 104.

51 Ibid.

52 Thomas Fletcher, 'All Yorkshiremen are from Yorkshire, but Some are More "Yorkshire" Than Others: British Asians and the Myths of Yorkshire Cricket', *Sport in Society* 15, 2 (2012), 228.

53 Ibid.

54 Thomas Fletcher, 'The Making of English Cricket Cultures: Empire, Globalization and (Post) Colonialism', *Sport in Society* 14, 1 (2001), 19.

55 Ratna *et al.*, 'Getting Inside the Wicket', 7.

56 Ian MacDonald, Sharda Ugra and Andy Sellins, *Anyone for Cricket? Equal Opportunities and Changing Cricket Cultures in Essex and East London*, quoted in Dominic Malcolm, '"Clean Bowled?" Cricket, Racism and Equal Opportunities', *Journal of Ethnic and Migration Studies* 28, 2 (2002), 309–310.

57 Joseph Maguire, 'Sport, Racism and British Society: A Sociological Study of England's Elite Male Afro/Caribbean Soccer and Rugby Union Players', in Grant Jarvie, ed., *Sport, Racism and Ethnicity* (London: Routledge, 1991), 96.

58 Ian Thomas, 'James Peters the 1st Black Rugby Player', www.blackhistorymonth.org.uk/james-peters-the-1st-black-rug/4566978699, accessed 21 August 2015.

59 Tony Collins, *A Social History of English Rugby Union* (London: Routledge, 2009), 102.

60 Ibid.

61 Maguire, 'Sport, Racism and British Society', 116.

62 Ibid., 115.

63 Ibid.

64 Coakley, *Sports in Society*, 340.

65 Ibid.

66 David Stread, 'Sport and the Media', in Barrie Houlihan, *Sport and Society*, 2nd edition (London: Sage, 2008), 340.

67 Daniel Burdsey, 'One Man Named Mo: Race, Nation and the London 2012 Olympic Games', *Sociology of Sport Journal* 33, 1 (2016).

68 Ibid., 17.

69 Ibid.

70 Daniel Burdsey, 'The Technicolor Olympics? Race, Representation and the 2012 London Games', in John Sugden and Alan Tomlinson, eds, *Watching the Olympics: Politics, Power and Representation* (London: Routledge, 2011), 76.

71 Burdsey, 'The Technicolor Olympics?', 75.

72 David Dee, *Sport and British Jewry: Integration, Ethnicity and Anti-Semitism, 1890–1970* (Manchester: Manchester University Press, 2014).

73 *Hendon Times*, 1 April 1960, quoted in David Dee, 'There is no Discrimination Here', 128.

74 *Jewish Chronicle*, 1 April 1960, in Dee, 'There is no Discrimination Here', 130.

75 Dee, 'There is No Discrimination Here', 119.

76 Hendrik Buchheister, 'Yid Army: Football Teams: Jewish Identities Questioned', 4 October 2013, *Der Spiegel*, www.spiegel.de/international/europe/football-why-tottenham-and-ajax-fans-have-a-jewish-identity-a-926095.html, accessed 28 August 2015.

77 Daniel Burdsey and Sean Gorman, 'When Adam met Rio: Conversations on Racism, Anti-Racism and Multiculturalism in the Australian Football League and English Premier League', *Sport in Society* 15, 5 (2014), 577–87.

78 Football Regulatory Commission, 2014.

13

RACISM AND EUROPEAN FOOTBALL

Mark Doidge

In July 2015, the FC Ufa and ex-Arsenal player Emannuel Frimpong was sent off for reacting to Spartak Moscow fans who aimed racist chants at him throughout the game. Three years earlier, members of the Landscrona fan-group at Zenit St. Petersburg wrote an open letter to the club stating that they should not sign 'dark-skinned players' or 'sexual minorities'. Despite media stories to the contrary, these episodes are not unique to Russia or Eastern Europe. In January 2013, Kevin-Prince Boateng, AC Milan's Ghanaian midfielder, walked off the pitch in a friendly match against Pro Patria. He had received sustained racist abuse from the home fans and was supported by his teammates in his decision to leave the field. These small numbers of examples demonstrate the pervasiveness of racism in football across Europe. Yet these events do not only take place in the football stadium. The British anti-racism organisation Kick It Out released findings into racism in English football in May 2015. Not only did they reveal that racism continues to be a major problem in English football, but they demonstrated how it was finding new mediums of expression. Social media in particular was frequently used to target players. While at Liverpool in 2015, the Italian striker Mario Balotelli received over 8,000 abusive tweets, half of which included racist comments. Frequently, fans are the only ones blamed for racism by the authorities and media. It would be a fallacy to argue that these attitudes do not occur elsewhere in the football hierarchy, particularly given the paucity of non-white players in administration and coaching across Europe. Indeed, details of text messages sent between former Cardiff City manager Malky Mackay and his sporting director Iain Moody in 2013 showed how racist and anti-Semitic language was used to denigrate players and agents.

What these examples show is how pervasive racism is in European football. The demographic constitution of European nations has changed, with greater migration, and this is reflected in the composition of football teams. This rapidly changed after the passing of the *Bosman* ruling in 1995. Jean-Marc Bosman played for SRC Liège in the Belgian first division. His contract expired in 1990 and he wanted to sign for Dunkerque in France. Liège refused to sanction the move after there was a disagreement over transfer fees. Bosman was forced to train with the reserve team and had his wages reduced. With the support of FIFPro, the players' union, Bosman successfully challenged the Belgian football federation's regulations that permitted this situation. The European Court of Justice saw the Bosman case as a restriction on the movement of workers, in contravention of EU law. After the ruling, players were free to move between

EU countries and permitted to move at the end of their contract without a transfer fee imposed. This coincided with a dramatic economic transformation of European football. New television deals and corporate sponsorship packages dramatically increased the income of clubs, who then purchased a range of star players from across the globe. The make up of teams across Europe changed dramatically.

Despite these changes, racism has been part of European football for decades. The imperial and colonial histories of European nations witnessed players from across empires playing in early football matches. The conflation of nationhood and race in the late nineteenth century had an impact on sport. Clearly this reached its nadir between the World Wars, when nationalist ideology explicitly excluded those who did not conform to the notion of *jus sanguinis*, or citizenship by bloodline. Jews, gypsies, and non-nationals were excluded from sports clubs and national teams. Despite this ideology, rules were flexible. Mussolini permitted South American-born footballers with Italian families to play for the Italian World Cup winning teams for 1934 and 1938.[1] Since the 1970s European legislatures have introduced equality laws to tackle structural racism. Yet it should not be assumed that making racism illegal automatically stopped its practice. As previously noted, racism still occurs in football across Europe. As a result, charities and organisations like Kick It Out in England and Never Again in Poland have been established to raise awareness of the problem and campaign to remove racism from the sport. This chapter locates racism in European football and shows that the focus has been on racism from fans, but not in the hierarchies of the game. It also outlines the anti-racism organisations that have campaigned tirelessly to try to eradicate racism from football.

Racism and European football

In his essay 'The Sporting Spirit', George Orwell traced the growth of competitive sports to the rise of nationalism. 'Serious sport', Orwell argued, 'has nothing to do with fair play. It is bound up with hatred, jealousy, boastfulness, disregard of all rules and sadistic pleasure in witnessing violence: in other words it is war minus the shooting.' Orwell's analysis correctly focused on the negative and divisive aspects of football. It divides rival teams into winners and losers. It also acts as a vehicle for various forms of identity. Since the nineteenth century, football has been a ritual that permits people to perform their local and national identities through symbolic victory over rivals. The roots of the game can be traced back to before the sport became codified. Localised identity in Italy manifested itself in the intra-city rivalries displayed in the *palio* in Siena, *palio marinario* in Livorno, and the violent football game of *calcio fiorentino* in Florence.[2] Indeed, hooligan rivalries have been formed through the symbolic violence of masculine fan groups gaining superiority over opponents.[3]

Although nationalism is important in understanding racial and ethnic differences in football, it is not the only reason. A growth in localism during the 1970s and 1980s across Europe has also contributed to a heightened sense of localised identity in football.[4] This has been particularly acute in Italy, where there has been a long-standing identification with the locale long before the formation of the nation-state. Historical city-states preceded the nation of Italy and ensured that the Italian state has struggled to impose itself on citizens. This localism, or *campanilismo* has enhanced the identity of football fans in Italy, and has been incorporated into the identity of the *ultras*.[5] Localism entered the political arena in the 1980s with the growth of the Northern League, who openly sought cessation from Italy. As Podaliri and Balestri argue, 'This link to the small "mother country", which is very close to extreme right-wing values, facilitate racist and xenophobic behavioural patterns inside the stadia.'[6] This was reflected in chants and banners such as 'Bergamo is a Nation, all the rest is South', and 'Brescia to the people from Brescia'. At the same time, chants and banners denigrated the south of Italy, particularly Napoli, who was performing well in Serie A, by declaring 'Welcome to Italy' or 'Forza Etna' ('Go Etna').[7] This 'territorial discrimination' has continued into the twenty-first century and was linked to racism by the Italian authorities in 2013.[8] This ritualistic abuse highlights how groups become racialised and situated in a hierarchy of difference.

Racism (and other forms of abuse) has to be situated within fan rivalries.[9] Understanding broader football fan culture helps to locate the abuse that occurs in the sport. De Biasi and Lanfranchi have argued that the 'importance of difference' is central to the *ultras'* identity.[10] Highlighting what 'we' dislike, is reasserting what 'we' are not; denigrating rivals is part of this ritual. Abuse is directed at those that do not fit into what Back *et al.* call a 'structure of antipathy'.[11] Racism is part of this wider performance of abuse. As King highlights, racist abuse falls into a hierarchy.[12] When fans sing 'I'd rather be a Paki than a Turk' they are implicitly saying that being Pakistani is considered to be culturally and morally low in the list of nations; being Turkish is judged as worse.

Various markers of difference are utilised by fans to distinguish them from their rivals. Often, it can be related to club colours, symbols, or players.[13] Race, nation, and ethnicity can be added to this list.[14] In each case, these symbols are not absolute but relative and contingent on specific contexts. For example, Back *et al.* use the example of a black England fan attending a game against Scotland and noticing someone from Combat 18 (a far-right group).[15] There was an acknowledgement that the common enemy that day was Scotland, not each other. It is for this reason that fans who chant racist abuse at a rival black player can equally valorise their own players from black and ethnic minorities. Acceptance is contingent on various factors, including localised notions of nationhood, masculinity, and class.[16]

Despite the links to nationalism and localism, racism in European football is not always ideologically or politically motivated. Racism manifests itself in the stadium in two broad ways. There are fans who are ideologically motivated and politically driven. These fans are members of far-right organisations and seek to use football to promote their ideological beliefs. This is 'instrumental' or 'real' racism.[17] In contrast, there is 'organic' or 'accidental' racism.[18] This is when the crowd respond to events on the pitch, and use chants that can be considered racist, but without wider political intent. This form of abuse is usually aligned to the 'importance of difference' in broader football culture. Fans (and players) see denigration of rivals as a way of giving their team an advantage. It also helps foster group identity by reinforcing what they are not. This is achieved by highlighting and extenuating these markers of difference such as skin colour, height, hair (or lack of it), and perceived masculinity.

Understanding racism also needs to be culturally understood. Europe is a diverse continent that has many different historical and geographical distinctions. The colonial history of some Northern and Western European nations has facilitated certain patterns of migration and they have become multicultural much earlier. Eastern European nations had severe restrictions on migration in the Soviet era, while some Southern European nations have historically been spaces of emigration rather than immigration. It is this complexity that makes clear we should look at *racisms*. This helps identify the phenomenon's heterogeneous nature. As Garland and Rowe argue, this is important in 'moving away from singular conceptions of racism, which seek to explain it as though it were a unitary phenomenon, and towards an understanding which recognises the plurality of racisms'.[19] While racism based on skin colour is a clearer marker of distinction, other forms of ethnic abuse remain strong across Europe. Anti-Romany and anti-Jewish abuse remains culturally strong in parts of Eastern and Southern Europe and is not seen as racist in the same way as abuse directed at players of African origin.[20] For example, the term 'Jew' is used pejoratively in Poland to denigrate rivals. Teams and groups of fans are associated with Jewish founders or players and this is then turned into a term of abuse. In particular, Cracovia are targeted as being Jewish, even though the majority of their fans are Catholic. Similarly, fan groups at Lazio have chanted anti-Semitic abuse at Livorno and Roma fans for their perceived Jewish heritage. Consequently, anti-racist measures find resistance and/ or confusion when implemented across the continent.

The problem with the term 'racism' is that it implies there are separate and distinct races. There is no 'black' or 'white' race, but attributes are assigned to individuals based on phenotypes, like skin colour. Garland and Rowe seek to move towards racialisation as an approach to the phenomenon as this reinforces its socially constructed nature, rather than assume that race is predetermined.[21] In some jurisdictions, racism is seen as only directed against people with black skin. This issue was highlighted by Burdsey, who observed that a black–white dualism emerged in anti-racism campaigns in the 1960s; this dualism 'remained dominant and unchallenged in English football for longer than in other institutions'.[22] Effectively this rendered other ethnic groups, such as British Asians, absent from attention. Significantly, outside of Britain, the black–white dualism of Anglo-American discourse does not have the same history.[23] As diverse migration patterns have affected various European nations differently, ethnicities are also utilised.

As Back *et al.* demonstrated, 'common sense' understandings of abuse are located within fan rivalries.[24] Referring to skin colour (or any other marker of difference) is not always seen as racism. When the former Prime Minister of Italy, Silvio Berlusconi, complimented Barack Obama for being 'young, handsome and sun-tanned', it was not deemed offensive in Italy. Indeed, many anti-Berlusconi protestors showed solidarity with Obama by blackening their faces. Something similar occurred in Treviso in 2001 when one of their players was racially abused; the rest of the team 'blacked up' to show solidarity.[25] The problem here is that in the Anglo-Saxon world, especially in the UK and USA, this is seen as an insult based on a long-standing minstrel tradition that sought to mimic African culture.

Racism in European football is highly nuanced and complicated; abuse is not automatically racism. The case of Mario Balotelli highlights the complexity of this phenomenon.[26] Balotelli has played for AC Milan and Inter in Italy and Manchester City and Liverpool in England. He was born to Ghanaian migrants in Palermo who were unable to afford his medical care when he fell ill as a child. Two years later Balotelli was adopted by a white Italian family from Brescia. While at Inter, he was subjected to a wide range of abuse from rival fans. The most common was '*se saltelli, muore Balotelli*' ('If you jump up and down, Balotelli dies'). This is not automatically racist as the same chant was aimed at Cristiano Lucarelli, a Livorno player who was noted for his communist politics. Yet Balotelli is simultaneously a threat to the rival team, and seen as a symbol of difference to the fans. His perceived attitude and petulance deemed him inferior and not worthy of the masculine world of football. Further analysis of the abuse targeted at Balotelli also highlighted that many racialised slurs were incorporated into the abuse, including comments like 'There are no Black Italians'. This is not to say that *all* people abusing Balotelli are racist, but some are using racist language. Understanding the nuances of racism will hopefully help challenge this abuse in football stadiums.

Structural racism

Much of the academic and media focus has been on racism in the stadium. Racism is always seen as a problem of a minority of fans attending matches. What the Malky Mackay case showed in Britain is that managers and coaches also hold racist attitudes and use racist language. It is a fallacy to think that only fans hold views that are widespread elsewhere in society. Burdsey argues that the blight of racism has not disappeared in England, and recent events have only reinforced it.[27] Yet these examples are often attributed to individuals.[28] The examples of Luis Suárez and John Terry were attributed to individual players, while the example of Chelsea fans aggressively pushing a black Parisian off a metro train in the French capital were seen as a minority.

While great strides have been made, it does not mean that racism has been eradicated in European football. 'Common sense' arguments state that football cannot be racist precisely because there are players from numerous ethnicities on every team. Extending this logic, it would be possible to argue that nineteenth-century plantation owners were not racist because their slaves were black! Burdsey observes:

> Overly optimistic views of progress neatly sidestep questions around power and politics, and ignore the fact that to look beyond the multiethnic spectacle on the pitch, in Europe at least, football remains a primarily white institution: games are watched by crowds of predominantly white supporters, controlled by white match officials, and teams are run by white (male) managers, coaches, owners and directors.[29]

Structural issues remain within football, including exclusion of members of many different groups from access to the game. Old white men remain in positions of power within the sport.

Much of this approach is due to a growing individualisation of racism across Europe, predominantly in Northern Europe. Coinciding with a similar neoliberal approach in other areas of society, success and failure are individualised. Wealth accumulation and career success are seen as rewards for individual hard work and enterprise, while the poor are seen as feckless and lazy. As part of broader neoliberal processes across North America and Europe, structural issues are marginalised as governments seek to justify their reduction in the role of the state. This situation has also occurred in regards to racism. Goldberg states that 'in diluting, if not erasing, race in all public affairs of the state, neo-liberal proponents nevertheless seek to privatize racisms alongside most everything else'.[30]

Through this 'colour-blindness', racial neoliberalism removes states' or institutions' obligations to deal with racism. As Goldberg argues, 'the individualization of wrongdoing, its localization as personal and so private preference expression, erases institutional racisms precisely as conceptual possibility'.[31] By locating it as the individual failure of the person engaging in racist behaviour, or the lack of hard work by the person of colour who has not succeeded, then the authorities can absolve themselves of responsibility. Ultimately, 'colour-blindness works as an ideology by obscuring the institutional arrangements reproducing structural inequalities and does so in a way that justifies and defends the racial status quo'.[32] Moreover, colour-blindness is publicly argued by predominantly white populations who suggest that they do not see colour. This is particularly apposite in football as club owners and administrators deny that race is an issue.[33] Long *et al.* show that those in power often place the blame for lack of minority ethnic players and fans on the groups themselves.[34] More pertinently, Ratna suggested that white coaches and administrators in the women's game thought that the lack of British Asian footballers was due to issues within South Asian communities, rather than racism.[35]

Denial is often the starting point for clubs and football authorities. Back *et al.* argued:

> the typical 'public' response of football clubs and individuals associated with the game to allegations of racism has historically been one of denial: denial that the problem exists at any significant level at individual clubs or amongst players, denial that there is a problem within the game more generally and, on occasion, denial that racism exists itself as a problem in society.[36]

Denial of structural issues is even more pronounced. Long and McNamee have highlighted the slow and conservative attitude towards change within the administration of football.[37] As noted earlier, 'common sense' arguments are identified to show that there cannot be racism as there are many different nationalities and ethnicities playing the game. This argument, as Burdsey states, does not deny that racism existed; it argues that racism has disappeared.[38] This aligns with the broader categories of racism identified by Back *et al.* and Müller *et al.*, where racism was motivated by politically ideological groups.[39] These have been removed and consequently any racism is 'accidental'[40] or comes down to individual failure.

Responses from governing bodies and clubs are wildly different across Europe. Governing bodies simply deny racism or pass a superficial sanction. After the Suárez and Terry incidents in 2011, the president of FIFA, Sepp Blatter, stated that these issues should be dealt with by shaking hands at the end of the match. This attitude was also clear after the sending off of Emmanuel Frimpong in Russia in July 2015. The general director of Ufa, Shamil Gazizov, said the taunts were 'an unfortunate incident' and that Frimpong was in the wrong and 'sometimes you even have to hold back the tears and just put up with it'. These attitudes locate racism within the broader culture of abuse in football. Players have to demonstrate hegemonic masculinity, develop a thick skin, and demonstrate that they are physically and psychologically able to deal with the rigours of the game. Sensitivity to abuse is identified as an individual weakness rather than a structural issue.

In keeping with these attitudes, governing bodies have failed to successfully challenge the systemic racism within the game. Where sanctions are imposed, the fines amount to a few hours' wages for star footballers or clubs. For example, the Italian football federation fined Juventus €20,000 and ordered them to play a match behind 'closed doors' for the various episodes of abuse directed at Mario Balotelli.[41] To put this into context, they fined Inter's manager Jose Mourinho €40,000 for making a crossed-arm 'handcuffs' gesture after his team had two players sent off, which insinuated that the federation was corrupt and were trying to prevent Inter from winning the title. As Doidge states, 'When accusations against the Federation are punished more severely than widespread racist abuse, there is little surprise that the problem continues.'[42] Elsewhere, the Italian federation has suggested that players enter the field with 'No Al Razzismo' banners. These empty symbolic gestures have been reflected elsewhere in Europe and represent the 'non-performativity' of anti-racism in sport.[43]

Racist attitudes pervade all hierarchies of football. The Malky Mackay case in England illustrates the discussions and views held in private by management. The disclosure of private texts between the former manager of Cardiff, Mackay, and his sporting director, Iain Moody, illustrated how groups were identified on the basis of their perceived race or ethnicity. Black players were seen as going to jail, South Koreans as dog-eaters, and Jews as money grabbing. Twelve months after the case was leaked to the media, the English FA took no action, stating it had no jurisdiction as there was a 'legitimate expectation that these messages were only for the eyes of the other person'. A similar approach was taken with Richard Scudamore, the chief executive of the Premier League, when it was alleged he had sent sexist emails. As they were private, he escaped censure. In contrast, Paul Elliot, the former player and trustee of the Kick It Out anti-racism campaign, was forced to resign by the FA after a private text emerged in which Elliot used the 'N-word' in an argument with a business partner. The 'non-performativity' of anti-racism reflects your position in the hierarchy as well as your skin colour.

Similar issues occur across Europe. Club presidents have made racist comments about players and have not been sanctioned. The president of Palermo, Maurizio Zamparini, described the former Chelsea and Fiorentina player Adriano Mutu as a 'crafty little gypsy'.[44] When Mario Balotelli moved to AC Milan in 2013, the brother of the club's president (and former prime minister) and editor of *Il Giornale* newspaper, Paolo Berlusconi, invited attendees at a rally for his brother's political party to come back for a party and meet 'the nigger of the family [Balotelli]'. In the summer of 2014 the Italian football federation held its elections for president. The favourite, Carlo Tavecchio, made a speech that lamented the number of foreign players in Italy and suggested they were the reason for Italy's failure at the World Cup in Brazil. As part of this speech, he referred to Opti Poba, a fictional player 'who was previously eating bananas and now is a first team player for Lazio'. Tavecchio inferred that players from Africa were monkeys and not worthy of playing in Italy. Sadly, Tavecchio was still elected as head of the Italian football federation. This illustrates how many presidents and administrators are ignorant or wilfully blind to the issues of racism in sport.

Despite the failures of national football federations to adequately tackle racism in football, UEFA has finally begun to provide a uniform approach across Europe. While some of this can fall into the 'non-performativity' of anti-racism, UEFA has started to take a moral stance. The European football federation has introduced a zero-tolerance approach to racist chanting by fans in European competitions. They have also lent their support to national federations, such as Italy, to sanction racist abuse in national leagues. UEFA work in partnership with Football Against Racism Europe (FARE) and other European anti-racism groups to communicate a clear anti-racism message. These actions are vital if the issue of racism across Europe is to be addressed. There needs to be clear boundaries and an unambiguous approach. However, it is also important that UEFA and these groups work with fans to educate them and explain how and why racist actions are unacceptable.[45] Taking a moralising tone will push certain masculine fan groups into acts of resistance, some of whom feel persecuted by the authorities. In some cases, sanctions bring about the very behaviour the punishment is attempting to stop as the fans resist and rebel against authority.[46] Fines should be used to encourage education schemes and stadium closures should only be the last resort. It is imperative that authorities and groups work with fans as they often have led the way in challenging racism in football.

Anti-racism in European football

The failure of the authorities to tackle racism in football has resulted in players and fans taking the initiative themselves. The 1990s were a significant time for the politicisation of football fans in Europe.[47] The economic changes that transformed the sport into a global media spectacle encouraged many fans to mobilise to challenge the changes as they felt that fans were losing control of their clubs, and owners were focused on extracting profits rather than good sport. Many of these Independent Supporters Associations and *ultras* groups incorporated anti-racism and anti-discrimination into their activities. Other groups also emerged to challenge racism in football. This coincided with many black players openly criticising racism in the game. In the past they were encouraged to develop a thick skin, as was suggested for Emmanuel Frimpong in Russia. By the 1990s, the players from the third generation of immigrants in Britain, Germany, and the Netherlands were increasingly vocal about racism. It was the combination of fans and players that helped challenge the conservatism and inaction of the clubs and authorities.

Ironically, it was the actions of a white player, Eric Cantona, which helped propel the issue of discrimination into the public spotlight in England.[48] In 1995 Manchester United's mercurial French striker was sent off in a game against Crystal Palace. As he trudged off the pitch towards the changing room, he suddenly jumped into the crowd, feet first, and struck a Crystal Palace fan called Matthew Simmonds square in the chest. This kung fu kick became an instant media sensation and Cantona was roundly condemned. He was banned from playing for ten months and ordered to undertake community engagement work. This situation also highlighted the abuse that was directed at Cantona by Simmonds. Cantona's nationality was invoked and he was told to 'fuck off back to France', alongside some other choice words. For decades, footballers of Afro-Caribbean heritage have been abused in similar and more systematic ways and told, like Emmanuel Frimpong, to 'turn the other cheek'. Cantona received similar abuse and reacted. Although he received widespread condemnation from the authorities and media, as a white European, Cantona remained in a privileged position. Had he been less skilful, or of Afro-Caribbean heritage, it is unlikely he would have been allowed to recover his career.

Many grassroots, fan-led anti-racism initiatives emerged during the 1990s. In Poland, the *Nigdy Więcej* (Never Again) association formed in 1992 to challenge the growing racism in the country after the fall of communism. Highlighting the conflation of racism and fascism during this period, the *Bündnis antifaschistischer Fanclubs und Faninitiativen* (BAFF, Association of Antifascist Fan Clubs and Fan Initiatives) was formed in Germany in 1993. This name was changed to the Association of Active Football Fans in 1998. In Britain, the first anti-racist fan group was established in 1994 under the title of Leeds Fans United Against Racism and Fascism. Again, this highlighted the mistaken link between fascism and racism. Not all racists identified as fascist, so challenging their behaviours required a more nuanced approach. These organisations utilised similar approaches to raise awareness, lobby authorities, and directly challenge racist behaviour.

Italy was the site of one of the more innovative projects to challenge the growing racism in stadiums. The Emilia-Romagna section of *Unione Italiana Sport Per tutti* (UISP) helped establish *Progetto Ultra*, an organisation that sought to work with the hardcore fans, the *ultras*, in order to educate them about racism and fascism. *Progetto Ultra* was also important because it became a space to break down barriers between rival fans and discuss a wide range of issues that affected *ultras* and fans. *Progetto Ultra* is no longer funded, but its legacy remains with the *Mondiali Antirazzisti* ('Anti-Racist World Cup'). This annual event began in 1997 and takes place in Emilia-Romagna every July. Over 200 teams attend and the format has been expanded to include other sports like basketball, cricket, and rugby. Crucially, the tournament is non-competitive and seeks to be an inclusive space that can break down barriers between groups.[49] The challenge for the *Mondiali*, as with other anti-racist initiatives, is to reach beyond those groups who already engage in anti-racism activities.

Kick It Out in England demonstrates the successes and challenges of anti-racism campaigns in football. Let's Kick Racism Out of Football was launched by the Commission for Racial Equality and the Professional Footballers' Association in 1993. It changed its name to Kick It Out in 1997. When the campaign was launched, the *Alive and Still Kicking* report highlighted how many clubs did not see racism as a priority.[50] More strikingly, some clubs did not want to be associated with the campaign since they believed that fans might think they were racist. Since then, the campaign has been successful in raising awareness of racism in football, not just in stadiums, but in relation to under-representation of minority groups in administration and coaching and codes of practice within the amateur game. Kick It Out has worked seriously with the authorities to tackle the issue of racism, as well as clearly reporting levels of racist abuse. It has developed ways to make it easier to report racist abuse through education of clubs and stewards, as well as launching an app for smartphones that allows fans to anonymously report abuse.

As the campaign has developed, it has also attracted some criticism. Working closely with the authorities can lead to accusations that it is not working with fan groups or players. Much of the funding comes from the FA, Premier League, and Professional Footballers' Association. Since the Premier League has rescinded funding for Supporters Direct (an organisation to campaign for fan democracy) after critical comments made by former chief executive Dave Boyle, organisations like Kick It Out can be viewed as politically compromised. Yet, this has to be seen in light of the limited funds and a small number of staff. A year after the Suárez and

Terry incidents, a number of black footballers refused to wear Kick It Out T-shirts that called for an end to racism. Jason Roberts was the most vocal of the protesters, arguing that Kick It Out was not strong enough to challenge the authorities. Roberts believed that the T-shirts were an empty gesture and the organisation needed to show they were strong enough and represented his experiences of football. While these organisations and campaigns have achieved some relative success, the fact that racism is still being discussed within European football shows that alternative approaches need to be utilised.

Anti-racism initiatives like Kick It Out and Never Again are significantly underfunded and this limits the impact they can make. They also tend to operate independently of fan groups, which can lead to resentment from supporters. In Germany there is an alternative approach to challenging fans' anti-social behaviour. These fan projects work with fans to educate them about the impact of their actions. They are partly funded by the club and the regional authorities and work as social work projects. Importantly, the role of the football club is vital when communicating with fans.[51] At Borussia Dortmund, for example, the fan project has access to the stadium for workshops, which are attended by the star players. This helps to create a clear link between the football club and the anti-racism message. As fans remain more loyal to the club, rather than the football federations, rival fan groups, or anti-racism organisations, the message becomes unsullied by perceived political connotations. More importantly, Borussia Dortmund actively works with the fan project and other fan groups to listen to their suggestions as to how to tackle discrimination. The club supported an initiative, organised by the *ultras* group The Unity and the fan project, to visit Auschwitz. Borussia Dortmund lent the fan project their team bus so young fans could see the potential impact of racism, and its links to German and Dortmund history.

Poland has recently adopted a similar scheme, called *Kibice Razem* ('Fans United') and trialled at seven different clubs.[52] Because of the different civil society traditions in each European nation, there are a variety of challenges for these schemes. In Poland, the *Kibice Razem* is almost building civil society from its base. There is a reason fan projects started in Germany – there is a more cooperative culture between the state and community groups. The libertarian traditions of British political culture means that this approach would be more complicated in England. Football Unites, Racism Divides (FURD) in Sheffield is rather unique in this respect. It is a youth work organisation that works with the local youth community to educate and support their life choices. They work with both football clubs in Sheffield (Wednesday and United) and visits schools and prisons. They set up an initiative called Streetkick, which took inflatable goals to different neighbourhoods and used football as a way of educating players on the impact of racism.[53] The success of this approach has resulted in its adoption by fan projects in Germany as groups and campaigns share ideas across Europe.

The difficulty for anti-racism groups is that differences and rivalry are seen as fundamental parts of the game by the dominant masculine groups that claim legitimacy over the sport. As Ratna shows, it is not possible to tackle discrimination of female British Asians by only focusing on racism.[54] Anti-sexist agendas are also important for the inclusion of women from black and ethnic minority groups. In recent years, FARE, Kick It Out and the Football Supporters' Federation (FSF) have expanded their focus to include other forms of discrimination. Kick It Out has changed its subtitle to 'Tackling Racism & Discrimination', while FARE also has anti-homophobia campaigns. The FSF has launched the 'Fans for Diversity' campaign under the stewardship of former West Ham United player Anwar Uddin. This project seeks to bring in fans from all its communities, including fans who are disabled, LGBTQI, and black and ethnic minorities. Strikingly, fans with disabilities have also been less visible in these campaigns. Organisations like Level Playing Field and Centre for Accessibility in Football Europe (CAFE) are raising awareness of this issue. Slowly, the different organisations are becoming more collaborative, which is important when communicating a clear message.

There is a clear European approach to anti-racism and discrimination developing across the continent. While the 1990s saw a number of nationally based organisations emerge to tackle the problem of racism, the twenty-first century has seen European-wide groups established. These include CAFE, the European Gay and Lesbian Network, and Football Supporters Europe. Specifically related to racism and discrimination, Football Against Racism Europe was established from a variety of anti-racism groups, supporters associations, and fan projects from across Europe in 1999. FARE is supported by UEFA and helps organise the fan embassies at UEFA events like the European Championships. These spaces help communicate anti-racism messages and the UEFA 'respect' agenda.

Conclusion

Football's popularity is unsurpassed as a global sporting activity. It can bring people together from different backgrounds, ages, and genders. But it also provides opportunities to distinguish yourself and your group from others through abuse, violence, racism, and discrimination. Racism remains one of the most prevalent anti-social behaviours associated with football. From sustained abuse directed at Mario Balotelli in England and Italy to Zenit St Petersburg fans calling for the club to only sign Slavic or Scandinavian players, racism is a pervasive problem in European football. For racism to be eliminated from the game, it requires action from *all* sections of football. This includes the fans themselves, governing bodies, media, politicians, and players. UEFA and some national federations have reinforced a clear message in an attempt to underline the importance of anti-racism, but some fans view their actions with suspicion. Likewise, anti-racism campaigns like FARE, Kick It Out, and Never Again are important in producing the literature, guidance, and training to help educate various groups about the extent and various ways racism manifests itself. But they also have to be careful not to be seen to be distant from football fans.

It is important to understand the nuanced and shifting nature of racism in football. Often racism is located in inter-club rivalries and is used as another form of abuse to denigrate rivals. Not all racism is ideologically driven. While certain fan groups, like the *ultras*, want to be confrontational, not all fans do. Rather than immediately enforcing sanctions that impact all fans, or making empty gestures advocating 'no to racism', authorities need to engage in educational projects that communicate the impact of racism and abuse to fans, coaches, and directors. These approaches have worked well with FURD, fan projects, and *Kibice Razem*. They need to be safe spaces that allow trust to be built and cross-cultural understanding fostered. The danger of treating all fans as potentially racist will only succeed in alienating these fans and potentially make the situation worse.

Most importantly, authorities have to recognise that racism is not only committed by fans. There are structural issues impacting racism, and the continued under-representation of women, disabled, LGBTQI, and people from black and ethnic minorities in administration, boardrooms, and coaching of the game highlight that there is a long way to go before racism is eliminated from European football. Football is a powerful tool that can potentially bring people of different backgrounds together. There are many fan groups and anti-racism campaigns across Europe and they are sharing ideas and experiences and providing spaces that help to remove barriers and promote cross-cultural understandings. It is important to acknowledge that football unites people in a shared passion and that should be the focus.

Notes

1 S. Martin, *Football and Fascism* (Oxford: Berg, 2004).
2 M. Doidge, *Football Italia: Italian Football in an era of Globalisation* (London: Bloomsbury, 2015); M. Doidge, 'Il Calcio as a Source of Local and Social Identity in Italy', in U. Merkel, ed., *Identity Discourses and Communities in International Events, Festivals and Spectacles* (Basingstoke: Palgrave Macmillan, 2015).
3 G. Armstrong, *Football Hooligans: Knowing the Score* (Oxford: Berg, 1998); E. Dunning, P. Murphy, and J. Williams, *The Roots of Football Hooliganism: An Historical and Sociological Study* (London: Routledge, 1988); R. Spaaij, *Understanding Football Hooliganism: A Comparison of Six Western European Football Clubs* (Amsterdam: Vossiuspers UvA – Amsterdam University Press, 2006); Doidge, *Football Italia*.
4 A. King, *The European Ritual: Football in the New Europe* (Aldershot: Ashgate, 2003).
5 Doidge, *Football Italia*.
6 C. Podaliri and C. Balestri, 'The Ultras, Racism and Football Culture in Italy', in A. Brown, ed., *Fanatics! Power, Identity and Fandom in Football* (London: Routledge, 1998), 95.
7 Doidge, *Football Italia*.
8 M. Doidge, *Anti-racism in European Football: Report to UEFA* (Brighton: University of Brighton, 2015).
9 L. Back, T. Crabbe, and J. Solomos, *The Changing Face of Football* (Oxford: Berg, 2001).
10 R. De Biasi and P. Lanfranchi, 'The Importance of Difference: Football Identities in Italy', in G. Armstrong and R. Giulianotti, eds, *Entering the Field: New Perspectives on World Football* (Oxford: Berg, 1997), 87–104.
11 Back *et al.*, *The Changing Face of Football*.
12 King, *The European Ritual*.
13 M. Doidge, '"If You Jump Up and Down, Balotelli Dies": Racism and Player Abuse in Italian Football', *International Review for the Sociology of Sport* 50, 3 (2015), 249–64.
14 Back *et al.*, *The Changing Face of Football*.
15 Ibid.
16 Ibid.
17 Ibid.; F. Müller, L. van Zoonen, and L. de Roode, 'Accidental Racists: Experiences and Contradictions of Racism in Local Amsterdam Soccer Fan Culture', *Soccer & Society*, 8, 2–3 (2007), 335–50.
18 Back *et al.*, *The Changing Face of Football*; Müller *et al.*, 'Accidental Racists'.
19 J. Garland and M. Rowe, *Racism and Anti-Racism in Football* (Basingstoke: Palgrave, 2001), 52.
20 Doidge, *Anti-Racism in European Football*.
21 Garland and Rowe, *Racism and Anti-Racism in Football*.
22 D. Burdsey, *British Asians and Football* (London: Routledge, 2007), 105.
23 J. Van Sterkenburg, 'Thinking "Race" and Ethnicity in (Dutch) Sports Policy Research', in J. Long and K. Spracklen, eds, *Sport and Challenges to Racism* (Basingstoke: Palgrave Macmillan, 2010); Doidge, 'If You Jump Up and Down, Balotelli Dies'.
24 Back *et al.*, *The Changing Face of Football*.
25 Doidge, *Football Italia*.
26 Doidge, 'If You Jump Up and Down, Balotelli Dies'.
27 D. Burdsey, *Race, Ethnicity and Football: Persisting Debates and Emergent Issues* (London: Routledge, 2011).
28 D. Burdsey, 'One Week in October: Luis Suárez, John Terry and the Turn to Racial Neoliberalism in English Men's Professional Football', *Identities: Global Studies in Culture and Power* 21, 5 (2014), 429–47.
29 Burdsey, *Race, Ethnicity and Football*, 5.
30 D.T. Goldberg, *The Threat of Race* (Oxford: Wiley-Blackwell, 2009), 331.
31 Goldberg, *The Threat of Race*, 362–3.
32 J. Rodriguez, 'Color-blind Ideology and the Cultural Appropriation of Hip-Hop', *Journal of Contemporary Ethnography* 35, 6 (2006), 645.
33 Burdsey, 'One Week in October'.
34 J. Long, P. Robinson, and K. Spracklen, 'Promoting Racial Equality within Sports Organisations', *Journal of Sport and Social Issues* 29, 1 (2005), 41–59.

35 A. Ratna, 'A "Fair Game"? British Asian Females' Experiences of Racism in Women's Football', in J. Magee, J. Caudwell, K. Liston, and S. Scraton, eds, *Women, Football and Europe: Histories, Equity and Experiences* (Oxford: Meyer and Meyer Sport, 2007), 77–96.

36 Back *et al.*, *The Changing Face of Football*, 164.

37 J. Long and M. McNamee, 'On the Moral Economy of Racism and Racist Rationalizations in Sport', *International Review for the Sociology of Sport* 39, 4 (2004), 405–20.

38 Burdsey, *Race, Ethnicity and Football*.

39 L. Back, T. Crabbe, and J. Solomos, 'Beyond the Racist/Hooligan Couplet: Race, Social Theory and Football Culture', *British Journal of Sociology* 50, 3 (1999), 419–42; Back *et al.*, *The Changing Face of Football*; Müller *et al.*, 'Accidental Racists'.

40 Müller *et al.*, 'Accidental Racists'.

41 Doidge, *Football Italia*.

42 Doidge, *Football Italia*, 160.

43 S. Ahmed, 'The Non-Performativity of Anti-Racism', *Meridians: Feminism, Race, Transnationalism* 7, 1 (2006), 104–26; K. Hylton, 'How a Turn to Critical Race Theory Can Contribute to Our Understanding of "Race", Racism and Anti-Racism in Sport', *International Review for the Sociology of Sport* 45, 3 (2010), 335–54.

44 Doidge, *Football Italia*.

45 Doidge, *Anti-racism in European Football*.

46 Doidge, *Anti-racism in European Football*; Doidge, *Football Italia*.

47 King, *The European Ritual*.

48 Back *et al.*, *The Changing Face of Football*.

49 D. Sterchele and C. Saint-Blancat, 'Keeping it Liminal: The Mondiali Antirazzisti (Anti-racist World Cup) as a Multifocal Interaction Ritual', *Leisure Studies* 34, 2 (2015), 182–96.

50 AGARI, *Alive and Still Kicking* (London: Advisory Group Against Racism and Intimidation, 1996).

51 Doidge, *Anti-racism in European Football*.

52 Ibid.

53 R. Johnson, 'Football Unites, Racism Divides', in C. Kassimiris, ed., *Anti-Racism in European Football: Fair Play for All* (Plymouth: Lexington Books, 2009).

54 A. Ratna, '"Taking the Power Back!": The Politics of British-Asian football players', *Young: Nordic Journal of Youth Research* 18, 2 (2010), 117–32.

14

MIGRATION AND INTEGRATION IN GERMANY

Sebastian Braun and Tina Nobis

Introduction

Writing a review article for an international handbook on 'race and ethnicity' that summarizes and represents the relevant scientific publications on this topic in Germany is a challenging assignment. In Germany, the concept of 'race' has been disavowed for historical reasons and the term 'ethnicity' also plays a rather marginal role in social sciences of sport in the country. Given this, a chapter that focuses on research in this field in Germany must look for scientific discussions that address associated topics.

Such topics are found in research on social integration and sport, which has evolved since the 2000s from a somewhat marginal field to a discipline characterized by increasingly intensive research. While research into racism in this context has retained a more marginal status[1] and has recently come to focus on fan cultures, in recent years a growing number of studies has addressed constructs such as 'integration' and 'culture'. Building upon a variety of theoretical traditions, an increasing number of sport social scientists have investigated the opportunities and achievements for integration offered by sport, focusing on the micro-level of individuals and the meso-level of sports clubs.

The focus in this context is on a population for whom the term 'individuals with migrant background' has become established in political and scientific parlance. According to the official definition, this group comprises around 16 million people in Germany:

> all foreigners and naturalized foreigners, all individuals who immigrated as ethnic Germans to the territory of today's Federal Republic of Germany after 1949, and all German citizens born in Germany with at least one parent who immigrated to Germany or was born in Germany as a foreign citizen.[2]

This chapter will review and discuss the above research publications on social integration and sport. To understand precisely which topics are addressed in German research and why, which theoretical concepts and terms are used, and which methods are applied, the chapter first outlines the central starting points for the scientific discussions on 'sport and integration' conducted in Germany. We then go on to describe the conceptual and theoretical points of reference in research on integration and sport in Germany and present empirical studies at both the micro-level and meso-level. In a final conclusion, this review then summarizes the key results and research needed in the future.

Points of reference of German research on integration and sport

In Germany, the gradual establishment of research on integration and sport appears not to be entirely random. It coincides with discussions on integration mechanisms in migrant societies at the socio-political levels and in sports federations, which have certainly impacted its establishment as a branch of research.

Since the 2000s at the latest, migration and integration have become central topics for public debate and are no longer marginalized on the periphery of social dialogue. Whether concrete governmental integration policies, migratory movements by refugees, or Islamophobia in German society, the normatively charged issue of 'successful' integration seems to play a role in all instances. One of the basic issues discussed within a socio-political context, for example, is whether – and if so, how – an individualized, multiethnic, and multi-religious society which has long oriented its narrative identity along a specifically 'German approach' of cultural homogeneity will be able to maintain social stability and cohesion.[3]

In view of this public debate, it is hardly surprising that even influential German sports federations such as the German Olympic Sports Confederation (Deutscher Olympischer Sportbund – DOSB), the German Football Association (Deutscher Fußball-Bund – DFB), and others have given increasing attention to the topic of integration in the last 15–20 years. The DOSB, the German umbrella organization and representative of sports associations and sports clubs in German politics, has underlined the special role played by Germany's roughly 91,000 sports clubs in the integration of migrants. Political players in the field of sport politics and policy, such as political parties and public administrations, are also convinced of these roles. Using attractive and accessible slogans such as 'The language of sport is universal' or 'Sport brings people together', stakeholders advertise the opportunities for social integration offered by sport and designed to be activated through various measures, including state-funded support schemes.[4]

These trends presumably correspond with the fact that since the mid-2000s, stakeholders in both sports federations and sport politics have stepped up their efforts in initiating and supporting projects that investigate the integration opportunities offered by sports clubs. Most major scientific research projects (in terms of funding periods and amounts, publication formats and outputs) in this field are based on such funding initiatives and policies. Where sports federations are concerned, both the DOSB and various state sports federations and sports associations have commissioned or funded a number of evaluation studies, companion research projects, and expert reports. However, the Federal Office for Migration and Refugees (Bundesamt für Migration und Flüchtlinge – BAMF) and the Federal Institute of Sports Science (Bundesinstitut für Sportwissenschaft – BISp), as two authorities operating under the Federal Ministry of the Interior (Bundesministerium des Innern – BMI), and various state ministries have also provided substantial funding for research into integration and sport.

These structural framework conditions of research funding and the question of the genesis of research topics – with its relevance from the perspective of the sociology of knowledge – are both likely to leave their marks on the field of research on integration and sport. First, it is not surprising that research projects commissioned, funded, or supported by sports federations, sport politics, or public administration bodies address issues that, at least to some extent, fall into the spheres of responsibility of these supporters. Second, researchers are also always bound by their specific positions and perspectives in the social space, which, in turn – generally subconsciously – influence their questions, conceptual decisions, and study designs. Research into integration and sport has, therefore, gradually become established as a discipline in which numerous sport scientists identified topics of research and to which they applied their established conceptual and theoretical, methodical and empirical approaches; also – and particularly – because of the current debate over integration-related issues in 'Germany as a country of immigration' in sport politics and sports federations.

Based on these considerations and observations, the specific design and focus areas of research on integration and sport, which is characterized by relatively close groupings of stakeholders from science, politics, and sports federations, may not come as a surprise. The following sections therefore aim at demonstrating that most research efforts are directed both conceptually and empirically at the issues of integration, inclusion, and intercultural openness at sports clubs – issues that are also much debated in sports federations and sport politics; however, with a few exceptions, issues such as racism, exclusion and discrimination are addressed only marginally and from the perspective of their role as obstacles to integration. This review aims to show that current research focuses on the integration achievements of sports clubs, while other settings within that research play more of a marginal role. In addition, this review illustrates that research on integration and sport primarily takes the form of applied research that clearly references social practice in Germany.

Conceptual points of reference

From a conceptual perspective, research on integration and sport in the sport since 2000 has primarily examined issues of integration-related achievements by sports clubs at the micro-level for individuals from migrant backgrounds. This perspective has been extended more recently by meso-level studies addressing sports clubs as organizations that can either open or restrict specific structures for integration processes. The two interrelated perspectives can be summarized under the labels of 'integration within and through sport' and 'integration achievements by sports clubs'.

Integration within and through sport: the micro-level

To provide a conceptual framework for the integration achievements by sports clubs, which are analysed within the context of the population of individuals with migrant backgrounds, research on integration within and through sport predominantly references two basic positions. These two positions have their points of reference in decades of debate by sports science and sports politics over the justification of the role of sport in Germany. In this context, the concepts of 'education for sport' and 'education by sport'[5] were coined in discussions on the role of physical education and school sports from the 1970s onwards. This discussion was later taken up in an extra-curricular context in concepts such as 'socialization for sport' and 'socialization by sport' and developed further in the context of sports clubs in particular.[6] At the turn of the millennium these conceptual points of reference were once again relatively straightforwardly transferred to research on integration within and through sport by developing the analogous interrelated concepts of 'integration within sport' and 'integration through sport'.

The first position of integration within sport focuses on active participation in sport, and in sports clubs in particular, by individuals with migrant backgrounds. The hypothesis generally investigated by researchers is that an educationally justifiable lifestyle in modern society includes engagement in sport, and that therefore participation in sport in everyday life and the acquisition of sport skills make good sense.[7] This hypothesis associates participation in sport by individuals from a migrant background with opportunities to participate in society, obviating the need for any further justifications for opening spheres for participation in sport or providing target-group-oriented sports services.

With reference to this first position, the second position of integration through sport references 'the effects that engaging in sport has for integration into society'.[8] According to this position, the permanent interactive processes in sport-related action-based situations, and in sports clubs in particular, result in the establishment of a special sphere of values which provides individuals from a migrant background with the possibility of acquiring and strengthening competences and dispositions. Based on the above position when applied to integration research, individuals from a migrant background are then assumed to be able to transfer these competences and dispositions – anchored as habitual processes – to other spheres of life, consequently enabling them to act more meaningfully, reasonably, and successfully there too.[9]

To provide a conceptual framework for the potential effects on integration, research on integration within and through sport has so far mainly applied the integration concept defined by Esser, who distinguishes between four dimensions of integration: placement, meaning the opportunities to access positions and rights; culturation, referring to the acquisition of knowledge and competences; interaction, relating to the formation of social relations and networks; and identification, standing for the development of emotional bonds.[10] Research on integration within and through sport adopted these concepts – albeit with slight modifications depending on the context – to analyse and discuss the various dimensions of integration through sport.[11]

However, beyond these dimensions, research on integration within and through sport has so far neglected to identify or systemize precise concepts or to concentrate on possible spill-over effects. Given this, the research papers in this field address a rather unclear mix of competences and dispositions. In addition, the logical next question – namely the investigation of precisely which mechanism could be used to transfer the competences and dispositions acquired in sport to other contexts in life – has so far remained largely unanswered.[12]

Integration achievements by sports clubs: the meso-level

Apart from discussions on integration into and through sport at the micro-level, recent years have produced an increasing number of research papers that focus on the meso-level of sports clubs (and sometimes also sports federations). These research papers, while offering a variety of conceptual reference points, indicate priorities in the field of research on clubs, associations, and federations, and on both system theory and actor theory. This field thus falls back on a classic tradition of research in German-language sports sciences, which has focused for decades on the analysis of sports clubs as voluntary associations with particular attention to their organizational structures, but also their organizational cultures, self-image, and perspectives and actions.[13]

The organizational theory analyses on the special structures of voluntary associations developed by Horsch in the 1980s and 1990s, using sports clubs as examples, play a critical role in this branch of research.[14] They include the following characteristics: voluntary membership, as no one can be forced to join a sports club; alignment of goals with members' interests, as correlation of these two aspects is a 'conservation commandment' for sports clubs to avoid membership cancellations; democratic decision-making structures, as a prerequisite for members being able to express their interests; voluntary work, to implement the interests of members in social practice; and autonomy, ensured via voluntary work and membership fees. These structural characteristics form a central background in the numerous surveys conducted at sports clubs in Germany, which also play an important role in research on integration within and through sport,[15] and in specific surveys conducted at sports clubs participating in integration programmes, as well as special surveys of sports clubs founded by and for migrants.[16]

Some of these papers also point out the connection of 'integration' and 'marginalization', an aspect frequently given too little attention in the prevailing discourse on the integration opportunities and achievements offered by sports clubs. In this context, the notion of *Wahl-Gemeinschaften* ('Communities of Choice'), coined by Strob and relevant in research into sports clubs, was adopted in research on integration within and through sport,[17] and the issue of the social closure of sports clubs examined with the help of Bourdieu's theory.[18] While these papers base their arguments on rational actor theory, other studies base their conceptualization of the closure processes at sports clubs on system theory. In this context, research differentiates between direct and indirect 'exclusion by others' in sports clubs on the one hand, and 'self-exclusion' by individuals from a migrant background on the other, in order to use this theoretical basis in practical applications such as conceptually justified counselling for sports clubs and associations with the aim of recruiting junior professional athletes.[19] Against this background, special significance is granted to research papers that address the concepts of 'intercultural opening' and 'diversity management' at sports clubs in order to answer practical questions on the action programmes of sports clubs.[20]

Normative points of reference

A fundamental problem of most research papers so far has been the virtual absence of any differentiated explanation of the normative backdrop against which the empirical results are surveyed and discussed.[21] Admittedly, numerous studies show a normative bias in favour of the general idea of assimilation. They more or less implicitly assume that persons from a migrant background would assimilate into the established structures and norms of sport in sports clubs over the longer term or that discrepancies in sports participation, voluntary engagement, or choice of the type of sport between individuals with and without migrant background would decrease successively. These studies also include several more or less explicit lines of argument referencing pluralist models of integration and cultural equivalence. For example, they refer to migrant sports clubs as the 'standard case' of self-organization in a civil society and to new types and forms of sport as an 'enhancement' of sports at sports clubs, or claim intercultural openings at sports clubs to be an alternative concept to the general ideas of assimilation. However, this unclear picture and, in particular, the fact that the underlying normative models of integration are not addressed in greater detail are only surprising to a certain extent. In Germany as a country of immigration, integration concepts are certainly among the concepts most heatedly discussed, clearly revealing the complex mixture of scientific findings, policies, and contemporary diagnosis of research on integration in the field of sports sciences.

One example of the above is the question of ideal team constellations and interactions in sports clubs, which has largely been avoided so far. Most studies agree on the highly questionable nature of the widespread idea that activities in a team at a sports club contribute de facto automatically to social integration. The normative desired integration effects are not by-products of engaging in sports, but result from sophisticated educational arrangements, which in turn require target-group-specific measures. However, studies addressing possible opportunity structures and educational arrangements in sports clubs to promote 'integration effects' have been somewhat rudimentary so far, in spite of the focus on applied research and the relatively high number of evaluations of programmes related to integration within and through sport. Research papers frequently target a – normatively desired – rise in the share of migrants in sports clubs. However, they largely fail to provide answers to questions such as the specific groups into which the new members are – and, from a normative perspective, should be – integrated. This approach, while largely obscuring the concepts of assimilation and pluralism as analytical concepts to describe empirical phenomena, also largely avoids reference to these concepts as normative models of integration that are also controversial in socio–political discourse.

Empirical research on integration within and through sport: the micro-level

Any attempt to systematize the relatively diverse empirical studies that investigate questions of integration within and through sport first reveals that research activities have intensified considerably since the 2000s. A detailed presentation of the results of these studies is therefore impossible within the scope of this review article.[22] The second fact that becomes evident is that most publications focus on empirical findings on the issue of integration within sport. As a comparison, empirical research on issues related to integration through sport may be described as rudimentary.

The available studies are based on analysis and evaluation of various data sets, including secondary analyses of quantitative data that had originally been surveyed against the backdrop of other scientific interests. Examples particularly include various population surveys and youth (sport) studies, which also surveyed the migrant background of respondents, their participation in sport in various settings, particularly in sports clubs, and sometimes also the actors' 'social orientations'.[23] These studies are complemented by qualitative studies, many of which focus on investigating participation in sports by girls from migrant backgrounds.[24] Finally, a number of quantitative and qualitative evaluation studies address issues related to the accessibility of various target groups from migrant backgrounds by means of integration efforts in and through sport.[25]

A screening of this large number of studies reveals that young people's engagement in sports clubs has been particularly well researched. Although specific information on membership rates varies from study to study, all of them show that young people from migrant backgrounds are under-represented in sports clubs. However, increasingly differentiated socio-structural analyses proved that this finding by no means applies to all young people with migrant backgrounds. To take adequate account of the heterogeneity of individuals with migrant backgrounds, recent research has focused on investigations of gender differences, but also issues related to young people's countries of origin, social origin, and degree of religious beliefs. These variables have emerged time and again as relevant factors influencing young people's membership in sports clubs.[26]

Some studies also examine sporting activities by young people with and without migrant backgrounds.[27] In recent years a few publications have also compared participation in sport by children[28] and adults.[29] However, the scope and degree of detail in all these publications are hardly comparable to studies that address young people and the setting of sports clubs.

Compared with the number of empirical studies examining issues of integration within sport, there are only modest numbers of empirical studies on *integration through sport* for individuals from migrant backgrounds. The few studies that generally examine the integration achievements by sports clubs while focusing on young people primarily include cross-sectional data that permit few final conclusions as to whether statistically significant relationships can be interpreted as the result of participation in sport and/or membership of a sports club. In keeping with the above, Mutz and Burrmann recently summed up the available empirical results and assigned them to the abovementioned four concepts of social, cultural, (everyday) political, and structural integration:

> As far as integration effects are concerned, it must first be noted that while many studies validate these effects in theory, the status of empirical research is very far from

being able to supply satisfactory evidence of these effects. The greatest evidence can certainly be found for the achievements of sport in the field of social integration. In this context, sports clubs are seen as contact points and meeting places, offering enormous opportunities for children and young people in particular to form communities. Interethnic contacts and friendships are reported more frequently by young people who engage in sport than by non-athletes. In these studies, migrants' integration into everyday politics through sport is generally limited to their appointment to offices in sports clubs or informal participation in sports club activities. At least at informal level, engagement by young people with migrant background is hardly less common than that of their peers without migrant background. In terms of achievements in cultural and structural integration, scepticism is justified. At first glance, validation of the effects, such as language acquisition and a sense of belonging, seems possible to a certain extent. However, as participation in sport is preceded by social selection of participants, the results are inconclusive unless other socio-structural variables are also considered in parallel.[30]

The approaches used to interpret different rates of activity and participation of individuals with and without migration backgrounds, by contrast, have become far more differentiated. Admittedly, research to date has failed to develop an encompassing theoretical framework that conclusively combines the various explanatory approaches. So far, publications have tended to supply a list of possible explanatory approaches, while failing to systematically identify exactly which empirical phenomena might be interpreted by which explanatory approach. At the same time, there are increasing numbers of multi-causal explanatory models. In this context, the research conducted firstly references the 'paradigm of cultural difference'. Studies that refer to Turkish or Muslim girls in particular address differences in perceptions of sports and body issues, educational style, and gender expectations that may impact specific sports practices.[31] However, as this interpretation approach may lead to over-emphasis of cultural differences while the variety and dynamism of migrant lifestyles and ways of life are ignored, these differences are also discussed against the backdrop of social inequalities.[32] In this context, some authors focus on the socioeconomic status of young people, while others put more emphasis on preferences related to social milieu and lifestyle.

Last but not least, these studies rarely mention approaches to interpretation that refer to discrimination mechanisms and practices. The topic of foreignness has seen a particular revival in recent years; given this, studies have also pointed out phenomena of perceived and experienced discrimination, everyday racism, and open or subtle practices of marginalization which may cause people to terminate their membership in a sports club.[33] However, overall empirical research on questions of integration within and through sport is still, first and foremost, a discourse on the positive aspects that predominantly addresses the integration opportunities offered by sports clubs.

Empirical research on integration achievements by sports clubs: the meso-level

As research on integration within and through sport has been established, publications focusing on the meso-level and, in particular, the integration achievements by sports clubs have also been completed. Compared to the research at micro-level as outlined above, the first aspect to be noted is that the number of publications in this field is significantly smaller. The second aspect that becomes evident is that the authors that may be categorized in this discipline focus on different conceptual frameworks. As thematic priorities also vary and sometimes conflict, this chapter will be restricted to an initial attempt at systematizing the studies of differently designed research. Presumably, the authors would not necessarily consider themselves as working in the same research discipline or identify a shared cognitive interest. However, our assessment allows some topics to be identified, which have been addressed in recent years. These topics include integration achievements by sports clubs examined (1) from the perspectives of sports club organization and (2) sports club culture, with both perspectives (3) also explicitly applied to sports clubs for people with migrant backgrounds. In addition, there have been (4) analyses of the perspectives and actions of sports clubs and associations.

(1) Many empirical studies concerning the integration achievements by sports clubs focus on their structural characteristics. They are designed as applied sports clubs surveys and are generally supported by actors in sports politics and/or sports federations. One example comprises 'sport development reports', which are produced every two years and claim to be representative of all sports clubs in Germany. They address a host of issues, including integration.[34] In addition, some studies are available on sports organizations that are restricted to selected social spheres.[35] There are also evaluation studies on integration programmes within and through sport that analyse the structural characteristics of sports clubs.[36] While these studies are not directly comparable in terms of their fundamental thematic orientation, they all frequently present the structural characteristics of the various sports clubs at a descriptive level, recording aspects such as membership structures and target groups in addition to human, financial and space-related resources. These studies further link these structural characteristics with individual dimensions of integration efforts, e.g. integration-specific actions, processing them in applied contexts of argumentation.

(2) In addition to the investigation of structural characteristics, the organizational cultures of sports clubs have increasingly moved to the fore. Studies on this topic investigate more or less explicitly how organizational cultures impact processes of integration and exclusion. Examples that should be mentioned here are papers that argue from a theoretical background in organizational sociology, but also system theory, which address practices and mechanisms of exclusion and social closure. These papers have one thing in common: they all stand out to a certain extent from the prevailing discourse of positive aspects of integration within and through sport. Membership in a sports club may be terminated if, in a sport setting, foreignness is created and experienced through informal membership expectations, if individuals from a migrant background feel they are confronted with prejudice and everyday racism, or if members from a migrant background are met with expectations of assimilation.[37]

(3) Research across these two thematic priorities comprise studies addressing the structures and cultures of sports clubs founded by, and reserved for, migrants (migrant sports clubs). These studies describe the characteristics of those sports clubs and seek to link these descriptions with issues of integration achievements. Research on organizations founded by and for migrants intensified from the 1990s onwards.[38] However, more recent studies investigating the structures, conditions of development and integration achievements of sports clubs for individuals from migrant backgrounds are also available.[39] Nevertheless, to date this topic has been primarily addressed by smaller empirical studies, local case studies of individual groups of people from migrant backgrounds, or studies of individual sports. In addition, hardly any of these research efforts have been continued in recent years. While some years ago this topic could still have been expected to become a 'new' focal topic for research on integration within and through sport, it may now be regarded as a discipline that has not been researched in depth.

(4) Another more marginal area of investigation focuses especially on the internal perspectives of sports federations and sports-related intervention programmes in integration efforts. On the

one hand, document analyses reviewed integration-specific opinions and ideals of the DOSB (e.g. the views of sports federations regarding the integration opportunities offered by sports organized in clubs or perceptions of integration).[40] On the other hand, these internal perspectives have been examined in evaluation studies by the largest sport-related integration programme, bearing the characteristic title of 'Integration through Sport', which the DOSB has now carried out for roughly 25 years with government funding. On the basis of qualitative interviews with the programme officials, studies have repeatedly analysed the perspectives of integration opportunities and the understanding of integration, but also of concepts such as intercultural openings of sports clubs that receive subsidies from the programme.[41]

Conclusion

It is apparent that the concepts of race and ethnicity play little role in the German-speaking context, particularly in research on sports science. Against this backdrop, this chapter focuses more on associated topics and debates primarily related to the issues of 'sport, integration and migration'. These issues have experienced a dynamic boom since the 2000s and have advanced from a marginal subject to a discipline characterized by intensive research. In this context, the intensification of research efforts appears to be anything but coincidence: it has occurred in parallel to fundamental social and political discourse related to the question of Germany as a country of immigration and the associated controversial debate on successful integration policies. In this context, sport – and sport in sports clubs organized by sports federations in particular – is not only assigned a function of relevance for the success of the integration of immigrants; the sports federations also set themselves goals in this area.

Against this backdrop, it is hardly surprising that in Germany the research on integration and sport that is described in this chapter primarily comprises investigations concerning sports clubs characterized by a relatively close constellation of actors from the worlds of science, politics, and sports federations. Research in the field of sport sciences, the social policies of sports federations and governmental sport policies are closely integrated into research on integration and sport. This focus may be driven by mutual support and strengthening, but may also be due to the fact that structural integration achievements for individuals and societies had been attributed to sports clubs long before research on integration and sport related to the migration debate became established. Apparently, there is little or no perception of these integration achievements involving other sport-related settings (e.g. commercial sports service providers such as gyms or dance studios, reception of sport in the media, stadiums or public screenings of sports events). These basic and positively invested assumptions of the special integration achievements of sports clubs extend through studies focused on system theory, as well as through studies addressing socialization theory and civil society that have dominated perceptions of the specific integration achievements by the sports clubs in Germany.

This hints at a further characteristic of the papers submitted in Germany. Another noticeable fact is that discussions primarily – albeit not exclusively – revolve around issues of integration and sport, while discussions of exclusion and marginalization are far more rare. While a group of authors has increasingly examined discrimination practices and mechanisms of social closure over recent years, empirical studies that explicitly investigate issues of exclusion, marginalization, discrimination, or racism based on elaborate theoretical frameworks are still few and far between. In other words, research on integration and sport, as indicated by the concepts and terms it chooses, remains a discourse on positive factors, focusing primarily on research into processes of integration within and through sports clubs instead of research into processes of exclusion and marginalization in the broad field of sports.

On the one hand, this narrow research focus means that some subject areas are only marginally addressed. However, in this context it must be mentioned that in recent years an increasing amount of research has succeeded in closing gaps in the literature, with significant advancements made in empirical research regarding engagement in sport by young people with and without migrant backgrounds and – to a lesser degree – empirical research regarding integration achievements by sports clubs. In this context, numerous valuable studies have been submitted and differentiated empirical findings and presented interpretations have helped research on integration within and through sport to grow into an increasingly central research discipline with a focus on social sciences.

However, a final glance at these works indicates first that development of a theoretical framework has occupied a low priority to date. Although various interpretations have been assembled and offered to explain divergences in engagement in sport, they mostly represent an eclectic collection of individual fragments which still need to be combined to form a "new" theoretical framework. Second, most of the available studies fail to reference overarching concepts of integration; even studies that report on the concepts of assimilation or pluralism generally fail to penetrate to the level of empirical operationalization.

Third, a fundamental task for the future design of research on integration within and through sport is important to mention. No matter whether research references the paradigm of cultural difference, whether empirical analyses differentiates between people with and without migrant backgrounds, or whether sports clubs promote intercultural openings, by far the majority of the studies continue to subscribe to the paradigm of difference. While an increasing number of studies point out the problems of reification and warn against the dangers of singularity, neither theoretical nor data models have been developed so far in which the 'migration background' of the people surveyed is not defined a priori as an independent variable. Given this, binary codes and the marking of differences are largely retained in the current works of research.

Notes

1   For exceptions, see Bernd Bröskamp and Thomas Alkemeyer, *Fremdheit und Rassismus im Sport: Tagung der dvs-Sektion Sportphilosophie vom 09.-10.1994 in Berlin* (Sankt Augustin: Academia, 1996). See also Gerd Dembowski and Jürgen Scheidle, *Tatort Stadion:Rassismus, Antisemitismus und Sexismus im Fussball* (Köln: PapyRossa, 2002); G.A. Pilz, 'Fangewalt, Rechtsextremismus und Diskriminierung im Fußballsport', in Günther Deegener and Wilhelm Körner (eds), *Gewalt und Aggression im Kindes- und Jugendalter: Ursachen, Formen, Intervention* (Weinheim: Beltz, 2011).
2   Statistisches Bundesamt, *Bevölkerung und Erwerbstätigkeit: Bevölkerung mit Migrationshintergrund – Ergebnisse des Mikrozensus* (Wiesbaden: Statistisches Bundesamt, 2014).
3   Cf. Berthold Löffler, *Integration in Deutschland: Zwischen Assimilation und Multikulturalismus* (München: Oldenbourg, 2011).
4   Tina Nobis, 'Multikulturelle Zivilgesellschaft? Sportverbände und –vereine als Akteure der Integrationsarbeit', in Sebastian Braun, ed., *Der Deutsche Olympische Sportbund in der Zivilgesellschaft: Eine sozialwissenschaftliche Analyse zur sportbezogenen Engagementpolitik* (Wiesbaden: Springer, 2013), 46–9.
5   Cf. the basic premise of Dietrich Kurz, *Elemente des Schulsports* (Schorndorf: Hofmann, 1990).
6   Jürgen Baur and Ulrike Burrmann, 'Sozialisation zum und durch Sport', in Kurt Weis and Robert Gugutzer, eds, *Handbuch Sportsoziologie* (Schorndorf: Hofmann, 2008), 230–8. See also Sebastian Braun and Jürgen Baur, 'Zwischen Legitimität und Illegitimität – Zur Jugendarbeit in Sportorganisationen', *Spectrum der Sportwissenschaften* 12 (2000), 53–69.
7   Dietrich Kurz, *Elemente des Schulsports* (Schorndorf: Hofmann, 1990).
8   Michael Mutz and Ulrike Burrmann, 'Integration', in Werner Schmidt, Nils Neuber, Thomas Rauschenbach, Hans P. Brandl-Bredenbeck, Jessica Süßenbach, and Christoph Breuer, eds, *Dritter Deutscher Kinder- und Jugensportbereicht: Kinder- und Jugendsport im Umbruch* (Schorndorf: Hofmann, 2015), 256.

9   Sebastian Braun, 'Voluntary Associations and Social Capital: Inclusive and Exclusive Dimensions', in Matthias Freise and Thorsten Hallmann, eds, *Modernizing Democracy: Associations and Associating in the Twenty-First Century* (New York: Springer, 2014).

10 Hartmut Esser, *Soziologie: Spezielle Grundlagen. Band 2: Die Konstruktion der Gesellschaft* 2 (Frankfurt am Main: Campus, 2000).

11 Jürgen Baur, 'Kulturtechniken spielend erlernen: Über die Integrationspotenziale des vereinsorganisierten Sports', *Treffpunkt: Magazin für Migration und Integration* 16, 3 (2006), 3–9. See also Sebastian Braun and Sebastian Finke, *Integrationsmotor Sportverein: Ergebnisse zum Modellprojekt 'spin – sport interkulturell'* (Wiesbaden: VS Verlag für Sozialwissenschaft, 2010). Christa Kleindienst-Cachay, Klaus Cachay, and Steffen Bahlke, *Inklusion und Integration: Eine empirische Studie zur Integration von Migrantinnen und Migranten im organisierten Sport* (Schondorf: Hofmann, 2012).

12 Sebastian Braun, 'Sozialintegration, Systemintegration und Integration über sozialstrukturelle Bindungen: Integrationsleistungen freiwilliger Vereinigungen in traditionellen und aktuellen Gesellschaftsbeschreibungen', in Jürgen Baur and Sebastian Braun, eds, *Integrationsleistungen von Sportvereinen als Freiwilligenorganisation* (Aachen: Meyer and Meyer, 2003), 88–108.

13 For an overview, see Bernd Bröskamp, 'Migration, Integration, interkulturelle Kompetenz, Fremdheit und Diversität: Zur Etabilierung eines aktuellen Feldes der Sportforschung. Eine Sammelbesprechung', *Sport und Gesellschaft* 8 (2011), 85–94. See also Kleindienst-Cachay *et al.*, *Inklusion und Integration*; Klaus Seiberth, *Fremdheit im Sport: Ein theoretischer entwurf, Erscheinungsformen, Erklärungsmodelle und pädagogische Implikationen* (Tübingen: Eberhard-Karls-Universität, 2010).

14 Heinz-Dieter Horch, *Strukturbesonderheiten freiwilliger Vereinigungen. Analyse und Untersuchung einer alternativen Form menschlichen Zusammenarbeitens* (Frankfurt am Main: Campus, 1983). See also Heinz-Dieter Horch, *Strukturbesonderheiten freiwilliger Vereinigungen. Analyse und Untersuchung einer alternativen Form menschlichen Zusammenarbeitens* (Frankfurt am Main: Campus, 1992).

15 Christoph Breuer, ed., *Sportentwicklungsbericht 2013/14: Analyse zur Situation der Sportvereine in Deutschland* (Köln: Sporverlag Strauß, 2015). See also Christoph Breuer, Pamela Wicker, and Martin Forst, 'Integrationsspezifische Organisationsleistungen und -herausforderungen der deutschen Sportvereine', in Sebastian Braun and Tina Nobis, eds, *Migration, Integration und Sport: Zivilgesellschaft vor Ort* (Wiesbaden: VS Verlag für Sozialwissenschaften, 2011), 45–61; Kleindienst-Cachay *et al.*, *Inklusion und Integration*.

16 See Jürgen Baur, ed., *Evaluation des Programms 'Integration durch Sport'* (Potsdam: Universität Potsdam, 2009). See also Braun and Finke, *Integrationsmotor Sportverein*.

17 Burkhard Strob, *Der vereins- und verbandsorganisierte Sport: Ein Zusammenschluss von (Wahl) Gemeinschaften?* (Münster: Waxmann, 1999).

18 Sebastian Braun, 'Assoziative Lebenswelt, bindendes Sozialkapital und Migrantenvereine in Sport und Gesellschaft. Vergemeinschaftungsformen als Wahlgemeinschaften des Geschmacks', in Sebastian Braun and Tina Nobis, eds, *Migration, Integration und Sport: Zivilgesellschaft vor Ort* (Wiesbaden: VS Verlag für Sozialwissenschaften, 2011), 29–43.

19 Steffen Bahlke, Carmen Borggrefe, and Klaus Cachay, 'Weltmeister werden mit euch! - aber wie? Theoretische Überlegungen zum Problem der Unterrepräsentanz von Migrantinnen und Migranten im Handball', *Sport und Gesellschaft* 9, 1 (2012), 38–61.

20 Petra Gieß-Stüber, Ulrike Burrmann, Sabine Radtke, Bettina Rulofs, and Heike Tiemann, eds, *Expertise: Diversität, Inklusion, Integration und Interkulturalität: Leitbegriffe der Politik, sportwissenschaftliche Diskurse und Empfehlungen für den DOSB und die dsj* (Frankfurt am Main: Deutscher Olympischer Sportbund, 2014). See also Bettina Rulofs, 'Diversity Management: Perspektiven und konzeptionelle Ansätze für den Umgang mit Vielfalt mit organisierten Sport', in Sebastian Braun and Tina Nobis, eds, *Der Deutsche Olympische Sportbund in der Zivilgesellschaft: Eine sozialwissenschaftliche Analyse zur sportbezogenen Engagementpolitik* (Wiesbaden: Springer, 2011), 83–97.

21 See, for example, Michael Mutz and Ulrike Burrmann, 'Integration', in Werner Schmidt, Nils Neuber, Thomas Rauschenbach, Hand P. Brandl-Bredenbeck, Jessica Süßenbach, and Christoph Breuer, eds, *Dritter Deutscher Kinder- und Jugendsportbericht: Kinder- und Jugendsport im Umbruch* (Schorndorf: Hofmann, 2015), 255–71.

22 For a summary see Mutz and Burrmann, 'Integration'; see also Kleindienst-Cachay *et al.*, *Inklusion und Integration*.

23 See Braun and Nobis, *Migration, Integration und Sport*. See also Ulrike Burrmann, Michael Mutz, and Ursula Zender, eds, *Jugend, Migration und Sport: Kulturelle Unterschiede und die Sozialisation zum Vereinssport* (Wiesbaden: Springer VS, 2015); Michael Mutz, *Sport als Sprungbrett in die Gesellschaft? Sportengagements von Jugendlichen mit Migrationshintergrund und ihre Wirkungen* (Weinheim and Basel: Beltz Juventa, 2012); Michael Mutz and Silvester Stahl, 'Mitgliedschaft junger Migranten in

eigenethnischen Sportvereinen: Eine Sekundäranalyse auf der Basis des Ausländersurveys', *Sport und Gesellschaft* 7, 2 (2010), 255–71.

24 See Burrmann *et al.*, *Jugend, Migration und Sport*. See also Christa Kleindienst-Cachay, *Mädchen und Frauen mit Migrationshintergrund im organisierten Sport* (Baltmannsweiler: Schneider Hohengehren, 2007); Yvonne Weigelt-Schlesinger, Klaus Seiberth, and Thorsten Schlesinger. 'Fußballerinnen mit Migrationshintergrund in der Schweriz', in Silke Sinning, Jonathan Pargätzi, and Björn Eichmann, eds, *Frauen- und Mädchenfußball im Blickpunkt* (Münster: Lit, 2014), 219–32.

25 See Baur, *Evaluation des Programms*. See also Anne Rübner Burrmann, Sebstian Braun, Tina Nobis, Ronald Langner, Michael Mutz, Anabel Marquez-Lopez, and Mareike Rickert, 'Ziele, Konzeption, und Wirkungen sportbezogener Integrationsarbeit aus Sicht der Funktionsträger/innen des DOSB-Programms "Integration durch Sport"' (2014), www.integration-durch-sport.de/fileadmin/fm-dosb/arbeitsfelder/ids/files/downloads_pdf/downloads_2014/Evaluation_programm_integration_durch_Sport_2013.pdf, accessed 11 August 2014; Ulf Gebken and Sören Vosgerau, eds, *Fußball ohne Abseits: Ergebnise und Perspektiven des Projekts 'Soziale Integration von Mädchen durch den Fußball'* (Wiesbaden: Springer VS, 2014).

26 See Baur, *Evaluation des Programms*. See also Ursula Boos-Nünning and Yasemin Karakaşoğlu, 'Kinder und Jugendliche mit Migrationshintergrund und Sport', in Werner Schmidt, Ilse Hartmann-Tews, and Wolf-Dietrich Brettschneider, eds, *Erster Kinder- und Jugendsportbereicht* (Schorndorf: Hofmann, 2003), 319–38; Braun and Finke, *Integrationsmotor Sportverein*; Nancy Fussan and Tina Nobis, 'Zur Partizipation von Jugendlichen mit Migrationshintergrund in Sportvereinen', in Tina Nobis and Jürgen Baur, eds, *Soziale Integration vereinsorganisierter Jugendlicher* (Köln: Sportverlag Strauß, 2007); Marie-Luise Klein and Christa Kleindienst-Cachay, eds, *Muslimische Frauen im Sport* (Düsseldorf: LSB Nordrhein-Westfalen, 2004); Christa Kleindienst-Cachay and Carmen Kuzmik, 'Fußballspielen und jugendliche Entwicklung türkisch-muslimischer Mädchen', *Sportunterricht* 56, 1 (2007), 11–15; Christa Kleindienst-Cachay, *Mädchen und Frauen mit Migrationshintergrund im organisierten Sport* (Baltmannsweiler: Schneider Hohengehren, 2007); Michael Mutz, *Sport als Sprungbrett in die Gesellschaft? Sportengagements von Jugendlichen Mit Migrationshintergrund und ihre Wirkungen* (Weinheim und Basel: Beltz Juventa, 2012). Mutz and Burrmann, 'Sportliches engagement jugendlicher Migranten'; Mutz and Nobis 'Strategien zur Einbindung von Migrantinnen integration durch Sport'.

27 See Fussan and Nobis, 'Zur Partizipation von Jugendlichen mit Migrationshintergrund in Sportvereinen'; Michael Mutz and Ulrike Burrmann, 'Sportliches engagement jugendlicher Migranten in Schule und Verein: Eine Re-Analyse der PISA- und der SPRINT-Studie', in Sebastian Braun and Tina Nobis, eds, *Migration, Integration und Sport: Zivilgesellschaft vor Ort* (Wiesbaden: VS Verlag für Sozialwissenschaften, 2011).

28 See Thomas Lampert, Gert Mensink, Natalie Romahn, and Alexander Woll, 'Körperlich-sportliche Aktivität von Kindern und Jugendlichen in Deutschland: ergebnisse des Kinder- und Jugendgesundheitssurveys (KiGGS)', *Bundesgesundheitsblatt Gesundheitsforschung Gesundheitsschutz* 50, 5–6 (2007), 634–42. See also Michael Mutz, *DOSB Expertise: Die Partizipation von Migrantinnen und Migranten am vereinsorganisierten Sport* (Frankfurt am Main: Deutscher Olympischer Sportbund, 2013).

29 See Baur, *Evaluation des Programms 'Integration durch Sport'*. See also Braun and Nobis, *Migration, Integration und Sport*; and Christoph Breuer, ed., *Sportentwicklungsbericht 2013/14: Analyse zur Situation der Sportvereine in Deutschland* (Köln: Sporverlag Strauß, 2015).

30 Mutz and Burrmann, 'Integration'.

31 Thomas Alkemeyer and Bernd Bröskamp, 'Einleitung: Fremdheit und Rassismus im Sport', in Bernd Brösekamp and Thomas Alkemeyer, eds, *Fremdheit und Rassismus im Sport: Tagung der dvs-Sektion Sportphilosophie* (Sankt Augustin: Academia, 1996), 7–40. See also Ursula Boos-Nünning and Yasemin Karakaşoğlu, *Viele Welten leben: Zur Lebenssituation von Mädchen und jungen Frauen mit migrationshintergrund* (Münster: Waxmann, 2005); Bernd Bröskamp, *Körperliche Fremdheit: Zum Problem der interkulturellen Begegnung im Sport* (St. Augustin: Academia, 1994); Gunter Gebauer, 'Der Körper als Symbol für Ethnizität', in Bernd Bröskmap and Thomas Alkemeyer, eds, *Fremdheit und Rassismus im Sport: Tagung der dvs-Sektion Sportphilosophie* (Sankt Augustin: Academia, 1996), 81–4; Marie-Luise Klein and Christa Kleindienst-Cachay, eds, *Muslimische Frauen im Sport* (Düsseldorf: LSB Nordrhein-Westfalen, 2004). Christa Kleindienst-Cachay, Klaus Cachay, and Steffen Bahlke, *Inklusion und Integration: Eine empirische Studie zur Integration von Migrantinnen und Migranten im organisierten Sport* (Schondorf: Hofmann, 2012).

32 Alkemeyer and Bröskamp, 'Einleitung: Fremdheit und Rassismus im Sport'. See also Michael Mutz, *Sport als Sprungbrett in die Gesellschaft?*; Klaus Seiberth, *Fremdheit im Sport: Ein theoretischer entwurf. Erscheinungsformen, Erklärungsmodelle und pädagogische Implikationen* (Tübingen: Eberhard-Karls-

Universität, 2010); Fussan and Nobis, 'Zur Partizipation von Jugendlichen mit Migrationshintergrund in Sportvereinen'; Bernd Bröskamp, 'Migration, Integration, interkulturelle Kompetenz, Fremdheit und Diversität: Zur Etabilierung eines aktuellen Feldes der Sportforschung. Eine Sammelbesprechung', *Sport und Gesellschaft* 8 (2011), 85–94.

33 Heiko Meier and Ansagar Thiel, '"Starke Kulturen"? Sportvereine im Spannungsfeld zwischen struktureller Veränderung und Existenzsicherung', in Michael Krüger and Bernd Schulze, eds, *Fußball in Geschichte und Gesellschaft* (Hamburg: Czwalina, 2006). See also Mutz, *Sport als Sprungbrett in die Gesellschaft?*; Nobis, 'Einstellungen jugendlicher Sportvereinsmitglieder zur ausländischen Bevölkerung'; Jürgen Schwark, 'Rassismus und Ethnozentrismus im alltagskulturellen Sportsystem', in Marie-Luise Klein and Jürgen Kothy, eds, *Thnisch-kulturelle Konflikte im Sport* (Hamburg: Czwalina, 1998), 75–85; Klaus Seiberth, *Fremdheit im Sport: Ein theoretischer entwurf: Erscheinungsformen, Erklärungsmodelle und pädagogische Implikationen* (Tübingen: Eberhard-Karls-Universität, 2010); Klaus Seiberth, Yvonne Weigelt-Schlesinger, and Thorsten Schlesinger, "Fußballerinnen mit Migrationshintergrund in der Schweiz', in Silke Sinning, Jonathan Pargätzi, and Björn Eichmann, eds, *Frauen- und Mädchenfußball im Blickpunkt* (Münster: Lit, 2013), 219–32.

34 Christoph Breuer, Pamela Wicker, and Martin Forst, 'Integrationsspezifische Organisationsleistungen und -herausforderungen der deutschen Sportvereine', in Sebastian Braun and Tina Nobis, eds, *Migration, Integration und Sport: Zivilgesellschaft vor Ort* (Wiesbaden: VS Verlag für Sozialwissenschaften, 2011), 45–61.

35 Kleindienst-Cachay *et al.*, *Inklusion und Integration*. See also Sebastian Braun and Tina Nobis, *Migrationenorganisationen mit sportbezogenen Handlungsfeldern: Zusammenfassung zum Forschungsprojekt: Arbeitspapier des Forschungszentrums für Bürgerschaftliches Engagement* (Berlin: Humboldt-Universität zu Berlin, 2012).

36 Baur, *Evaluation des Programms 'Integration durch Sport'*. See also Braun and Finke, *Integrationsmotor Sportverein*.

37 Kleindienst-Cachay *et al.*, *Inklusion und Integration*. See also Heiko Meier and Ansagar Thiel, 'Starke Kulturen?'; Tina Nobis, 'Einstellungen jugendlicher Sportvereinsmitglieder zur ausländischen Bevölkerung', in Tina Nobis and Jürgen Baur, eds, *Soziale Integration vereinsorganisierter Jugendlicher* (Köln: Sportverlag Strauß, 2007), 331–52; Seiberth, *Fremdheit im Sport*; Klaus Seiberth, Yvonne Weigelt-Schlesinger, and Thorsten Schlesinger, 'Wie integrationsfähig sind Sportvereine? Eine Analyse organisationaler Integrationsbarrieren am Beispiel von Mädchen und Frauen mit Migrationshintergund', *Sport und Gesellschaft* 10, (2013), 174–98.

38 Valerie Amiraux and Bernd Bröskamp, 'Sportangebote islamischer Organisationen in Berlin', in Bend Brösekamp and Thomas Alkemeyer, eds, *Fremdheit und Rassismus im Sport: Tagung der dvs-Sektion Sportphilosophie* (Sankt Augustin: Academia, 1996), 109–30; Friedrich Heckmann, 'Sport und gesllschaftliche Integration von Minderheiten', in Harald Bammel and Hartmut Becker, eds, *Sport und ausländische Mitbürger* (Bonn: Friedrich-Ebert-Stiftung, 1985), 12–33. Marie-Luise Klein, Jürgen Kothy, and Gülsen Cabadag, 'Interethische Kontakte und Konflikte im Sport', in Wilhelm Heitmeyer and Reimund Anhut, eds, *Bedrohte Stadtgesellschaft: Soziale Desintegrationsprozesse und ethnisch-kulturelle Konfliktkonstellationen* (Weinheim: Juventa, 2000), 307–46; Thomas Schwarz, *Türkische Sportler in Berlin zwischen Integration und Segragation* (Berlin: Express Edition, 1987).

39 Diethelm Blecking 'Vom "Polackenklub" zu Türkiyem Spor: Migranten und FUßball im Ruhrgebiet und in anderen deutschen Regionen', in Beatrix Bouvier, ed., *Zur Sozial- und Kulturgeschichte des Fußballs* (Trier: Friedrich-Ebert-Stiftung, 2006), 183–98. See also Sebastian Braun and Tina Nobis, *Migrationenorganisationen mit sportbezogenen Handlungsfeldern: Zusammenfassung zum Forschungsprojekt: Arbeitspapier des Forschungszentrums für Bürgerschaftliches Engagement* (Berlin: Humboldt-Universität zu Berlin, 2012). Daniel Huhn, Hannes Kunstreich and Stefan Metzger, eds, *Türkisch geprägte Fußballvereine im Ruhrgebiet und in Berlin* (Münster: Westfälische Wilhelms-Universität Münster, 2011). Silvester Stahl, *Selbstorganisation von Migranten im deutschen Vereinssport* (Köln: Sportverlag Strauß, 2009); Dariuš Zifonun, 'Das Migrantenmilieu des FC Hochstätt Türkspor', in Sighard Neckel and Hans-Georg Soeffner, eds, *Mittendrin im Abseits: Ethnische Gruppenbeziehungen im lokalen Kontext* (Wiesbaden: VS Verlag für Sozialwissenschaften, 2008), 187–210.

40 Andres Göttlich, 'König Fußballs neue Kleider: Die Integrationsvorstellungen deutscher Sportverbände', in Sighard Neckel and Hans-Georg Soeffner, eds, *Mittendrin im Abseits: Ethnische Gruppenbeziehungen im lokalen Kontext* (Wiesbaden: VS Verlag für Sozialwissenschaften, 2008), 211–34. See also Tina Nobis, 'Multikulturelle Zivilgesellschaft? Sportverbände und -vereine als Akteure der Integrationsarbeit', in Sebastian Braun, ed., *Der Deutsche Olympische Sportbund in der Zivilgesellschaft: Eine sozialwissenschaftliche Analyse zur sportbezogenen Engagementpolitik* (Wiesbaden: Springer, 2013), 46–9.

41 Burrmann *et al.*, 'Ziele, Konzeption,und Wirkungen'.

15

IRELAND AND THE IRISH DIASPORA

Paul Darby

Introduction

It is somewhat of a truism that the 'Irish', defined here as those born and resident in the island of Ireland who consider themselves to be ethnically Irish as well as those who comprise the wider Irish diaspora, are often defined by their engagement in and relationship to sport. Sport possesses significant social, political, economic, and cultural significance for the Irish. Its centrality in Irish cultural life is exemplified by the fact that, despite being a relatively small geographical entity, Ireland, north and south, has produced a high number of world–class men and women athletes who have excelled at the highest levels of their chosen sport. In the case of boxing, for example, Ireland has a long and rich history of punching above its weight, with the Irish boxing landscape peppered with world titles in the professional code, and European, world and Olympic medals in the amateur version. The recent successes of Ireland's golfing quartet of McIlroy, Clarke, McDowell and Harrington, who won nine major titles between them between 2005 and 2015, is another case in point.

The significance of sport here, though, extends far beyond achievements at the elite level of competition. Sport has historically been a focal point in the lives of ordinary Irish men and women, a fact that can be measured by the numbers and commitment of participants as well as the emotional and financial investment of spectators. This passion for sport among the Irish is not only apparent within the confines of Ireland though. The Irish ebullience for various sporting codes is clearly manifest not only during international competition that features an Irish team or athlete, but also in the numbers who leave the Republic of Ireland and Northern Ireland on a regular basis during weekends between August and May to support various English and Scottish football (soccer) teams. Beyond this transient movement of sports spectators to locales outside of Ireland, those who have formed part of Ireland's long-standing diaspora have been no less passionate about sport. For some, sport has been the primary reason for their departure, and these sporting migrants have graced venues throughout the world. For the majority of those who have emigrated, though, the search for a better life, measured in social, political and economic terms, has been the key factor in their decision to leave Ireland. This is not to say that sport has been a marginal part of their lives in their new 'homes'. Rather, the Irish diaspora have brought their enthusiasm for various codes of sport to virtually all of those parts of the world that have sizeable Irish communities.

Sport has also long functioned as a conduit for the expression of both semantic and syntactical ethnic identities. Although Irish national teams in popular sporting codes such as football and rugby union and prominent individual Irish athletes and sports stars often generate celebratory and carnivalesque versions of Irishness, sport can also serve as a stage where dichotomous ethnic and national identities clash. The latter has been observed in the voluminous literature on sport and identity politics in Northern Ireland and it is not the intention of this article to revisit this ground. Rather, this chapter examines the role of sport in the construction and articulation of varying forms of Irish ethnic identity among the diaspora. The chapter begins by positioning the role of sport in this regard within the wider context of Irish emigration. This discussion provides a broad sweep of sports and their import in a range of diasporic contexts. Thereafter, the chapter focuses on the development of the Gaelic games in the USA and, more specifically, their role in enabling sections of the Irish émigré to construct and articulate their ethnicity.

Sport in the context of Irish emigration

The current worldwide Irish diaspora, estimated at around 70 million, is the result of a history of sustained emigration from Ireland that stretches back to the seventeenth century.[1] This process accelerated to such an extent in the nineteenth and twentieth centuries that Ireland quickly became the leading European nation in terms of out-migration as a proportion of its total population. In the period between 1815 and 1870, for example, the numbers emigrating from Ireland stood at between 4 and 4.5 million and by 1890 almost 40 per cent of all those people born in Ireland were living outside the country.[2] While Irish emigration has been diffuse, with émigré populations found on every continent, the USA, Britain, Canada and Australia have been the main ports of disembarkation for the Irish in their journeys around the world. This continues to be the case, particularly for those who have looked outwards in their quest to build a future following the recent global financial crisis and subsequent economic recession. Emigration, then, has clearly been prominent in Ireland's history. Indeed, the leaving of, or at least the potential of leaving, the island of Ireland has been so salient to the collective Irish psyche, that David Fitzpatrick, one of the leading analysts of Irish emigration, commented that, 'growing up in Ireland meant preparing oneself to leave it'.[3]

The Irish have contributed significantly to the societies in which they have migrated. For example, the great cities in the north-eastern part of the USA, particularly New York and Boston, were shaped, physically, politically, socially and culturally by the Irish diaspora. As the largest ethnic group in these expanding metropolises in the late nineteenth and early twentieth centuries, Irish workers provided the labour for the construction, infrastructure and sanitation projects, while Irish clergy formed the cornerstone of the Catholic Church. Once they had overcome nativist prejudice and crude stereotypes and acquired opportunities for social mobility, Irish businessmen, industrialists, publishers and entrepreneurs excelled.[4] Irish politicians played a leading role in urban and, later, national politics, and their success in this regard is epitomised by the entry into the White House of John F. Kennedy, a descendant of a Famine emigrant from County Wexford. As will be discussed shortly, the Irish also made a visible and lasting contribution to sports, not only in America but also in other host societies where they settled. Not all that the Irish brought to the New World was positive though. Deep religious and political differences between Anglo-Protestant and Irish Catholic were as evident in America and Britain as they were in Ireland. Indeed, so significant has sectarianism been to the dynamics of the Irish emigrant experience that Donald Akenson has argued, 'to study Irish history either of the homeland or of any part of the diaspora without considering sectarian divergences is not to study the Irish at all'.[5]

As has been observed elsewhere, the Irish contribution to and role in sport throughout the world has also reflected and been reflective of the sectarian and ethnic divisions that have blighted Ireland, north and south, through much of its recent history.[6] However, sport has not only provided countless hours of enjoyable distraction from the rigours of everyday life, it has also performed a number of other crucial functions. For some immigrants, sport eased their assimilation and facilitated a degree of acceptance in what could be hostile and unwelcoming environments. For others, proficiency and success in sports allowed for the promotion and preservation of a strong sense of ethnic pride and identity. The Irish émigré were by no means unusual in utilising sport as a means of both facilitating integration and marking oneself as distinctive. Indeed, it has been recognised that sport has served this dual purpose for a whole range of immigrant populations throughout the world.[7] In much the same way as other European immigrants, the Irish émigré were reluctant to completely discard their indigenous culture, traditions and identity. Thus, they strove to come to a position of accommodation, rather than complete assimilation or acculturation. As pragmatists they absorbed those cultural forms that would allow them to progress, socially and economically, in their new 'homes'. At the same time, they sought ways to maintain their links with the 'old country' and preserve and articulate their ethnic distinctiveness. Beyond the role of sport in terms of identity politics, involvement as participants or spectators provided occasions for Irish-born migrants and their descendants to come together and be sustained by mixing with like-minded individuals. The human contact and social interaction that sport encouraged also opened doors to the Irish in terms of acquiring work, accommodation and friends, all of which were crucial to surviving and prospering in Britain, the USA, Canada, Australia and all of the other destinations of the emigrating Irish.

These themes have been apparent in what can be described as an emerging literature on sport and the Irish diaspora. This scholarship has developed over the last decade or so, partly because of a growing acknowledgement of the socio-economic, political and cultural significance of sport for the Irish abroad and partly because of the growth and diversification of the field of Irish diaspora studies. This work has addressed a variety of sports, both those that the Irish brought with them on their travels and those that they encountered in new lands, and has examined a range of destinations where the Irish settled. It has also explored, either specifically or tangentially, the ways in which engagement in sport coalesces around the construction and maintenance of Irish ethnic identities in 'foreign' climes. For example, Wilcox, Reiss, Bjarkman and, to a lesser extent, McCaffrey and Ridge have all examined the significance and role of sports in the lives of the Irish in the USA in the late nineteenth and early twentieth centuries.[8] To a large extent, their work, with the exception of Ridge, has centred on the Irish role in American and British codes of sport including baseball, basketball, athletics and soccer.

Other studies of Irish involvement in sport in the USA have concentrated specifically on Gaelic games. These include the work of McGinn on hurling in New York in the eighteenth century, Black's unpublished doctoral dissertation on sport, gender, nationalism and the Irish diaspora in San Francisco, and Brady's unpublished postgraduate thesis on Gaelic Park, the home of Gaelic games in New York.[9] A number of those who have written more broadly on the Gaelic Athletic Association (GAA), particularly Humphries and de Búrca, have also commented, albeit briefly, on Gaelic games in the USA.[10] Darby's work is also significant in this regard and his research has uncovered, in a much more sustained way, the history and role of Gaelic games for the Irish émigré across America from the late nineteenth century to the current day.[11] Outside of the USA, other notable work on Gaelic sport abroad includes King's populist analysis of the global diffusion of hurling and his co-authored study with Darby on hurling and Irishness in Argentina, McCarthy's work on the GAA in Western Australia, Bradley's account of Gaelic sport in Scotland,

Ryan and Wamsley's study of hurling and Gaelic football in Toronto, Hassan's analysis of Gaelic games in Europe, and Moore and Darby's research on the GAA in London.[12] What connects this work is an acknowledgement of the role of these sports in allowing Irish migrants to build, maintain, and give voice to ethnic distinctiveness.

The same can also be said of the scholarship that has addressed the Irish diaspora and other codes of sport beyond the USA. This is particularly the case regarding the literature on the role of the Irish in Scottish football, and more specifically their place in the dynamics of the 'Old Firm' rivalry between Glasgow's two main football clubs, Celtic and Rangers.[13] Alongside this work on the 'Old Firm', a number of scholars have assessed the role of Celtic in the maintenance of Irishness among the Irish diaspora in Scotland, while others have touched on the same issue in relation to the Edinburgh club, Hibernian.[14] The contribution of Irish-Australians in the emergence of Australian sports culture has been addressed directly by Bairner and Horton and as part of broader histories of Australian sport by Adair and Vamplew and Cashman.[15] Ryan and Wamsley have also examined the role of sport for the Irish in Toronto in the opening decades of the twentieth century.[16] Space does not permit elaboration on the specific ways in which a variety of sporting codes across a wide range of diasporic settings have articulated and facilitated Irish ethnic identities. Instead, this chapter shifts its focus to analysing how Gaelic games have historically fed into and shaped Irish ethnicities abroad.

Gaelic games, ethnic identity and the Irish in America

That Gaelic games have played an important role in the maintenance of strong feelings of Irish ethnic identity beyond the island of Ireland should come as no surprise when one considers the national origins and development of the Gaelic Athletic Association, founded in 1884. The story of the Association has been the subject of much scholarship and reveals that it was established as a response to British cultural imperialism and a desire to rediscover and promote a strong, distinctive version of Irishness.[17] The emergence of Gaelic games in Ireland in the late nineteenth and early twentieth centuries was part of a wider Gaelic revival that sought to foreground Ireland's cultural heritage in the wider struggle for Irish independence from Britain.[18] While the extent to which the Association served as a stage for politicised ethnic identities has waxed and waned, largely in response to Ireland's relationship with Britain and the political situation in Northern Ireland, Gaelic sports in Ireland have remained almost exclusively Irish in terms of participation and consumption. The same can be said for much of its history in the USA, where the very act of becoming a member of the GAA or playing or watching Gaelic games invariably marked one as ethnically Irish or Irish American. While this has been important in the physical enactment of Irish immigrants' ethnic identity in America, the fact that the Association has long functioned as a conduit for the articulation of support for specific Irish causes has been equally significant in allowing Gaelic games to function as an explicit marker of Irishness. This is particularly evident in the long-standing relationship between Gaelic games in the USA and the wider political aspirations of Irish nationalism, and this is the focus for the rest of this chapter.

Irish nationalism as a significant expression of Irish Catholic identity in America emerged in the first half of the nineteenth century as the result of a combination of slow social, economic and political progress for Irish Catholic immigrants and an intense sense of Anglophobia.[19] It was the Great Famine, though, that did much to shape Irish ethno-nationalist expression in the New World. The Famine immigrants that poured into America in the mid-1800s adopted the motif of exile and saw Britain as responsible not only for their poverty and starvation in Ireland, but also for their exodus to what was for most of them an unwelcoming and deeply inhospitable country.[20] Thus, from the 1850s onwards Irish American nationalism became increasingly characterised not only by a love for Ireland, or at least an 'imagined', idealised vision of Ireland, but by a hatred of the British. Indeed, Irish nationalists in America in this period displayed what the great Irish poet William Butler Yeats described as a 'fanatic heart'.[21] The initial experiences of the Famine Irish in America, blighted as they were by nativism, poverty, disease and destitution, did little to assuage their acrimony towards Britain nor dampen their desire to see Ireland free of British influence. Indeed, the émigré of the second half of the nineteenth century believed that their progress, acceptance and recognition as fully fledged citizens of America could only be won through the achievement of emancipation in Ireland.[22]

Although there were fluctuations in levels and intensity of support, nationalism, of both the revolutionary and constitutional brands, became a key element of Irish ethnic identity in the second half of the nineteenth century. Joining revolutionary organisations, donating their dollars to parliamentary nationalism, attending political meetings dealing with the Irish question, joining Irish clubs and societies and voting for Irish politicians provided Irish Americans with an opportunity to develop and give vent to politicised versions of Irishness. Taking their lead from Irish nationalist thinking in Ireland around the importance of a revival of Irish culture, Irish American nationalists soon recognised that any contribution to separatist aspirations, politically, financially and militarily, would be much stronger and more coherent if it were built on a strong sense of cultural Irishness among the émigrés. Thus, in much the same way as occurred in Ireland, Irish cultural forms, literature and the Irish language were promoted in America as a way of achieving this end. The significance of sport in the British Empire and the role that American sports, particularly baseball, played in helping the Irish community assert themselves, develop a sense of ethnic cohesion and acquire self-esteem was not lost on the leaders of Irish American nationalism.[23] Thus, as it had done in Ireland, Gaelic sport in the USA also came to represent an important cultural mechanism for building and articulating an affinity for Ireland and the nationalist agenda and in doing so shaping Irish ethnicity in the New World.

This manifested itself in a whole range of ways from the inception of formally constituted Gaelic football and hurling clubs in the USA from the 1880s onwards through to the current day. The founders of these clubs were staunch Irish nationalists and they aligned their activities to the movement for Irish independence by naming their clubs after historical and popular nationalist personalities and organisations, and linking their activities to a whole host of nationalist organisations, of both the physical force and parliamentary kind.[24] This allowed Gaelic games to serve as a platform for feelings of Irishness that were rooted in 'imagined' romanticised, mythical and certainly 'invented' visions of Ireland as a rural idyll, populated by manly and sport-loving Celts.[25] In the opening decades of the twentieth century Gaelic sports remained an important marker of Irish ethnic identity. The linking of the Gaelic games to the campaign for Irish home rule and independence from Britain was particularly important in this regard. For example, between 1914 and the Easter Rising of 1916, GAA clubs, events and venues became key locales for fund-raising activities for militant irredentism. While this bolstered the coffers of the Irish National Volunteers as they prepared for revolution in Ireland, it also helped to forge an ethnicity among sections of the Irish diaspora that was characterised by a hostility and belligerence towards the continued British presence in Ireland.

From around the late 1920s the relationship between the GAA and these versions of ethnic identity began to decline. This was largely as a consequence of a broader transformation in the identities of Irish Americans and the decline of Gaelic games in the USA. In the minds of the majority of Irish Americans during this period, the signing of the Anglo-Irish Treaty in 1921, which created an autonomous 26-county Irish Free State and allowed the six-county Northern Irish state, had effectively resolved Ireland's relationship with Britain.[26] In addition, large swathes of the diaspora were bemused by the ensuing civil war in Ireland and felt increasingly alienated by some dimensions of post-partition Irish nationalism, not least a small isolationist *Gaelic* and socialist element. While there remained some support for a campaign for complete reunification, events in Ireland combined with greater levels of social mobility and cultural assimilation into American society ultimately led to less of a preoccupation with the affairs of the 'old country', and hence a more general decline in Irish nationalism as an expression of Irish Catholic identity. As McCaffrey succinctly put it: 'As the Irish achieved success and respectability in the United States, they became more American and less Irish.'[27] As a corollary to this, sporting and cultural forms that had previously been so closely linked to Irishness and the Irish nationalist cause experienced a serious decline. The Great Depression, immigration restrictions and the onset of the Second World War also contributed to this decline and by the 1940s organised GAA activity across America had virtually died out.

The hosting of the All-Ireland Gaelic football final in New York in 1947, the first and only time that this event has been staged outside the island of Ireland, did much to revive the popularity of Gaelic games in post-war America. While there were pockets of support for militant Irish republicanism in this period, the GAA fraternity was generally more concerned about sporting encounters and their participation in and consumption of Gaelic sport engendered a much more benign, culturally focused Irishness.[28] This changed with the onset of the conflict in Northern Ireland in the late 1960s. Many Irish Americans quickly reconnected with what had been a largely dormant version of Irishness, one that for some increasingly became characterised by an intense antipathy towards the Unionist establishment in Northern Ireland and the British presence in Ireland more generally. More politicised, belligerent and militant senses of Irishness quickly found expression within units of the GAA around the USA. This manifested itself in a range of ways from the early 1970s through to the signing of the Good Friday Agreement (GFA) in 1998, and was particularly, although not exclusively, prominent in New York where the GAA supported organisations from across the spectrum of Irish nationalism during the early years of the troubles. For example, when Irish nationalists in the north campaigned on issues related to civil rights, New York's Gaels were eager to help in whatever way they could. Likewise, when popular support for physical force republicanism gained momentum in Northern Ireland, they also came forward with support. This was especially evident in the close association that developed between the GAA and Irish Northern Aid (Noraid), an organisation that officially provided aid for the families of IRA prisoners in Northern Ireland but also canvassed openly for funds to arm the Provisional IRA.[29] That such a link developed is hardly surprising, given that those who were instrumental in setting up Noraid were all influential figures in the GAA.

Evidence of the explicit linking of Gaelic sports clubs with an overtly political agenda was not just specific to America's north-eastern seaboard. On the Pacific coast a similar rationale underpinned the establishment of the Ulster Gaelic Football Club (GFC) in San Francisco in 1986. The majority of those behind the founding of the club hailed originally from Northern Ireland and were republican in their political outlook. They clearly aspired to ensure that the club reflected their political orientation. Of the five key aims of the club, four dealt with its commitment to remembering, celebrating and supporting those who were involved in the movement for a united Ireland, and it was only the club's fifth aim that mentioned the promotion of Gaelic games and the culture of the Irish people.[30] The club strove to meet its objectives and satisfy its overtly political agenda in a number of ways. For example, a Political Wing Committee (PWC) was established to oversee and promote its republican underpinnings. Ulster also closely aligned itself with the activities of Noraid in San Francisco and there was significant cross-membership between both organisations. The club also organised remembrance masses for PIRA volunteers killed in the conflict in Northern Ireland and held an annual Easter Brunch, organised to commemorate and celebrate those who took part in the 1916 Easter Rising. In conducting itself in this manner, the Ulster club represented perhaps the clearest example in the late 1980s and early 1990s of GAA members not only accommodating a political component within their broader promotion of Irish cultural pastimes, but actually proactively using Gaelic games as a medium through which to foster a highly politicised Irish ethnicity in the USA.

As the 1990s progressed, political developments in Northern Ireland once again began to impact the nature of Irishness in America and as a corollary, alter the extent and intensity of the linkages between the GAA there and Irish republicanism. The shift towards a commitment to constitutional, non-violent republicanism that occurred in Ireland was also reflected in the USA, where the majority of those with republican sympathies either followed the official line of Sinn Féin and committed themselves to a peaceful, constitutional campaign for a united Ireland or simply allowed the more belligerent elements of their Irishness to slowly subside. Pockets of support for dissident republicans in Ireland who remain committed to a campaign of violence as a mechanism for Irish unification are still apparent in some quarters, and this has occasionally seeped, indirectly, into the activities of some GAA clubs. However, most members of the GAA in the USA are less inclined towards politicised expressions of their Irishness, preferring instead to concentrate on the cultural aspects of their ethnicity.[31]

By the beginning of the new millennium, other events fed into this process, perhaps most notably the GAA's response to dwindling rates of Irish immigration following the introduction of tighter border controls post-9/11. By the mid to late 1990s, the impact of the Celtic Tiger on Irish immigration into the USA had led to serious concerns about the survival of Gaelic games. The virtual cessation of Irish immigration following the imposition of much tighter border controls post-9/11 brought fears regarding the GAA's future in the USA to an apex. While some responded by calling on the GAA in Dublin to relax the regulations surrounding player transfers, other influential figures decided to move in an altogether different direction by embarking on a strategy that may aid the GAA's survival in quantitative terms but will, without question, alter the extent to which the Association functions as a bulwark of an exclusively Irish ethnic expression in the future. The fundamental reason for this is the fact that this strategy is rooted in a drive to promote Gaelic games to an American-born constituency and one not necessarily of Irish descent. This process has been particularly marked and innovative in San Francisco, where there has been a long-standing commitment to promoting Gaelic games among a broader American-born public. In recent years, the GAA in San Francisco has made considerable strides in opening up Gaelic sports to a wider constituency. For example, Gaelic football has been promoted in local schools; American-born only teams, such as the Celts, have been established at the junior level to provide a vehicle to allow young American players to progress beyond youth programmes; and hurling teams have been established at Stanford University and University of California, Berkeley. The Association has also drawn on information technology in an attempt to extend the reach of Gaelic games, with podcasts of matches available through iTunes and translation software being used to make the division's website available in Spanish, thus providing opportunities for clubs to tap into the sizeable Hispanic community in the Bay Area.

It should be noted that the emphasis on youth development programmes, particularly the promotion of Gaelic games to non-ethnically Irish American citizens, has not been uncontested and has raised questions in the minds of some Gaels about the *raison d'être* of the Association in post-9/11 America. As this chapter has demonstrated, the GAA has historically provided a platform for the preservation and articulation of Irishness in the USA and it did much to sustain

Gaelic games in times of difficulty. While GAA clubs have always drawn on non-Irish players when circumstances dictated, the recent drive to open up Gaelic games to a range of ethnic constituencies in the USA has the potential to create a body that is less distinctively Irish, at least in terms of membership. For some this is problematic, not least because it is viewed as a process that could undermine the deeply rooted, cultural and political significance of the GAA. While some feel that part of the essence of Gaelic sport might be lost in the drive to broaden its appeal, others welcome any moves aimed at making the GAA more inclusive and ethnically diverse. Indeed, for individuals involved in this process, the future of Gaelic games in the USA should be predicated not on their Irishness but rather purely on their aesthetic qualities as sporting pursuits.

Conclusion

This chapter has revealed that the ethnicity that has coalesced around and has been articulated through the GAA in the USA has been fluid, multi-faceted and has fluctuated through time and according to the broader socio-economic and political context that the Association has found itself in. In the late nineteenth century, involvement in Gaelic games allowed newly arrived Irish immigrants who had ultimately become citizens of the USA but who still saw themselves as ethnically Irish to identify themselves as part of the Irish nation. For those who joined an emergent GAA in this period, involvement in Gaelic games served as an extension of a belligerent, Anglophobic, politicised, ethnic version of Irishness, one that was fashioned by their experiences, real or imagined, of British repression in Ireland and of their experiences of exile in the USA. In the opening decades of the twentieth century, participation in or consumption of Gaelic games continued to serve this role. This was very much in evidence in the period leading up to the Easter Rising in 1916 and again during the Troubles in Northern Ireland (1969–98). That said, the extent to which the USA's Gaels drew on their sports specifically to express politicised versions of their ethnicity fluctuated, very often according to events in Ireland and the USA. For example, while the partition of Ireland and a subsequent decline in Irish American nationalism may have encouraged some to cling tighter to the GAA as a marker of a distinctive ethnicity, others drew on Gaelic games to retain and give vent to a relatively benign, culturally focused and ultimately liberal version of 'Irishness'. This process of flux and the waxing and waning of nationalist discourse within the GAA in the USA has been an ongoing process and one that continues today. Indeed, while the close relationship between the GAA and politicised versions of Irishness helped to sustain Gaelic games in the USA at various stages in its history, it is likely that the survival of these sports in the post-9/11 USA might be partly dependent on eschewing or de-emphasising the Association's long-standing linkages to ethnic versions of Irishness.

Notes

1   This estimate is based on a statistic cited in Mary Robinson's inaugural speech after assuming the post of President of Ireland in December 1990. O. O'Leary and H. Burke, *Mary Robinson: The Authorised Biography* (London: Hodder and Stoughton, 1998); F. D'arcy, *The Story of Irish Emigration* (Cork and Dublin: Mercier Press, 1999). It should be noted, though, that smaller-scale Irish emigration stretches back beyond this period.
2   D.H. Akenson, *The Irish Diaspora: A Primer* (Toronto: P. D. Meany Company, 1993).
3   D. Fitzpatrick, *Irish Emigration, 1901–1921* (Dundalk: Dundalgan Press Ltd, 1984), 30.
4   See L.J. McCaffrey, *The Irish Catholic Diaspora in America* (Washington, DC: Catholic University of America Press, 1997).
5   Akenson, *The Irish Diaspora*, 9.

6   P. Darby and D. Hassan, eds, *Emigrant Players: Sport and the Irish Diaspora* (New York: Routledge, 2008).

7   See, particularly, M. Cronin and D. Mayall, eds, *Sporting Nationalisms: Identity, Ethnicity, Immigration and Assimilation* (London: Frank Cass, 1998).

8   R.C. Wilcox, 'Sport and the Nineteenth Century Immigrant Experience', in M. D'Innocenzo and J. P. Sirefman, eds, *Immigration and Ethnicity: American Society – 'Melting Pot' or 'Salad Bowl'?* (Westport, CT : Greenwood Press, 1992), 177–89; R.C. Wilcox, 'The Shamrock and the Eagle: Irish Americans and Sport in the Nineteenth Century', in G. Eisen and D.K. Wiggins, eds, *Ethnicity and Sport in North American History and Culture* (Westport, CT: Greenwood Press, 1994), 54–74; S.A. Reiss, 'Sport, Race and Ethnicity in the American City, 1879–1950', in M. D'Innocenzo and J. P. Sirefman, eds, *Immigration and Ethnicity: American Society – 'Melting Pot' or 'Salad Bowl'?* (Westport, CT : Greenwood Press, 1992), 191–219; P.C. Bjarkman, 'Forgotten Americans and the National Pastime: Literature on Baseball's Ethnic, Religious, and Racial Diversity', *Multi-Cultural Review*, 1 (1992), 46–8; P.C. Bjarkman, *The Boston Celtics Encyclopaedia* (Champaign, IL: Sagamore, 1999); L.J. McCaffrey, *Textures of Irish America* (Syracuse, NY: Syracuse University Press, 1992); L.J. McCaffrey, *The Irish Catholic Diaspora in America* (Washington, DC: Catholic University of America Press, 1997); J.T. Ridge, 'Irish County Societies in New York, 1880–1914', in R.H. Bayor and T. J. Meagher, eds, *The New York Irish* (Baltimore, MD: Johns Hopkins University Press, 1997), 275–300.

9   B. McGinn, 'A Century Before the GAA: Hurling in 18th Century New York', *Journal of the New York Irish History Roundtable*, 11 (1997), 12–16; M.F. Black, 'Cultural Identity: Sport, Gender, Nationalism and the Irish Diaspora', PhD thesis, University of California, Berkeley, 1997; S. Brady, *Irish Sport and Culture at New York's Gaelic Park*, PhD thesis, School of Arts and Science, New York University, 2005.

10 T. Humphries, *Green Fields: Gaelic Sport in Ireland* (London: Weidenfield and Nicolson, 1998); M. De Búrca, *The GAA: A History*, 2nd edition (Dublin: Gill and Macmillan, 1999).

11 P. Darby, 'The Gaelic Athletic Association, Transnational Identities and Irish-America', *Sociology of Sport Journal* 27, 4 (2010), 351–70; P. Darby, 'Playing for Ireland in Foreign Fields: The Gaelic Athletic Association and Irish Nationalism in America', *Irish Studies Review* 18, 1 (2010), 69–89; P. Darby, '"Without the Aid of a Sporting Safety Net": The Irish Émigré in San Francisco and the Gaelic Athletic Association (1888–c.1938)', *International Journal of the History of Sport* 26, 1 (2009), 63–83; P. Darby, *Gaelic Games, Nationalism and the Irish Diaspora in the United States* (Dublin: University College Dublin Press, 2009); P. Darby, 'Emigrants at Play: Gaelic Games and the Irish Diaspora in Chicago, 1884–c.1900', *Sport in History* 26, 1 (2006), 47–63; P. Darby, 'Gaelic Games and the Irish Immigrant Experience in Boston', in A. Bairner, ed., *Sport and the Irish: Historical, Political and Sociological Perspectives* (Dublin: UCD Press, 2005); P. Darby, 'Gaelic Sport and the Irish Diaspora in Boston, 1879–90', *Irish Historical Studies* 33, 132 (2003), 387–403.

12 S. King, *The Clash of the Ash in Foreign Fields: Hurling Abroad* (Cashel: The Author, 1998); S. King and P. Darby, 'Becoming Irlandés: Hurling and Irish Identity in Argentina', *Sport in Society* 10, 3 (2007), 425–38; N. McCarthy, 'Irish Rule: Gaelic Football, Family, Work and Culture in Western Australia', *Australian Journal of Irish Studies* 3 (2003), 33–48; N. McCarthy, 'Enacting Irish Identity in Western Australia: Performances from the Dressing Room', *Sport in Society* 10, 3 (2007), 368–84; J. Bradley, *Sport, Culture, Politics and Scottish Society: Irish Immigrants and the Gaelic Athletic Association* (Edinburgh: John Donald Publishers Ltd, 1998); D. Ryan and K. Wamsley, 'A Grand Game of Hurling and Football: Sport and Nationalism in Old Toronto', *Canadian Journal of Irish Studies* 30, 1 (2004), 21–31; S. Moore and P. Darby, 'The Gaelic Athletic Association and the Irish Diaspora in London', in M. Ó Catháin and M. Ó hAodha, eds, *New Perspectives on the Irish Abroad: The Silent People?* (New York: Lexington Books, 2014), 55–71; D. Hassan, 'The Role of Gaelic Games in the lives of the Irish Diaspora in Europe', *Sport in Society* 10, 3 (2007), 385–401; S. Moore and P. Darby, 'Gaelic Games, Irish Nationalist Politics and the Irish Diaspora in London, 1895–1915', *Sport in History* 31, 3 (2011), 257–82.

13 See, for example, B. Murray, *The Old Firm: Sectarianism, Sport and Society in Scotland* (Edinburgh: John Donald Publishing Ltd, 2000); B. Murray, *Bhoys, Bears and Bigotry: Rangers and Celtic and the Old Firm in the New Age of Globalised Sport* (Edinburgh: Mainstream Publishing, 2003); G.P.T. Finn, 'Racism, Religion and Social Prejudice: Irish Catholic Clubs, Soccer and Scottish Society. I – The Historical Roots of Prejudice', *The International Journal of the History of Sport* 8, 1 (1991), 72–95; G.P.T. Finn, 'Racism, Religion and Social Prejudice: Irish Catholic Clubs, Soccer and Scottish Society. II – Social Identities and Conspiracy Theories', *International Journal of the History of Sport* 8, 3 (1991), 370–97; G.P.T. Finn, 'Faith, Hope and Bigotry: Case Studies of Anti-Catholic Prejudice in Scottish Soccer

and Society', in G. Jarvie and G. Walker, eds, *Scottish Sport in the Making of the Nation: Ninety Minute Patriots* (Leicester: Leicester University Press, 1994).

14 J.M. Bradley, *Celtic Minded: Essays on Religion, Politics, Society, Identity and Football* (Edinburgh: Argyll Publishing, 2004); T. Campbell and P. Woods, *Dreams and Songs to Sing: A New History of Celtic* (Edinburgh: Mainstream, 1996); J.R. Mackay, *The Hibees: The Story of Hibernian Football Club* (Edinburgh: Mainstream, 1986); J. Kelly 'Hibernian Football Club: The Forgotten Irish?', *Sport in Society* 10, 3 (2007), 514–36.

15 A. Bairner, 'Wearing the Baggie Green: The Irish and Australian Cricket', *Sport in Society* 10, 3 (2007), 457–77; P.A. Horton, 'The "Green" and the "Gold": the Irish-Australians and their Role in the Emergence of the Australian Sports Culture', *International Journal of the History of Sport* 17 (2000), 65–92; R. Cashman, *The Paradise of Sport: The Rise of Organised Sport in Australia* (Melbourne: Oxford University Press, 1995); D. Adair and W. Vamplew, *Sport in Australian History* (Melbourne: Oxford University Press, 1997).

16 D.P. Ryan and K.B. Wamsley, 'The Fighting Irish of Toronto: Sport and Irish Catholic Identity at St Michael's College, 1906–1916', *Sport in Society* 10, 3 (2007), 495–513.

17 W.F. Mandle, *The Gaelic Athletic Association and Irish Nationalist Politics, 1884–1928* (London and Dublin: Christopher Helm/Gill and Macmillan, 1987).

18 See, for example, M. Cronin, *Sport and Nationalism in Ireland: Gaelic Games, Soccer and Irish Identity Since 1884* (Dublin: Four Courts Press, 1999); M. De Búrca, *The GAA: A History*, 2nd edition (Dublin: Gill and Macmillan, 1999); A. Bairner and P. Darby, 'Divided Sport in a Divided Society: Northern Ireland', in J. Sugden and A. Bairner, eds, *Sport in Divided Societies* (Aachen: Meyer and Meyer, 1998), 51–72.

19 McCaffrey, *Textures of Irish America*.

20 K. Miller, *Emigrants and Exiles: Ireland and the Irish Exodus to North America* (Oxford: Oxford University Press, 1985).

21 Cited in Ibid., 94.

22 U. Ní Bhroiméil, *Building Irish Identity in America, 1870–1915: The Gaelic Revival* (Dublin: Fours Courts Press, 2003).

23 Reiss, 'Sport, Race and Ethnicity'; Wilcox, 'Sport and the Nineteenth Century Immigrant'; Ralph C. Wilcox, 'The Shamrock and the Eagle: Irish Americans and Sport in the Nineteenth Century', in G. Eisen and D.K. Wiggins, eds, *Ethnicity and Sport in North American History and Culture* (Westport, CT: Praeger, 1994), 55–74.

24 Darby, 'Without the Aid'; Darby, 'Immigrants at Play'; Darby, 'Gaelic Sport and the Irish Diaspora'.

25 'Imagined' and 'Invented' in the senses posited by B. Anderson, *Imagined Communities: Reflections on the Origins and Spread of Nationalism* (London: Verso, 1991); and E.J. Hobsbawm and T. Ranger, eds, *The Invention of Tradition* (Cambridge: Cambridge University Press, 1983).

26 McCaffrey, *Textures of Irish America*. The Anglo-Irish Treaty created a 26-county Irish Free State. The six counties of Northern Ireland, established under the *Government of Ireland Act* a year previously, opted out of the Irish Free State and in doing so established the Northern Irish state.

27 McCaffrey, *Textures of Irish America*, 154.

28 Darby, *Gaelic Games*.

29 B. Hanley, 'The Politics of NORAID', *Irish Political Studies* 19, 1 (2004), 1–17.

30 Ulster Gaelic Football Club, *Constitution*, San Francisco.

31 Darby, *Gaelic Games*.

16

RUSSIA AND THE SOVIET UNION

Sergey Altukhov

Territorial expansion was a feature of the powerful Russian empire throughout much of history. This required from its citizens not only obedience and keeping with the law, but also readiness to defend the boundaries and a "war footing" for "faith, tsar and motherland." The vast country stretched "from one sea to the other sea," from the Baltic and Black Sea in the West to the Pacific in the East. Russia was and is still inhabited by different ethnic groups. More than 200 different ethnic groups established their own communities on a vast territory that occupies one sixth of the world. These people migrated to various regions of the country, settled down there, adjusted to the landscape and very often readjusted it to their own needs. Members of these different ethnic communities suffered natural hardships, intrusions against their property, and disruption of their way of life. This encouraged adaptation and was the only way to survive and prolong their family ties, but sometimes the struggle led to the disappearance of ethnic population groups and dominance of others. In this chapter I consider historical sport developments among different ethnic groups in Russia and their cultural and social meaning in ethnicity making. This has been where scholarship, what little exists, has focused in terms of ethnicity and race in Russia. There have been, as outlined in Mark Doidge's contribution to this collection, recent racist incidents involving Russian football spectators; however, this is a new development linked to globalization in football.

Scientific concepts and terms

The Russian climate can be harsh, particularly during winter. Different ethnic groups had to invent the tools of their trade and use in-hand instruments to facilitate labor and defensive skills, varied weapons, and physical skills in order to survive. These activities, that elevated skills, strength of body, and marksmanship, had not yet been labeled "sport" and were not the same for people living in central, northern, southern, mountainous, lowlands, and other parts of the country. The social elite eventually converted these games into forms of entertainment. At first glance, the topic investigated here might seem dated and trivial. Moreover, it may seem too specific for the majority of readers. However, historically powerful and progressive scientific schools were established in Russia and its representatives are still involved in anthropological studies. Such great scientists as L.N. Gumilev, U.I. Semenov, U.V. Bromley, S.V. Lurie, and others were the first to complete this type of research. Tellingly, today the fundamental principles, hypotheses, and definitions mentioned in the scientific work of these scientists are no longer popular even in Russia. Tolerance and assimilation is the main focus among state leaders. Yet it is important to consider sport development among different ethnic groups and its meaning for people in these groups.

To be clear, one can imagine the situation when one team of footballers, Spartak Moscow, are going onto the field; they are Artem Rebrov, Jano Ananidze, Yura Movsisyan, Diniyar Bilyaletdinov, Vladimir Granat, Sergey Parshivlyuk, and others. There are differences in their appearance, though very little. They were all born in the same country – the Soviet Union. They all wear the same uniform, come to a football match by the same bus, and prepare for the match in the same clubhouse.

Is there any difference among them? There certainly is. One of them is a goalkeeper, two of them are defenders, two of them are half-backs, one of them is a striker. Yes, indeed, these are their positions on the playing field. They are not the same age. These footballers are also of different ethnicities. Artem Rebrov is Russian, Jano Ananidze is Georgian, Yura Movsisyan is Armenian, Diniyar Bilyaletdinov is Tartar, Vladimir Granat is Buryat, Sergey Parshivlyuk is Ukrainian. They were brought up in the same country, but their families speak different languages, have different cultural traditions and customs, and profess different religions.

It is important to be precise when defining ethnicity and race in the Russian and Soviet context. According to one definition, ethnicity is determined as

> historically settled on the territory a stable intergeneration aggregate of people having not only common traits but relatively stable culture features (including language) and mentality; they also have the consciousness of their unity and difference from other communities (self-consciousness) fixed in self determination (ethnicon).[1]

Ethnic groups in Russia are complex and have resulted from centuries of migration, the endurance of living in harsh climates and emergent identification with a region.

The outstanding Russian scientist Leo Gumilev created "passionate ethnic theory." He called all people who are eager to change their life and background "*passioner*" (derived from French).[2] His ethnic theory states that community "is formed on the basis of original behavioral stereotypes and exists as a system of integrity (structure), framed against another community, and which forms a common ethnic tradition for all its representatives."[3] Common behavioral stereotypes unite all ethnic members having definite connection to the landscape – ethnic place-based development. This stereotype, as a rule, includes language, political, and economic structures. Such a variant of behavior is called a national trait. Let us consider this in detail. For example, Europeans believe Russians are all people living in Russia and are thus "Russians." Even though not only ethnic Russian people live in Russia, but also people of more than 200 different ethnicities or nations and nationalities. And each of these ethnic groups has its own behaviors, cultural and ethno-national customs, and traditions. And together they are considered a superethnic group – the Russian people.

We must understand the difference between ethnicity and race in the Russian context. Race is a part of ethnicity. People of one race have generalizable external biological features in that they often have similar complexions, eye shape, hair, and other features. This classification scheme indicates biological, genetic, and eventually historical affinity among ethnic groups. Race and ethnicity categorization does not always coincide, however. People of different races can be included in one ethnic group. Yet it's not necessary for representatives of one race to be included in one ethnic group. The Chinese migration over the world makes this clear. They represent the Mongoloid race, but after a time they became a part of an American ethnicity, Australian ethnicity, and others. In Russia, a similar outcome has resulted due to centuries of migration and intermingling across vast expanses of territory, and thus the definitions differ.

Ethnic groups, having their own historical experiences, preferred to live at a social distance to oppose themselves and their background against the rest of the world. Ethnic groups practising agriculture were ready to defend their settlements and families more often than to attack others. As a rule, it took much time to build barns and houses. While adapting to life, people were under the influence of different climatic conditions. The adaptation process was unique and it was connected with ethnic inner culture. Ethnic inner culture, in its turn, had been forming relationship rules and regulations for people living in the same community. Further, I will consider the most illustrative historical examples of various patterns of sport among different ethnic groups in Russia, present-day ethnosport theory formation, and interethnic contradictions in the contemporary history of the country.

Great Russian ethnicity and sport

Water is the basis of life. Rivers and lakes became places of priority for Russian ethnic groups to make barns. Besides, in summer rivers could be a transport system and a place where people from all ethnic groups could go fishing. People learned to make boats and rafts to float along the riverbeds using sculls and they could also sail. It was important to master physical skills such as those of rowers, pilots, boatswains, and fishermen. These jobs, because of their extrinsic nature and ties to making a living, cannot easily be classified as "sport." But these people were worshiped and respected by members of their ethnic group.

During the reign of Peter the Great, the sailing and rowing fleet grew rapidly. On 12 April 1718, the Russian tsar established by decree the club called "the Neva fleet" and placed at their command 140 yachts and boats. The fleet had its own charter, instructions, signals, and special yacht flag. Prince Potemkin commanded the Neva fleet and because of this fact was called admiral of the Neva. To fulfill their duties, new club members had to be at sea once per week to improve their rowing and yacht management skills.

The "Red shirts" regatta in St. Petersburg was the first regatta which encouraged development of the sport of rowing in Russia. There were no bridges over the Neva and the Nevka in those days; people and cargo were carried by skiffs. Skiff-rowers wore red shirts and blue trousers. There were a few among them who were known to be the best at rowing. On Sundays, these skiff-rowers contested who would be the quickest to carry their passengers. And there was a large audience on the banks of the river. Rowers were very popular with the Russian people in the nineteenth century.

In winter, most of the rivers in Russia are frozen. This natural phenomenon provided perfect conditions for skating. Members of Russian ethnic groups could skate even in the thirteenth century. One can see examples of ancient skates in museums displaying archeological artifacts. The skates were made of polished horse bones with holes drilled on one side. Durable leather straps were threaded through the holes and tied a bone lace to a foot. There were also wooden skates. Then a narrow metal strip was fixed to a wooden lace. In winter people had to come up with ways to make their movement on the snow more comfortable and convenient. So they invented skis and sleds. Some experts assume people in northern countries could ski even 5,000 years ago. Skiers went out hunting along the vast snowy Russian land, and gathered wood. Usage of hauling sleds allowed them to improve their transport system in winter.

Skis and sleds were also useful in the army. Campaign packs of "ski warriors" were mentioned in fifteenth-century Russian chronicles. Prince Kurbsky, a ski warrior, campaigned along the

Irtish and the Ob' in 1479. This is recorded in other archival documents as well. There were ski detachments in the Emelian Pugachev riot army and also in the army of his opponent – tsar colonel Mikhelson. They both participated in the battle of the Tatischeva fortress.

Russian people had been hunting wild animals in the forests for a long time. It was hard to go in the deep snowdrifts without skis. In the north of the country along the Dvina river postmen delivered goods using skis – a mail service in Russia was established by Peter the Great in a decree of January 1704. However, it was only at the end of the nineteenth century that people began to ski in significant numbers, both in Russia and all over the world. Time and distance records were the main goals of the sport of skiing. Just imagine the Russian distance ski route from Moscow to Arkhangelsk, organized in 1923 – four skiers covered the 1,406 kilometers in 28 days.

Russian women also took part in skiing competitions. In 1935 five wives of Red Army commanders travelled on skis from Tumen to Moscow, walking for 95 days. In one year ten women from a power plant covered the 2,400 km distance from Moscow to Tobolsk on skis by walking for 40 days. And in 1937 five sportswomen went the farthest, 6,065 km on skis from Ulan-Ude to Moscow in 95 days. The weather was bad, 40–50 degrees below zero. But the most difficult and the longest ski route was covered by Russian officers Brazhnik, Egorov, Kupikov, Popov, and Shevchenko. They went 9,000 kilometers in 151 days, from Baikal to Murmansk. They walked through taiga and tundra where severe frost was sometimes 50 degrees below zero. Their record is considered to be unique in Russia and confirms the readiness of the Russian Empire's ethnic groups to live in extremely low winter temperatures.[4]

Russian people especially admired strong men. They were the heroes of fairytales and legends, and icons for boys. The hero Ilya Muromets could lay out a field without any help, and another hero, Mikula Selyaninovich, worked with a plough that nobody else could lift. Besides these and other legendary athletes, called *bogatyrs*, such as Alesha Popovich and Dobrinya Nikitich, there were a lot of strong people. And even in those times, they organized contests and single combat.

Russian cultural development from the thirteenth to the eighteenth centuries resulted from its victories over the Tartars, the Lithuanians, the German knights, the Swedes, the Poles, the Hungarians, the Bulgarians, and others. Russia had more than 160 military victories. It is clear that there was a military trend in physical training. When a boy living in a Russian community was 14 years old he became an adult. Military and physical training was necessary for every Russian man.

Special bands of men were regular warriors who had been trained in the Old Russian early feudal state. Men-at-arms were a group of regular warriors who lived in special fortified camps. Future men-at-arms trained for the army from 12 years old in special houses called quarters of the bodyguard. Men-at-arms training was the only known organized form of East Slavic military physical upbringing and education during the sixth to ninth centuries. They taught the boys directly during campaigns and battles.

The famous Russian historian S.M. Solovyev wrote about military physical qualities and appearance of the Slavs:

> the Slavs had peculiar skills of swimming and being under water for a long time in contrast to people from other tribes. They stayed under water lying on their back with cavate reed in the mouth; the head of the reed was on the surface of water so that the swimmer hidden under water could breathe. The Slavs were armed with spears, wooden bows and small arrows smeared with very active poison that even a skillful doctor could hardly help a wounded man. Some men had good and very heavy shields.[5]

Bygone Tale ("The Russian Primary Chronicle") written by monk Nestor of Kievo-Pecherskaya lavra in the beginning of the twelfth century was the first to provide information about ancient physical training. The book details that the ancestors of the Russians – Radimichi, Viatichi, Northmen – lived in the forest but at leisure "they organize gamesmanship among villages and all people from baby to adult came to participate in the games."[6] During the gamesmanship, they organized competitions in different leaps, wrestling, hand-to-hand fighting, bear wrestling, running games, archery, and horse races.

The first indication of a wrestling match goes back to 1197, when Dmitrovsky cathedral in Vladimir was built. There is a bas-relief depicting a wrestling scene of *bogatyrs* (strong men); it is one of many white stone ornamental monuments. Wrestlers wore simple knee-length body shirts with belts and embroidery along the selvedge hem. Such shirts were common among wrestlers in everyday life. Wrestling experts who have studied this depiction are sure that such a kind of wrestling as "arms span" and "belt zone" had already been invented at that time. Throws with the help of the legs were banned.[7]

Fistfight traditions have been evident in Russia for a long time. Some records say that fistfights go back to the tenth century, but we have a few other examples of fistfights as a necessary part of ancient gamesmanship. There were three kinds of fistfights – "hand to hand" ("self-to-self"), "wall to wall," and "couple – dogfight." "Self-to-self" fights were similar to old English boxing known as bare knuckle fights, but Russian fistfights were less cruel. Before a fight competitors hugged and kissed three times, showing a lack of enmity between them. When one of the fighters fell the fight was called, whereas in English boxing the beating of a fallen fighter continued (beating was banned only in 1743). However, the most popular fights in Russia were "wall-to-wall" fights; they were highly ranked among other ancient national contests. Boys were likely to play different games, but when they grew up all of them without exception took part in fistfights. As a rule, the men were devoted to them for their whole lives.[8]

"Couple – dogfighting" was wide-ranging and full of mischief. Everyone fought for himself against all the rest. It disappeared long ago. Fistfighting rules developed over many centuries before becoming standardized. Later, leg blows and throws using the legs were banned. There were some rules and regulations in different places, but eventually the rules became unified all over Russia. One of the rules even became a proverb emphasizing Russian generosity during a fight: "Don't beat a lying man."

Nearly everyone in Russia knows of legendary Russian sportsman Ivan Maximovich Poddubny, "champion of champions." Russian writer Maxim Gorky called him "the embodiment of our people's strength." Ivan Maximovich wore a world champion belt of honor in wrestling for 33 years. He wrestled through his advanced years and retired at the age of about 70. He lived to be 80 years old. There is a monument to Poddubny in Eisk. Weightlifters Yury Vlasov and Vasiliy Alekseev and outstanding Russian wrestler Alexander Karelin carried on the traditions of Russian wrestlers and athletes. A Great Russian ethnicity emerged over many generations, with the authority of Russia ultimately accepted by all regional sports federations.[9]

Cossack ethnicity and sport

"Cossacks" had been defending the frontiers since the sixteenth century and became a considerable part of Russian ethnicity. The word "Cossack" comes from the Turkish language and it means free-and-easy, independent person or a person who defends the country's frontiers. Russians, Ukrainians, steppe nomads, North Caucasus, Siberia, Central Asia, the Far East people, all became Cossacks. East Slav ethnicity dominated among Cossacks by the beginning of the twentieth century. Thus, according to Gumilev's theory, Cossack is a sub-ethnicity of the Great Russian ethnicity. Cossacks lived on the Don, in the North Caucasus, in the Urals, in the Far East, and in Siberia. Some Cossack communities were a part of a certain Cossack army. The Cossack way of life was semi-military in nature. The Cossack working language (lingua franca) is Russian, but included such dialects as: Donskoi, Kuban, Ural, Orenburgsky, and others. Cossacks read Russian literature. The Cossack population numbered 4.434 million people by 1917.[10]

Freedom, devotion to the army, love of country were the ideals instilled in Cossack children. Young Cossacks were prepared for both military and labor activity. Games, parades, hunting, feasts, and campaigns were regularly included among military physical exercises and there were a great number of different forms and means of physical training. Nineteen-year-old men (called preteens) were enlisted into service. Leaders appointed a convenient place where the atamans, old men, and preteens from neighboring Cossack villages gathered with their best high-bred horses and full armament: pikes, long guns (fusils), sabers, and bows.

Young Cossack contests took place in the presence of the ataman in the middle of the valley for two weeks or a month. Some young men showed their horses' tittup. The other contests were as follows. A group of horsemen in full armor rushed to the river before jumping into the water and crossing it; the winners received rewards from the ataman, such as bridles and weapons, and garnered great respect for their accomplishments. Fistfights usually took place in the evenings. Cossacks organized wrestling competitions, different kinds of running, ball games, leap frog, and other physical activities. Especially popular were shooting and races.[11]

Beginning from the first half of the twentieth century there were some changes in teaching techniques: domestic games were transferred into professional training. But domestic games were the most exciting feast for Cossacks. There is evidence that Cossack girls participated in competitions together with boys, especially stunts on horseback and even contests of *kulachki* – a sort of hand-to-hand fight. Games and sport competitions were the important part of Cossack feasts. Taking part in the competitions taught the participants rules of conduct and communication skills. Games were artistic in nature – including theatrical actions with songs, dances, riddles, and puzzles, counting rhymes, and other forms of folk art. Participating in the games had educational implications for the children, as they set goals (be the first and the best) and tried to achieve them. The games also influenced the personality, inclinations, and abilities of the children.

Ceremonies and feasts were connected with games and became a significant part of life. Competitions and contests were evident everywhere during feasts – such as races, hand-wrestling, long jump, fencing, weightlifting, stone-tossing, noose-throwing, wrestling, acrobatics, and tug of war over the river or a pit. In the present day, the Russian Ethnic Sport Federation has revived competitions in *kulachki* for men and Cossack domestic games as well.

Caucasian (Caucasus people) ethnicity and sport

Mountainous landscapes influenced the Caucasian way of life. Agriculture and cattle breeding was the main work of Caucasians. Flocks of sheep were considered signs of wealth and fortune. Struggles for new territories and new pastures were accompanied by fights against outlaws making forays – so-called *abreks* who raided cattle, robbed people, and took captives. Local people tell romantic stories of the *abreks'* bravery and devotion to their race and beliefs. The *abreks'* way of thinking of "one against all" made them real heroes.

Local people have an inclination for power and combat sport, and the Caucasus was the right place to develop different kinds of this sport. With Russian expansion into the Caucasus and farther to the south in the eighteenth and nineteenth centuries, local people were faced with not only internal problems but also with external ones. Severe mountain life and constant struggles against "uninvited guests" encouraged the development of people who were physically fit, obstinate, decisive, and strong-willed.

In ancient times almost every Caucasus village community had its own self-defense military – *druzhinas* (troops) – drawn from the local community. For the *druzhinas*, freestyle wrestling was a significant part of physical training. Feasts included this combat sport for mountaineers, with the contests taking place in tiltyards in the open air, with crowds of people in attendance. People greatly respected the winners.

There were real *bogatyrs* among them who were famous beyond the Caucasus. The most prominent was Mamma Makhtulaev; Russians know him by his pseudonym, Sali-Suleiman. This outstanding mountaineer was featured in many arenas. He beat most of the strongest wrestlers of the time. He was most proud, however, of his draw with the famous Ivan Poddubny. Sali-Suleiman was the first Dagestani wrestler who took part in international competitions, but local people remember other mountaineers and were surprised at their power and victories in wrestling. We know the legendary names of such wrestlers as Al-Klych Khasaev from Buglen and Osman Abdurakhmanov from Kikuni in Dagestan. The physical power of these *bogatyrs* was incredible. They were also skillful wrestlers and few people could keep their balance fighting against them.[12]

Horse races were the most popular and favorite contests among Caucasus people. The equestrians participating in the contests owned their own horses. Among the Chechen ethnic group living in the North Caucasus, it was a very popular tradition of initiation into manhood. There was a custom in which a 15–16-year-old Chechen went to his mother's brother with presents and the uncle gave him a horse; after this ceremony the boy was considered to be a man.

The final goal of mastering equestrian ins and outs was complete control of the horse by the riders due to the perfect education of the horse. Long-distance horse racing became like that in Europe after the joining of the Northern Caucasus and Russia. It provided the opportunity to compare the results of different breeds in different regions of the Northern Caucasus and to analyze the horses' speed and stamina.

Mountaineers were very good at shooting at clay jugs and stone tossing. Clay jug shooting competitions originated during ancient times. The dexterity of an equestrian and skill in archery (and later in gunfire) were necessary for this kind of sport. In the old days participants in clay jug shooting were young people, mainly from noble families. Stones for stone tossing were of different weight and form, depending on the age of the participant. The distance, goal, height and roofs were features of stone tossing. The most popular was flat stone tossing, with the stones weighing between 1–2 and 16 or more kilograms. In some places, flat stones were tossed from a turn, like a discus. In the Northern Caucasus, mountain stone rolling on the ground was very popular. The stones were made into the shape of a discus. The stone was rolled both to a goal and distance along a mountain slope, down small descents, and sometimes on a plain. The winner was considered to be the first to roll the stone the farthest and reach the goal. Young people's interest in stone rolling from the mountains to the goal over a distance wasn't accidental – it had applied military meaning.[13]

Yakutia ethnicity and sport

The Republic of Sakha (Yakutia) is one of the largest regions of Russia. The climate in Yakutia is extremely continental. The winter is long and the summer is short. April and October in Yakutia are winter months. Average temperature maximums of the coldest month – January – and the warmest month – July – are −21 and 26 °C. The absolute temperature minimum in the eastern mountains – in hollows, in cavities, and in other low places – can be up to –70 °C. The total cold period length is 6.5–9 months each year. Yakutia is a unique region in the Northern Hemisphere. Yakutia's indigenous peoples, in contrast to neighboring regions, have successfully maintained their unique, original, traditional physical culture. In particular, the Yakuts, the Evens, the Evenkis, the Yukaghirs, and the Chukchi living in the Republic of Sakha (Yakutia) have held on strongly to their sporting traditions. There are two primary reasons for this: the first was the great distance from the tsar of Russia; and the second was the late arrival (in the seventeenth century) of Russian people to the Yakutia region.

Customs, social traditions, and ceremonies are the main ingredients of ethnic self-identification in Yakutia. Yakutian ethnicity is not an exception to these rules. National feast traditions are one of the key markers of ethnic identity. Generally power and dexterity for the Yakuts was important. With a severe climate, when winter lasts eight months and summer lasts only one month per year, the physical features of people uniquely adapt to the environment.

Practically all people of the broad Yakut ethnicity (the Yakuts, the Evenkis, the Chukchi, the Kariaki, and others) are related to Mongols. Yakut ethnicity was the only ethnicity in the Republic of Sakha's contemporary territory. This ethnicity became assimilated, not only with less developed sub-ethnicity (the Lamuts, the Tungus, and the Chukchi) but with those, for example, who moved into the region of Russian, Ukrainian, and Cossack ethnicity. Men were involved in reindeer breeding, hunting, and fishing. Women took care of domestic chores and raised the children. Young men learned lessons from old community members and developed strength, dexterity, and ingenuity, since without these qualities it was impossible to survive the severe conditions in the north. Children's games supported and encouraged stamina.

National games were the main vehicle by which the northern children were brought into hunting, fishing, reindeer breeding, foraging, and keeping the house. Children up to 4–5 years old played with toys depicting boats, cards, reindeer, a dogsled tackle, or pottles for berries. The older boys practiced archery and noose tossing. Such games as "running like a bear," "hare leap," and "one-leg races" helped children to imitate animals' behavior.

Games for teens and young people were competitions such as "Stick pulling," "Wrestling," "Leaps over dog-sledge," "Skiing," "Boat racing – oblas," and "Leg wrestling." Girls were very active participants in the games among people of the north.[14]

The European physical education system was the basis of physical education programs for children in the Soviet Union, with gymnastics, track and field, game-oriented sports, ski racing, swimming, and skating forming part of the curriculum. With the severe weather conditions in Yakutia there were no swimming pools, skating-rinks, or gymnastic apparatus so much of the physical education program could not be fulfilled. "Teachers were forced to promote the program and students were discouraged to participate in sport so this damaged the physical education and health promotion system."[15]

Study of oral folk arts materials such as *olonkho* – or legends, tales, and stories – allows us to conclude that physical education among Yakutian native peoples was devoted to developing health, to increasing stamina, and to teach and improve movement skills necessary for life in the north. However, with globalization there has been alienation from traditional ethnic-based activities. Many families are deliberately detached from older-generation trades and crafts and, because of this, some traditions are dying out; it is difficult to maintain them in such a rapidly changing environment. New possibilities lead to gradual decrease in a community sense of ethnicity and desire for comfort and self-actualization beyond ethnic communities. And sport greatly influences these processes. Nowadays, freestyle wrestling in the Yakutia region is the number-one sport. No wonder that long ago national wrestling, called *khapsagai*, which means "dexterous" and "quick" in the Yakut language, was the favorite form of entertainment. Those particular qualities were necessary for every man to hunt in such vast and wild forests and survive when severe frost was 50–60 °C below zero. These qualities had been cultivated among northern people since childhood. Besides, *khapsagai* originally was a tactical kind of single battle. Yakut *bootours* (wrestlers) not only wrestled skillfully, but also combined wrestling with hand-to-hand fighting elements. Different kinds of arm movements are used in the fights.

Khapsagai rules are simple. To win a victory over a competitor it is necessary to make him touch the ground with any part of the body (except feet). Holds, grape vines with a leg, undercuts, grape vines, lifts of the competitor, all these moves have Yakut origins and their original names. Fights demand attention, dexterity, stamina, fixity, and observation. Every Yakuti region (*ulus*) has its own school of wrestling. *Khapsagai* brought up many outstanding freestyle wrestlers. The Yakuts enjoy the feast to welcome the summer, known as *Ysyakh*, and celebrate with wrestling. From the earliest times, winners of these contests became national heroes and were honored for their exploits. Legends about their feats on "the green rink" were passed on by word of mouth, from generation to generation.[16]

Sport palaces, stadiums, and swimming pools are being built in Yakutia in the twenty-first century. Conditions for planned sport development are being created in this vast territory. But one of the most important tasks is the conservation of traditional sports and Yakuts' cultural traditions and customs. Today the Yakut ethnicity consists of about 400,000 people.

Ethnosport in Russia and in the world

Many Russian experts are against commercial sporting projects and their expansion to different countries and continents as a result of globalization. Russian culture expert Alexsei Kylasov criticizes the Olympic system and the International Olympic Committee (IOC). His *Ringed Sport: Origin and Meaning of Contemporary Olympism* reveals negative trends in the IOC. This work was of great interest among Russian scientists. The result of Kylasov's scientific investigation was a theory of support for ethnosport.[17] He sees ethnosport as a complex of traditional kinds of physical activity, their conservation, and development techniques. Ethnosport theory is presented as an article in the *Encyclopedia of Life Support Systems* (EOLSS) produced by UNESCO.[18] According to the author, ethnosport has to support ethnically based cultural localization in the face of contemporary globalization conditions, and encourage cultural relativism principles that reinforce cultural equality of ethnic groups. The dominance of the European–American value system is dangerous and prevents sports institution development all over the world.

Methodologically important for ethnosport promotion is a neoconservative philosophy. The idea of ethnocultural diversity of sport is being developed in this context. There are a lot of scientific approaches to the preservation issue and cultural diversity propagation, including the works of Ernest Unger, Carl Shmidt, William Reigh, and their followers. Convergence theory, activity, rational choice theory, and postmodernist concepts are used, first in the works of Gilles Deleuze and Felix Guattari. Pierre Bourdieu's theory about cultural, social, economic, and religious fields had great methodological influence in showing the relationship of sport's macro-structures and agents on the micro-level.[19]

The Russian Ministry of Sports has delegated authority for the development of ethnic and national sports to regional governments. The Ministry of Sports decree of 14 February 2014 (Decree No. 83) "About confirmation of the basic kinds of sport for 2014–2018" covered "regional basic kinds of sport" and local authorities' responsibilities. But you will not see national and ethnic sports in this list. Table 16.1 shows some examples of "basic kinds of sport".

Table 16.1 Examples of regional sports

Region	Winter sport	Summer sport
Moscow city	Biathlon, bobsleigh, ski mountaineering, curling, speedskating, ski race, ski jumping, sledding, snowboard, figure skating, freestyle skiing, hockey	Badminton, basketball, boxing, cycling, cycling (mountain bike), cycling (track), high road cycling, water polo, volleyball, golf, rowing and canoeing, whitewater, rowing, judo, equestrian, track and field athletics, table tennis, yachting sport, swimming, water jump, trampoline tumbling, rifle and pistol shooting, rugby, synchronous swimming, modern pentathlon, amateur wrestling, Olympic gymnastics, clay target shooting, archery, tennis, triathlon, taekwondo, weightlifting, fencing, football, field hockey, rhythmic-sportive gymnastics
Smolensk region	Biathlon, ski race,	Olympic gymnastics
Chechen Republic	None	Boxing, judo, amateur wrestling, taekwondo, weightlifting, football
Republic of Sakha (Yakutia)	Biathlon, ski race	Boxing, judo, track and field athletics, swimming, rifle and pistol shooting, amateur wrestling, archery
Jewish Autonomous Region	None	Boxing

As we can see, there are no local traditions or customs offered in the "basic kinds of sport" of different ethnic groups inhabiting Russian regions. But the Ethnosport Federation of Russia is promoting national sport and organizes festivals, feasts, and competitions.

Contemporary interethnic conflicts in sport

There are many interethnic conflicts in the stadiums and outside in the run-up to the Russian FIFA World Cup in 2018. Every week after a football match, information is provided on football fans conflicts, and crimes. Sustainable development strategy is a focus of the World Cup legacy planning. Plans for the World Cup have been jeopardized by fan groups advocating discrimination and superiority of one ethnicity over others. Racism and its different ugly forms have not been widely seen yet. Ethnic problems are a characteristic feature not only of football but other kinds of sport. What are the reasons for this?

The contemporary history of Russia is keenly debated. There is no common ideology following the Soviet Union's collapse of 1989. People built-up communism in the Soviet Union. Current politicians and state leaders cannot offer key ideological goals for all ethnic groups inhabiting the vast country. Instead of this, they try to integrate the existing Western system of values and social practices, including in sport.

Despite all the financial resources put into sport, it has not become a unifying factor for Russian citizens. The Russian team victory in the Olympic Games in Sochi was a success. This victory was a mark of pride for Russia and its sportspeople. But not every citizen sees its value and prospects for the future. It is an impossible luxury for many people who are struggling to achieve prosperity. Sport, a social relationship, becomes part of a state capitalist system, with authoritarian development and regulations and rules in sport thus damaging competitiveness. Such state management of Russian sport results in the increased interest of youth in international sporting teams, particularly global football brands such as Real Madrid, Barcelona, Manchester United, and Bayern Munich. With new technologies many youth are now armchair watchers of sport instead of participants.

Relationships of fans to football clubs in Russia are very similar to how they were in England at the end of the last century. The members of the Security Council of Russia understand that fires and explosions in the stadiums, the mutual insults, fights, and hooliganism in fans are bad publicity before the World Cup 2018.

New capitalist relations appeared instead of former social relationship in the Soviet Union based on socialist principles. The new period of capitalist development in Russia allows natural resource moguls to become tycoons. At the same time, the bulk of the people are at a loss and suffer from loneliness. D.M. Keins explained the causes of this decay: "Capitalism is a strange conviction that the ugliest people using the ugliest motives influence the common good one way or the other."

The most serious problem emerging in Russia is discrimination and racism. A new oversight system of discrimination and many educational programs will be implemented during the World Cup in Russia, together with other organizers of the World Cup 2018. They are unlikely to eliminate racism. But we must realize that it is a difficult and long job to deal with young people's enlightenment and education. Racism, nationalism, and Nazism are forms of protest of many men with inferiority complexes because of unstable social positions and limited opportunities for achievement. And, to this author's great regret, this phenomenon may increase racial and ethnic tensions in Russia for the foreseeable future.

Notes

1   U.V. Bromley, *Ethnic Theory Essays*, 2nd edition (Moscow: LKI Press, 2008).
2   L.N. Gumilev, "Ethnogenesis and Ethnosphere," *Nature* 1 (1970), 335.
3   L.N. Gumilev, *Ethnosphere: History of People and History of Nature* (Moscow: Ecopros, 1993), 544.
4   N.A. Tuzhilin, *The World Around You: The Book for Inquisitives* (Simferopol: The Crimea, 1966), 357.
5   S.M. Solovyev, *Russian History from Ancient Times*, vol. 1 (Moscow: Socio-economic Literature Publishing House, 1962), 235.
6   *Tale of Bygone. Library of Ancient Russia Literature*, vol.1 (St. Petersburg, 1997 [Ipatievskoy Chronicle, 1997]).
7   B.R. Goloschapov, *Physical Culture and Sport History* (Moscow: Publishing House Academy, 2013), 76.
8   N.A. Tuzhilin, *The World Around You: The Book for Inquisitives* (Simferopol: The Crimea, 1966), 357.
9   Ibid., 358.
10 www.mgutm.ru/kazachestvo/history.php, accessed 20 October 2015.
11 Goloschapov, *Physical Culture and Sport History*, 320.
12 http://wrestdag.ru/history, accessed 20 October 2015.
13 Z.H. Ibragimova, *History of Sports Contests Development Among the Chechens in the Twentieth Century*. www.Kavkazoved.info/news/2013/12/11, accessed 20 October 2015.
14 B.R. Goloschapov, *Physical Culture and Sport History: Schoolbook for Academy Students* (Moscow: B.R. Goloschapov, 2005, 2008).
15 V.P. Kochnev, "Traditional Games and Yakutia Native Peoples National Kinds of Sport in Contemporary Physical Education System." www.dissercat.com, accessed 20 October 2015.
16 www.allsportinfo.ru/index.php?b=1&id=27551&I=40, accessed 20 October 2015.
17 A.V. Kylasov, *Ringed Sport: Origin and Meaning of Contemporary Olympism* (Moscow: AIRO XXI, 2010), 328.
18 A. Kylasov and S. Gavrov, *Ethnocultural Diversity of Sport: Encyclopedia of Life Support Systems (EOLSS), Sport Science* (Moscow: UNESCO/EOLSS, Magister Press, 2011), 462–91.
19 http://dikoepole.com/2011/11/17/etnosport, accessed 20 October 2015.

17

SOUTH AFRICA

Chris Bolsmann

One of the most poignant and enduring images of post-apartheid South Africa is President Nelson Mandela handing the William Webb Ellis trophy to François Pienaar, captain of the victorious Springbok rugby team in the 1995 World Cup. While the image reflects an important moment in South African sporting history, popularized by the Clint Eastwood film *Invictus*,[1] the broader context is often omitted. Only one of the South African players in a squad of 28 was black,[2] the majority of spectators were white and the apartheid-era South African flag was visible throughout the stadium. Twenty years on, elite rugby in South Africa remains overwhelmingly white. Of the 31 players who were part of the 2015 South African rugby world cup squad, eight were black. As a result, sport in South Africa remains a contested terrain in which demands for development, transformation, and redress are central. Race and ethnicity are pivotal to interpreting this sporting landscape. In this chapter, we will consider the role of race and ethnicity in shaping South African sport over a 150-year period.

Colonialism, segregation, and sport in South Africa

Sport played an important role in the British Empire. Soldiers, administrators, officials, businessmen, and workers took sport to all parts of the Empire. South Africa was no different and sport became a central component of local culture more generally and a significant reference point for the rest of the world.[3] Cricket was introduced to the Cape after the first British occupation (1795–1803). As early as 1808, advertisements appeared in the *Cape Town Gazette* with references to cricket matches between military regiments stationed in Cape Town.[4] The Dutch ceded control of the Cape to Britain in 1814 and this precipitated British immigration, exploration, and conquest in southern Africa. Colonialists settled in the eastern parts of the Cape colony after 1820 and founded the town of Port Elizabeth. The first recorded football match to be played in South Africa took place in the town in 1862. While it remains unclear whether the game played was association football or rugby or a combination of both, a 'colonial born' team was pitted against a 'home-born team' made up of white men.[5] Schools were established in towns for white children, while mission schools in rural areas catered for black children. In both instances, cricket was played by black and white school children.[6] Local sports clubs were established along segregated lines from the 1850s onwards. Association football was played in the 1870s in the Natal colony, which became known as 'the home of the game in South Africa'.[7] Football matches were also played in Bloemfontein, the capital of the Orange Free State Republic in the 1870s. The game spread throughout the Boer Republic in the 1880s, with clubs formed in Heilbron and Jagersfontein, among others.[8] White football clubs such as Pietermaritzburg County Football Club and the Natal Wasps Football Club were established in 1889 and 1880.[9] Soon thereafter, the Natal Football Association was formed in 1882. Not only were white cricket and football clubs established in Natal during this period, but Indian clubs too.[10]

Gold was discovered on the Witwatersrand in 1886 and Johannesburg quickly developed into a burgeoning town. Immigrants from around the world settled in the Transvaal and organized sport followed suit. Rugby clubs were formed in Pretoria, Potchefstroom, and Johannesburg and regular inter-town matches occurred.[11] The Wanderers' Club was established in 1888 in central Johannesburg and brought together a range of different sports codes for white athletes.[12] Organized sport became formally entrenched in South African towns during the 1880s and national sporting bodies were established, albeit for white sportsmen only. The South African Cricket Association (SACA) and the South African Rugby Board were formed in 1889 and the South African Football Association (SAFA) was established in 1892. The formation of national sporting bodies unified a range of sports codes across the British colonies of the Cape and Natal and the independent Boer Republics of the Transvaal and the Orange Free State. Sir Donald Currie, the shipping magnate, donated trophies to five sports codes in South Africa including cricket, football, and rugby. In addition, the fledgling national sports bodies canvassed for foreign tours to and from South Africa. The first such tour was by an English cricket 11 managed by Major Warton in 1889. The English tourists convincingly beat white representative sides in two matches in Port Elizabeth and Cape Town, respectively. The captain of the English team, Aubrey Smith, noted that the 'visit which, from all that I can see … is calculated to have so great an effect on the cricket of the Cape, not only amongst the white population, but even amongst the black [people]'.[13] While cricket matches had been staged between black and white South Africans prior to the tour, the tourists only faced white opposition in South Africa. Black and white spectators were segregated at sporting events in South Africa during this period and the *Potchefstroom Budget* noted that two English cricketers at the Newlands cricket ground in Cape Town sat with black spectators 'in sight of some thousands of spectators [and] the professionals in question were quite unconscious of any impropriety'.[14] The newspaper *Imvo Zabantsundu* founded and edited by John Tengo Jabavu, reported that a black South African cricket team would tour England in April 1889. However, without funding, adequate preparation, and a national governing body nothing came of the proposal.[15] Warton's team played a match in King William's Town and *Imvo Zabantsundu* reported that 'the sympathies of the native spectators were with the English'.[16] This would remain a trend for the next 100 years in South African sport.

In 1892, the English cricket team returned to South Africa led by Walter Read. The English tourists played a match at Newlands against a Malay team in March 1892. The South Africans acquitted themselves well against the tourists and in particular the fast bowler H. 'Krom' Hendricks and the batsman L. Samsodien, who scored 55, the highest by a South African against a touring side.[17] The English batsman, George Hearne, remarked that Hendricks was 'the fastest bowler in South Africa … [and] it wasn't pleasant. The balls flew over our heads in all directions.'[18] The South Africans recorded their appreciation of the game in the *Cape Times*, stating they hoped for 'similar kindness' in sporting events in the future.[19] SACA arranged for a South African cricket team to visit England in 1894. Harry Cadwallader, the secretary of SACA, identified 16 players who could tour England. Cadwallader included Hendricks in the list and in his role of sports editor of the *Cape Times* promoted the inclusion of Hendricks.[20] The Western Province Cricket Union (WPCU) did not support the inclusion of Hendricks in the team. The WPCU suggested players would be against 'a coloured man on equal social terms' being part of the team.[21] William Milton, the chair of the WPCU selection committee, stated '[T]hey wanted me to send a black fellow called Hendricks to England … but I would not have it.'[22] Milton was a close associate of the prime minister of the Cape Colony, Cecil John Rhodes, and in the broader context of Cape politics the inclusion of a black player would have been unacceptable. Rhodes pushed for further segregation in the Cape through the *Glen Grey Act* in which black political aspiration would be served by local authorities rather than the Parliament in Cape Town. Rhodes envisioned a 'native reserve … the natives should be in native reserves and not mixed up with whites at all'.[23] Moreover, 'the idea of a black player representing South Africa was politically dangerous and, for a large proportion of the white population, emotionally intolerable'.[24] South African cricketer A.B. Tancred went so far as to say it would be 'impolitic, not to say intolerable' should Hendricks be part of the tour.[25] The *Cape Argus*, sympathetic to Rhodes, stated in 1894 in relation to sport that '[t]he races are best socially apart, each good in their way, but terribly bad mixture'.[26] The South African tourists performed poorly in England and ironically played against K.S. Ranjitsinhji, the Indian batsman who represented Cambridge, Sussex, and England. Hendricks was further excluded from representing the Western Province cricket team during the Currie Cup tournament in Natal. The Natal side included the 'Coloured' player 'Buck' Llewellyn who also played football for Natal against the touring Corinthian Football Club in 1897.[27]

The Corinthian Football Club toured South Africa on three occasions in 1897, 1903, and 1907.[28] On each tour they only played against white opposition. In their match against the Orange Free State in 1897, a young black footballer, Joseph Twayi, was in attendance in the segregated ground of the Ramblers' Football Club in Bloemfontein. Twayi went on to captain the first South African football team to tour abroad in 1899 when he led the 'Kaffir' Football Club on a 50-match tour of Europe. The tour was supported by the white Orange Free State Football Association. In a scathing report regarding the tour, the *Cape Argus* noted:

> The whole affair is farcical as it is unsportsmanlike, and smacks very much of hippodrome. Western Province 'socker' enthusiast can scarcely credit the fact that a gang of Kafirs should seriously be expected to give an exhibition worthy of the name.[29]

The Western Province Football Association raised the issue of the tour at the SAFA annual general meeting held in Bloemfontein in September 1899. It was resolved 'that before a coloured team can be sent by an affiliated Association permission must be obtained from the South A[frican] Association'.[30] The *Cape Times* wrote that:

> It is hoped that the English sporting press and public will take the same view of such a burlesque of the game as the niggers are bound to provide.... The governing body of the Association football seems to have quite ignored the proceedings in connection with this nigger troupe. This is all very well in a way, and no doubt silent contempt is often the best way [of] treating matters unworthy of notice, but the present case is, we submit one of which a very great deal of notice should be taken. The question is, what attitude did the Orange Free State Football Association take up in this matter, and how was it that the organizers of the tour were allowed to slip out of the country with their hirelings almost unheeded?[31]

George Parker, manager of the 1897 touring Corinthian side and author of *South African Sports* (1897), stated that a 'strong line of distinction is drawn between the white and black population in South Africa, consequently the membership of athletic clubs is strictly confined to whites'.[32] The South Africans met first-class professional opposition throughout their tour. They lost all their matches, bar one draw in Britain and the north of Ireland, and defeated a French team in Roubaix. During the tour the South African War broke out and the tourists consistently sided with their hosts and collected revenue for their war effort. Moreover, Twayi hoped a British victory would help the plight of black South Africans. Twayi returned to South Africa, was active in Bloemfontein politics and the precursor to the African National Congress (ANC) founded in 1912. Despite their groundbreaking tour in 1899, they have been airbrushed out of South African sports history until recently.[33] South Africans competed in the 1904 St. Louis Summer Olympics in the marathon and tug-of-war events. Three South Africans ran in the marathon, with Len Tau and Jan Mashiani finishing in ninth and twelfth place respectively. Both athletes were black and they too were removed from official South African Olympic history.[34]

War, union, and sport segregation

In the aftermath of the South African War, a number of British and South African cricket, football, and rugby teams toured both countries. In particular, the 1903 British rugby tour of South Africa has been referred to as a 'tour of reconciliation', while the Springbok rugby tour to Europe in 1906 comprised Afrikaner and English players.[35] Yet, this reconciliation was between Dutch- and English-speaking white South Africans only. This can be understood in the broader context of the development towards the Union of South Africa proclaimed in 1910. Central to Union was the exclusion of black South Africans through the *Natives Land Act* of 1913, restricting the purchase of land and consolidating segregation more generally. In sporting terms, a range of national associations were established for different 'racial' groups during this period. The South African Coloured Cricket Board (SACCB) was formed in 1902 and arranged national tournaments for cricketers. In football, the South African Indian Football Association was formed in 1903.[36] In 1913, the Durban District Indian Cricket Union (DDICU) affiliated to the SACCB and competed nationally on a non-racial basis. This early attempt at non-racial sport was short-lived, with Indians restricting sporting contact to fellow Indians and India.[37]

A South African Indian football team toured India in 1921–22.[38] Christopher's Contingent, as the team was known, was made up primarily of footballers from Durban who played against European opposition, among others in India. An Indian team toured South Africa in 1934 and SAIFA corresponded with the local white and African football authorities to arrange matches with the Indian tourists.[39] The whites-only SAFA refused to play matches against the tourists and no matches were played against African sides either.[40] The refusal to play against the tourists was not surprising considering that the Constitution and Rules of SAFA stated members had to be 'of full European descent'.[41] SAFA had earlier rejected an invitation to play against mixed teams in Java in 1931.[42] While SAIFA made seemingly progressive overtures to African and white football associations, they too were concerned with racial representation of their teams. Rule 27 of the SAIFA constitution stated that the association was comprised of Indians who were defined as 'that player born of [an] Indian father irrespective of the mother's nationality'.[43] While 'Coloured' footballers regularly played for the three Indian football teams in Kimberley, they were unable to represent the provincial team in the Sam China Cup.[44] Moreover, the executive council of SAIFA agreed that in matches between an All-Indian team and a South African, the team would be composed of 'Indian Players only, representative of all sections, if possible'.[45] During this period, the South African African Football Association was formed in 1932 and the South African Coloured Football Association in 1933.

In rugby, a New Zealand Services Team toured South Africa in 1919. 'Ranji' Wilson was excluded from the touring team due to his Anglo-West Indian heritage.[46] The whites-only Springbok team toured New Zealand in 1921. In a match against a Maori XV, a South African journalist reporting on the game stated:

> the most unfortunate match was ever played … it was bad enough having to play a team officially designated 'New Zealand Natives', but the spectacle of thousands of Europeans frantically cheering on a band of coloured men to defeat members of their own race was too much for the Springboks, who were frankly disgusted.[47]

Springbok player Hugo Scholtz, who toured in 1921, wrote in more diplomatic terms: '[t]he Maori is an excellent sportsman, plays very keenly with fine spirit and is hard man to beat'.[48] When the New Zealand All Blacks visited South Africa in 1928, they refused to select Māori players for the tour.[49] Similarly, in cricket the white South African Springboks objected to playing against Anglo-Indians in matches on the tour of England in 1929.[50] When the Springboks returned to New Zealand in 1937, the issue of playing against Māoris resurfaced. The Western Province rugby official, J.D. de Villiers, declared:

> [T]he Board should take steps to ensure the prohibition of Maoris taking part in matches. He was of the opinion that if players were asked to play against Maoris, they would refuse at all costs. Players would definitely not play against coloured people. Parents would not allow their sons to do so.[51]

The South African Rugby Board (SARB) adopted a more conciliatory approach, suggesting matches against Māoris could be scheduled. The Springboks, however, did not play against a Māori team, although several provincial teams included Māoris and two represented New Zealand against the visitors.[52] A number of European football sides toured South Africa prior to the outbreak of war in 1939. Teams included the English FA Amateur team that toured on four occasions. African spectators were granted permission by local officials to watch the touring sides at reduced prices, in inferior segregated seating.[53] African spectators continued to support foreign sides playing against white South African opposition.[54] In the aftermath of the Second World War, decolonization, the establishment of the United Nations, and the rejection of racism and discrimination more generally, South Africa, and South African sport in particular, was thrust into the international spotlight.

Apartheid, boycotts, and multinational and non-racial sport

The National Party (NP) won the 1948 election in South Africa and ushered in the system of apartheid. The term was first used during the war by Afrikaner leaders in the NP. In 1944, Daniel Malan, the future nationalist prime minister (1948–1954) noted 'I do not use the term "segregation", because it has been interpreted as fencing off but rather "apartheid", which will give the various races the opportunity of uplifting themselves on the basis of what is their own.'[55] The nationalist government introduced a range of laws to enforce apartheid, including the *Population Registration Act* of 1950, which established a national register in which a person's race was classified and the *Group Areas Act* of 1950 enforced racial segregation in residential areas. While there were no laws prohibiting playing of mixed sport in South Africa, '[t]here was no need … custom and "tradition" kept sport segregated'.[56] This was considered 'an old national custom' and the 'vast majority of South Africans' support racial segregation and 'have no desire to part from it'.[57] In boxing, Ronnie van der Walt was South African welterweight champion who was classified as Coloured in 1951. While van der Walt lived in Coloured areas he was accepted in white boxing circles as white. He applied for reclassification as a white person after winning the title in 1966 but this was denied and his boxing licence was withdrawn.[58]

In 1951, the white football association SAFA applied for readmission to football's world governing body FIFA. SAFA had first joined FIFA in 1910 but followed the lead of the English FA and withdrew from the world body in 1926. SAFA's application was accepted and it became the sole representative for South African football at FIFA. This position was immediately challenged by the South African Soccer Federation (SASF), established in 1951, who applied to FIFA for membership. SASF brought together the African, Coloured, and Indian football associations. FIFA rejected the SASF application, stating only one national federation could represent football in the country. SAFA came under pressure to address the emergence of SASF from FIFA and considered amending its racist clause in its constitution, which restricted membership of the association to 'Europeans' only. SAFA added the clause: 'save such affiliated members who cater for and control Non-European Football Associations, and whose Constitutions have been approved by this Association'.[59] Moreover, SAFA informed SASF that they were welcome to join SAFA and did not need to apply to FIFA for membership. The proposed amendment was rejected and only in 1956 did SAFA remove its racist clause after pressure from FIFA.[60]

In table tennis, the black South African Table Tennis Board was formed in 1948. It applied to and was granted affiliation to the international federation. This was at the expense of the white organization.[61] Similarly, applications by black cricketers, weightlifters, and body builders were lodged with international organizations.

The minister of the interior, T.E. Dönges, issued the regime's first sport policy in 1956, and stated that inter-racial competitions were prohibited and sport would remain segregated and separately organized.[62] Racially mixed sport in South Africa was prohibited and no team representing the country abroad would be mixed either. White touring teams would play white South African teams and black touring teams would play against black South African teams only. In addition, black sports organizations seeking international affiliation and membership had to do so under the auspices of the white equivalent body in South Africa. Moreover, individuals and organizations who challenged this position were barred from overseas travel. The nationalists' sport policy was a reaction to increased international pressure against apartheid sport. Activist and school teacher Dennis Brutus formed the Coordinating Committee for International Recognition of Sport in 1955. The committee lobbied for the recognition of black sports associations by international federations.[63] Brutus and South African author Alan Paton were part of the South African Sports Association (SASA) formed in 1958. SASA endorsed the principle of non-racialism in South African sport.[64] South African sport increasingly came under the spotlight internationally when 500 people demonstrated at the Cardiff Empire Games against the selection of the South African team. A West Indies team scheduled to play in South Africa against black cricketers was called off. Significantly, not only did black South Africans support touring teams against white opposition, black cricket spectators in Johannesburg booed the South African team facing Australia. SASA launched the South African Non-Racial Olympic Committee (SANROC) in 1962 with the goal of isolating apartheid sport. SASA and SANROC set out to assist non-racial South African sports bodies with international recognition, and oppose overseas tours of South Africa and teams selected on the basis of race.

The apartheid state was brutal in its suppression of opposition to apartheid. In March 1960, over 50 protestors were killed by the South African police in Sharpeville. Activists were harassed, banned, and imprisoned. Brutus was banned, shot by the police and imprisoned on

Robben Island for his opposition to apartheid sport. He continued his campaign against apartheid South Africa while in exile from the mid-1960s onwards. In 1961, South Africa left the Commonwealth and became a republic and lost its seat on the Imperial Cricket Conference (ICC); despite this, tours continued. Apartheid South Africa became an increasingly problematic issue for international sports organizations, particularly the International Olympic Committee (IOC). In an era of decolonization, African and Asian states were able to exert pressure on the IOC and FIFA. In the build up to the 1964 Olympic Games in Tokyo, the IOC banned South Africa from participation and insisted they renounce racial discrimination in sport and permit competition between black and white athletes in the country for the ban to be overturned. The South Africans offered to include seven black athletes in their team of 62 athletes, yet this token gesture was insufficient for the IOC to rescind the ban.

Demonstrations against white players' participation at Wimbledon in tennis further isolated apartheid sport. The white South African cricket team were met by widespread protests while on tour in Australia and New Zealand in 1964. In tennis, a Davis Cup match in Norway was disrupted and protestors disrupted a bowling tour of Britain. In rugby, a South African team toured New Zealand in 1965 and played against Māoris. On the team's return to South Africa, H.F Verwoerd, the South African prime minister, insisted the New Zealand rugby team to tour in 1967 did not include Māoris. While the New Zealanders had agreed to a similar request in 1960, the 1967 tour was cancelled. In the build up to the 1968 Olympic Games in Mexico City, African and Asian members of the IOC threatened to withdraw from the Summer Games should South Africa participate in the event.[65] The Mexicans, faced with the prospect of boycotts by a number of African and Asian teams, did not invite the South African team to participate in the games. This represented a major victory for the anti-apartheid movement generally and for sport in particular. One of the most significant episodes in apartheid sport related to Cape Town cricketer Basil d'Oliveira. As a talented coloured cricketer in South Africa, d'Oliveira's opportunities were limited. He moved to Britain in 1960 and played first-class cricket and took up British nationality. He was selected for the English cricket team in 1966. d'Oliveira was included in the English team to tour South Africa in 1968. South African prime minister B.J. Vorster stated: 'It's the team of the anti-apartheid movement. We are not prepared to accept a team thrust upon us – it's a team of people who don't care about sports relations at all.'[66] Vorster declared the player would not be welcome in South Africa and as a result the tour was cancelled. In rugby, the Springboks toured Britain and Ireland in 1969/70 and the tourists were met by large-scale demonstrations by the Stop the Seventy Tour protest movement.[67] The team were also met by protests on their tour of Australia in 1971, where a State of Emergency was declared in Queensland.[68] South African sport was increasingly isolated by the end of the 1960s, and in 1970 the IOC voted to expel South Africa from the Olympic Movement and FIFA followed suit in 1976.

In an attempt to placate international opposition to apartheid and sway public opinion, Vorster introduced the policy of multinationalism in South African sport. Mixed teams from traditional sporting partners Australia, Britain, and New Zealand would be welcome in South Africa, but would not play against locally mixed opposition. Abroad, mixed South African teams could play in international competition such as golf and tennis, among others. Within South Africa, teams of racially defined 'nations' could play against each other at the national level but no mixed sport was permitted at provincial and local levels. Football in particular was considered by the apartheid regime as a vehicle for testing the policy of multinationalism.[69] Piet Koornhof, the minister of sport, suggested football could be used as a 'guinea pig' for experimenting with multiracial sport.[70] Lucrative sponsorships were received from the alcohol, automobile, and tobacco industries.[71] In rugby, multiracial 'invitation' teams were played rather than multiracial national teams. Multinationalism reinforced segregation along racial lines in apartheid South Africa, part of the broader policy of Bantustans and 'independent' homelands. Some sporting spaces were desegregated, such as professional football, boxing, and road running.[72] Internationally, apartheid sport became the focus of the 1976 Olympic Games in Montreal. In protest against the New Zealand rugby tour of South Africa in the same year, over 20 African states withdrew from the games due to the participation of the New Zealand Olympic team in Montreal. One of the outcomes of the 1976 Olympic boycott was the Commonwealth Statement on Apartheid in Sport, signed in 1977. Also known as the Gleneagles Agreement, it was adopted by heads of government of Commonwealth states who declared their opposition to apartheid sport.[73] Despite the Gleneagles Agreement, South Africa competed internationally in foreign tours and tournaments while foreign teams toured locally. In 1981, the New Zealand Rugby Union invited the Springboks to tour the country on the proviso that players be selected on merit. Errol Tobias was included in the touring party. He had made his debut as the first black South African to play for the Springboks in 1980 on a tour of South America. The Springbok team's tour of New Zealand was met by protest and demonstrations, with two games cancelled and pitches invaded by activists.

Within South Africa, anti-apartheid activists challenged racism within sport. The South African Council of Sport (SACOS) was established in 1973 and subscribed to the principles of non-racialism, rejected multinationalism, and demanded the end of apartheid. SACOS initially negotiated with white sport organizations until the mid-1970s, but this was replaced by non-collaboration. SACOS president Hassan Howa argued that 'no normal sport in an abnormal society' was possible. SACOS subscribed to the position that non-racial sport could not participate in or be associated with racial or multinationalism in sport.[74] By 1979, F.W. de Klerk, the minister for sport, allowed sports associations the right to administer affairs free of state intervention and multinationalism was replaced by multiracialism. At the local level, schools were granted autonomy in school sport administration. Yet this resulted in numerous racist incidents in which black athletes were barred from participation at white schools. The attempts at reform were superficial and interventions in assisting black sport were part of the broader strategy of regaining admission into the international sporting arena without leaving lasting infrastructural legacies or benefits.

'Rainbow nationalism' and the transformation of sport

In February 1990, former minister of sport de Klerk freed a range of political prisoners and unbanned political parties. This resulted in a process of negotiations that culminated in Nelson Mandela being elected as the first democratic president of South Africa in April 1994. In the sporting arena, negotiations between rival sports administrators occurred against the backdrop of broader political negotiations at the national level. For many of the white sports authorities, the lure of international competition facilitated negotiations with non-racial sports bodies. In 1991, the Indian Cricket Board invited a South African team to play in the country. An all-white South African team lost the One Day International series against India. The IOC invited South Africa to participate in the 1992 Olympic Games in Barcelona. A mixed South African team walked under an interim Olympic flag and two silver medals were won in 1992 by white athletes in athletics and tennis.

Sport is an important reference point in post-apartheid South Africa. The major male sports of cricket, football, and rugby have all achieved varying degrees of success since 1994. The rugby Springboks, in particular, have won two World Cup titles in 1995 and 2007 respectively. Mandela's act of wearing the Springbok jersey in 1995 not only legitimized the use of an apartheid symbol in post-apartheid South Africa, but also suggested sport could become a vehicle of nation-building more generally. The slogan 'One Team, One Country' was adopted as part of the process of inclusion.[75] Pienaar recalled: 'As players, unlike any Springbok side before us, we had been able to feel the committed support of the entire country.'[76] While rugby remains the only sporting code in South Africa not to replace the Springbok as the official symbol after 1994, it had become 'the sport that would help to catalyse the building of a "rainbow nation" predicated on a common identity, a common sense of "South Africanness"'.[77] Yet the references to a 'common identity' are problematic, as a cursory glance at the dominant male sports highlight cricket and rugby as overwhelmingly white while football is black.[78] Moreover, 'Afrikaner men have been strikingly over-represented in rugby'[79] on the field, on the sidelines, and in the boardrooms.

Since the early 1990s, a range of developmental programmes were initiated to identify and nurture future black players in a wide range of sports, in cricket and rugby in particular, with varying degrees of success. Moreover, transformation of sporting codes remains an important agenda for a range of actors in South African sport.[80] The ruling ANC and numerous politicians have called for the transformation of predominantly white sports. Again, this has been met with varied degrees of success. An important feature of the post-apartheid sporting landscape has been the hosting of international sporting events. The FIFA World Cup is the largest single-sport mega-event, and South African football authorities indicated their desire to host the event soon after their readmission into the international fold in 1992.[81] FIFA noted that a World Cup in South Africa, would 'generate significant unity amongst ethnic groups [and] the legacy compared to the investment needed will be a great contribution to the country'.[82] The mass daily newspaper the *Sowetan* gushingly claimed hosting the event would be 'endorsing the South African miracle created in 1994' and that 'ours comes tantalisingly close to a true African bid … the benefits will not only spill over into the poorest parts of our country … our neighbours will also reap the benefits'.[83] The local organizing committee exclaimed that South Africa was 'the gateway to Africa' and 'as true African representatives'.[84] The 2010 World Cup was a success for South Africa. The organizers put on a world-class event without major incidents or concerns. FIFA, in particular, did financially well from the event, generating over $4.2 billion in tax-free profits.[85] Danny Jordaan, chief executive of the local organizing committee for 2010, remarked 'Blatter [former FIFA president] is very happy. This has been the most successful [tournament] in their history.'[86] Yet, South Africa 2010 represented 'a thoroughly middle-class occasion; a gathering of global elites [and a] First World show superimposed upon a putrid, demeaning Third World squalor'.[87]

The FIFA 2010 World Cup highlighted some of the contradictions facing South African sport. On the one hand, South Africa was able to host a successful mega-event, generate profits for the international body and general goodwill during the event; yet on the other, the long-term legacies are less tangible. The South African men's football team were the first host nation to be knocked out of a World Cup after the first round, the team continues to fall down FIFA's world rankings, and the local game attracts few spectators and the standard of play is poor. The stadia remain underutilized and expensive to maintain. Cricket and rugby consistently perform at the highest level on the international stage, yet these sports remain overwhelmingly white, from the players through to coaching officials and administrators. Sport remains highly contested in South Africa. Over 20 years have passed since Mandela's gesture of reconciliation, yet race and ethnicity remain central to understanding and explaining post-apartheid South African sport.

Notes

1 Clint Eastwood, *Invictus* (Warner Bros. Pictures, 2009).
2 The author recognizes that race designation has no scientific validity. For the purposes of this chapter, I refer to black, coloured, Indian, and white used in relation to apartheid legislation and post-1994.
3 For a good overview of the early links between sport, Empire and race within South Africa, see John Nauright, *Long Run to Freedom: Sport, Cultures and Identities in South Africa* (Morgantown, WV: Fitness Information Technology, 2010).
4 Bernard Hall, Richard Parry, and Jonty Winch, 'More Than a Game', in Bruce Murray and Goolam Vahed, eds, *Empire & Cricket: The South African Experience 1884–1914* (Pretoria: UNISA, 2009); and Bruce Murray and Christopher Merrett, eds, *Caught Behind: Race and Politics in Springbok Cricket* (Johannesburg and Scottsville: Wits University Press and University of KwaZulu-Natal Press, 2004).
5 Lloyd Hill, 'Reflections on the 1862 Football Match in Port Elizabeth', *South African Journal for Research in Sport, Physical Education and Recreation* 33, 1 (2011), 81–98.
6 Andre Odendaal, *The Story of an African Game* (Cape Town: David Philip, 2003).
7 George Parker, ed., *South African Sports* (London: Sampson Low, Marston, 1897), 86.
8 Chris Bolsmann, 'The 1899 Orange Free State Football Team of Europe: "Race", Imperial Loyalty and Sports Spectacle', *International Journal of the History of Sport* 28, 1 (2011), 81–97.
9 Alfred Gibson and William Pickford, eds, *Football and the Men Who Made It* (Cape Town: D.E. McConnel and Co., 1906).
10 Goolam Vahed, 'Deconstructing "Indianness": Cricket and the Articulation of Indian Identities in Durban, 1900–32', *Culture, Sport, Society: Cultures, Commerce, Media, Politics* 6, 2–3 (2003), 144–68.
11 Ivor Difford, *History of South African Rugby* (Wynberg: Spendly Press, 1933); also see David Black and John Nauright, *Rugby and the South African Nation* (Manchester: Manchester University Press, 1998).
12 Thelma Gutsche, *Old Gold: The History of the Wanderers Club* (Cape Town: Howard Timms, 1966).
13 Jonty Winch, '"I Could a Tale Unfold': The tragic Story of "Old Caddy"', in Bruce Murray and Goolam Vahed, eds, *Empire & Cricket: The South African Experience 1884–1914* (Pretoria: UNISA, 2009), Murray & Vahed, *Empire & Cricket* 55.
14 Ibid.
15 Ibid., 57.
16 Ibid.
17 Ibid., 59.
18 Ibid., 65.
19 Ibid., 59.
20 Ibid., 65.
21 Ibid.
22 Ibid., 66.
23 Quoted in Martin Meredith, *Diamonds, Gold and War: The Making of South Africa* (London: Pocket Books, 2007).
24 Winch, 'I Could a Tale Unfold', 67.
25 Ibid.
26 Quoted in Martin Meredith, *Diamonds, Gold and War*, 267.
27 Christopher Merrett, 'Sport and Race in Colonial Natal: C.B. Llewellyn, South Africa's First Black Test Cricketer', *Natalia* 32 (2002), 19–35.
28 Bolsmann, 'The 1899 Orange Free State'.
29 *The Cape Argus*, 10 August 1899, 7.
30 *The Friend of the Free State and Bloemfontein Gazette*, 1 September 1899.
31 *Cape Times*, 21 September 1899, 5.
32 *The Football Evening News*, 2 September 1899, 3.
33 Bolsmann, 'The 1899 Orange Free State'.
34 South African Olympic and British Empire Games Association, *Springboks ... Past and Present: A Record of men and Women Who Have Represented South Africa in International Amateur Sport 1888–1947* (Pietermaritzburg: The Natal Witness, 1947).
35 Paul Dobson, *Bishops Rugby: A History* (Cape Town: Don Nelson, 1990), 44; Albert Grundlingh, Andre Odendaal, and Burridge Spies, eds, *Beyond the Tryline* (Johannesburg: Ravan Press, 1995); Dean Allen, 'Tours of Reconciliation: Rugby, War and Reconstruction in South Africa, 1891–1907', *Sport in History* 27, 2 (2007), 172–89; J. Nauright, 'Colonial Manhood and Imperial Race Virility:

British Responses to Colonial Rugby Tours', in J. Nauright and T. Chandler, eds, *Making Men: Rugby and Masculine Identity* (London: Routledge, 1996), 121–39.

36 Peter Alegi, *Laduma! Soccer, Politics and Society in South Africa* (Scottsville: University of KwaZulu-Natal Press, 2004), 18.

37 Vahed, 'Deconstructing'.

38 Chris Bolsmann and Goolam Vahed, '"They are Fine Specimens of the Illustrious Indian Settler": Sporting Contact Between India and South Africa, 1914–1955' (unpublished paper).

39 South African Indian Football Association, 17 March 1934. Historical Papers, William Cullen Library, University of the Witwatersrand, A2764.

40 Southern Transvaal Football Association Minutes of the Executive Committee, 3 May 1934, 'Indian Football Team'. South African Football Association Gauteng.

41 South African Football Association, Circular to Divisional Association, February 1930. Historical Papers, William Cullen Library, University of the Witwatersrand, AG3365.

42 South African Football Association, Meeting 4 September 1931. Historical Papers, William Cullen Library, University of the Witwatersrand, AG3365.

43 South African Indian Football Association Annual General Meeting, 14 August 1920. Historical Papers, William Cullen Library, University of the Witwatersrand, A2764.

44 South African Indian Football Association, 28 July 1928. Historical Papers, William Cullen Library, University of the Witwatersrand, A2764.

45 Ibid.

46 Greg Ryan, 'Anthropological Football: Maori and the 1937 Springbok Rugby Tour of New Zealand', *New Zealand Journal of History* 34, 1 (2000), 60–79.

47 Douglas Booth, *The Race Game: Sport and Politics in South Africa* (London: Frank Cass, 1998), 23.

48 Hugo Scholtz, 'The Springboks in New Zealand', in Ivor Difford, ed., *History of South African Rugby* (Wynberg: Spendly Press, 1933), 386.

49 Booth, *The Race Game*, 23.

50 Robert Archer and Antoine Bouillon, *The South African Game* (London: Zed Books, 1982).

51 Ryan, 'Anthropological Football', 76.

52 Ibid.

53 Southern Transvaal Football Association Minutes of the Emergency Committee, 16 July 1936.

54 Peter Alegi, *Laduma!*; Nauright, *Long Run to Freedom*; J. Nauright, '"Bhola Lethu": Football and Urban Popular Culture in South Africa', in G. Armstrong and R. Giulianotti, eds, *Football in the Making: Developments in the World Game* (London: Macmillan, 1999), 189–200.

55 Quoted in Hermann Giliomee, *The Afrikaners: Biography of a People* (Charlottesville: University of Virginia Press, 2003), 475.

56 Booth, *The Race Game*, 58.

57 Ibid.

58 Ibid.

59 SAFA, South African Football Association, Minutes of Special General Meeting, 11 October 1952. Historical Papers, William Cullen Library, University of the Witwatersrand, AG3365.

60 Chris Bolsmann, 'White Football in South Africa: Empire, Apartheid and Change, 1892–1977', *Soccer and Society* 11, 1–2 (2010), 29–45.

61 Archer and Bouillon, *The South African Game*.

62 Richard Lapchick, *The Politics of Race and International Sport: The Case of South Africa* (Westport, CT: Greenwood Press, 1975).

63 Christopher Merrett, '"In Nothing Else Are the Deprivers So Deprived": South African Sport, Apartheid and Foreign Relations', *International Journal of the History of Sport* 13, 2 (1996): 146–65.

64 Booth, *The Race Game*.

65 Ibid.

66 Odendaal, *The Story*, 175.

67 Peter Hain, *Don't Play with Apartheid: Background to the Stop the Seventy Tour Campaign* (Sydney: Allen & Unwin, 1971).

68 David Black and John Nauright, *Rugby and the South African Nation* (Manchester: Manchester University Press, 1998).

69 Chris Bolsmann, 'Professional Football in Apartheid South Africa: Leisure, Consumption and Identity in the National Football League, 1959–1977', *International Journal of the History of Sport* 30, 16 (2013), 1947–61.

70 Bolsmann, 'Professional Football'.

71 Anne Kelk Mager, *Beer, Sociability, and Masculinity in South Africa* (Bloomington, IN: Indiana University Press, 2010); Peter Alegi and Chris Bolsmann, 'From Apartheid to Unity: White Capital and Black Power in the Racial Integration of South African Football, 1976–1992', *African Historical Review* 42, 2 (2010), 1–18.

72 Booth, *The Race Game*.

73 Malcolm Templeton, *Human Rights and Sporting Contacts: New Zealand Attitudes to Race Relations in South Africa, 1921–94* (Auckland: Auckland University Press, 1998).

74 Booth, *The Race Game*.

75 Edward Griffiths, *One Team One Country: The Greatest Year of Springbok Rugby* (London: Viking).

76 François Pienaar, *Rainbow Warrior* (London: CollinsWillow, 1999), 203.

77 Ashwin Desai, ed., *The Race to Transform: Sport in Post-Apartheid South Africa* (Cape Town: HSRC Press, 2010); Chris Bolsmann and Cora Burnett, 'Taking South African Sport Seriously', *South African Review of Sociology* 46, 1 (2015), 1–6.

78 Ashwin Desai and Zayn Nabbi, '"Truck and Trailer": Rugby and Transformation in South Africa', in Sakhela Buhlungu, John Daniel, Roger Southall, and Jessica Lutchman, eds, *State of the Nation: South Africa, 2007* (Cape Town: Human Sciences Research Council Press, 2007).

79 Isak Niehaus, 'Warriors of the Rainbow Nation? South African Rugby after Apartheid', *Anthropology Southern Africa* 37, 1–2 (2014), 68–80; Albert Grundlingh, *Potent Pastimes: Sport and Leisure Practices in Modern Afrikaner History* (Pretoria: Protea Book House, 2013).

80 Desai, *The Race to Transform*.

81 Chris Bolsmann, 'Representation in the First African World Cup: "World-class", Pan-Africanism, and Exclusion', *Soccer and Society* 13, 2 (2011), 156–72.

82 FIFA, *Inspection Group Report for the 2010 FIFA World Cup* (Zurich: FIFA, 2004), 8.

83 *Sowetan*, 'Why We Deserve the 2010 Games', 14 May 2004.

84 Scarlett Cornelissen, '"It's Africa's Turn!": The Narratives and Legitimations Surrounding the Moroccan and South Africa Bids for the 2006 and 2010 FIFA Finals', *Third World Quarterly* 25, 7 (2004), 1293–310; John Nauright, 'Global Games: Culture, Political Economy and Sport in the Globalized World of the Twenty-First Century', *Third World Quarterly* 25, 7 (2004), 1325–36.

85 *The Witness*, 8 July 2011.

86 Richard Calland, *Mail & Guardian*, 9–15 July, 2010, 24.

87 *Mail & Guardian*, 9–15 July, 2010, 24; Richard Calland, Lawson Naidoo, and Andrew Whaley, *The Vuvuzela Revolution: Anatomy of South Africa's World Cup* (Auckland Park: Jacana, 2010), 175.

18

USA

Rob Ruck[1]

The shadows of slavery and its aftermath long distorted the study of sport's connection to race and ethnicity in the USA. Scholars, public intellectuals, and the public discussed race's nexus with sport almost exclusively as a binary matter involving African-Americans and Caucasians. Both of these groups were largely portrayed as homogeneous racial aggregations, their internal class, ethnic, and regional differences muted. Meanwhile, indigenous people and immigrants from North America, the Caribbean basin, Asia, and the Pacific were pushed to the sidelines as the African-American struggle to gain access to the mainstream of sport drove the overarching historical narrative. Stressing a before-and-after dynamic, scholars addressed either the impact of African-Americans' exclusion from, or their subsequent inclusion in, the nation's sporting life. Painting with a broad brush, they treated segregation as lamentable and integration as redemptive, but neither segregation's upside nor integration's downside were broached.

This binary approach also distorted and downplayed study of the disparate European immigrant communities that began forming in the USA during the nineteenth century. Little was made of old country traditions that shaped immigrants' sporting lives in their new homes. Instead, importance was placed on gaining access to the sporting mainstream and succeeding at the highest levels once there.

The sons and grandsons of mid-nineteenth-century immigrants from Ireland were lauded for rising to the upper ranks of boxing and baseball, and Irish-American athletic accomplishments were considered as evidence of their successful Americanization. This was part of the Irish, as some argued, "becoming white." As they gained a degree of power in the workplace, local politics, the church, and sport by the early twentieth century, Irish-Americans enjoyed substantial economic mobility and were portrayed as having assimilated into society. Melding into white America, their acceptance was facilitated by their symbolic success in the boxing ring and on the baseball diamond, as well as by skin color.[2]

The arrival of later waves of European immigrants from Southern, Eastern, and Central Europe, like that of the Irish diaspora before them, brought a virulent nativism to the surface. But unlike African-Americans, these new immigrants and their children were not denied the chance to prove themselves in most sporting venues. Indeed sport, especially baseball, was thought to be a meritocracy, a vehicle that affirmed white immigrants and their sons' capacity to overcome the disadvantages of class or nationality, and thus prove themselves worthy of citizenship: of being considered as Americans. Like the Irish, these varied wayfarers were ultimately perceived as Europeans whose whiteness underscored their capacity to Americanize. The stigma these new immigrants faced gradually faded, especially after the *Quota Acts* of the 1920s curtailed immigration from the parts of Europe from which they hailed. By the end of the Second World War, their children and grandchildren had gained a larger degree of acceptance. That opportunity to fit in and be perceived as American citizens, however, was denied to those who were not Caucasian.

A few of the new immigrants' descendants, like Hank Greenberg or Joe DiMaggio, were lionized as athletic icons and regarded as harbingers of Jewish or Italian acceptance. But little attention was paid to the connections between sport and the Jewish or Italian-American communities from which they emerged. Instead, the emphasis on segregation and the perception of race as a black or white affair diverted attention from the distinctive sporting patterns that had taken shape among these diverse European-American communities at a time when they had yet to be recognized as white by many native-born Anglo-Saxons. That binary also ignored class and skin color tensions within the African-American community; instead, it treated them as one homogeneous mass.[3]

But during the 1960s and 1970s, the civil rights movement and a turn toward social history triggered a sea change in the ways in which historians and other scholars connected sport to race and ethnicity. The energy generated by the civil rights struggle, especially as it morphed into a black power movement, spurred efforts to uncover the critical arenas where African-Americans exerted control over their own sporting lives. Meanwhile, social and labor history, which drew strength from the social and political movements taking to the street, identified common sporting ground in which parallels regarding the roles and meanings of sport could be drawn across racial and ethnic boundaries. Though the racial binary continues to hang over the study of sport in the USA, it no long remains unchallenged, sucking up all the oxygen in the academy.

Sport was a terribly underdeveloped field of study in the USA until the 1970s. While European scholars were in the vanguard of those investigating the social and historical importance of sport, American academics lagged behind. Their studies of sport in North America focused on institutional and biographical actors but lacked in-depth analysis and did not resonate with either a larger scholarly audience or the public. The stress on teams and champions also fostered an almost exclusive focus on boys and men. Women, who were on the unacknowledged side of the gender binary, never entered the frame and their absence was rarely questioned, much less challenged. Few poked into what Lara Putnam described as "the spaces of informal sport in non-white, working class communities (streets, alleys, fields) [that were] open to girls."[4] When notions of race became part of the discussion, they usually concerned the institutional racism that segregated American sport all the way from the professional level down to scholastic play and neighborhood recreational facilities. Other more ambiguous or complex aspects of sport's racial nexus were ignored.

Most scholars and journalists addressing these issues decried segregation's unfairness, underscored the lost opportunities or difficulties men like Fleetwood Walker, Jack Johnson, or Jessie Owens encountered, or heralded their against-the-odds triumphs. Only a few intrepid African-American public intellectuals and scholars, notably Edwin Henderson and Ocania Chalk, sought to legitimize African-American sport during the decades when a color line prevailed. Their work also dealt primarily with institutional sport and its pantheon of heroes, but these pioneers began to address some of the class differences among African-Americans and how that affected sport.[5]

By changing the point of view, and looking at matters from the other side of the color line, scholars ventured beyond a narrative of victimization. Instead of depicting African-Americans as at the mercy of segregated professional leagues and colleges, they began exploring what sport meant to the creation of a sense of community on the local and national levels. They recovered a sporting scene that had been downplayed because it was the by-product of segregation and, for some, an embarrassing or guilt-inducing reflection of those times. These efforts, along with the social history sensibility that infused many scholars and public intellectuals, explored how sport figured into constructing different notions of race and racial identity. They allowed a more nuanced sense of class, ideas of respectability, and identity to emerge.[6]

The new social history, moreover, prompted a history-from-below perspective that energized the study of sport. Since then, the story of African-Americans in sport has been rescued from the condescension of a limiting binary narrative that revolved around integration. Scholars subsequently expanded the definition of race to bring indigenous peoples, Hispanics, Asian-Americans, and Pacific Islanders into the story and delved into the ways in which Irish, Italian, Jewish, and other European immigrants used sport to shape and comfort their lives. Asking new questions and looking at the past from a different vantage point, they are reshaping our sense of the nation's sporting past.[7] They are bringing girls and women, as well as new questions regarding sexuality and sport, into the conversation.

Perhaps it was inevitable, as Patrick Miller and David Wiggins wrote in the preface to their edited volume, *Sport and the Color Line*, that what they called the "long and arduous struggle to relegate Jim Crow to the sidelines in American sport during the course of the twentieth century" took center stage in both popular and academic consciousness.[8] While the failure to reconstruct American society after the Civil War marred sport, as it did most aspects of life, the essays that Miller and Wiggins assembled showed how much sport illuminated these larger socio-political realities. They divided their book into three sections: "Sport and Community in the Era of Jim Crow," "The Ordeal of Desegregation," and "Images of the Black Athlete and the Racial Politics of Sport." The essays in the volume offered a comprehensive picture that stretches from the sporting institutions that African-Americans built in segregated community and educational institutions to the significance of barrier breakers like Joe Louis and Jackie Robinson, and transcendent figures like Muhammad Ali and Michael Jordan.

That Wiggins was the volume's co-editor should come as no surprise. Perhaps no other scholar has written more widely about the black sporting experience in the USA. His essays, ranging from the play of slave children, portraits of largely forgotten nineteenth-century black boxers and jockeys, the efforts of African-American journalists like Wendell Smith, to the debate over genetics, race, and sport, became the starting point for other scholars.[9] Previous efforts stressed the barriers excluding African-Americans from a whites-only sporting mainstream and obscured the world that African-Americans created for themselves on the other side of the color line. Wiggins and his fellow travelers began to look at the ways in which African-Americans socialized and entertained themselves on plantations during slavery and in free black communities in the North before and after the Civil War. Wiggins, whose scholarly coming of age was shaped by the reemergence of an emphasis on slavery and race in the academy as well as the ethos of the 1960s, drew upon the slave narratives conducted by the Works Progress Administration and edited by George Rawick. They brought African-American voices into the conversation; scholars like Wiggins kept them there.[10]

Wiggins was not the only scholar to re-cast the connections between race, sport, and ethnicity in new and revealing ways. Some of that work maintained an institutional and biographical focus; other studies soon began posing new questions and approaches. Randy Roberts' biographies of boxers Jack Johnson, Jack Dempsey, and Joe Louis, Jules Tygiel's *Baseball's Great Experiment: Jackie Robinson and His Legacy*, and Peter Levine's *Ellis Island to*

Ebbets Field: Sport and the American Jewish Experience are scholarly yet exceptionally accessible and revealing narratives anchored in contexts that tell stories about sport, race, and ethnicity.[11] They went well beyond the uncritical hagiography that characterized most earlier biographies of athletes. Others followed in their wake.

Steven Riess, Linda Borish, and Jeffrey Gurock developed American Jewry's sporting experience in a number of articles and books, including women in the story. Others did much the same with the Irish.[12] George Kirsch and his co-editors assembled a comprehensive encyclopedia of ethnicity and sport in the USA, bringing sports like lacrosse, Gaelic football, European-American gymnastic societies, and *bocce* into the discussion.[13] But these sports and their ethnic ties remain relatively understudied, at least in comparison to the scholarly and popular emphasis on sport in African-American urban communities.[14]

Many of these and related studies beg the question as to whether their subjects are collectively defined by race, nationality, religion, or a combination of such markers. Moreover, to what degree did these collective identities evolve or disintegrate over time. While these classifications can be elastic and mutable, they can also oversimplify matters and sometimes confuse as much as they clarify. Perhaps it is best to think of these categories as overlapping, ambiguous, and malleable, instead of static and definitive distinctions.

In addition to considering the damage wrought by segregation, these new interlocutors asked what the sporting world that African-Americans created meant for African-Americans, as well as for other races, and for sport itself. They focused on African-American sport where it was most able to develop – in the urban North – and examined its evolution from the Civil War through the Great Migration, the Second World War, and the civil rights movement. By looking at the Negro Leagues as a by-product of the Great Migration to the North rather than as a sorry spectacle resulting from segregation, different points of emphasis emerged. The Negro Leagues, black sandlots, and other institutions that African-Americans created for themselves revealed that sport was a force for cohesion after the tumultuous Great Migration. Baseball and boxing bridged differences among African-Americans based on place of birth, social class, and skin color. They lent a sense of national identity to African-Americans scattered across a greater geographical area. Sport also offered a cultural counterpoint to the discrimination encountered in the workplace or in politics, one where African-American power and ability fostered a stronger self-image. The shift in focus meant that new questions emerged regarding the nature of integration in sport and what was lost in the process. Integration caused the death of independent black baseball; as a result, the black community lost a significant degree of control over its own sporting life. As that turn of events affected the role that sport would play in African-American communities, sport was increasingly perceived more as a way out of the community than a way to create the social capital to build it. Not only the Negro Leagues but other black institutions – newspapers, historically black colleges and universities, and businesses – often suffered because of the ways in which integration occurred. They lost the captive clientele that segregation had created and found it difficult to compete with better capitalized, white-owned concerns after integration. The consequences of how sport and other institutions integrated have continued to plague African-Americans.

The cultural turn, critical race theory, and gender studies also inspired new questions. In 1989, Susan Birrell called for a conception of race "as a culturally produced marker of a particular relationship of power, to see racial identity as contested, and to ask how racial relations are produced and reproduced through sport." Others, notably John Hoberman, Adrian Burgos, and Ben Carrington, have ably answered her call.[15] In 1994, a few years after Birrell's challenge, Jeffrey Sammons wrote a prodigious critique of scholarship pertaining to race in North America. After comprehensively surveying the field, he concluded that its "scholarship remains wedded to dated methods, limited theory, and narrative structure." Sammons called for greater use of newer research methods and more openness to multidisciplinary and cultural approaches. In the last 20 years, as a younger cohort of scholars embraced new ways of studying race and sport, some of his challenge has been answered. These scholars are posing new research questions that reflect the intellectual work that molded their formative years.

Ironically, the study of the Negro Leagues opened up a more transnational agenda for the study of sport in the USA. A two-way flow of players between the USA and the Caribbean basin has characterized professional baseball for over a century. Significant numbers of Latinos, especially Cubans, played in the Negro Leagues, while those able to cross the color line that had been drawn in the 1890s entered white professional baseball. Meanwhile, hundreds of Negro Leaguers and major leaguers played winter ball in and around the Caribbean. This flow of Caucasians, descendants of the African diaspora, indigenous people, and mixes thereof within professional baseball confused both participants and the sporting public as to notions of race and nationality. Oftentimes, it was not so easy to determine a person's nationality or race. In the early 1900s, black teams sometimes masqueraded as Cubans in order to skirt racial boundaries and play to larger crowds.

In Latin America, a more fluid and nuanced definition of race prevailed, one that ventured beyond the binary racial code of the USA. Racism's contradictions became more apparent when men who were teammates in Cuban or Mexican winter leagues went their segregated ways in the USA during the summer season. After integration, darker-skinned players from the Caribbean often found themselves in trouble after unwittingly – or defiantly – transgressing the racial code in the American South.[16]

In writing about Jackie Robinson, the Negro Leagues, and the barnstorming black ballclubs who were part of this transnational circuit, Jules Tygiel, Donn Rogosin, Neil Lanctot *et. al.* brought an increasingly transnational dimension to their work. Adrian Burgos went even further, questioning notions of racial categories in baseball, a pastime prized as much in parts of the Caribbean basin as in the USA.[17] Alan Klein expanded this transnational picture by studying baseball on the border between the USA and Mexico, emphasizing a different set of racial, cultural, and national tensions.[18]

Black and Latin baseball were inextricably linked by their relation to major league baseball's racial policies. After Jackie Robinson's success opened the way for Latin players with darker complexions, their numbers in the major leagues edged upward throughout the 1950s and 1960s and then exploded. So did the Hispanic American population in the USA, which would outnumber people of African descent in the nation by the early twenty-first century. The number of Latinos in major league baseball, meanwhile, surpassed that of African-Americans. In recent years, Latinos have comprised over one-quarter of all major leaguers and 40+ percent of minor leaguers. The Latin cohort is currently more than three times larger than the number of African-Americans in major league baseball. Their presence meant that questions of race and nationality in sport became salient and that they could no longer be seen as simply a matter of black and white. The growing number of Japanese and Korean players has brought another group of athletes to the field. A few outliers from Southeast Asia and Africa might join them within the decade, injecting even more nuances to popular and scholarly understanding of race and ethnicity in American sport.

Baseball was the harbinger of American sport's globalization, one that has brought Africans, Canadians, West Indians, Polynesians, Australians, Japanese, and others to compete in the USA, especially at the collegiate level, in recent years. These border-hopping players have become part of the conversation. Africans compete in collegiate track and field and basketball as well as on the road-racing and marathon circuit. Some come as seasonal sporting migrants who train and compete (and often attend school) but retain residency in their homelands. Other African boys moved here in high school to play basketball and seek college scholarships and/or a path to professional play. The sons of other African émigrés who were born or grew up here have become a presence in high school football. This trend reflected the large increase in African migration to the USA.[19] While only about 80,000 Africans resided in the USA in 1970, their numbers have more or less doubled every decade since, reaching 1.6 million in recent years, or about 4 percent of the foreign-born population. Many go on to play NCAA ball and a select few will make it to the NFL. Similarly, Haitian boys who grew up playing football in Florida and Polynesians, especially Samoans and Tongans, who did the same in Hawai'i, California, and Utah have appeared at higher levels of the game. Samoan football and rugby players, South African swimmers, Jamaican runners, Brazilian volleyball players, and soccer players from several continents reflect American sport's increasingly global as well as its racially and ethnically mixed make-up.

Scholars have reaffirmed the importance of viewing questions of race and ethnicity in sport from more transnational and global perspectives. Theresa Runstedler demonstrated the power of those connections in her study of Jack Johnson and the global color line at the turn of the twentieth century. Walter LaFeber addressed how, a century later, another black American sporting icon, Michael Jordan, became the face of American sport in an age of global capitalism. Both were iconic figures not just in the USA but around the globe. The difference in how Johnson and Jordan were perceived could hardly be more striking. Johnson was seen in heavily racialized ways while Jordan's athletic and commercial success meant that his race mattered far less than his global celebrity and marketing cachet. Lara Putnam has written about some of these transnational dynamics in boxing, describing how fighters with some African ancestry circulated in a circum-Caribbean world and transcended nationality. She describes how boxing, in contrast to cricket, "offered a vocabulary of identification centered not on island and empire but on nation and race." Penny Von Eschen placed African-Americans in the context of anti-colonialism and the Cold War, while Amy Bass plumbed the 1968 Mexico Olympics and its impact on what she calls the "Making of the Black Athlete." These studies reflect how well sport's racial nexus can be used to get at deeper issues and offer a tantalizing glimpse of future work.[20]

As the presence of a more international group of athletes changed the racial conversation about US sport, scholars of sport followed in pursuit. Much of this terrain remains unexplored and will entice younger scholars in the years ahead. But while the transnational study of sport is reaching critical mass, more localized studies of the role of sport in Hispanic American, Asian-American, indigenous, and Pacific Islander communities have remained underdeveloped. So have broader interpretive accounts.

For that to change, a solid evidentiary base must be built for each of these demographic groups as well as an understanding of how they fit into the larger narrative of sporting history. It's difficult to analyze sport in a vacuum, much less develop interpretive frameworks when the narrative is absent or ambiguous. Who played? Why did they play and what roles did sport play for them? How did they organize their sporting institutions, be they clubs, teams, leagues, or community institutions? What were the internal fissures over class, religion, color, or gender that factored into sport? Who had the power to define and control sporting life in the community? To what degree did they interact with mainstream, Caucasian sport?

Answers to these questions emerge from the building blocks of sport history – biographies and memoirs of athletes, team histories, and studies of grassroots community institutions, as well as the factories, reform groups, and governments that intervened in community sport with their own agendas. They allow scholars to attempt to describe both context and trajectory. Invariably, two fundamental questions that have defined much of American sporting history should be answered for each demographic. How did sport relate to that group's larger effort to

"Americanize" and how did their sporting history fit into sport's evolution from community-based pastime to global capitalism?

Given the incredible diversity among the portion of the US population dubbed as Latino or Hispanic American, it's understandable that few would dare tackle research that attempted to cast them as a unified group. Some Hispanic Americans reside on land that was their ancestral home long before the USA took that territory over. Others hail from Mexico, the Caribbean basin, or South America; they and their predecessors arrived in different historical moments and faced dramatically different receptions. They brought different sporting traditions with them as part of their cultural baggage. Class and racial diversity further complicated their experiences, more so than for the disparate descendants of the African diaspora that formed the African-American population of the USA due to the latter's experience with slavery. Perhaps that explains why there have been fewer community studies of Latino sport along the lines of those that looked at the role of sandlot and Negro League baseball in Kansas City, Newark, Philadelphia, and Pittsburgh.[21] Nor has a native-born Hispanic gained the celebrity that propelled Jack Johnson, Joe Louis, and Muhammad Ali into the global limelight. Only Puerto Rican-born Roberto Clemente, who became a pan-Caribbean hero after the 1971 World Series and his subsequent death en route to Nicaragua after the 1972 earthquake devastated the Central American nation, has received comparable attention.[22]

To generalize about indigenous people is even more difficult than it is to treat Hispanic Americans as homogeneous. The number of indigenous groups, their differing lifestyles and political economies, and the varied ways in which they encountered European power turn such efforts into Herculean tasks. But a growing number of more focused studies have launched the examination of particular groups in specific locales. They look at the complex set of relationships between these disparate groups and sport's mainstream in many of the ways in which scholars have considered African-Americans, Hispanic Americans, and European immigrant groups. But they also raise other questions, including notions of traditional religion that might pertain more to indigenous peoples and their varied experiences. Efforts to universalize these experiences and discuss indigenous people and sport in a more comprehensive way will likely emerge only when these more specific studies have established a solid foundation.

Biographies of Jim Thorpe, Chief Bender, and Billy Mills, explorations of basketball on the reservation, studies of running and lacrosse, as well as dozens of other investigations are under way.[23] Joseph Oxendine's *American Indian Sports Heritage*, Jeffrey Powers Beck's *American Indian Integration of Baseball*, and Peter Nabokov's *Indian Running* are among them.[24] Richard King has edited volumes, *Native Americans in Sports* and *Native Athletes in Sport and Society*, whose authors address several of these questions, while Frank Salamone edited a volume that focuses on questions of identity and culture. John Bloom's *To Show what an Indian Can Do: Sports at Native American Boarding Schools*, which captures the often contradictory impact of sport as both a means of assimilation and of resistance, is part of that project. Matthew Gilbert Sakiestewa has focused on Hopis and running and David Wallace Adams and Tom Benjey have written about the Carlisle Indians, whose star, Jim Thorpe, remains the best known indigenous athlete in US history.[25] These scholars pose a raft of questions and help readers understand the role and meaning of sport from an indigenous vantage point, not simply as a function of exclusion and discrimination within a mainstream sporting world.

US imperial expansion in the Pacific forced other groups of people to become part of the nation's sporting story. These demographics often carried dual identities. While their origins were in the Hawaiian islands, the Samoan archipelago, the Federated States of Micronesia, and Guam, they were also perceived as members of a broader designation known as Pacific Islanders. Still other people from this region have migrated to the USA from Japan, Tonga, Fiji, and elsewhere. Their experiences with the USA have varied considerably. Hawaiian islanders endured a demographic disaster as well as the loss of their autonomy, while those living on Tutuila and the Manu'a islands that became the territory of American Samoa were better able to withstand these epidemiological and political traumas.

A small but vibrant group of academics are exploring these sporting connections. Some describe and analyze the evolution of sport among Asian-Americans and Pacific Islanders on the mainland and in Hawai'i. Sayuri Guthrie Shimuzu's sweeping history of Japanese baseball in a pan-Pacific context connects Japanese communities in Hawai'i and the mainland to a larger narrative that reveals a tension between becoming "American" and holding on to native culture.[26] That transnational context is virtually unavoidable for scholars of Asian-Americans, Pacific Islanders, and sport. It is also evident in Samuel Regalado's *Nikkei Baseball: Japanese American Players from Immigration and Internment to the Major Leagues* and Joel Franks' books about "Asian Pacific cultural citizenship" and a barnstorming squad made up of a diverse population of Hawaiians, as well as Robert Fitt's biography of Hawaiian Wally Yonamine, who made his mark on two sports in two countries.[27]

Lauren Shizuyo Morimoto's dissertation on barefoot football leagues in sugarcane and pineapple towns on Kaua'i shows that Japanese in the diaspora played something other than baseball. Linda Espana-Maram devotes part of her study of working-class Filipinos in Los Angeles to the role of boxing, the most popular pastime among Filipino immigrants and their descendants in Hawai'i and the mainland, and one that has figured prominently in conceptions of masculinity. Rachel Joo connects the growing numbers of Korean athletes in the USA to a larger global diaspora and plumbs the roles they played across the Pacific.[28] Vicente Diaz's exploration of football in Guam examines how race, gender, identity, and American empire coalesced in the youth football league established there.[29]

Scholars have also begun to plumb the extraordinary contributions of Samoans in football and raise questions regarding how sporting identities have been reformulated in ways that bring together race, nationality, gender, and culture. Questions of masculinity and racial identity are central to a fascinating piece by Ty P.K. Tengan and Jesse Makani Markham, "Performing Polynesian Masculinities in American Football: From 'Rainbows to Warriors'." Markham led the way in placing Samoan football players in the archipelago and the USA on the map in a master's thesis that tracks the growing involvement of Samoans and members of the diaspora in high school, college, and professional football.[30]

Lisa Uperesa's studies of football and culture in American Samoa and among Samoan communities in the USA expand upon Markham's pioneering work. Taken together, they establish a critical framework for understanding Samoan sport. Markham systematically sketches the political economy of football for Polynesian boys and how they make their way from Big Boyz and youth football to higher levels of the game. He also explores cultural concerns that Uperesa is developing to an unprecedented degree in her current work. An exceptional piece of research and scholarship, her revised dissertation will become the launching point for future scholars. Uperesa and Markham make clear why Samoans are significantly over-represented in football at each level of the game. While comprising only a tiny sliver of the population, they often dominate high school football in Hawai'i and parts of California.[31]

This Polynesian micro-culture of sporting excellence in football begs a question that has long roiled the study of sport and race. What causes such clusters to emerge? Are they due to some inherent genetic advantage or, as Uperesa and Markham suggest, the product of an enduring culture, socioeconomics, and the growth of a sporting infrastructure? This argument is redolent of ones that have raged in both barrooms and arenas, as well as in journals and classrooms, where many declare that sporting excellence is a matter of collective racial athletic superiority. David Epstein's *The Sporting Gene* is a welcome addition to the discussion. It focuses on particular genetic patterns and variations that allow groups of outliers to emerge in sport and perform at exceptionally high levels. It also helps explain why different individuals respond better to certain conditions and training regimens than others. But history, class, culture, and environment are more relevant factors. There are few if any "sports genes" that affect broader demographic groups.

Culture matters more than other factors in the Samoan case. A still-strong traditional culture that stresses discipline, collectivism, and hierarchy has been reinforced by military and religious (especially Church of the Latter Day Saints) connections. That's a perfect recipe for football. Uperesa underscores how much *fa'a samoa*, "in the way of Samoa," has influenced the making of Samoan football. Her deeply anthropological interpretation is grounded in both sport and Samoa's fiercely competitive culture. Nobody has isolated a "warrior gene" that might explain the athletic brilliance of a Junior Seau or Troy Polamalu. But Uperesa and Markham take apart the ways in which a warrior identity has been racialized and exploited, as well as analyze how and why it matters.

As the study of sport in the USA reaches critical mass and attracts a younger cohort of scholars who have engaged with sport in different ways than those who preceded them, a new agenda will emerge. Sport history is now attracting significantly greater numbers of female scholars who grew up after Title IX took effect and with more exposure to cultural studies along the way. Their experiences and sensibilities will break the gender binary, which like the black and white racial binary, has distorted understanding of sport. They will incorporate women and gender into the story of race, ethnicity, and sport in new, more substantive, ways. They will answer the question posed by Jennifer Bruening, "Are all the women white and all the blacks men?" when it comes to the study of sport. They will consider representations of the body, the construction of gender, and questions yet to be formulated.[32] They might ask, Lara Putnam suggests, how "racialized perception and norms regarding gender and sexuality" shaped the "kinds of admiration, attention, and acceptance … open to which athletes."[33]

This will constitute both a generational and philosophical shift. The study of sport has always been at its strongest when it draws upon the best prevailing historical scholarship of society. The generation of scholars who were made in the 1970s and 1980s drew insight from the popular movements animating the nation and demanding attention to race and the roles and status of women. They were schooled in social and labor history and their work reflected these concerns. But new cohorts of younger scholars profoundly influenced by feminism and cultural studies are exploring new questions and coming up with new answers. They will draft the next edition of sport's historical connections to race and ethnicity.[34]

Notes

1 I want to thank Lisa Uperesa and Lara Putnam for their suggestions and insight regarding this chapter.
2 Bryan Di Salvatore, *A Clever Base-Ballist: The Life and Times of John Montgomery Ward* (New York: Pantheon, 1999); Steven A. Riess, *Touching Base: Professional Baseball and American Culture in the Progressive Era* (Urbana and Chicago, IL: University of Illinois Press, 1990); see also James R. Barrett, *The Irish Way: Becoming American in the Multiethnic City* (New York, NY: Penguin: 2012).
3 Peter Levine, *Ellis Island to Ebbets Field: Sport and the American Jewish Experience* (New York, NY: Oxford University Press, 1992); Richard Ben Cramer, *Joe DiMaggio: The Hero's Life* (New York, NY: Simon & Schuster, 2000); Jack Moore, *Joe DiMaggio: A Bio-Bibliography* (Westport, CT: Greenwood Press, 1987); Nicholas P. Ciotola, "Spignesi, Sinatra, and the Pittsburgh Steelers: Franco's Italian Army as an Expression of Ethnic Identity, 1972–1977," *Journal of Sport History* 27, 2 (2000), 271–89.
4 Lara Putnam, "The Panama Cannonball and the Queen: Migrants, Sport, and Belonging in the Interwar Greater Caribbean," *Journal of Sport History* 41, 3 (2014), 401–24.

5   Edwin B. Henderson, *The Black Athlete: Emergence and Arrival* (New York, NY: Publishers Company, 1968); Ocania Chalk, *Pioneer of Black Sport: The Early Days of the Black Professional Athlete in Baseball, Basketball, Boxing, and Football* (New York, NY: Dodd, Mead, and Company, 1975); see also Art Rust, Jr., *Get that Nigger Off the Field* (New York, NY: Delacorte Press, 1976); Art Rust, Jr. and Edna Rust, *Joe Louis, My Life* (New York, NY: Harcourt Brace Jovanovich, 1978).

6   The study of the Negro Leagues played a role in this shift. As Jules Tygiel's *Baseball's Great Experiment* (New York, NY: Oxford University Press, 1983); Don Rogosin, *Invisible Men: Life in Baseball's Negro Leagues* (New York, NY: Macmillan, 1985); Janet Bruce, *The Kansas City Monarchs: Black Baseball's Champions* (Lawrence, KS: University Press of Kansas, 1985); Rob Ruck, *Sandlot Seasons: Sport in Black Pittsburgh* (Urbana and Chicago, IL: University of Illinois Press, 1986); Michael Lomax, *Black Baseball Entrepreneurs 1860–1901* (Syracuse, NY: Syracuse University Press, 2003); Neil Lanctot, *Fair Dealing and Clean Playing: The Hilldale Club and the Development of Black Professional Baseball, 1910– 1932* (Jefferson, NC: McFarland, 1994); Neil Lanctot, *Negro League Baseball: The Rise and Ruin of a Black Institution* (Philadelphia, PA: University of Pennsylvania Press, 2008); and others recaptured the story of black baseball, they began framing the narrative in dramatically different ways. See also William J. Baker, *Jesse Owens: An American Life* (New York, NY: Free Press, 1986); Thomas Hauser, *Muhammad Ali: His Life and Times* (New York, NY: Simon & Schuster, 1991); Gerald Early, "The Black Intellectual and the Sport of Prizefighting," *The Kenyon Review* 10, 3 (1988), 102–17; Gerald Early, *Tuxedo Junction: Essays on American Culture* (New York, NY: Ecco Press, 1990); Gerald Early, *The Culture of Bruising: Essays in Literature, Prizefighting, and Modern Culture* (New York, NY: Ecco Press, 1993); Arthur R. Ashe Jr., *Hard Road to Glory: A History of the African-American Athlete* (New York, NY: Warner Books, 1988); Arthur Ashe and Arnold Rampersad, *Days of Grace: A Memoir* (New York, NY: Knopf, 1993); Al-Tony Gilmore, *Bad Nigger: The National Impact of Jack Johnson* (Port Washington, NY: Kenniket Press, 1975); Jeffrey T. Sammons, *Beyond the Ring: The Role of Boxing in American Society* (Urbana and Chicago, IL: University of Illinois Press, 1988).

7   John Bloom and Michael Nevin Willard, eds., *Sports Matters: Race, Recreation, and Culture* (New York, NY: New York University Press, 2002) includes several essays that might chart the way.

8   Patrick B. Miller and David K. Wiggins, eds., *Sport and the Color Line: Black Athletes and Race Relations in Twentieth-Century America* (New York, NY: Routledge, 2004), vii.

9   David Wiggins, *Glory Bound: Black Athletes in a White America* (Syracuse, NY: Syracuse University Press, 1997).

10 Rawick was the editor of *The American Slave: A Composite Autobiography*, which was a 41-volume set of oral histories of former slaves. The interviews were conducted by the Works Progress Administration during the New Deal. Rawick's *From Sundown to Sunup: The Making of the Black Community* (Westport, CT: Greenwood Press, 1972) was volume 1 of *The American Slave*; Wiggins, *Glory Bound*.

11 Randy Roberts, *Papa Jack: Jack Johnson and the Era of White Hopes* (New York, NY: Free Press, 1983); *Jack Dempsey: The Manassa Mauler* (Urbana and Chicago, IL: University of Illinois Press, 2003); *Joe Louis: Hard Times Man* (New Haven, CT: Yale University Press, 2010); Chris Mead, *Champion: Joe Louis, Black Hero in White America* (New York, NY: Charles Scribner Sons, 1985).

12 Steven A. Riess, *Sport and the American Jew* (Syracuse, NY: Syracuse University Press, 1988); Linda Borish, "Jewish Women in the American Gym: Basketball, Ethnicity and Gender in the Early Twentieth Century," in Leonard Greenspoon, ed., *Jews in the Gym: Judaism, Sports, and Athletics*, vol. 23 (West Lafayette, IN: Purdue University Press, 2012); Jeffrey Gurock, *Judaism's Encounter with American Sports* (Bloomington, IN: Indiana University Press, 2005); Linda Borish, "American Jewish Women's Voices in Sport History: Heritage and Identity in Documentary Film and Research," in Kalle Voolaid, ed., *People in Sport History: Sport History for People, Proceedings of the International Society for the History of Physical Education and Sport*, ISHPES Seminar (Tartu, Estonia: Estonia Sports Museum, International Society for the History of Physical Education and Sport, 2011), 108–20; Rob Ruck, Maggie Jones Patterson, and Michael P. Weber, *Rooney: A Sporting Life* (Lincoln, NE: University of Nebraska Press, 2010); Peter Redmond, *The Irish and the Making of American Sport, 1835–1920* (Jefferson, NC: McFarland & Co., 2014).

13 George B. Kirsch, Othello Harris, and Claire E. Nolte, eds., *Encyclopedia of Ethnicity and Sports in the United States* (Westport, CT: Greenwood Press, 2000); also see George Eisen and David K. Wiggins, eds., *Ethnicity and Sport in North American History and Culture* (Westport, CT: Greenwood Press, 1994).

14 Soccer clubs formed by European immigrants flourished in St. Louis, Pittsburgh and other cities yet have escaped scholarly treatment commensurate with the roles they played in these working-class environs; for a history of the sport in Washington, DC, see Charles Parrish and John Nauright, "Senators, Darts, Whips, and Dips: The Evolution of Soccer in Washington D.C.," in C. Elzey and

D. Wiggins, eds., *DC Sports: The Nation's Capital at Play* (Fayetteville, AR: University of Arkansas Press, 2015), 147–64.

15 Susan Birrell, "Race Relations Theories and Sport: Suggestions for a More Critical Analysis," *Sociology of Sport Journal* 6 (1989), 212–17; John Hoberman, *Darwin's Athletes: How Sport Has Damaged Black America and Preserved the Myth of Race* (Boston, MA: Houghton Mifflin Company, 1997); Adrian Burgos, *Playing America's Game: Baseball, Latinos, and the Color Line* (Berkeley and Los Angeles, CA: University of California Press, 2007); Ben Carrington, *Race, Sport and Politics: The Sporting Black Diaspora* (London: Sage, 2010). See also Theresa Runstedtler, *Jack Johnson, Rebel Sojourner: Boxing the Shadow of the Global Color Line* (Berkeley and Los Angeles, CA: University of California Press, 2012); Walter LaFeber, *Michael Jordan and the New Global Capitalism* (New York: W.W. Norton, 2002); Putnam, "The Panama Cannonball"; Penny Von Eschen, *Race Against Empire: Black Americans and Anti-colonialism, 1937–1957* (Ithaca, NY: Cornell University Press, 1997); Amy Bass, *Not the Triumph but the Struggle: The 1968 Olympic Games and the Making of the Black Athlete* (Minneapolis, MN: University of Minnesota Press, 2002).

16 Rico Carty endured one such incident in Atlanta that resulted in a beating. Rob Ruck, *The Tropic of Baseball: Baseball in the Dominican Republic* (Lincoln, NE: University of Nebraska Press, 1998).

17 Adrian Burgos, *Playing America's Game: Baseball, Latinos, and the Color Line* (Berkeley and Los Angeles, CA: University of California Press, 2007); Adrian Burgos, *Cuban Star: How One Negro League Owner Changed the Face of Baseball* (New York: Hill & Wang, 2011).

18 Allen Klein, *Baseball on the Border: A Tale of Two Laredos* (Princeton, NJ: Princeton University Press, 1997). Klein has written three other books about baseball that invariably deal with race: *Sugarball* (New Haven, CT: Yale University Press, 1993); *Growing the Game: The Globalization of Major League Baseball* (New Haven, CT: Yale University Press, 2006); and *Dominican Baseball: New Pride, Old Prejudice* (Philadelphia, PA: Temple University Press, 2014); Rob Ruck brings the stories of African-Americans and people from the Caribbean basin together in a context defined by their relationships with major league baseball in *Raceball: How the Major Leagues Colonized the Black and Latin Game* (Boston, MA: Beacon Press, 2011).

19 United States Census Bureau, "African-Born Population in U.S. Roughly Doubled Every Decade Since 1970, Census Bureau Reports," Release Number: CB14-184, The Foreign-Born Population From Africa, 2008–2012.

20 Runstedtler, *Jack Johnson*; LaFeber, *Michael Jordan*; Putnam, "The Panama Cannonball," 403; Von Eschen, *Race Against Empire*; Bass, *Not the Triumph but the Struggle*.

21 Janet Bruce, *The Kansas City Monarchs*; James Overmyer, *Queen of the Negro Leagues: Effa Manley and the Newark Eagles* (Lanham, MD: Scarecrow Press, 1998); Ruck, *Sandlot Seasons*; Donn Rogosin, *Invisible Men: Life in Baseball's Negro Leagues* (New York, NY: Atheneum, 1983); Leslie Heaphy, *The Negro Leagues 1869–1960* (Jefferson, NC: McFarland, 2013).

22 David Maranis, *Clemente: The Passion and Grace of Baseball's Last Hero* (New York: Simon & Schuster, 2006); Kal Wagenheim, *Clemente! The Enduring Legacy* (Chicago, IL: Olmstead Press, 2011); Bernardo Ruiz, *Clemente* (American Experience, Public Broadcasting System, 2008).

23 Kate Buford, *Native American Son: The Life and Sporting Legend of Jim Thorpe* (New York, NY: Alfred A. Knopf, 2010); Tom Benjey, *Doctors, Lawyers, Indian Chiefs: Jim Thorpe & Pop Warner's Carlisle Indian School Football Immortals* (Carlisle, PA: Tuxedo Press, 2008); John M. Yeager, *Our Game: The Character and Culture of Lacrosse* (New York, NY: Dude Publishing, 2006).

24 Joseph Oxendine, *American Indian Sports Heritage* (Lincoln, NE: University of Nebraska Press, 1995); Jeffrey Powers-Beck, *The American Indian Integration of Baseball* (Lincoln, NE: University of Nebraska Press, 2004); Peter Nabokov, *Indian Running: Native American History and Tradition* (Santa Barbara, CA: Capra Press, 1981).

25 Richard C. King, ed., *Native Americans in Sports*, 2 volumes (Armonk, NY: M.E. Sharpe, 2003); Richard C. King, ed., *Native Athletes in Sport and Society: A Reader* (Lincoln, NE: University of Nebraska Press, 2005); Frank A. Salamone, ed., *The Native American Identity in Sports: Creating and Preserving a Culture* (Lanham, MD: Scarecrow Press, 2013); John Bloom, *To Show What an Indian Can Do: Sports at Native American Boarding Schools* (Minneapolis, MN: University of Minnesota Press, 2000); Matthew Gilbert Sakiestewa, "Marathoner Louis Tewanima and the Continuity of Hopi Running, 1908–1912," *Western Historical Quarterly* 43, 3 (2012), 324–46; Matthew Gilbert Sakiestewa, "Hopi Footraces and American Marathons, 1912–1930," *American Quarterly* 62, 1 (2010), 77–101; David Wallace Adams, "More Than A Game: The Carlisle Indians Take to the Gridiron, 1893–1917," *Western Historical Quarterly* 32, 1 (2001), 25–53.

26 Sayuri Guthrie Shimuzu, *Transpacific Field of Dreams: How Baseball Linked the United States and Japan in Peace and War* (Chapel Hill, NC: University of North Carolina Press, 2012).

27 Samuel O. Regalado, *Nikkei Baseball: Japanese American Players from Immigration and Internment to the Major Leagues* (Urbana and Chicago, IL: University of Illinois Press, 2013); Joel S. Franks, *Crossing Sidelines, Crossing Cultures: Sport and Asian Pacific American Cultural Citizenship* (Lanham, MD: Rowman & Littlefield, 2000); *Asian Pacific Americans and Baseball: A History* (Jefferson, NC: McFarland, 2008); *The Barnstorming Hawaiian Travelers: A Multiethnic Baseball Team Tours the Mainland, 1912–1916* (Jefferson, NC: McFarland, 2012); Robert K. Fitts, *Wally Yonamine: The Man Who Changed Japanese Baseball* (Lincoln, NE: University of Nebraska Press, 2008).

28 Lauren Shizuyo Morimoto, "The Barefoot Leagues: An Oral (Hi)story of Football in the Plantation Towns of Kaua'I," PhD thesis, Ohio State University, 2005; Linda Espana-Maram, *Creating Masculinity in Los Angeles's Little Manila: Working-Class Filipinos and Popular Culture, 1920s–1950s* (New York: Columbia University Press, 2006); Rachel Miyung Joo, *Transnational Sport: Gender, Media, and Global Korea* (Durham, NC: Duke University Press, 2012).

29 Vicente M. Diaz, "'Fight Boys, 'til the Last…': Islandstyle Football and the Remasculinization of Indigeneity in the Militarized American Pacific Islands," in Paul Spickard, Joanne Rondilla, and Deborah Hippolite, eds., *Pacific Diaspora: Island Peoples in the United States and Across the Pacific* (Honolulu: University of Hawai'i Press, 2002), 169–94.

30 Ty P.K. Tengan and Jesse Makani Markham, "Performing Polynesian Masculinities in American Football: From 'Rainbows to Warriors'," *International Journal of the History of Sport* 26, 16 (2009), 2412–31; Jesse Wind Markham, "An Evolving Geography of Sport: The Recruitment and Mobility of Samoan College Football Players 1998–2006," MA thesis, University of Hawaii at Manoa, 2008.

31 F.L. Uperesa, "Fabled Futures: Development, Gridiron Football, and Transnational Movements in American Samoa," PhD thesis, Columbia University, 2010; F.L. Uperesa, "Fabled Futures: Migration and Mobility for Samoans in American Football," *The Contemporary Pacific* 26, 2 (2014), 281–301.

32 Jennifer E. Bruening, "Gender and Racial Analysis in Sport: Are All the Women White and All the Blacks Men?" *Quest*, 57, 3 (2005), 330–49; Lisa Doris Alexander suggests that studying "how and why historically black colleges and universities fostered and celebrated female athletic participation long before Title IX was implemented can provide a far more comprehensive and well-rounded understanding of the black historical experience" in her "Sports History: What's Next" contribution to "State of the Field: Sports History and the 'Cultural Turn'," *Journal of American History*, 101 (2014), 148–72; see also: Rita Liberti, "'We Were Ladies, We Just Played Basketball like Boys': African American Womanhood and Competitive Basketball at Bennett College, 1928–1942,", *Journal of Sport History* 26, 3 (1999), 567–84; Jennifer H. Lansbury, "'The Tuskegee Flash' and the 'The Slender Harlem Stroker': Black Women Athletes on the Margin," *Journal of Sport History* 28, 2 (2001), 233–52.

33 Personal correspondence, 20 July 2015.

34 See the roundtable re: "State of the Field: Sports History and the 'Cultural Turn'," *Journal of American History* 101, (2014), 148–72, in which Amy Bass addresses some of these questions and Lisa Doris Alexander, Adrian Burgos Jr., Daniel A. Nathan, Randy Roberts, and Rob Ruck respond.

19

SPORT AND MUSLIMS OR MUSLIMS IN SPORT, POST-9/11

Mahfoud Amara

Introduction

The question of Islam and Muslims in Europe and in the West took a drastic turn after the 9/11 attack in Manhattan, and the 7/7 bombings which occurred the day after London had won its bid to host the 2012 Olympics. Muslims are being put under more scrutiny by states' security apparatus, the media, and the mushrooming research centres specialized in the study of 'Islamism', 'terrorism' and 'radicalism'. The tension provoked by these two events and other terrorist attacks in Europe, followed by the important US-led military operations in the Middle East, has had repercussions for different domains, including sport. Muslim visibility (or over visibility for some) whether in relation to the question of the veil (hijab) in sport, the expression of Islamic faith in sport (e.g. fasting during sport competitions) or in relation to sport marketing, such as the case of Qatari investment in the international sport market, is increasingly contested today on ideological bases. It is even equated, particularly within right and far-right movements, as another (soft) strategy for the 'Islamization' of Europe in particular, and the West in general. The chapter, informed by a few years of observation of media portrayal of Muslims in sport post-9/11, is organized around the following three aspects: hijab and the 'Islamization' of sport; Arab-Muslim investment in sport as a means for 'soft power'; and sport and the question of integration of Muslims as a challenge to citizenship and national identity debates.

Hijab and the 'Islamization' of sport

The press in Europe, Australia, North America, particularly in Quebec province in Canada, is full of articles debating the presence of the hijab in sport and the demand of Muslim women to wear the hijab or other forms of adaptation of the traditional veil in the sport arena (basketball court, football pitch or swimming pool, to name but a few). The question of the veil in sport or in society in general becomes a contested space to conquer, by government, political movements, representatives of Muslim communities and different feminist groups. The visibility of the veil in public space post-9/11 created a dilemma. For some it is yet another form of provocation and example of disloyalty to Western nations (and culture). For others, accepting the presence of and respecting the veil is a form of resistance against the growing Islamophobic propaganda, but also for the protection of Western values of democracy and tolerance of diversity. For veiled Muslim women, the hijab is a form of resistance and identity expression against an anti-Muslim stereotype. Governments are torn between security discourse, symbolized by the ban of the full veil (or burqa) in some European countries, the discourse of nationalism, fuelled by the war against the enemy of the Western way of life, and that of tactical politics toward far-right voters. In France and Quebec province in Canada, where there is the tradition of *laïcité* in the sense of separation between politics and religion in public space, reducing the visibility of the veil, including in sport whether at recreational or at elite level, is promoted in political and media spheres as a weapon against *communitarisme* (community closure on ethnic or religious bases). Hence the protection of social cohesion, or as known in Quebec, *accommodement raisonnable* (reasonable accommodation), which can be translated as the balance between diversity and national (Canadian) values.

The question of the veil in sport has triggered a number of newspaper articles and political debates (Figure 19.1). We can cite, for instance, the decision by Swiss sport authorities requiring Sura Al-Shawk to either remove her headscarf or stop competing in basketball.[2] In 2007 a referee ruled that 11-year-old Asmahan Mansour could not wear a hijab during a game at the Canadian indoor soccer championships held in Montreal. Quebec's soccer federation argued that Asmahan Mansour of Ottawa was given the choice of taking off her hijab or not playing in a Sunday tournament in nearby Laval. The reason put forward was that her hijab violated a no-headgear rule set down by the sport's governing body for 'safety' reasons.[3] This ban was also extended to Sikh turbans.[4] In 2008 the supreme tribunal in Switzerland rejected the demand to exempt boys and girls from Muslim communities from practising swimming in mixed classes because according to Swiss law it was against the policy for integration and equal rights. In 2009, a French woman (who had converted to Islam 17 years ago) was refused the right to swim in a communal swimming pool in Emerainville in France because she wore an 'Islamic swimming suit' she had bought in Dubai.[5]

Another place where the question has taken a politico-ideological turn is in relation to the veil in the Olympics. I argued elsewhere why the hijab in the Olympics is opposed, or at least contested, by feminist movements such as Atlanta Plus, an association that campaigns for the promotion of women's rights in the Olympics. The argument put forward is that the hijab in

Banning Muslim Head Scarves

■ Bad idea ■ Good idea

	Bad idea	Good idea
France	22	78
Germany	40	54
Netherland	46	51
Spain	48	43
Great Britain	62	29

Figure 19.1 Europeans debate the scarf and the veil.[1]

sport is invasive (a threat) and runs counter to the values of women's emancipation. For veiled athletes themselves, the hijab in the Olympics should be celebrated as a form of cultural plurality and an example of the IOC's openness towards diversity. The lift of the ban on the veil in sport by international federations has allowed for the first time the participation of female athletes from Saudi Arabia and Qatar at the 2012 Olympic Games. The participation of Saudi Arabia's judoka Wojdan Shaherkani, which lasted only 1 minute and 22 seconds, was particularly attractive to the media.[6] Farooq and Sehlikoglu highlighted how Muslim women athletes were represented in Orientalist 'exotic' terms, as 'strangers' and 'out of place':

> Once Muslim women's presence at the Olympics was conflated with culturally embedded, socially constructed, and locally produced public and political discourses of fear and suspicion, individual reporters transmitted messages about the sporting Muslim female subject that characterized 'Her' presence at the Olympics as strange, incompetent and out-of-place. This was evident in mediated representations of Muslim sportswomen across the UK and France, North America, Canada and Australia, where the notion of the 'oppressed Arab lady', the 'helpless veiled woman', the novice and child-like, almost immature, athletic woman was used to purport familiar messages about Muslim women's sense of strange(r)ness, 'Their' athletic incompetency and the extent to which they were 'outsiders' (or out-of-place) at the Olympics.[7]

Arab-Muslim investment in sport as means for 'soft power'

Dubai, Abu Dhabi, Manama and Doha are associated today with sport entertainment and are promoted as a must-see destination for sport tourists and fans of speedboat racing, car racing and golf, to name a few. The urban landscape of cities in the Gulf Cooperation Council (GCC) is being shaped by sports at multiple levels. As part of their overarching economic strategy to diversify their economies beyond the hydrocarbon industry, the UAE, Bahrain and Qatar have all sought to invest in alternate sectors and – through hosting and sponsoring sporting mega-events, sponsoring international sport clubs and investing directly in sport clubs and sport products – the sports sector has emerged as one new locus being actively developed. This pattern is also being followed to a certain extent (but with a less aggressive marketing approach), by other GCC countries.

Several of the GCC states have demonstrated a desire to improve their sport performance standings – by seeking a FIFA ranking and more Olympic medals – and to enhance their engagement in the business of sport, through the sponsoring of and direct investment in top sport leagues and events. Countries in the Arabian Peninsula have embarked on a worldwide campaign of investment in the international football industry, through bidding for and staging major football tournaments, sponsorship and even direct ownership of European football clubs (e.g. Manchester City, Paris Saint-Germain aka PSG, FC Barcelona). The other strategic sector is sport broadcasting. Qatar Sport Network BeINsport is now competing worldwide with other giant sport networks such as SKY, FOX, Canal Plus and ESPN. For some, these investments are welcomed as they boost the global economy of sport. For others, Arab investment in European football is also perceived as a threat to the identity (and hegemony) of European football clubs. Identity would include also 'Christian' values of European football clubs – as with the case of Real Madrid, which made a decision to remove the traditional Christian cross from its logo after signing a three-year deal with the National Bank of Abu Dhabi.[8]

Qatari investment in the European sport market has been received with more controversy by European media. Qatar Sport Investment (QSI), which is the sport arm of the Qatar Investment Authority, first acquired 70 per cent shares of PSG. In June 2012 the rest of the shares (30 per cent) were bought by QSI from the US company Colony Capital, making QSI the sole owner of the club. The purchase of PSG is part of a wider Qatari investment in France. Al-Jazeera (now BeINSport) bought parts of the broadcasting right of the French league from 2012–13 for €61 million per year, and paid the same amount for the broadcasting (including on internet and mobile) of 133 matches in France of the UEFA Champions League.[9] In a similar manner to the controversy around Dubai Ports investment in the USA (rejected for security concerns), the increasing visibility of Qatar opened the door for speculation in Europe in general, and in France in particular, about the true agenda behind its global investments in sport, as well as in other sectors. It is estimated that Qatar has invested €6 billion in France. The Qatar Investment Authority has shares in: France Telecom (1 per cent), Lagardere (13 per cent), LVMH (1 per cent), Total (3 per cent), Veolia (5 per cent), Vinci (8 per cent), Vivendi (5 per cent).[10] For the French media, Qatar investment in sport in France cannot be explained in mere economic terms. The far-right movement, represented by Marine Le Pen's *Front National*, goes so far as to accuse Qatar of *Islamizing* France, in reference to Qatar's proposed project to invest in the outskirts of French cities, populated by French of North African/Muslim communities, known as les *Baulieus*. The same narrative is reproduced by French media with different political tendencies:

Les musulmans dans la mire du Qatar: Après l'immobilier et le foot, l'émirat investit discrètement dans l'islam hexagonal en finançant des mosquées et soutenant l'Union des organisations islamiques de France. [Muslims the target of Qatar: after property and football, the Emirate invests discreetly in French Islam in financing Mosques in favour of the Union of Islamic Organizations (labelled as close to the international movement of Islamic brotherhood)].[11]

Le Qatar, « un pays entre monopoly et islam radical » : Après une enquête d'un an sur le Qatar, Christian Chesnot et Georges Malbrunot, spécialistes du Moyen-Orient, dévoilent les deux visages de cet Etat « caméléon ». [Qatar 'between monopoly and radical Islam': after an investigation of one year, Christian Chesnot and Georges Malbrunot, specialists of the Middle East, reveal the 'chameleon' faces of this state.[12]

Royaume-uni. Le Qatar achète un quartier d'affaires à Londres. Le Qatar et un investisseur canadien viennent de s'emparer d'une partie de Canary Wharf, le quartier d'affaires le plus important de Londres après la City. [The United Kingdom, Qatar bought the Business quarter of London. Qatar and another investor from Canada (not mentioned in the main title) took over part of Canary Wharf, one of the most important centres of business and the City.[13]

Les projets d'investissements du Qatar en France, dans le secteur sportif ou pour relancer l'activité dans les banlieues, continuent de susciter des interrogations dans la classe politique, où l'idée d'une commission d'enquête parlementaire commence à faire son chemin. Après avoir investi dans le secteur sportif, au Paris-Saint-Germain (football et handball) et dans l'achat de droits de diffusion TV, puis sur le marché de l'art, le Qatar s'intéresse depuis fin 2011 aux banlieues françaises, auxquelles il voulait dédier à l'origine un fonds de 50 millions d'euros. L'initiative a été reportée avant les élections en France, afin d'éviter son instrumentalisation politique. La présidente du Front national, Marine Le Pen, avait notamment accusé le Qatar 'd'investir massivement' sur une base communautaire dans les banlieues, où vivent de nombreux musulman. [The investment project of Qatar in France, in the sporting sector or to re-launch activities in the suburbs, continue to raise questions within the political class, hence the idea of establishing a parliamentary commission. Following Qatar's investment in the sport sector, Paris-Saint-Germain (football and handball) and in acquiring sport TV rights, then is the Arts Market, Qatar has been interested since 2011 in French suburbs to which they want to dedicate initially 50 million euros. The initiative was postponed until after presidential elections to avoid political interference. The president of National Front, Marine Le Pen, notably accused Qatar of 'investing massively' in Parisian suburbs on a community basis where many Muslims live].[14]

On another level, due to globalization of sport brands, global mobility of athletes of Muslim culture or the increasing religiosity of Muslims in the West who want to be visible in the public domain, a number of cases were reported in the media about athletes refusing to wear, for instance, football shirts sponsored by gambling and alcohol companies or protesting against the legalization of sport betting. The risk for global brands, including non-alcoholic beers, to lose customers in their traditional (non-Muslim) market is real, as was the case for the Australian beer company Coopers 'accused of "supporting terrorism" and "lowering yourself to a minority" because it received *Halal* accreditation for its malt extract products'.[15]

Muslims and sport as a challenge to 'integration' policies

The 7/7 bombings in London fostered an atmosphere of fear and brought to the surface the debate around multicultural policy in Britain. Trevor Phillips, chairman for the Commission on Racial Equality, in April 2004 argued that Britain's policy of multiculturalism had gone too far and that there was a need to ensure that a core of British values remained intact.[16] There was evidence, in some areas of government and the quasi-government sector, of a shift away from a dominantly multiculturalist agenda (which had come to be seen as encouraging 'separateness') and towards interculturalism to promote common interests and a shared sense of belonging.[17]

The question of Islam in sport in Europe and elsewhere was confronted in a number of ways. The demand by Muslims to accommodate sport to their culture and religious beliefs is perceived as a sign of disintegration or non-assimilation of European values of citizenship and community cohesion; even more as a defiance of national (secular) values of universalism, social cohesion and national unity. In France, where the confrontation between two visions of citizenship – French republicanism and cultural pluralism – is the most contentious, the Muslim community's desire for women-only swimming is becoming the centre of electoral campaigns. This is to measure the loyalty of candidates for different elections at local and national levels to the French republican value of *laïcité* in the anti-clerical sense of disassociating politics from religion and preservation of public space from religious interference. Martine Aubry, previously the head of the socialist party and the mayor of Lille, was highly criticized for allowing the allocation of a specific time for women (mainly Muslim) in a public swimming pool.[18] She and the socialist party, now in power, have been accused by the conservative party and far-right movements of seducing electorates among Muslim communities to the detriment of secular values of France and its assimilationist/republican model. In Australia, Toffoletti and Palmer explain, from a transnational feminist approach, how

> public policy has responded to the perceived problems of social cohesion, integration and difference among Australian Muslims through government interventions such as

the 'People of Australia' Multicultural Policy of which a key initiative is the Multicultural Youth Sports Partnership (MYSP).[19]

Testa points out that since the 9/11 terrorist attacks in the USA, radicalization and Islamophobia seem to be the most recurrent topics: 'radicalization in particular can be promoted by a perception of unfair treatments and distrusts in the political system of the country where communities live'.[20] And we can add where they were born. According to Saeed:

> in today's Britain, especially after 9/11 and the beginning of the so-called War on Terror, British Muslims have been identified as a group of potentially 'false nationals' and systematically constructed as the Other. A discourse has been produced which directly links European Muslims with support of terrorism, fundamentalism, 'illegal immigration' and Orientalist stereotype.[21]

The sense of being under surveillance, isolated and marginalized, are reiterated in interviews we undertook with representatives of Muslim communities, asking them about their access to sport provision and funding targeting ethnic minorities in cities such as Leicester and Birmingham, known for their high percentage of Muslim populations in comparison to the national average. Interviewees' responses emphasized the question of prejudices relating to Muslim communities in the UK, particularly after the 9/11 and 7/7 terrorist attacks. These are reflected in the following responses:

> it appears that the whole Muslim community is being put in the dock and made answerable for the criminal activities of a tiny, tiny number of people. All these pressures that are on us have created an atmosphere of fear among the Muslim community. It is a community that feels under siege. They have got a siege mentality in their mind. To bring up their confidence in themselves we need the outside forces to understand when they are looking into the Muslim community ... what is it they want to do. The majority are law abiding citizens. In fact Islam is a law, Shari'a based faith, and within this Shari'a faith base our love for justice, law and order is very strong.[22]

Some interviewees expressed resentment at what they perceived as uneven treatment of different faith communities:

> since 9/11 everybody is talking about targeting faith communities ... asking faith communities to talk to each other ... but it is a nonsense (nothing is happening in reality). They are not thinking seriously about the subject.... The Muslim community is not receiving any money ... the local authority did not put any penny here (i.e. in the building of the Central Mosque). They give churches more money. Every church (in the area) has been supported by the central government, but not mosques. These have all been built by the community.[23]

With the growing number of so-called 'home grown Jihadists' who integrated with different armed groups to fight in Syria, Iraq and sub-Saharan Africa, the question of radicalization among Muslim youth and how sport is used as a means of political mobilization for militant Islam caught the attention of Western media. The French magazine *Le Point* asks how sport can be a source of radicalization. To explain what is meant by 'radicalization' and how serious it is, its article provides some examples reported by the French Intelligence Bureau (*les Renseignement Generaux*) in a lengthy document of 13 pages transmitted to the government:

> *Les RG ont ainsi remarqué que des joueurs de football d'une équipe de Perpignan prient sur la pelouse devant des arbitres médusés ; ou encore que des éducateurs sportifs fichés par les services de renseignements comme musulmans salafistes encadrent néanmoins des adolescents en déployant des tapis de prière dans les gymnases. Le titre du document écrit par le Service central du renseignement territorial (SRCT) est sans équivoque : « Le sport amateur vecteur de communautarisme et de radicalité ».* [The General Intelligence Bureau noticed that football players of a team in Perpignan were praying on the pitch in the presence of referees who were astonished; furthermore sport educators listed by the Intelligence Bureau as *Salafists* were supervising adolescents and providing prayer matrices in the changing room. The title of the document written by the Central Service of Territorial Intelligence is clear 'amateur sport a vehicle for communautarisme and radicalization'.[24]

Others advocate for development through sport, and promoting in contrast the idea of using sport for deradicalization and reintegration into society: 'Bringing together people from different backgrounds in a variety of settings, such as the classroom, housing projects and the sports field reduces their prejudice about members of the other group.'[25] Already after the invasion of Iraq the old (colonial) notion of civilizing processes through sport was resurrected by the USA-established and -led Coalition Provisional Authority, to govern post-Saddam Iraq, to win the hearts and minds of Iraqi youth:

> As a government program, it consists of 3,000 staff and 130 youth centres across Iraq…. The 130 youth centres will be our principal instrument for reaching the youth of Iraq … the sports aspect tends to get most of the attention. Iraq, like most Arab countries, takes sports very seriously…. Soccer stars are more highly regarded than government leaders. That's why sporting events are so important. It will really bring this society back to life…. For us to complete our mission here, we have to complete the 'de-Baathification', complete the reorganization of government programs and position new Iraqi people into government – people who have the necessary qualifications and have no part of the corrupt past.[26]

The interim government's strategy utilizes sport to stop the youth from being recruited by anti-occupation groups:

> Sport is so important to young Iraqis, especially now. If they are not at school or playing sports they will be targeted by terrorist organizations, religious fundamentalists or other criminals, and the interim government has agreed that sport has to be promoted amongst the young.[27]

Similar thinking is driving today's strategy to counter radicalization of American citizens and preventing them from joining 'global Jihadism'. In Minneapolis in the USA, site of the country's biggest Somali community, sport (particularly soccer) is deployed to target young Somalis in the Cedar Riverside neighbourhood.[28] In Canada, Jonathan Wade, 14-year veteran of the Canadian Forces, promotes the idea:

The Canadian government could very well work with the Muslim communities on the youth programs. Having the young Muslims involved in sports, arts and other hobbies related or not to religion would greatly benefit them. As a matter of fact, involving any at-risk kids in sports and arts could keep them off the streets. They should also be playing with kids of their age from different backgrounds and religions.[29]

Conclusion

The visibility of Muslims in sport, their claim to local authorities and local leisure centres to cater for their sporting needs as Muslim citizens or athletes, and demands for accepting Muslim religiosity in sport, symbolized by the veil or fasting if Ramadan falls during a sport competition, are being increasingly interpreted and debated in politico-ideological terms in Western societies. This is particularly true post-9/11. Sport is becoming a contested terrain to defend the expression of diversity and pluralism, for some, and for the protection of Western secular values from '*Islamization*', for others. Adapting sport brands and logos to meet Islamic cultural and religious requirements is perceived as a way to surrender to '*Islamist ideology*'. Accepting investment from wealthy Middle Eastern funds is being put under severe scrutiny due to Western state security and sovereignty concerns, and can even be subject to parliamentary debate, as with the case of Qatar's investment in sport in France. Is this suspicion unique to/or targeting only Muslims' culture and religion? Notwithstanding the apparent anti-Muslim sentiments provoked by the attacks in the USA and other European cities, one could argue that similar narratives can be reproduced regarding 'the visibility' of Chinese investors in the USA, Europe and Africa, or the dominance of Chinese products in the global market. There are also suspicions in Muslim societies over the 'invasion' of American products and globalization of so-called 'Western sports', defined as poisonous imports from the West, which draw the nation of Muslim Believers (Muslim *Ummah*) from their true societal and political concerns. The trauma of 9/11 and the 'War on Terror' that followed signalled the shift of geo-politics, including in relation to the power dynamics between the West and majority Muslim countries, and the question of Muslim presence in the West, of which the questioning of and 'mode of thinking'[30] about Muslims' visibility in the geo-politics of sport is a by-product.

Notes

1   R. Morin and J.H. Menasce, 'Europeans Debate the Scarf and the Veil', Pew Research Centre (20 November 2006), www.pewglobal.org/2006/11/20/europeans-debate-the-scarf-and-the-veil, accessed 1 October 2015.

2   J. Dacey, 'Muslim Angered by "Unjust" Headscarf Sport Ban', swissinfo.ch (9 September 2009), www.swissinfo.ch/eng/Specials/Islam_and_Switzerland/News_and_views/Muslim_angered_by_unjust_headscarf_sport_ban.html?cid¼463872, accessed 14 September 2015.

3   N. Wyatt, 'Rules Forbid Hijab, Says Quebec Soccer Federation', TheStar.com (26 February 2007), www.thestar.com/News/article/185923, accessed 12 April 2015.

4   BBC.com, 'Quebec Soccer Federation Defends Turban Ban' (4 June 2003), www.bbc.com/news/world-us-canada-22771425, accessed 10 June 2015.

5   AFP, 'Musulmane interdite de piscine pour port "du burkini"', *Tribune de Genève*, 12 August 2009, www.tdg.ch/actu/monde/musulmane-interdite-piscineport-burkini-2009-08-12, accessed 3 March 2015.

6   E. Addley, 'Saudi Arabia's *Judoka* Strikes Blow for Women's Rights at Olympics', *Guardian* (3 August 2012), www.theguardian.com/sport/london-2012-olympics-blog/2012/aug/03/saudi-wojdan-shaherkani-women-olympics, accessed 8 February 2015.

7   S. Farooq and S. Sehlikoglu, 'Strange, Incompetent and Out-Of-Place: Media, Muslim Sportswomen and London 2012', *Feminist Media Studies* 15, 3 (2015), 363–81.

8   *Guardian*, 'Real Madrid Drop Christian Cross from Club Crest in Middle East' (27 November 2014), www.theguardian.com/football/2014/nov/27/real-madrid-christian-cross-abu-dhabi-crest, accessed 1 March 2015.

9   B. Garcia and M. Amara, 'Media Perceptions of Arab Investment in European Football Clubs: The Case of Malaga and Paris Saint-Germain', *Sport and the European Union Review* 5, 1 (2013), 5–20.

10 *Marianne Magazine* 'Comment ils ont livré la France au Qatar', *Marianne Magazine*, 820 (January 2013), 5–11.

11 W. Le Devin, 'Les musulmans dans la mire du Qatar', *Liberation* (26 April 2003). www.liberation.fr/societe/2013/04/26/les-musulmans-dans-la-mire-du-qatar_899408, accessed 15 March 2015 (translated by the author).

12 S. Briclot, 'Qatar, "un pays entre monopoly et islam radical"', *Le Parisien* (28 March 2003), www.leparisien.fr/magazine/grand-angle/le-qatar-un-pays-entre-monopoly-et-islam-radical-26-03-2013-2672465, accessed 10 July 2015 (translated by the author).

13 J. Sinnige, 'Royaume-uni. Le Qatar achète un quartier d'affaires à Londres', *Courrier International* (30 January 2015), www.courrierinternational.com/ article/2015/01/30/le-qatar-achete-un-quartier-d-affaires-a-londres, accessed 30 January 2015 (translated by the author; author's comment in parentheses).

14 *Le Point*, 'L'action du Qatar en France suscite de plus en plus de réserves à droite' (1 October 2012), www.lepoint.fr/politique/l-action-du-qatar-en-france-suscite-de-plus-en-plus-de-reserves-a-droite-01-10-2012-1512146_20.php, accessed 15 March 2015 (translated by the author).

15 G. Barila, 'Coopers Defends Halal Accreditation for Malt-Extract Products', *The Advertiser* (11 February 2014), www.adelaidenow.com.au/news/south-australia/coopers-defends-halal-accreditation-for-maltextract-products/story-fni6uo1m-1226823960243, accessed 4 February 2015.

16 T. Baldwin and G. Rozenberg, 'Britain Must Scrap Multiculturalism', *The Times Online* (3 April 2004), www.timesonline.co.uk/tol/news/uk/article1055221.ece, accessed 1 November 2008.

17 M. Amara and I. Henry, 'Sport, Muslim Identities and Cultures in the UK, an Emerging Policy Issue: Case Studies of Leicester and Birmingham', *European Sport Management Quarterly* 10, 4 (2010), 419–43.

18 M. Veron, 'Aubry a-t-elle vraiment réservée des créneaux de piscine à des musulmans', *L'express Magazine* (30 March 2012), www.lexpress.fr/actualite/politique/aubry-a-t-elle-vraiment-reservee-des-creneaux-de-piscine-a-des-musulmanes_1098551.html, accessed 1 December 2012.

19 K. Toffoletti and C. Palmer, 'New Approaches for Studies of Muslim Women and Sport', *International Review of the Sociology of Sport* [online] 2. DOI: 10.1177/1012690215589326.

20 A. Testa, 'Engaging in Sport: The Islamic Framework', in A. Testa and M. Amara, eds, *Sport in Islam and in Muslim Communities* (London: Routledge, 2015), 2.

21 A. Saeed, 'The Influence of the Nation of Islam and Islam on British Ex-offenders: Malcom, Mohammed and Redemption', in A. Testa and M. Amara, eds, *Sport in Islam and in Muslim Communities* (London: Routledge, 2015), 125.

22 Amara and Henry, 'Sport, Muslim Identities and Cultures in the UK', 432.

23 Ibid., 434.

24 *Le Point*, 'Comment le sport peut être source de radicalisation' (15 October 2015), www.lepoint.fr/societe/comment-le-sport-peut-etre-source-de-radicalisation-15-10-2015-1973735_23.php, accessed 15 October 2015.

25 H. White, 'Tackling Radicalization through Sport', *International Initiative for Impact Evaluation* (13 July 2015), http://blogs.3ieimpact.org/?s=sport+and+radicalisation, accessed 15 July 2015.

26 J. Quinn, 'Eberly Hopes Sports Can Instill a "Civil Society" in Iraq', *Intelligence Journal* (16 July 2003), www.highbeam.com/doc/1P2-9187300.html, accessed 1 October 2011.

27 *The Scotsman*, 'MBE for Getting Iraq Back' (4 December 2004), www.scotsman.com/news/scotland/top-stories/scotsman-coaching-iraq-on-to-triumph-1-1017262#axzz3prloJazF, accessed 14 December 2004.

28 M. Jordan and T. Audi, 'A Test Case for "Deradicalization",' *Wall Street Journal* (6 May 2005, www.wsj.com/articles/a-test-case-for-deradicalization-1430944585, accessed 20 May 2005.

29 J. Wade, 'Canada Needs a Stronger Deradicalization Program', The Sentinel Analytical Group (1 April 2015), http://thesentinel.ca/canada-needs-a-stronger-deradicalization-program, accessed 1 April 2015.

30 M. Klare, 'The New Geopolitics', *Monthly Review* 55, 3 (2003), http://monthlyreview.org/2003/07/01/the-new-geopolitics, accessed 12 September 2015.

INDEX